Learning For All 1

Curricula for Diversity in Education

Learning For All

The other volume in the series:

Volume 2 Policies for Diversity in Education
Edited by Tony Booth, Will Swann, Mary Masterton and Patricia Potts

This reader is one part of an Open University integrated teaching system and the selection is therefore related to other material available to students. It is designed to evoke the critical understanding of students. Opinions expressed in it are not necessarily those of the course team or of the University.

If you would like to study this course, please write to The Central Enquiries Office, The Open University, Walton Hall, Milton Keynes MK7 6AA, for a prospectus and application form. For more specific information write to The Higher Degrees Office at the same address.

Learning For All 1

Curricula for Diversity in Education

Edited by
Tony Booth, Will Swann, Mary Masterton and Patricia Potts

ROUTLEDGE
London and New York
in association with
The Open University

First published 1992
by Routledge
11 New Fetter Lane, London EC4P 4EE

Simultaneously published in the USA and Canada
by Routledge
a division of Routledge, Chapman and Hall, Inc.
29 West 35th Street, New York, NY 10001

Typeset in 10/12 pt September regular by Leaper & Gard Ltd, Bristol
Printed and bound in Great Britain by
Mackays of Chatham PLC, Chatham, Kent

British Library Cataloguing in Publication Data

Curricula for Diversity in Education. – (Learning
For All; 1)
I. Booth, Tony II. Series
375.0010941
ISBN 0–415–07184–4

Library of Congress Cataloging in Publication Data applied for.

Contents

Figures viii
Tables ix
Contributors x
Acknowledgements xiii

Introduction 1
Tony Booth

Part 1 Teaching for diversity 7

1 Collaborative classrooms 9
Susan Hart

2 Opening doors: learning history through talk 23
Chris Morris

3 Getting it true: notes on the teaching of poetry 36
Fred Sedgwick

4 Primary science: starting from children's ideas 53
Pamela Wadsworth

5 What will happen if . . .?: an active approach to mathematics teaching 63
Adrienne Bennett with Honor Williams

6 Setting the agenda: student participation on a multi-media learning scheme 76
Stuart Olesker

7 Hardening the hierarchies: the National Curriculum as a system of classification 83
Will Swann

Part 2 Support for learning 103

8 Evaluating support teaching 105
Susan Hart

9 A new role for a support service 114
Linda Harland

10 An extra radiator?: teachers' views of support teaching and withdrawal in developing the English of bilingual pupils 124
John Williamson

11 In the driving seat?: supporting the education of traveller children 136
Chris Mills

12 Chris Raine's progress: an achievement to be proud of 143
Alyson Clare

13 Signing and talking in a Leeds primary school 150
Beate Schmidt-Rohlfing

14 Expanding horizons: microtechnology and access to the National Curriculum 156
Christopher and Rowena Onions

Part 3 Changing special curricula 169

15 Becoming a reflective teacher 171
Mel Ainscow

16 Conductive education: contrasting perspectives 183
Mike Oliver and Virginia Beardshaw, with an introduction by Will Swann

17 'Totally impractical!': integrating 'special care' within a special school 193
Jenny Corbett

18 Returning to the basics: a curriculum at Harperbury Hospital School 200
Dave Hewett and Melanie Nind

Part 4 Children and young people under pressure 211

19 Lassies of Leith talk about bother 213
Gwynedd Lloyd

20 Bullying in two English comprehensive schools 224
Colin Yates and Peter Smith

21 From school to schemes: out of education into training 236
Robert Hollands

22 Stressing education: children in care 249
Felicity Fletcher-Campbell

23 Adolescents, sex and injecting drug use: risks for HIV infection 253
Marina Barnard and Neil McKeganey

24 Affected by HIV and AIDS: cameos of children and young people 270
Philippa Russell, with an introduction by Tony Booth

25 Blood relations: educational implications of sickle-cell anaemia and thalassaemia 277
Simon Dyson

26 Hell guffawed: Joseph Meehan starts secondary school 284
Christopher Nolan

Part 5 Representing practice 291

27 What counts as research? 293
Lawrence Stenhouse

28 Finding a voice 304
Extracts by Micheline Mason, Ved Mehta, Doug Mellor and Rosemary Sutcliff, with an introduction and discussion by Patricia Potts

29 Close observation 317
Extracts by Patrick Easen, John Joseph Gleason, Robert Hull and James Pye, with an introduction and discussion by Patricia Potts

30 Approaches to interviewing 332
Patricia Potts

31 *Le mot juste*: learning the language of equality 340
Caroline Roaf

32 Writing clearly: contributing to the ideal comprehensibility situation 345
Margaret Peter

Index 349

Figures

2.1 Poem about a bombing raid: stage 1 31
2.2 Poem about a bombing raid: stage 2 31
2.3 Poem about a bombing raid: final version 32
5.1 How do you make a 3 × 3 × 3 cube? 64
5.2 Assessing the best buy: measuring canfuls in the bottle 73
13.1 Asima's communication with deaf peers, hearing peers, mainstream teachers and support staff in one school day 154
15.1 Format for recording progress using an objectives approach 174

Tables

8.1 Ideas associated with the individual approach and the whole curriculum approach 107
8.2 Implications for support teaching 108
8.3 Criteria for evaluating support teaching 109
20.1 Percentage of pupils who reported being bullied at school 227
20.2 Whom pupils report as usually the worst bullies 228
20.3 Whom pupils report as trying to put a stop to it when a young person is being bullied 229
20.4 Percentage of pupils who reported bullying other young people in school 230
20.5 Number of reports of being bullied in school, and of bullying other young people 232
25.1 Approximate incidence of sickle-cell and thalassaemia traits amongst different ethnic groups in N.W. Europe 278

Contributors

Mel Ainscow is a Tutor in Special Educational Needs at the Cambridge Institute of Education.

Marina Barnard is a Research Fellow at the Social Paediatric and Obstetric Research Unit, University of Glasgow.

Virginia Beardshaw is Director, King's Fund London Initiative.

Adrienne Bennett is a teacher at Watergate Special School, Isle of Wight.

Tony Booth is a Senior Lecturer in Education at The Open University.

Alyson Clare is Head Teacher of Ravenstonedale Endowed School, Cumbria.

Jenny Corbett is a Senior Lecturer in the Department of Education Studies, Polytechnic of East London.

Simon Dyson is a Senior Lecturer in Health Studies, Leicester Polytechnic.

Patrick Easen is a Lecturer in Education, University of Newcastle upon Tyne.

Felicity Fletcher-Campbell is a Senior Research Officer at the National Foundation for Educational Research, Slough, Berkshire.

John Joseph Gleason is an Associate Professor of Special Education at Rhode Island College, USA.

Linda Harland is a Senior Lecturer in Primary Education, Thames Polytechnic.

Susan Hart is a Tutor at the Cambridge Institute of Education.

Dave Hewett is a freelance consultant to Education and Social Services Departments.

Robert Hollands is a Senior Lecturer in Sociology, Sunderland Polytechnic.

Robert Hull is a freelance writer and lecturer with twenty-five years' teaching experience.

Gwynedd Lloyd is a Lecturer in Special Educational Needs, Moray House College of Education.

Micheline Mason is a disability equality trainer and campaigner.

Mary Masterton is a Course Manager at The Open University.

Neil McKeganey is a Senior Research Fellow at the Social Paediatric and Obstetric Research Unit, University of Glasgow.

Ved Mehta is a writer living in New York.

Doug Mellor is a tiler.

Chris Mills is a Curriculum Support Teacher for travellers' children, Cambridgeshire.

Chris Morris is a Senior Advisory Teacher for English, Dudley.

Melanie Nind is Special Needs Co-ordinator at Enfield College.

Christopher Nolan is a writer living in Dublin.

Stuart Olesker is a Lecturer and Co-ordinator of the Multi-Media Scheme at Portsmouth College of Art Design and Further Education.

Mike Oliver is a Reader in Disability Studies at Thames Polytechnic.

Christopher Onions is a freelance child psychologist and educational adviser.

Rowena Onions is an infants teacher at Nanstallon County Primary School, Cornwall.

Margaret Peter is Editor of the *British Journal of Special Education*.

Patricia Potts is a Lecturer in Education at The Open University.

James Pye is Mature Students Adviser at Oxford Polytechnic.

Caroline Roaf is Co-ordinator for Special Needs at Peers School, Oxford.

Philippa Russell is Director of the Voluntary Council for Handicapped Children at the National Children's Bureau.

Beate Schmidt-Rohlfing is a teacher of the deaf in a Leeds primary school.

Fred Sedgwick is a freelance lecturer and writer. He was a primary head teacher for sixteen years.

Peter Smith is a Reader in Psychology at the University of Sheffield.

Lawrence Stenhouse was Director and Professor of Education at the Centre for Applied Research in Education, University of East Anglia. He died in 1982.

Rosemary Sutcliff is a writer living in West Sussex.

Will Swann is a Lecturer in Education at The Open University.

Pamela Wadsworth is a Project Officer at the SPACE Project, King's College, London.

Honor Williams is Research and Development Coordinator at the Mathematics Centre, West Sussex Institute of Higher Education.

John Williamson is a Lecturer in Education, University of Newcastle upon Tyne.

Colin Yates is a youth and community worker in London.

Part 1

Teaching for diversity

Chapter 1

Collaborative classrooms

Susan Hart

In this chapter Susan Hart describes some of the results and conclusions of a study of collaborative learning environments in primary classrooms. The project began with the aim of investigating the use of collaborative activities by teachers under normal classroom conditions, but reached the conclusion that collaboration in the classrooms observed involved much more than 'group work'. The research turned to describing the collaborative learning environment which teachers sought to foster. To develop such an environment, teachers aimed to create a self-supporting framework, in which pupils could work independently of the teacher, using the resource of other pupils and contributing actively to their own learning. Teachers taught pupils how to make use of this environment by structuring collaborative work, supporting pupils in working together and demonstrating the purposes and processes of collaboration.

1 BACKGROUND TO THE PROJECT

A busy afternoon in an infant classroom. Eileen, the class teacher, is working with a group of boys who are inventing an adventure story about the castle they have just constructed together. Two girls (just turned 6) approach; they want to make a television. Is it all right? Eileen nods absently, still engrossed in the work of the group. The girls disappear in the direction of the junk modelling box. When they re-emerge, a morning later, they have made a television set, a video recorder with space to insert cassettes, three appropriately sized cassettes labelled with the names of the programmes and three alternative pictures of 'scenes' from each cassette to fit the TV screen. The model is presented with some pride to the class. Its working are explained, with an invitation to 'watch' the videos or offer suggestions about other films to include.

What were these girls learning through this activity? Where did the idea come from and how did it relate to their developing interests, understandings and skills? Does such spontaneous activity have a legitimate place in the National Curriculum? And what did they gain from doing it together?

This chapter is about the possibilities for creating learning environments which encourage children to work and learn collaboratively. It is about ways of organising learning activities so that children expect and are able to help one another, to share ideas, to comment constructively upon one another's work, to recognise and use one another's resources in ways which support and enhance learning.

The chapter tells the story of a small-scale research project which set out to study how experienced teachers were developing 'collaborative' methods of working.[1] The project ran into difficulties when we discovered that the forms of 'collaboration' being developed in the classrooms observed were more all-pervasive yet apparently less structured and organised than had been anticipated. The findings drew attention to the contrast between the teacher-initiated models of 'group work' which at the time offered the *only* practical insights and guidance available in the literature (e.g. Barnes and Todd 1977, Tann 1981, Biott and Clough 1983, Slavin 1983, Johnson *et al.* 1984) and the long-standing commitment of many primary teachers to promoting independence and self-direction in learning. With hindsight, it was obvious that teachers whose practice reflected these aims would be seeking strategies for encouraging collaboration which allowed room for spontaneous, child-initiated (*as well as* teacher-led) collaborative activity. Yet nowhere in the existing research or literature does this need appear to be acknowledged, let alone addressed. In this chapter, I describe how the work in these classrooms has helped to highlight this neglected area, and offer a first tentative analysis of the processes involved. I suggest that, in spite of appearances, these processes are every bit as carefully organised and crafted as those involved in setting up 'group work', and I propose some starting points for further discussion and development.

We did not expect or intend that the project should address issues of this kind. It had been set up with a directly practical focus: to provide insights and resources which would help teachers in initial training to prepare themselves to use activities involving collaborative work between children. Since there was little practical guidance available in the literature and most previous research had not been carried out under normal classroom conditions, we decided to enlist the help of a number of experienced teachers who were using 'collaborative approaches successfully. The intention of the project was to investigate how teachers across the primary age-range used collaborative tasks as an integral part of their normal classroom activity and what they did to enable the children to work effectively together.

The kinds of activities which we had in mind were problem-solving and investigations, collaborative writing, reading and discussion about books and poems in pairs and groups, group picture or collage making, group construction tasks, group activities on the computer: the sorts of activities whose value is widely accepted and which might be included in the repertoire of any teacher, regardless of differences in overall teaching style.

We made it a condition that, as far as possible, teachers and pupils should be observed working in their usual way. We wanted our findings to reflect normal classroom processes rather than the circumstances dictated by the needs of a research programme. It did not occur to us that 'working in their usual way' might prove to be so different from what we were expecting that work on the project would be brought virtually to a standstill.

2 WHEN 'COLLABORATION' IS NOT 'GROUP WORK'

The following examples illustrate the sorts of problems we encountered when we tried to apply our notion of 'shared tasks' in these classrooms.

> *Example 1:*
> Two 3rd year juniors were engaged in design and construction tasks. One was having difficulty fitting wheels on his police car. The other left his work briefly to lend a hand. They talked together and worked out how to solve the problem. He returned to his own tasks. Some moments later another problem arose. He offered help again, then continued with his own work.

The first striking feature of the collaboration we observed was that most of it was associated with *individual* rather than *shared* tasks. This was puzzling because in our minds 'collaborative learning' was about children working together on the *same* tasks, with the shared experience providing the context and reason for interaction. No doubt the sort of collaboration recorded in this example could be found in any classroom, whether the teacher intended it or not. However, from the teacher's comments it was clear that it was very much intended. The activity had been planned so that when children helped one another they would be using principles applied in problem-solving on one of the tasks and applying them in a new form on the other. Planning for collaboration therefore did not necessarily imply planning collaborative tasks.

> *Example 2:*
> Four boys decided to write a story together. They requested permission to work on their own in a small area immediately outside the classroom, collected paper and felts, decided between them how to take turns to scribe. The boys not scribing joined in by offering ideas and producing elaborate pictures, inventing new details to enliven the narrative as they developed their pictures. Enthusiasm was sustained over a number of weeks, read out in instalments to the class and eventually produced as a book.

A second characteristic of the collaboration in these classrooms was that so much of it appeared to arise spontaneously. When children were engaged in sustained collaborative activity in pairs or groups, this had in most cases been initiated by themselves, albeit with the teacher's blessing. This did not fit with the idea of 'collaborative activities' which we had set out with because we had formulated our questions in terms of the *teacher's* decision making. We had been trying to understand the *teacher's* purposes and actions in enabling successful collaboration to take place. If the teacher had had no obvious part in planning or organising an activity, it was difficult to see what might be learnt from it that would be of help to other teachers.

> *Example 3:*
> Four girls were seated round a table, each writing individually. One girl stopped the others to ask advice about how to write down the ghostly sound of a door opening. She made the sound she wanted to write, and the other girls made suggestions. Combinations of letters were discussed and rejected on various grounds. Eventually a solution was decided upon, along with a word such as 'squeaked' to help convey the sound intended.

Although an impressive example of children sharing and exploring ideas together, this could not reasonably be called a 'collaborative group activity' of the sort we were anticipating. It was simply a conversation in which the group was significant only in so far as any communication requires two or more people to support it. This example drew attention to an important difference between 'group work' as a way of *classifying* classroom situations and 'group work' as a teaching-learning *strategy*: a way of creating learning opportunities. In this example, the teacher had not 'set up' a group-learning experience. It arose from the child's writing, from her awareness of audience and her commitment to communicating with them.

> *Example 4:*
> Four middle infants were making a castle using a construction kit. As they built in each new feature, they discussed how it would help to defend the castle from attackers. Noticing the creative/fantasy element in their talk, the teacher encouraged them, once the castle was finished, to make up a story together about what happened in the castle, while she wrote their ideas down for them. They later typed these up on the computer and made the story into a book.

In this case, the teacher's involvement in the collaborative writing was the problem from our point of view. We had been assuming that it was the *absence* of the teacher which created the unique benefits of collaborative learning. This would allow children to take over control of a task, and allow teachers time to work intensively with individuals and groups. This example revealed the possibilities for developing collaborative learning with the teacher present. Working as a group, and supported by the teacher's skilful questioning, the children together could extend and develop each other's thinking in ways which a teacher with only one child could not.

> *Example 5:*
> Three middle infants were looking at wood-lice through a magnifying glass. Each had a glass and a wood-louse. They were working side by side but there was very little exchange of ideas and observations.

Perhaps most challenging of all was the discovery that in these classrooms there was rarely any obligation to work collaboratively. In this example, the children were grouped to enable collaboration to occur, but they chose to work individually. We expected that if a task was set as a group task, then it should be done as a group. The teacher's purposes in selecting it as a 'collaborative' activity would be undermined if some children worked individually. In this activity, the teacher saw the choice to observe silently, to reflect upon what was observed individually as legitimate and as educational as engaging in an animated discussion. The children's choice ought therefore to be respected.

To summarise, the reality of collaborative learning in these classrooms differed from our expectations in a number of important respects. We had been looking for tasks that were:

1 planned by the teacher with a specific educational purpose;
2 worked on as a pair or group without the continual presence of the teacher;
3 sustained over a period of time.

But we found forms of collaboration that were more often:

1 spontaneously initiated by the children to suit their purposes;
2 associated with individual tasks;
3 of relatively brief duration.

Teacher-initiated collaboration was more often associated with individual than with shared tasks. Sustained collaboration was usually initiated by pupils themselves, or else it required the presence of the teacher for all or part of the time.

The experience of these classrooms called into question our assumption that 'using collaborative methods of working' meant 'setting tasks which children work on together'. It clearly had very different meanings in these teachers' minds, but although we talked about these together, it was not so easy to put them into words.

One teacher expressed what she was trying to do as follows:

> What I'm interested in is trying to promote more of the sort of spontaneous collaboration, where shared interests emerge from an activity the children are engaged in, and they develop it together.

She alerted us to the possibility that 'using collaborative methods of working' could also mean 'helping children to create collaborative activities for themselves'. There could be two distinct ways of thinking about the teacher's rôle in promoting collaboration:

1 *A direct role* where collaboration occurs as a direct result of the teacher's involvement: the teacher decides when collaboration should occur and why, and sets the processes in motion, for example, by asking children to read and comment on one another's work, by setting a task structured in such a way that the children need to talk to one another and collaborate with one another in order to accomplish it.

2 *An indirect role* where the teacher creates the conditions which will allow the children to initiate collaborative activities themselves in response to interests, purposes and needs arising from their activities.

The teachers in our study did use strategies which came into the first category, but it was the second which was the key to understanding the all-pervasive quality of the collaboration and the self-sufficiency of the children which had so impressed us, allowing the teacher uninterrupted periods of time for working with individuals and groups. The problem with the second version, however, is that because collaboration appears to be spontaneous and may be far removed in space and time from the groundwork which the teacher has laid, the relationship between the two can never be directly established, but only inferred. We set out to try to find evidence of those links in order to understand what made the spontaneous collaboration possible. We looked at the contexts in which it arose and the purposes for which it happened. We tried to work out what conditions were needed to support it, and the teacher's part in creating these conditions. Then we tried to link all of this with the strategies the teacher was actually observed to use in her interactions with children elsewhere in the room.

We realised that, like a complex collaborative jigsaw, it was impossible to understand the whole simply through a careful study of each of the parts in isolation. For these teachers, the development of 'collaborative methods of working' had moved beyond discrete tasks, contexts and settings (deciding for a particular activity between individual and group working), towards an approach in which collaboration was being developed as an integral element of the learning environment as a whole. Rather than 'structuring *tasks* for collaboration', it was more a process of 'structuring a *learning environment* for collaboration', with each of the elements contributing something to the whole and therefore needing to be understood in relation to the whole. Developing a 'collaborative classroom' did not mean suddenly insisting that everyone works together all the time (as some teachers fear may happen if enthusiasm for 'group work' gets out of hand), but rather creating conditions which would allow the collective resources of the group to be used to support and enhance across the whole range of classroom activity.

3 TOWARDS COLLABORATIVE CLASSROOMS

From the teachers' comments and our own observations, we built up a picture of some of the processes involved in creating these conditions. We now had two new questions:

1 How do teachers set about creating an environment which encourages children to learn from and with one another?
2 How do they develop children's ability to make effective use of the opportunities for collaboration which the environment provides?

The task for the teacher might be understood in terms of two interconnected functions:

1 creating a *self-supporting* framework which encourages and enables the children to operate independently of the teacher, thus freeing the teacher to use time as productively as possible;
2 developing the *range and quality* of collaborative activity which the children are able to initiate for themselves, by directly structuring and facilitating a variety of collaborative experiences, and modelling skills and strategies for pupils to take on for themselves.

Creating a self-supporting framework

In the following analysis, most of the examples have been drawn from one classroom of 9–11 year olds where we were studying collaboration in writing. However, the analysis also draws on all the situations we observed.

Children as resources

Child to teacher [showing completed draft]:	Shall I write it out in neat now?
Teacher to child:	Have you asked anyone else except me? Go and find Jenny and ask her what she thinks.

The self-supporting framework builds on the children's existing collective resources: their knowledge and experience, their social relationships, their capacity to support and stimulate one another through shared interests and concerns. It requires the teacher to demonstrate the significance which she places upon the children's resources and judgements. In this example, it would have been easy for the teacher to have made the child's decisions for her. Instead, the teacher reinforces the responsibility which she wants the children to exercise over their own learning, and the support they can offer to one another without needing to turn to her for confirmation.

Supportive relationships

> You have to reinforce all the time the need for them to listen to one another, to show interest in what each other has to say, to respect one another's views.... They have to know that the environment is a safe one, that you will step in if the children are nasty to each other or put one another down.... This takes about six weeks – just as you're about to hand in your notice, it suddenly clicks and they are doing it themselves without you having to say anything.

Trusting relationships between children are a crucial determining factor if we want them to collaborate spontaneously. It is essential to have a 'safe' environment, in which rights, responsibilities and mutual respect are explicitly negotiated with the children and, if necessary, enforced by the teacher. Several of the teachers used 'group building' activities to help children to feel good about one another and about themselves, so that they would want to enjoy the social benefits of working together, as well as the benefits of sharing ideas.

Organisation

> Five minutes into the lesson. All the children are already settled and working. The teacher has given no instructions about what to do, apart from nodding when a few children asked if it was 'writing workshop'. She is already seated and working with a group of children.

A self-sustaining environment requires forms of classroom organisation and management which support independence. All the teachers emphasised the importance of clearly established rules and routines about access to resources and the range of options open to children, so that the minimum of direct teacher intervention is required.

Commitment

Me to child: What are you going to write about today?
Child: We can write about anything!

The degree of self-sufficiency described in the previous example is unlikely to be attained if the tasks children are engaged in command only minimal commitment and personal involvement. In the classrooms we observed, the teachers achieved this commitment through negotiated choice or, as in the case of the 'writing workshop', giving complete choice over the content and the process of learning. The children persisted with the same piece of writing from week to week, taking up from where they had left off usually without a murmur.

The teacher did not assume that children would be able to make these choices, without receiving help in how to choose. This was built into the developing environment from the start, and continued to receive attention as and when the opportunity arose to help the children expand their existing range of choices.

Control

The element of choice and control extended also to whether children wrote individually or collaboratively.

> I asked Kerry how she decided whether to write on her own or with another person. She gave her answer in terms of her own distinction between

> 'creative' and 'personal' writing. She said that she chose to write with other people when she wanted to write a story, because other people helped to think of more ideas, and it was more fun. But when she wanted to write about herself, which only she knew about, then she wrote it alone.

In the early stages of the term most of the children were writing individually, although there was a fair degree of collaboration over spelling, ideas for writing and reading one another's work. Gradually, collaborative writing (writing in pairs, threes, fours and sustained over a number of sessions) began to increase. All of these groups were rooted in social relationships, and were initiated by the children because they found it useful and enjoyable to work together.

Quality and scope of activities

> A group of children were using some workcards designed by the teacher to give them experience of working independently and helping one another over difficulties. Noting the somewhat limited kinds of talk generated, the teacher commented that this no doubt reflected the limitations of the activities themselves: 'That's about as much as you could expect to get out of them.'

The teacher's comment reflects her conviction that the impetus for collaborative learning arises from the processes of the task, rather than its structure. In earlier examples, the boy trying to solve a design problem and the girl trying to spell a particular sound, the children turned to others for support because their tasks gave rise to questions which needed talking through. Individual tasks can do this as well as pair or group tasks. Pair or group tasks will not stimulate worthwhile collaboration unless they engage children's interest and involvement, and are sufficiently flexible and challenging to allow for a range of responses. Whether tasks are undertaken individually or collaboratively is not so important. What is vital is that they should generate the kinds of questions which can be explored through interaction with others.

Developing the range and quality of collaborative activity

Freed from managing aspects of learning which children can provide for themselves and for one another, the teacher uses opportunities as they arise with individuals and groups to inject new purposes for collaboration, develop appropriate skills and strategies and model processes which the children will later be able to use for themselves.

Understanding purposes for collaboration

> James was stuck. He had had a good idea for a story the previous lesson and spent much time preparing a detailed picture to start it off. Taking it up again this

> lesson, inspiration left him. The teacher, seeing what the problem was, drew the group together and suggested a 'brainstorm' of ideas to help him get started again. She suggested all the children offer names of possible characters who could be included in the story. James could then choose the ones that he thought would be most interesting. He went off with a list of ideas, and was later observed totally engrossed, having covered two sides of A4.

If children are to be able to seek out opportunities for collaboration themselves, they need to understand the purposes which collaboration can serve. Here the teacher uses James's block to create a group experience in which all the children could see how collaboration could help them to overcome a sudden loss of inspiration. Some weeks later the same group was observed brainstorming spontaneously about their writing.

Providing opportunities to experience collaboration

> Following a day out by the river, the class were asked in pairs to make a picture or a model of something they had seen or done the previous day. A range of different media were offered for pairs to choose from.

Some children may need to experience the pleasures and benefits of collaboration before they will spontaneously choose to work together on joint activities. By suggesting or initiating such activities, the teacher legitimates collaboration in the children's eyes. By involving everyone, the teacher included certain children who were frequently excluded from spontaneous groups, to give them experience of cooperative work. She also created some mixed-sex pairs to begin to address the tendency to self-select into single-sex groups.

Countering resistance to collaborative work

> Two girls sat down to make a picture together of the river they had seen the previous day. Dawn took her pencil and firmly drew a line down the centre of the sheet of paper they were supposed to be sharing. Each girl drew her own picture in her own section of the paper.

It could be that collaborative working was simply inappropriate for this girl's needs on this occasion. Nevertheless, we need to bear in mind that children bring with them expectations and prejudices derived from previous experience in and out of school. The teacher may need to take action to counter resistance to collaboration, to raise awareness of the value of discussion and actively to promote mixing across race, gender, class and ability divisions.

words classify and devalue students and to avoid the pitfalls of jargon.

REFERENCES

Booth, T. and Coulby, D. (eds) (1987) *Curricula for All: Producing and Reducing Disaffection*, Milton Keynes: Open University Press.

Booth, T., Potts, P. and Swann, W. (eds) (1987) *Curricula for All: Preventing Difficulties in Learning*, Oxford: Basil Blackwell.

Booth, T. and Swann, W. (eds) (1987) *Curricula for All: Including Pupils with Disabilities*, Milton Keynes: Open University Press.

National Curriculum Council (NCC) (1989) *A Curriculum for All: Special Needs in the National Curriculum*, London: National Curriculum Council.

Potts, P. and Booth, T. (1987) *Teaching for Diversity*, Milton Keynes: Open University Press.

students as a human and cultural resource is one in which education takes place together in common, comprehensive schools and colleges; in which there is the minimum of separation on the basis of competence and appearance. Similar principles happen to form the starting points, too, of the National Curriculum Council guidance on 'special needs in the National Curriculum' called, coincidentally, *A Curriculum for All* (NCC 1989). The ways such principles inform and are informed by the details of policy and practice, by the joys, troubles and conceits of experience in education, provide the unifying themes of our books.

Many authors have made contributions to the books and while we have sought chapters which illustrate the themes of our course there is not a unanimity of perspective. In our negotiations with authors, in the process of drafting and redrafting chapters and in the final editing, we have tried to keep jargon to a minimum. We see the books as contributing to the development of the education system as a whole rather than being preoccupied with a group of pupils and schoolworkers who carry the label of 'special needs'. We avoid talking of 'children with special needs' because it misleadingly implies a dividing line between ordinary and extraordinary, or special, students and curricula. Nevertheless some of our contributors use that language and we have not paraphrased it. We are aware too that classification systems in bookshops and libraries tend to reinforce the notion of 'special needs' as a separate sector of education.

We have reflected the variety of contexts for learning in our choice of chapters for the two books. Policy issues are frequently neglected in a consideration of difficulties in learning and we have tried to give them a thorough examination in our second book. However, we have not made an artificial split between policy and practice. Policy is made both in committee rooms and classrooms. Nor do we take a narrow view of the curriculum. The curriculum is what students learn at school and college. There is the written Word, in National Curriculum folders and school development plans, and the curriculum as constructed together by pupils and teachers. There are also lessons, intended and unintended, which do not appear on any syllabus but are picked up in classroom, corridor and playground. These may be among the most memorable and long-lasting.

THE CONTENTS OF THIS BOOK

This book, *Curricula for Diversity in Education*, is about educational practice and about some of the children and young people whose concerns need to be considered in developing that practice. It is a large book but we have tried to retain coherence, particularly within sections. It contains thirty-two chapters, eleven of which have been previously published (Chapters 16, 28 and 29 with new introductions and commentary). Each chapter is preceded by a brief italicised editorial introduction describing its contents and where necessary providing background information.

Part I, 'Teaching for diversity', looks at active and collaborative learning strategies which use the grouping of pupils as part of the way pupils' needs are recognised and supported. There are examples of the way the teaching of science, poetry, maths and history can build from the diverse starting points of students. There is a glimpse of the way young adults with disabilities can be encouraged to organise their own learning within a 'multi-media scheme'. The section finishes with a critique of the theory of learning which underpins the National Curriculum.

Part 2 is called 'Support for learning'. It charts the changes that have taken place in attempts to resolve difficulties in learning in schools from withdrawal support for basic skills, to support for individuals within class groups across the curriculum, to an emphasis on creating the conditions in which diverse groups can learn. It examines the problems that changing expectations can create for teachers. It provides examples of work supporting traveller children, a child with Down's syndrome in a rural primary school, bilingual deaf pupils using English and British Sign Language to communicate, and the developments in micro-technology to support students with disabilities.

Part 3, 'Changing special curricula', is concerned with changes in the identification of and curricula for special groups of students. One educator charts his adoption and subsequent move away from behavioural objectives as the foundation of curriculum planning for students who experience difficulties in schools. This is echoed by a report of work with adult students categorised as having profound and multiple learning difficulties who live in a hospital. Another teacher looks at the history of attitudes and segregation within a school for pupils categorised as having severe learning difficulties. There are accounts of the differing views of conductive education for children with physical disabilities.

Part 4, 'Children and young people under pressure', is a reminder of the variety of groups who may be vulnerable in education and the way priorities for our attention may change. There is the voice of disaffected 'lassies' from Scotland and the writing of Christopher Nolan, painstakingly headtyped, of his experience as a young person with a disability in a Dublin school. Bullying in two Sheffield schools is quantified, and the reactions of young people to the Youth Training Scheme are explored. There is a plea for the education of children in care to be given due importance. Two chapters are devoted to children and young people affected by HIV and AIDS. One looks at attitudes to HIV and AIDS among young people in a Scottish town, where injecting drug use is common. A second provides cameos of boys and girls who are either HIV positive themselves or whose lives are affected by the infection in family members.

Part 5, 'Representing practice', reflects on approaches to basic research in education: observing, describing, interviewing and recording. A legacy from Lawrence Stenhouse is used to ask 'What counts as research?' and is followed by an examination of personal accounts as a way of understanding difficulties in education, the variety of interviewing styles, ways of observing and describing the events of classrooms. We are urged in the last two chapters to consider the way

Teacher support in initial stages

> An interest in kestrels had developed among a group of boys after seeing one in a London street during a school trip. The teacher supported the group while they worked through topics and questions relating to kestrels which they might be able to pursue further. She helped them to organise a process of gathering information by drawing up a list of possible sources, and setting them writing letters.

The presence of the teacher may be needed initially in order to help children to collaborate before they are ready to tackle activities on their own. This teacher afterwards remarked that she could not just 'set' activities such as problem-solving or project work of this kind and expect the children to be able to manage on their own. She expected to take them through the process several times, demonstrating the skills and strategies involved, and gradually increasing the amount which they were able to tackle independently, before they could manage by themselves.

Modelling processes

Through her interactions with children in response to their work, the teacher also models processes of actively listening to and responding to ideas, questioning, exploring and sharing which the children will then be able to use for themselves. At the simplest level, the teacher shows the children how to receive the content of one another's writing and ask questions which invite the writer to tell more about what she knows or wants to say.

Monitoring the uses to which collaboration is put

> A child was writing a poem in Bengali and passing it on to another boy to translate for him. The teacher expressed concern that, although he could write quite well in English, he only did so when writing collaboratively with his friend (who was absent); she thought that collaboration might be becoming an avoidance strategy, to get out of the frustrating task of attempting to write in English.

In this class, writing in the children's home language was encouraged and reinforced. Books and pieces of writing in all languages were regularly produced. However, the teacher was still alert to the possibility that some children might use collaboration as a cover. The benefits of collaboration could not be taken for granted, but needed to be continually reappraised. Was collaboration being used to serve the interests and individual learning needs of the children in her class?

To summarise, the analysis has shown how collaborative experiences initiated by the teacher can be used to help create the conditions which make future spontaneous collaboration possible. Through her interactions with the children, the teacher is engaged in a continual process of crafting and recrafting the environment, building on their existing collaborative resources, and gradually extending the range of collaboration which children choose and are able to engage in by themselves.

4 IMPLICATIONS FOR THE NATIONAL CURRICULUM

So what are the implications to be drawn from our study with regard to the implementation of the National Curriculum?

The programmes of study give greater emphasis to oral communication, to planned cooperative work amongst pupils and to talk as a medium of learning than has perhaps generally been given in the past. As well, group styles of classroom management are being seen as a means of freeing teacher-time to engage in the close observation and recording of individual development which the assessment procedures require. Our research findings have a bearing on each of these areas.

Language and learning

The research has drawn attention to the many ways of creating worthwhile opportunities for talk and collaboration, for learning in a group and as a group other than structuring tasks for cooperative working. The implication for in-service education of teachers (INSET) is that, rather than placing exclusive emphasis on 'group work', it would be more appropriate for the issues to be presented at a more general level and discussion encouraged of a range of different strategies and their practical implications. This would provide a much-needed flexibility, showing that National Curriculum requirements can be met in a range of ways according to children's needs and teachers' preferred ways of working. For teachers and children who have not had much experience of collaborative methods of working it would offer the opportunity to explore, as a starting point, the potential of individual activities for generating worthwhile collaboration. For teachers who feel uncomfortable about imposing 'group work' on children, it recognises the possibility that collaboration may be promoted by *indirect* means. And for teachers already using (or wanting to adopt) the approach described here, it acknowledges and reflects their wider concerns, offering a framework which allows for the possibility of building in collaboration as an integral feature of teaching and learning across the whole range of classroom activity.

Collaborative classroom management

The research has drawn attention to the possibilities for developing a collaborative style of classroom management which effectively frees quality teacher time but is not subject to the limitations associated with management structured on the basis of cooperative groups.

'Group work' leaves the initiative and the onus for managing the environment with the teacher. The approach described in this chapter contains the basis from which collaboration can become self-generating. Because there is no polarisation between individual and group activities, there is no need for a radical shift from individual to group working. Building a collaborative learning environment is not about whether or how often children are working individually or in groups. It is about creating an expectation that children will share ideas, help one another and make the most of one another's resources while the teacher is busy elsewhere. It is about helping them to recognise the resources that they have to offer one another and to use them effectively in response to individual interests and learning needs. It is a gradual process, starting out from where teachers and children are and developing little by little, under their control, at a pace both feel comfortable with. It means making the development of collaboration a priority, and giving to it the same careful thought and planning as is given to other areas of children's development. It needs an understanding of how all the parts contribute to the whole, so that new elements of collaboration can be introduced as and when appropriate, with the children's confidence and understanding being developed until they are ready to take over the initiative for themselves.

Perhaps most of all, it needs staying power, realism and a belief that it is something worth working for. To quote one of the teachers involved in our study:

> Outsiders come in and they think it's wonderful. It all looks so easy, but it isn't easy and it isn't wonderful. It takes blood, sweat and tears to do it. I think this is the only way to teach these kids, but you have to be committed to this way of teaching to make it work.

NOTE

1 The Collaborative Learning Project was set up at Thames Polytechnic in January 1988. Edith Jayne was the director, I was the researcher, and a team of colleagues from the School of Primary Education collaborated in discussion of issues arising from the project. Teacher colleagues who collaborated in the project included Liz Allen, Ros Bailey, Kathy Kelly, Gillean Paterson, Patti Prior, Eileen Sarup and Carole Hunt. Their contribution to the development of these ideas is warmly acknowledged.

REFERENCES

Barnes, D. and Todd, F. (1977) *Communication and Learning in Small Groups*, London: Routledge & Kegan Paul.

Biott, C. and Clough, D. (1983) 'Cooperative group work in primary classrooms', *Education 3–13*, 11 (2), pp. 33–6.

Johnson, D. W., Johnson, R. T., Holubec, E. and Roy, P. (1984) *Circles of Learning*, Virginia: Association for Supervision of Curriculum Development.
Slavin, R. (1983) *Cooperative Learning*, New York: Longman.
Tann, S. (1981) 'Grouping and group work', in B. Simon and R. Willcocks (eds), *Research and Practice in the Primary Classroom*, London: Routledge & Kegan Paul.

Chapter 2

Opening doors
Learning history through talk

Chris Morris

This chapter gives an account of a project which involved part-time integration from a special school into a mainstream primary school – a growing practice in recent years. For one term, a class from a special school for pupils described as having moderate learning difficulties worked for one morning each week with a class from a mainstream primary school. The project was about the Second World War. The methods involved active collaborative learning, with a strong emphasis on talk. The work was based around interviews, conducted by pupils, with people who lived in the local area during the war. One aim was to organise learning activities so that the two groups of pupils would have real reasons to work together and learn from each other. Chris Morris, one of the teachers involved, describes how the project was organised, how pupils responded and how the project altered the two groups' conceptions of each other.

1 INTRODUCTION

This chapter tells the story of a collaborative curriculum project which involved pupils and teachers from two schools in Dudley, in the West Midlands. One of the schools, Russells Hall, is a mainstream primary school; the other, Sutton, is a special school for children identified as having moderate learning difficulties. The project ran for one morning a week over fourteen weeks in the autumn and winter of 1990/1. Its theme was the Second World War. Our aim was to develop a learning environment and a series of activities in which all pupils would be able to participate actively, and collaborate together. The project was built around interviews, conducted and recorded by the pupils, with a number of people who had lived through the war in Dudley. The interviews were supported by a range of other experiences and activities based on film, tape, conversation and text. By the end of the project we hoped that the pupils would produce a thirty-minute 'radio programme' on audio-tape, encompassing some of the materials, ideas and information they had accumulated during the project. The term's work was not to be seen as leading up to the audio tape. Instead, the tape was to be a corollary of the active learning in which all the pupils had been involved.

Talk was to be the central strategy for learning. Language was to be used as a means for learning, not merely as a way of demonstrating what had been learnt. We saw language development as a social process, not as a series of individual skills to be mastered in turn. The activities would demand collaborative work, role allocation and sharing. To a large extent, pupils would assume control over the learning process.

2 THE SETTING

The schools

Russells Hall School is on a large housing estate about one mile from the centre of Dudley. It has 232 pupils. Pupils transfer to secondary school at 12. Russells Hall estate is not typical of its immediate surroundings as only 6 per cent of the population are aged 10 or under while 52 per cent of the estate population are 50 or over. Pupils from ethnic minorities account for only 4 per cent of the school roll. Parents are generally supportive and regularly visit the school both as adult helpers or to talk to staff. Average attendance at Parents' Evenings is very high.

Organisation within the school emphasises whole-staff participation in management, cross-phase teams in curricular areas and whole-school planning strategies.

There are about ninety pupils at Sutton School. Originally it catered for pupils from 5 to 16, but local reorganisation means that eventually the school will only accommodate children of secondary school age. Pupils are now only admitted at 8 or older.

A large proportion of the children have been referred to the school from mainstream schools where they have frequently been seen as having severe behaviour problems. Staff at Sutton feel these often arise from an unsuitable curriculum. Many of the problems experienced by the pupils are regarded by the Sutton staff as a result of emotional troubles that have been ignored by mainstream schools.

Parental involvement in the school is limited. The children live outside the immediate neighbourhood and this accounts for the difficulty in persuading parents to visit the school although great efforts have been made to improve upon this. The children travel to school by coach and taxi. Obviously this creates difficulties when staff wish to arrange extra-curricular activities.

For many years there was no whole-school curriculum policy at Sutton. Recently, however, there have been many new initiatives; the school has moved away from a 'basic skills' approach and now provides a much more relevant and purposeful curriculum. The impact of the National Writing Project[1] on the school resulted in many new learning strategies.

The pupils and teachers

The project involved some 45 Year 7 (age 11) pupils: 32 from Russells Hall and 13 from Sutton. We agreed that all pupils from the relevant classes would be involved and no pupils with potential behaviour problems would be excluded. The teachers were Linda Whittall, deputy head at Russells Hall and with responsibility for language within the school, Verena Ranford, the teacher of the 11 year olds at Sutton School and also with a responsibility for language, and Chris Morris, senior advisory teacher for English in Dudley. As the teachers all had full-time commitments outside the project, they were only able to meet when the pupils were working on the project. Although the original intention was to devote every Thursday morning during the autumn term to the project, the time spent each week was less than a morning as pupils from Sutton School had to be transported one and half miles to Russells Hall, and other events such as school assemblies delayed the start each Thursday. It soon became apparent that the working time each week would be limited to about two hours.

Preconceptions

Before the first day of the project, both groups had been given a very general outline of the activities in which they would be involved. They knew they would be working in groups of six or seven pupils from both schools. Many of the Sutton pupils were very apprehensive about their first visit to Russells Hall. Although they were the same age, they thought the Russells Hall pupils would be much bigger than them. Some Sutton pupils expressed worries about being picked on by the 'bigger ones' and were concerned about going into the same playground. The other major worry was that the Russells Hall pupils would be much better at the work. Julie said, 'Will we have to show them our work?' Other comments included 'What'll happen if we can't do the work?' and 'Can't we work on our own?' There was a general nervousness about producing writing. Dipak's question: 'Do we have to write?', voiced a common anxiety.

The Russells Hall pupils were far less apprehensive. They referred to Sutton as 'the soft school' and had a general view of Sutton pupils as 'backward'. They wanted to know how much help they would have to give the Sutton pupils. When discussing the different resources they might use, they expressed an unrealistic concern as to whether Sutton pupils would be able to use the books from the school library.

3 THE PROJECT

Week 1: learning to work together

On the first day of the project, pupils were arranged in six groups of about seven pupils, usually five from Russells Hall and two from Sutton. In future weeks, the groups would sometimes be rearranged because of absences and other factors. For most of the first session the pupils watched a video about living in Britain during the war and looked through printed resources. The experience was a salutary one for most of the pupils. The Russells Hall pupils were immediately able to see that their new working partners opted for as wide a range of activities as they did and joined in with as much interest. The Sutton pupils quickly noticed that Russells Hall pupils, whom they had imagined would be perfect writers and illustrators, sought help from the teachers and each other and often found it difficult to locate required information. Within the very first hour, in fact, there was an obvious revision of expectations.

At this stage the pupils appeared to be working well together, but we were aware that they were unnaturally polite. Neither group of pupils behaved towards their new peers as they normally did towards their classmates. At break, although the Russells Hall pupils took the Sutton pupils outside, the two groups did not really mingle or play together. By the end of the morning, some collaboration was evident but it was mainly along practical lines, with Russells Hall pupils showing Sutton pupils how to use the photocopier or where paper was kept. At the end of the session there was a very ostentatious saying of goodbye and promises from both groups to 'see you next week'.

We felt that the interaction and integration had exceeded our expectations. Initial reserve was beginning to disappear. Pupils had started to talk about the material. On a purely informative level the Russells Hall pupils had started to ease the entry of the Sutton pupils into their school.

Both groups of pupils had enjoyed the experience. Russells Hall pupils' comments were along the lines of 'Can't they come back this afternoon?' but also included: 'Dipak can draw well' and 'Marcelle thinks I'm a really good writer.' The Sutton pupils were very relieved to have been accepted by their new partners. Comments included 'Scott helped me with the photocopying', 'Can we stay in the groups because I really like working with Bobby?' and 'Why couldn't we stay all day?'

Week 2: research

During this session, the six groups watched a tape/slide presentation on the Second World War. While one group was involved in this, other groups continued with the previous week's general research. Pupils quite spontaneously related the tape/slide sequence back to the research they are carried out. For example,

Rachel (RH): Here's some of the land women [indicating a picture in a library book].
Craig (S): They got to work hard.
Rachel (RH): It's better than being bombed in towns.
Neil (S): They're the same as evacuees.

During this session teachers noticed how quickly most of the pupils related the information in the tape/slide sequence and in books from the library to modern fictional recreations – not just to films such as *Hope and Glory* but also to the series *Dad's Army* which had recently been repeated on television. One slide about careless talk and spies immediately provoked comments about an episode from *Dad's Army*. Marcelle (S) said 'They thought strangers might be Germans.' A slide of children with gas masks provoked Wayne (RH) to comment on Mickey Mouse designs placed on gas masks to encourage children to wear them, and Stephen (S) to say they didn't bother to wear them very often. Later one of the teachers noticed that Stephen had written a short piece about the provision of gas masks that concluded: 'No real gas attack ever took place and so by the middle of 1940 most people had stopped carrying their masks.'

Marcelle (S) objected that a film sequence of people going to an air-raid shelter was inaccurate as there was no earth on the shelter roof. She then showed the rest of her group a piece of her writing from earlier that day: 'People would often gow vegetbles on top Anderson shefter in the 18 inhes (46 cm) for earh.' By the end of the morning pupils were discussing the materials, relating the different activities and using information already gained and also beginning to think in terms of a wide-ranging, long-term project in which they were all involved.

Week 3: preparing to interview

The third session was devoted to developing the ability to interview others and to drafting questions for the following week's visitors, who would be able to recall the war. The start of this session was one of the very few occasions when we specifically told the pupils how to conduct part of an activity. Before the pupils were given the opportunity to interview each other about any subject, they were instructed to try to avoid questions which would only require monosyllabic responses, and, instead, think of questions that would encourage extended answers. At first some still found this difficult, as they practised on each other.

Terry: Do you like Grange Hill [a TV programme about a school]?
Julie: Yes.

Most pupils eventually resolved the difficulty for themselves.

Samantha: Why do you like school dinners?
Chris: Because they give you different choices and you can sit with your friends and it's better... in the winter it's better than walking home.

By the end of the session the groups had started to map out the areas for questions to be used with the visitors. We did not tell pupils how to organise the interviews, only that they were all to participate.

Weeks 4 to 7: interviewing

During session four we gave groups an hour to organise themselves, sort out their questions and decide who would operate tape-recorders, when to change interviewers, and related issues. It was now that gender became a significant factor. Many of the girls wanted to ask about domestic details such as rationing, clothes and saying goodbye to boyfriends while the boys frequently said they wanted to interview the men to find out if they had been on active service or if they had killed anyone.

Although we had three rooms for the sessions, conditions were very cramped and there were last minute hitches with pupils discovering their recorders wouldn't work or the plug points were too far from the place allocated for the interviews. By the time the interviews were to start, there was an atmosphere prevalent that might best be described as 'heightened excitement'.

The six interviewees were retired people from Dudley. The Sutton pupils knew two of them: the retired caretaker of the school and his wife. Another was a governor who frequently came into Russells Hall. None of the pupils had ever met the other three visitors. Each interviewed two people.

It soon became apparent that a crucial factor was the readiness of interviewees to take up areas referred to in the questions. Many pupils were still asking closed questions that did not encourage or prompt elaborated answers. In some cases, the interviewee was able to help out and almost suggest further questions. In others, they gave very precise and literal answers and nothing more. Where this happened, certain pupils in each group were clearly more aware of the problem than others; they were the ones who changed the nature of the questions.

For example, one group interviewed Mrs Glews first. Many of the initial questions were of exactly the type the previous week's session had been intended to prevent.

Stephen (S): Did you have a boyfriend?
Mrs Glews: Yes.

But most of the groups had at least two members who were able to rectify the situation. Often one of the pupils would immediately intervene with a more open question when the interview was becoming stilted by inappropriate questions that did not provoke extended replies. The poorer questions came from pupils from both schools and the intervention with more suitable questions would also come from Sutton as well as Russells Hall pupils:

Marcelle (S): Can you describe the bombing raids?
Mrs Glews: Well first of all you heard the sirens go off and then you all went down to the shelter and you could hear the planes coming over. When they were loaded they were very low and you kept hearing the bombs drop and wondering was it your turn next. By the time the bombs dropped it was too late because the plane had passed

over, so it was when you were hearing the planes you were worried.

Child: Were you still at school in the war?

Mrs Glews: No.

Tina (RH): What sort of things did you do in the war?

Mrs Glews: Well I was at work at Grainger and Smith's offices. The fire station was over the road. I was a part-time fire-woman and we used to go on duty as soon as we left work at night.

At the end of the first session of interviews, there was inevitable frustration. Some of the groups found that the sound quality was so poor as to make it difficult to listen to the recordings. Others found they had not even recorded all of the interviews. Perhaps the most important feature of the morning was that all the groups had discovered that there are definite skills to be used in interviewing. Many of the questions did not encourage informative or useful replies and in these cases pupils discovered they had not thought of enough questions or areas for inquiry in the time allocated. Neil, from Sutton, who had joined the school during the first week of the project (after causing severe behavioural problems at his previous schools) commented: 'You've gotta have good questions or they don't say enough.'

We made one change for the second week of interviewing. Each group would interview just one person. The pupils had obviously reflected upon their experience because this session was much more successful with more searching and carefully worded questions. There was an interesting dilemma here for the teachers. It would have been easy to instruct the interviewees to give extended answers to questions that only required a yes or no response. Although this would have provided the pupils with much more information on the Second World War, we decided that it would take a significant amount of control away from the pupils. It was essential they worked through the problems for themselves. The first part of week 5 saw the groups consciously working out ways of conducting more successful interviews. They reduced the number of questions, leaving more room for follow up – this despite the fact that some groups had apparently run out of questions the previous week. They noticeably changed the nature of their questions. It was also evident that some of the interviewees were more relaxed during this session and more willing to develop their answers. The first sessions had obviously been a useful learning experience for all concerned.

There was a more relaxed and unstilted feel to the interviews.

Sam (RH): What was it like in an air-raid shelter?

Mrs Glews: Well you just got used to it really; you didn't have to go at night if you didn't want to. We used to have one in our garden. We were fortunate really as we didn't have a lot of, you know, bombing round here but we used to go in. You'd got your milk and your sugar and all sorts of rations. And probably a book or a crossword puzzle or something you could do when you were down there, you know.

Dipak (S): How did you know whether the planes were English or German when you were in the air-raid shelter?

Mr George: Well, the German planes had a tendency to have a different note to the British planes and you never got many British planes over at night anyway. Mainly, when the air raids started which in the winter was about ... the sirens used to go off ... somewhere round about, what, six o'clock next morning or five o'clock. They used to drone over.

Child: What work did you do in the school holidays?

Mr Hill: Yes, now, during the war most men between 19 and 38 got called up and they went into the army, navy, airforce and fire-brigade or they had been drafted into factories to make tanks, aeroplanes and munitions so some things, areas, like farming were very short of labour. Now there are times on farms when they need a lot of people to help out. When they're picking fruit and picking potatoes, things like that. From school we used to go and help on farms, organised from school. We'd go on our bikes and take our lunch. I remember we went to a place about three miles from school, to a place called Sugarloaf Farm.

Weeks 8 to 10: working on the material

After four weeks every group had interviewed four of the original subjects, plus others who came in for a single session, and they had all accumulated a great amount of material. The crucial question now was the extent to which the pupils had understood the content, assimilated the main themes and were able to place the various memories, anecdotes and factual information in a relevant context.

The next three sessions were devoted to working on material in various ways, transcribing short sections of interviews, producing illustrations, writing factual accounts of events and poems based on what had been gleaned during the preceding weeks. It is impossible to give a full account of all the activity that took place but a look at one, a poetry session, will give a flavour of the whole.

A group had decided to write about a bombing raid. They based their poem on interviews with three informants, a scene from Hope and Glory and tapes of eye-witness accounts. They started by brainstorming sights and sounds, and produced two lists, shown in Figure 2.1.

The second stage was to produce a sequence of ideas, and in a genuinely collaborative discussion to which all pupils contributed the sequence in Figure 2.2 was decided upon.

With Wayne (RH) acting as scribe, the first draft was written and then revised:

Bombing raid
Screaming
Bang
boom
explode whistling
Shouting
Planes
Guns
air raid sirn
Planes crashing

Fire Smoke bodys
Solider running Fire engins
crying, lost children planes
leaked planes Houses on Fire

Figure 2.1 Poem about a bombing raid: stage 1

① air raid sirn ② Planes ③ Guns ④ Bombs whistling ⑤ Silance ⑥ explosin
⑦ Smoke ⑧ Flames ⑨ Children crying ⑩ Shouting ⑪ Houses on Fire
⑫ fire engins ⑬ Shouting for Help ⑭ Bodys

killer bombs

The sirns waled, the sirne ecoced through the Steetts
as the planes (zoomed) across the sky Droamed
There was a quick burt of Ack Ack Fire
Then a whistling of Bombs all around.
Suddley ~~Silence~~ There was slince
Then a ruble ~~the~~ a boom
~~boom~~ getting louder like a volcano
The Sky Filled smoke and flame's Black Bright orange leeping
in the middle of the noise a child crying
Then the Shouting of People traped in the ruble
House in Flames all around
The loud ringing of Fire engins rushing to the Fire
More and more voices (Shouing) For Help Screaming
Body lieing ~~every~~ all around.
*

through the air
across the sky

Figure 2.2 Poem about a bombing raid: stage 2

1 'The sirns waled' was changed to 'The sirns ecoed through the streets' by Jessica (RH).
2 'Zoomed' was changed to 'droaned' by Neil (S) who recalled Mr Hill talking abut planes droning in the distance.
3 'Suddenly silence' was collaboratively changed to 'There was silence'.
4 'Rumble' became 'boom' because Imran (S) said it sounded more scary.
5 'Black bright orange leaping through the air across the sky' was introduced by several pupils.
6 'Shouting' was changed to 'screaming' by Wayne (RH).

The final version, which met with the approval of all pupils, appeared in the form of Figure 2.3.

The sirens eccoed through the street
As the planes Droamed across the sky
There was a quick burst of Ack Ack Fire
Then a whistling of Bombs all around
Suddley there was slince
Then a rumble, Then a boom
getting louder like a Volcano
The Sky Filled with black smoke and Bright orange Flames leping through the air

In the middle of it all a child crieing
Then the Shouting of People traped in the ruble
Houses in Flames all around
The loud ringing of Fire engins rushing to the Fire
More and more voices screaming for Help

Bodys lieing every where.

Figure 2.3 Poem about a bombing raid: final version

Week 11: Christmas truce

The last session before Christmas was taken up with an activity unrelated to the topic. All the children made Christmas decorations in the form of silhouette pictures of snowmen, Father Christmas, reindeer and other festive objects. For the first time the pupils did not work in six groups but just sat at the tables as they chose. By now the groups were fully integrated: pupils from both schools, who had not worked together before, did so. They helped each other and shared ideas without prompting from their teachers. There were forty-seven children working on a very practical activity for a whole morning in one room. At no time were there any tensions or disputes over space, sharing of materials or any other potential points of conflict. Obviously this session would not have been possible if the pupils had not spent the preceding ten weeks on a common project where they were fully occupied in collaborative work.

Weeks 12 to 14: towards the end

The three sessions allocated to the project after Christmas were reduced to two by other unavoidable activities in both schools. The two sessions were a mixture of going through tapes and other materials, editing and adapting these for a thirty-minute radio programme, watching a documentary of a 1944 Lancaster raid on Germany and reflecting on the project as a whole.

One of the reasons for watching a raid on Germany was to provide some balance, as the pupils had all listened to accounts of raids on this country. By this stage, most of the pupils had seen news footage of the Gulf War at home on television. Several pupils from both schools said lucidly that there is no fairness in war and everyone suffers. It is difficult to generalise, but we all thought that the pupils related their work on the Second World War to the current conflict in the Gulf. They appeared to be more aware of the misery and realities of war than might otherwise have been expected.

As the material for the 'radio programme' was sifted and sorted, a picture of the pupils' intentions emerged. They wanted to present a collage of what they had discovered in the format of a modern day local radio programme.

Scott (RH): If it's a radio programme we can put anything on it.
John (S): About all of it . . . or just . . . sort of part of it.
Sam (RH): We could just do a year and everything but . . . you see . . . everything that might be happening then.
Scott (RH): And we can have jokes and things like they do now.

In addition to fully appreciating the significance and context of much of the material they wanted to use, pupils also intended to create new material themselves by acting roles as if they were there at the time. Scott explained the choice of a modern radio magazine format to report on the events of 1944: they all knew what a modern programme was like, but had only heard extracts from wartime broadcasts.

For the final tape a small production team of seven from the two schools was formed and they spent an extra day on this activity.

4 CONCLUSION

The social interaction between the two groups was both a major benefit that emerged, and a major justification for the project. The real evidence of successful integration occurred after the first two weeks. Initially the pupils behaved very politely and in an overconsiderate way. By the third week, if a pupil from one school felt that a pupil from the other school was taking up too much space, or holding the microphone at the wrong angle, or not performing a task quickly enough, they would be told. At this stage the six groups started to think of themselves as genuine groups for the project and began to regard each other as equal participants. The 'false dawn of courtesy' was over and the pupils really did accept each other. If a dispute arose over, for example, which questions to ask an interviewee, the ensuing discussion polarised pupils into groups that did not correspond to their schools.

The benefits from the oral work fell into three categories. The pupils from Sutton gained from the experience of mixing with a wider range of pupils than they normally encounter. In some of the initial interviews, the Russells Hall pupils were quicker to realise the need to ask open questions. The Sutton pupils followed their example. Once the interviews were underway, the majority of pupils could not be identified by the interviewees as belonging to a particular school. Second, any Russells Hall pupils who tried to dominate proceedings found that when they had finished, other pupils from both schools picked up on and developed points not covered by their questions. Finally, both groups progressed in the same way when they realised that a basic structure containing some predetermined questions was very important but that scope for flexibility and improvising questions was equally important.

Both groups started out with many misconceptions as to the likely ability and aptitude of the others. It wasn't only the pupils who displayed these attitudes, they were evident to a lesser extent among the teachers as well. We were surprised to realise that instead of two distinct groups there were a range of speakers and writers with an overlap and no clear demarcation between schools. It was a salutary experience for many pupils to hear, during a collaborative writing session, a whole series of vivid images and even a suggestion about what is required in order to create poetry, forcefully expressed by a Sutton pupil.

By the end of the project, perhaps the most important message to have emerged was that language development is an incremental, integrated process. The wider and more varied the opportunities that are provided for pupils to use language for a real purpose, the greater the success that will follow. Throughout the project, all the pupils understood the process in which they were involved and were able to make significant choices and exert control, both individually and collaboratively. All three teachers were adamant that despite the lack of time for consultation, the lack of space and resources and other problems that had nothing to do with the curricular rationale behind the project, it had been a great success. But the project belonged ultimately to the pupils and they should have the last words.

Bobbie (RH): It was better working with pupils from another school 'cos everyone's good at different things so the more people in the project, the more things we can do.

Acknowledgements

We should like to acknowledge the assistance of Caroline Fawcus and Teresa Kennard in the production of this book and its companion volume *Policies for Diversity in Education.*

Introduction

Tony Booth

Learning for All is a series of two books concerned with the education of children and young people who experience difficulties in learning or who have disabilities. They cover the age range from pre-school through to further education though they concentrate on the years of compulsory schooling. This book carries the title *Curricula for Diversity in Education* and the second book is titled *Policies for Diversity in Education.*

The books are readers for an Open University course with the same general title – *Learning for All.* The great majority of the contents of these books is being published for the first time. They are intended as a new contribution to the field.

The books are a continuation of a project in which we have been engaged for many years. This is reflected most closely in a previous series of books, *Curricula for All* (Booth *et al.* 1987, Booth and Coulby 1987, Booth and Swann 1987), and with a pack for teachers: *Teaching for Diversity* (Potts and Booth 1987). Within our project, the resolution of difficulties in learning is seen as part of the task of creating an education system that is responsive to all learners, irrespective of their gender, skin colour, background, level of attainment, abilities or disabilities.

Difficulties in learning arise when students are unable or unwilling to respond to what they are expected to learn. We are more concerned, then, with making curricula appropriate for the diversity of learners than with the identification of students with learning difficulties. The number of students with learning difficulties in any group will vary with the nature and quality of teaching. A group in a special school for students designated as having severe learning difficulties may all be actively engaged in learning, an A-level History group may all have lost the thread of the industrial revolution.

Teaching and learning take place within interacting contexts which are at varying removes from students and teachers. For example, there are the size and composition of groups; the organisation and morale of schoolworkers and students; the location, history and community of a school; the resources that are available to, and those that are used by, schools and within a student's family; the nature of government legislation; the attitude of teachers and others to educational law. All such contexts create enabling and constraining pressures on teachers and students and hence contribute to the production and resolution of difficulties in learning.

Workers in schools and colleges experience a perpetual stream of pressures and distractions. Yet the demands made on teachers conflict over time and between local and central government, school governors and parents. Such outside pressures are a poor foundation on which to construct an approach to teaching and learning.

Currently, the 1988 Education Act is providing the biggest challenge to relationships between teachers, pupils and curricula in state schools. While some of its intended effects seem inescapable, since it changes the balance of power between central and local governments and the schools, its intentions will inevitably be transformed as it works its way through the digestive tract of the education system. Its effects will be modified, too, because from its inception it contained contradictions which meant that it was impossible for it to be consumed as a whole. Apart from the fact that a so-called National Curriculum was designed to apply to only part of the education system, the National Curriculum introduced an entirely new core syllabus for 14–16 year olds which entailed their own forms of assessment only shortly after the 16+ GCSE had replaced O-level and CSE examinations. Other contradictions involve the unrealistically complex and time-consuming approach to assessment of 7, 11 and 14 year olds and the specification of core subjects, such as Modern Languages, for which teachers are in short supply, without the diversion of resources to train teachers to teach them.

It is very likely that the degree of specificity of the National Curriculum, as well as the belief that the ten attainment levels are comparable between attainment targets or subjects, will be modified over the next couple of years. So will the unprecedented faith of central government that teachers obey educational law without incorporating it into their own belief structures and existing practice.

Our reasons for action, in education as elsewhere, must be personally owned. We argue that the way we teach, the conditions for learning we create, have to be based on a set of carefully considered principles which form a more permanent framework within which all the competing pressures can be interpreted and assessed. We see the 1988 Act as a significant force, which is recognised in the subject matter of several of the chapters in these books, but it cannot supersede our own responsibility for decisions about the way children and young people are educated.

We are interested in supporting the development of an education system which recognises, values and provides for diversity. It is one which seeks to reduce the formidable pressures within our society, and hence our schools, to value students according to their competence or appearance. It would be absurd for us to pretend a concern for the welfare of those who experience difficulties in learning or have disabilities if we were to regard them as less than equal members of schools and society. An education system which values the diversity of its

Craig (S): I liked the project. There were lots of things to do and more people to do them with.

NOTE

1 National Writing Project materials are published by Thomas Nelson, in the form of eleven 'theme packs' and supplementary in-service material.

Chapter 3

Getting it true

Notes on the teaching of poetry

Fred Sedgwick

Fred Sedgwick shows how poetry can be made accessible to diverse groups of children of primary school age. He discusses the benefits for all learners of listening to, reading and writing poetry. As they work with poetry, children are able to reflect on what they know, to extend their understanding and to make new discoveries. Poetry can help children to learn about themselves, about the world around them and about their relationship to the world. Poetry, Sedgwick says, is a valuable tool for learning of all sorts. Not only does it help children come to terms with deeply felt emotions and powerful personal experiences, it is also a means to investigate the natural world about us. Fred Sedgwick stresses the need in working with poetry to make space for children's provisional, exploratory thoughts by encouraging group talk, drafting and redrafting. Children who find it hard to write with paper and pencil can compose in alternative ways: difficulty in writing need be no barrier to poetry.

> . . . Breughel,
> You'll know them if I can get them true . . .
>
> (Seamus Heaney, *The Seed Cutters*)

1 LISTENING TO POETRY

A group of 5- and 6-year-old infants are sitting on the carpet. The teacher, Beth, recites eleven seconds of poetry once they are quiet.

> Elsie Marley's grown so fine
> She won't get up to feed the swine
> But stays in bed till eight or nine!
> Lazy Elsie Marley!

As she says the word 'Lazy', her eyes widen with mock – or acted – or real (it's hard to tell) shock. She doesn't ask the children about the poem, but, after a moment's silence and a questioning look, goes on:

I met an old man by the sea,
his beard was long and grey;
his coat was torn, his face was worn,
but still he stopped to play.

We played Charades and I-spy,
Hopscotch and Drop-Down-Dead;
I asked him when his birthday was,
and this is what he said:

'Tuesday the last of Never,
Wednesday the first of When,
Thursday the third of So-I've-heard;
clap hands and ask again!'

We played at Forfeits, Hunt-the-Fish,
Knock-Knock and Guess-the-Word;
I asked his birthday once again
and this is what I heard:

'Sunday the first of Sometimes,
Monday the last of What?
Friday the twelfth of Suit Yourself,
Saturday Mark-the-Spot.'

I asked his birthday one last time;
he rose, and shook his beard;
and this was what he said to me
before he disappeared:

'Wednesday the ninth of Nothing,
Friday the fifth of Some;
Tuesday the last of Time-was-Past,
Time-Is and Time-to-come.'

(John Gohorry, in Sedgwick 1990)

That is one minute of poetry, and it's obvious that the children are happy. The teacher's skill in reading is similar to her colleague's skill – Jim who plays the guitar, and who can engage a whole school with three chords learned in a folk club in Hitchin twenty years ago and his performance of Tom Paxton's 'Marvellous Toy'.

But Beth isn't just the owner of a skill, she is also the owner of a passion. The poems' particular mixture of the ordinary and the magical has entranced her many times, as it now entrances the children, whom she does not patronise, as her eyes widen over Elsie's idleness. She half-sings, Rex Harrison-like, the line before each of the refrain verses in the Gohorry poem. This is a haven of verbal pleasure which the teacher evidently shares, as she relishes not only the sounds and meanings of the poems, but the feel of the words on her tongue and her palate.

Beth has practised her craft, of course, and as she reads the second line of each poem, thereby confirming the piece's rhythm, the children look up expectantly. All the children: bright, kempt Juliette, who hears poems at home and whose eyes never leave Beth's face; and Jamie, whose 'mother doesn't care' (as Jimmy Adair put it in a John Walsh poem) and 'who stays up half the night, you see' (Walsh 1960).

Malcolm, who is statemented, and has 'severe learning difficulties' (as the educational psychologist puts it) or who is 'dyslexic' (as his parents, encouraged by the local Dyslexia Institute, put it) or whom 'you just can't do anything with' (as several of his teachers have put it), mouths the words as Beth reads and smiles broadly as she finishes.

Here, for once, he perceives his environment in as full a way as his teacher and the other children. There is no serious dislocation between his view of reality and his teacher's, as there is (for example) when Beth says 'Can you draw a line between these two crosses ...'. There is almost always, as in that example, a gap between how children and adults see the world, and that gap is even wider when the children are perceived as having special needs and the adults are teachers. With poetry, this gap is reduced; even, at times, destroyed.

Another teacher, Lucy, reads to a group of 10- and 11-year-old children the same day. She begins by saying, 'We all know that Sean and Michael had a bit of a barney today' (Sean and Michael smile sheepishly at each other) ... 'and everyone else wanted to see ... Here's a poem about a fight ...'.

There's a big fight on the playground today –
  Two big boys from Mr Magee's
Are knocking the daylights out of each other
  Under the trees.

The girls are silent and staring
  And Clare whispers 'Stop it Paul'
As the fighting gets wilder and feet jab out
  And fingers maul.

I watch, and I'm glad it's not Joe
  And me in that horrible space –
Not my stomach winded, not my nose bleeding,
  Not my burning face.

The sky is bright. Two planes fly
  Out from the base, while one
Boy holds the other down with his knee
  And breathes 'You done?'

There's a fight on the playground today –
  Paul Topple from Mr Magee's
Is crushing the daylights out of John Randall
  Under the trees.

(Fred Sedgwick, in Sedgwick 1990)

She then goes on to read an account of a fight in Keith Waterhouse's *There Is a Happy Land* (1957) and to talk about fights in general. No one in the room is excluded, as they might be from a maths activity that some of them can't do; or from a games session, where physical prowess is such an important factor.

Poetry for both Beth and Lucy is about things that are familiar: the beach, the playground, laziness, fighting. It is not about Grecian Urns, like Beauty or Truth. It has the knack of making the usual unusual, the ordinary extraordinary, the commonplace special. And vice versa.

In its way of saying 'Look again', it is educational. It makes us engage with the world around us. It is not, as far as Beth or Lucy are concerned, about escape from tedium but about using the imagination to come to a provisional understanding of a view of reality. Each poem, as Robert Frost said, is a 'temporary stay against confusion'. This is true whether you are reading poetry, listening to it or writing it. Poetry's ability to cast things in a kind of temporary order, to defy the destabilising effects of time, if only for a moment, will be a recurrent theme of this chapter.

Both teachers keep on their desks, beside the National Curriculum ring binders, the registers and all the other tedious impedimenta of a teacher's working life, a pile of books of poems, which they use for short sections of time throughout the day. (I have listed these at the end of the chapter.) They never read in anything longer than ten-minute sessions. 'The idea is,' says Lucy, 'to make poetry part of everyday life, like laughter or lunch or maths or television . . . I abhor the poetry voie that makes it special, churchy –'" '– though', Beth interrupts, 'you have to be true to the rhythm in a poem, that's vital, the lifeblood of the thing . . .'

Recently, a boy in the school died. Now Lucy reads to her solemn class 'Tracey's Tree':

Last year it was not there,
the sapling with the purplish leaves
planted in our school grounds with care.
It's Tracey's tree, my friend who died,
and last year it was not there.

Tracey, the girl with long black hair
who, out playing one day, ran
across a main road for a dare.
The lorry struck her. Now a tree grows
and last year it was not there.

Through the classroom window I stare
and watch the sapling sway.
Soon its branches will stand bare.
It wears a forlorn and lonely look
and last year it was not there.

October's chill is in the air
and a cold rain distorts my view.
I feel a sadness that's hard to bear.
The tree blurs, as if I've been crying
and last year it was not there.

(Wes Magee, in Sedgwick 1990)

Poetry is unique in its ability to comment on such things in a classroom. It is the art that faces up, that follows 'to the bottom of the night', that legitimises the illegitimate, that makes temporarily bearable what is unbearable. 'I like a look of agony, because I know it's true' wrote Emily Dickinson. Certainly this sometimes brings about risks of embarrassment or distress. Sometimes children cry in poetry sessions, not to mention Beth and Lucy. More often, though, there are looks of wonder and smiles of recognition. A poem can stop time, while we remember Tracey, or Joe. At least, that's the feeling I get at the best of my poetry-reading moments.

2 READING POETRY

That power is even greater for the children when they read poetry by habit, sitting on scatter cushions in the library, perhaps, or at their desks. Then they can pause in a reading to worry out a meaning, and to discuss it with each other. The intense experiences – first, the ones the poem describes or enacts, and, second, the ones that the children have had that the poem helps make comprehensible for them – these experiences can be prolonged, mentally and emotionally, as long as the children want. On the other hand, their power over a film, a video or a TV programme is usually nil. Such modern techniques take time away.

It is possible to intensify poetry's power over time if we take on the implications of Rosenblatt's transactional theory, which is well described in Benton *et al.* (1988). This depends on the notion that 'Every time a reader experiences a work of art, it is in a sense created anew ...' Rosenblatt says that each poem is essentially an interaction between writer and reader. We might imagine a single-seater plane crashing in the desert because the pilot has been taken ill and died. According to Rosenblatt's theory, the poem is like the noise the crash makes, and if there was no one to hear the crash – no ear drums for the waves to bang against – there can have been no noise.

Analogously: no reader, no poem. The words on the page constitute a lifeless text until the poem is evoked (literally, 'called forth') by the reader, who is given an autonomy as powerful as the writer's when she gets deep into a text, using all her mental, emotional and physical experiences – and makes a poem of it: evokes it.

The Russian poet Marina Tsvetaeva adds another dimension to this when she says that 'reading is complicity in the creative process' (quoted in Brodsky 1987). That 'complicity' adds an important element of subversion: it is not difficult to think of texts that have been changed into fiery poems, novels and philosophies by their being thirstily read: evoked.

Getting children talking about texts in groups after reading them is one way of giving them this power with texts. Here is an extract from a transcript of a group of 8 year olds talking, without their teacher's presence, after reading together 'Anne and the Field-Mouse' by Ian Serrailier. The children depicted in Serrailier's poem, having watched a mouse frightened by a pheasant, chalk

> ... in capitals on a rusty can:
> THERE'S A MOUSE IN THOSE NETTLES. LEAVE
> HIM ALONE. NOVEMBER 15TH. ANNE.

Lisa: One day I was, um, outside when there was a load of lizards down the bottom of our garden. And a worm came up and slithered over one ...

John: Right, Have you ever seen, say if your cat hit a bird, have you ever seen it?

Ian [largely inaudible]: Cat ... bird ... porch ...

Joan: One day, my mum hates birds, right, so my cat, um, um, killed one and brought it indoors and my mum screamed and my da – my brother had to pick it up and take it outside.

John: Have you ever buried an animal?

Ann: You've said that!

John: I've got to talk about it. Have you ...

[long pause]

John: Have you ever ... put them in ... buried the animal yourself? ...

Children do not get enough opportunities to talk without the teacher's presence. In this short example, we see the apparently sturdy John (who has, in effect, chaired the meeting throughout) struggling through to the expression of his anxiety about the death and burial of animals: this was after much chat and jockeying for position. We have to risk that chat and that jockeying for such possible coming to terms with things.

Talking in small groups about anything without the supervising presence of a teacher is educational because it is heuristic: it helps children to set up possibilities, and to knock them down, and to set up new ones. It helps them negotiate meanings, both linguistic and social. And the presence of a teacher contaminates the process, all too readily short-circuiting learning with interventions.

This is similar to the contaminating presence of a man, however sympathetic, in a woman's group, or an education tutor in a staffroom, as teachers talk about changing their practice. The power of individuals to grasp autonomy for themselves depends on their ability to proceed in groups without the powerful outsider.

3 WRITING POETRY

But, arguably, the greatest power comes when children write. Then the teacher has the privilege of completing the text's change into a poem by reading it.

A case record

A small girl swinging

When first they pushed me
I was very scared.
My tummy jiggled. I was
Unprepared.

The second time was higher
And my ears
Were cold with whisperings
Of tiny fears.

The third time up was HIGH,
My teeth on edge.
My heart leapt off the bedroom
Windowledge.

The fourth time, oh, the fourth time
It was mad.
My skirt flew off the world
And I was glad.

No one's pushing now,
My ears are ringing.
Who'll see across the park
A small girl swinging?

Who'll hear across the park
Her mother calling,
And everywhere her shadows
Rising, falling?

(George Szirtes, in Sedgwick 1989)

I read this poem to a group of 10- and 11-year-old children, pointing out to them the physical immediacy of phrases like 'tummy jiggled', 'ears/Were cold' and 'teeth on edge'. We talked about the poem's movement. Caroline said that the poem 'went up and down like the swing'. With John's help, I developed this. The short lines seem to enact this movement: 'When you said "ears" the swing seemed to stop and turn back . . .' Then I asked the children to write about some experience they could recall that had something physical about it.

We collected a list of possibilities on the blackboard. They came up with: swimming pools, rain on the window, roundabouts, bikes, swings, a concert, in bed, first day at school, sports day, going upstairs and (improbably) a night club. I said they were to write notes on large pieces of rough paper and that it didn't matter (I always say this now) about spelling. This initial gathering of information was to be done in silence.

This silence is important, and usually neglected in primary schools. I'm writing this prose now in a domestic quiet broken only by a blackbird outside my window, and a car starting up and revving. The human voices I can hear are inconsequential, like stray punctuation marks, or figures in a Paul Klee painting. These things hardly disturb me, as I tap these words out.

But when we ask children to write, we often ask them to work in an atmosphere where all sorts of noises compete for attention. I offer the ones who want some silence that silence. If I can't manage it in a quiet room, or a temporary study, I impose it on everyone at least for a short time.

After the note-taking, the children arranged themselves in groups of three or four, and made suggestions to each other about their notes. They had to ask each other about one element in the writing that they wanted to know more about, and each writer had to act on this question. Finally, they would be told (though they didn't know this at the beginning) to make fair copies of their poems, taking on any of the suggestions they'd agreed with, as well as things that occurred to them later.

What follows are some of their poems, some notes by me and their teacher Hazel's comments (in brackets) on their ability as writers and any other things relevant to their work; 'xxx' signifies crossings-out:

Caroline (10 years 5 months)

My hair jumps as I first go into the deep end
    splashing like a dolphin.
The bubbles crowd my eyes. It stings.
As I hold them I slowly sink to the deep dark bottom. No end to
    where I fall.
I'm lost forever.
Jump up for air!
    Echoes play in my mind.

Here is Caroline's first draft:

> My hair jumps as I first
> go into the deep end
> splashing like a dolfin
> The bubbles crowd my eyes
> It stings
> As I hold them
> I sink to the deep
> dull bottom
> No end to were I fall
> I'm lost forever
> Jump up for air!
> echoes play in my xxxxx mind spin
> sink to the bottem
> ecoes play in my mind
> waves push me to the side

> splash
> my hair crowds
> my face

Note how Caroline's long line in her final version enacts her meaning: going down and down, 'no end . . .'. Also, note her rough notes scribbled on the paper till she was ready for the ideas in them.

(Caroline takes her time, is very methodical. Will draft and re-draft. Thorough.)

Matthew S. (11 years 2 months)

Matthew S. wrote (and his final copy was identical to his draft):

> Spin fast, spin slow,
> let the winter wind blow.
> Spin slow, spin fast
> let the spring wind blow
> Spin fast, spin slow
> let the summer breeze blow
> Spin slow, spin fast,
> let the autumn wind blow
> spin fast spin slow
> let the fast wind blow.

Matthew S. said to me 'I can't start, I haven't got any ideas . . . I don't know what to do.' I merely made encouraging noises and left quickly. When I came back to him five minutes later he'd written his first two lines. 'That's great.' 'Yes, but I don't know what else to write.' 'How about repeating that line, like a chorus . . .' (We'd used repetition in earlier sessions.) Matthew S. looked uncertain, but bent down to his paper again.

(Matthew S. is very worried about creative writing, or any kind of writing, really ... prefers practical things ... has never been above average in language all his school life. He is not the sort of child usually considered open to the notion of writing, reading, or listening to poetry.)

Matthew A. (11 years 2 months)

The speed running like a wildcat
a tight grip on the handlebars
a frightening experience keeping balance
can't stop the brakes are locked

I can't watch as I reluctantly move forward
my blood veins cold, my heartbeat 100 miles an hour
I jump and my bike disappears

One solid brick wall explodes

His draft:

the speed running like a wildcat
a tight grip on the handel bars
a frightning experean keeping ballence
cant stop the brakes are locked as I
relucktetle move ford
100 miles an hower

I carnt watch as I speed closer
my blood runs cold my hart beet
100 miles an hower
one solid brick wall explods in piecers
xxxx xx x xxx
I x jumped and my bike disappers.

Matthew A. has taken on the notion of drafting, of provisionality, better than the others. His first sheet of paper is an encouraging and meaningful shambles: you feel something might grow. As he is writing about speed, it isn't surprising that there is a breakneck quality about his work. His second draft shows several improvements: notably the climactic line is now last.

(Matthew A. loves creative writing, will do it above everything else. One of the girls said 'He is not like the other boys, he doesn't like playing football, he's softer.' He gets going quickly. He writes stories as well as poems, chapters and chapters, and he's good at telling a story. He's easily distracted from anything that isn't creative writing, though, very up-and-down. He doesn't finish maths.)

Ricki (11 years 2 months)

Ricki wrote (there was no change from his draft):

The Roundabout

As we were getting faster
I was getting sick taste
in my mouth.
The bars on the seat
are pushing on my
side because its going
to fast.
The wind blowing
in my face as we
got faster and faster.
I can hear the
wind howling in my
ears,
I see a little blur
as we slow down.
We stop.

Ricki was another reluctant starter. I extravagantly praised the 'sick taste' phrase early on.

(Negative about writing, especially creative writing, will put it off and get out of it if he can. Very bright mathematically. I don't know if that's fair, what you said once, that he's the school bully – he certainly has to be top dog. He's violent, yes, domineering, has a vile temper. He doesn't run out of school as much as he used to, does he? . . . It's down to once or twice a term . . . Certainly not someone you'd ever expect to enjoy poetry!)

Here are some general points to be made about this work:

First, notes are scribbled on large sheets of poor quality paper. This is to suggest as strongly as possible that the first words written down about anything important are almost never 'right' – whatever that might mean in this context. On rough paper, clichés and clumsy constructions are allowed and then debated. Spelling errors are legitimate too, because they can be dealt with when the important thing, the composition, is (provisionally, at least) finished. There are few things more obstructive to the composing impulse than those word books children queue up with, or those erasers they use to correct the first spelling mistake, often in the first word.

One of the problems with traditional remedial teaching has been that spelling and neatness are fetishes. Whatever effect this has on the children's futures as clerks, it maims creative instinct. It lengthens the odds on any serious chance of learning taking place, and of time being held up while the child is absorbed in what Ted Hughes calls 'a raid on the subconscious'.

Children perceived as 'special needs cases' can be rewarded by recognition of the fact that writing need not be by pencil on paper. Indeed, many writers have no contact with 'pencil and paper skills'. They use secretaries, dictaphones and

Amstrads. Children should have the opportunity to compose with scribes, tape recorders and word processors, thus gaining the opportunity to write without the dispiriting failure of knocking impotently against problems of spelling and punctuation.

Here, as an example, is a boy with a reading test score of 79 dictating his poem 'To the Sun':

You burn people's skin
when you're angry.
You are an octopus
trying to catch the clouds,
you are an image
changing every minute.

Second, the doodles are valuable. Adults often doodle in order to help themselves concentrate, and as the pencil strays around an apparently irrelevant line, in an apparently different activity – much like this paragraph, come to think of it – we might ask what the mind is doing.

An analogous state of affairs is described somewhere by T.S. Eliot, who says that while the reader works at subduing the difficulty of a poem, the poem is doing its emotional work on him. Similarly, as the hand wanders in a doodle, the mind is free to concentrate on something at the back of it: in this case, the ideas just put before the children.

One can take this a stage further: drawing. Often I suggest to children that the piece of paper could be used for learning about the subject they've decided on, or which I've given them, in any way they feel is right. So, rather than beginning with words, they might sketch. For this freedom to be effective, of course, drawing has to be part of the school's (or at least the class's) tradition. I would hypothesise that as they draw, and the front of the mind is focused on *that* activity, the back of the mind is reflecting subconsciously, or even unconsciously, on the words they might use. This is another potentially liberating factor for the child with linguistic difficulties: her ability to draw has a value in the writing lesson.

Third – note how in places punctuation, or lack of it, often enacts the movement. The clearest example here is Matthew A.'s work. If the teacher had red-pencilled her way down this, she would have destroyed the boy's at least partially successful attempt to convey the speed and panic of the experience. For another example, see Paul's poem on p. 49 ('I feared more than those . . .').

4 CONCLUSION

Most of us insufficiently understand the power of poetry as a tool for learning for humans of all abilities. McNeil (1986) suggests this power well in her book about Emily Dickinson, who

> uses her art to break open received certitudes. She is a heuristic poet, a poet of investigation, of knowledge as value. Her poetry experiences and argues and questions . . . the Dickinsonian 'process' is passionate investigation . . .

There are so many writers who say that writing is a process of discovery, or investigation, rather than a record of it:

> How can I tell what I think till I see what I say? (Auden, in Bagnall 1973)
>
> How many of us in fact discover our convictions from what we write, instead of writing in obedience to known convictions? (Geoffrey Grigson 1982)
>
> When writing poems, I do an experiment all the time with a possible 'Yes' or 'No' answer. (Miroslav Holub 1985)
>
> You change as you write, you change yourself, you change the way you think . . .' (Doris Lessing, in Harrison 1983)

Poetry is at the centre of our learning, whether we are (as the disc jockeys used to say) 8 or 80; whether we are 'highly gifted' or 'disadvantaged'. I would like to suggest that poetry helps the writer to learn about three things.

First we learn about ourselves. We can readily learn about our bodies through writing. Here is a 9 year old boy writing about something quite ordinary (down to earth, in fact) – his foot:

> Smooth, soft skin.
> Hard at the end
> with a curly-whirly pattern on top.
> Small, round, bouncy, like little marbles
> with a shiny coating . . .

(Some of these examples are taken from my book *Lighting Up Time* (Sedgwick 1990).)

This child had been asked to look at his foot carefully 'as if he's never seen it before'. These are his initial notes. But there is something more profound that can happen. This next piece shows a child learning about his own nature through an acceptance of an implicit invitation to write about it. Paul is a child subject to terrifying tantrums, and this behaviour is, needless to say, unwelcome in all the main places where he lives: home, the games field, the classroom . . . Paul is a child with a severe emotional special need, and here poetry breaks into his life and satisfies that need for as long as the poem takes, both to be written and to be reflected on.

Here he is writing a poem based on a prose version (that I had scribbled) of a poem by Stephen Spender (idea from Brownjohn 1980). The Spender is 'My parents kept me from children who were rough':

I feared more than those
bizarre animals
those mysterious
sounds
were
unfriendly

They were foul-mouthed
and they
glanced
at me
wildly

They wore fragments
of torn velvet

I was invisible through the remote lakes

I was trying to act scarce

The second thing you learn about as you write is the world around you. Here is a 7 year old writing 'To a worm':

> Slither, slimy, moving along, you're wet all over. Soggy, just like a lump of flesh. Slithering along when the rain has been falling. You weak long line crawling along, you look as if you have no bones . . .

Again, this has the status of an authentic attempt to learn about our world through looking, and then to find words that come close to getting things true. It is a first draft of a poem, or a description. It fits many of the statements of attainment in Science in the National Curriculum:

> Pupils should:
>
> observe familiar materials and events in their immediate environment, at first hand, using their senses . . . identify simple differences . . . make a presentation of their research and investigation . . . be able to recognise similarities and differences between living things . . .

The third entity writing can teach us about is the relationship between ourselves and our world, and that is, at least in part, a linguistic relationship. In other words, writing can teach us about language. James Reeves (1958) wrote that 'we attempt to teach children to write by making them write in prose. We should teach them to write verse.' Writing is best taught by the vigilant avoidance of cliché that poetry demands.

Here is a 9 year old learning about, first, a cat, and, second, language:

His eyes are a brighter green than they seem.
His tongue is a deadly poisonous serpent.
It moves slowly, cautiously towards the door, back arching,
legs moving,
sliding away across the floor, then enjoying every moment of
its milk.

In the poetry lesson we discard the second-hand phrase (such as 'deadly poisonous serpent') and forge a relationship between the object observed and the fresh words that might be used to describe it, to get it true. Thus 'furry' and 'cuddly' have been discarded here, and we have those tentative adverbs 'slowly' and 'cautiously'.

Each poem is a research project into the difference between the world and ourselves. It is the centre of the best Personal and Social Education: it is at the crux of what Philip Toogood calls the whole curriculum: Me and the rest of the world.

If we fill the room with things to write about: skulls, stones, shells, conkers, mirrors, photographs, paintings, sculptures, toadstools, books, models, rotting fruit, bits of car engines, old mowers – even the cleaner's things – this research takes life.

Or we can follow the example of one teacher/poet who brings into school an old bowl, the rim of which he runs his finger round. The bowl sings in a quavering, high-pitched way, and *surprises* the children into poetry.

ACKNOWLEDGEMENTS

Hazel Hollow who helped with the writing section. Seamus Fox, Margo Barker, Jill Pirrie and Vicki Muller, whose readings of a draft lead to several improvements.

REFERENCES

Auden, W. H. (1973) 'How can I tell what I think till I see what I say?', in N. Bagnall, *New Movements in the Study and Teaching of English*, London: Temple Smith.
Benton, M., Teasey, J., Bell, R. and Hurst, K. (1988) *Young Readers Responding to Poems*, London: Routledge.
Brodsky, J. (1987) *Less the One*, London: Penguin.
Brownjohn, S. (1980) *Does It Have To Rhyme?*, London: Hodder & Stoughton.
Grigson, G. (1982) *The Private Art*, London: Allison & Busby.
Harrison, B. T. (1983) *Learning Through Writing*, Windsor: NFER-Nelson.
Holub, M. (1985) Interviewed by Dennis O'Driscoll, *Poetry Review* 75 (3), October.
McNeil, H. (1986) *Emily Dickinson*, London: Virago.
Reeves, J. (1958) *Teaching Poetry*, London: Heinemann.
Sedgwick, F. (1989) *This Way That Way*, London: Mary Glasgow.
—— (1990) *Lighting Up Time 1*, Bury St. Edmunds: Triad.
Walsh, J. (1960) *The Roundabout by the Sea*, Oxford: Oxford University Press.
Waterhouse, K. (1957) *There Is a Happy Land*, London: Michael Joseph.

LUCY AND BETH'S POETRY BOOKS

John Agard
Say It Again Granny (Bodley Head)
I Din Do Nuttin (Bodley Head)

Allan Ahlberg
Please Mrs. Butler (Kestrel)
Heard It On the Playground (Kestrel)

James Berry
When I Dance (Oxford University Press)

Charles Causley
Figgie Hobbin (Puffin)
Jack the Treacle Easter (Macmillan)
Early in the Morning (Puffin)
The Puffin Book of Magic Verse (Puffin)
The Puffin Book of Salt-Sea Verse (Puffin)

John Cotton, L.J. Anderson and U.A. Fanthorpe
The Crystal Zoo (Oxford University Press)

John Cotton and Fred Sedgwick
Two by Two 'Hey' and 'The Biggest Riddle in the World' (Mary Glasgow)

Walter de la Mare
Peacock Pie (Faber)

John Mole
Boo to a Goose (Peterloo)
The Mad Parrot's Countdown (Peterloo)

Judith Nicholls
Midnight Forest (Faber)
Popcorn Pie (Mary Glasgow)

James Reeves
Collected Poems (Faber)

Michael Rosen
Wouldn't You Like to Know? (Kestrel)
Mind Your Own Business (Kestrel)

Shel Silverstein
A Light in the Attic (Cape)

Kit Wright
Rabbiting On (Kestrel)

Hot Dog (Kestrel)
Cat Among the Pigeons (Kestrel)

Anthologies
Edward Blishen, *The Oxford Book of Poetry for Children* (Oxford University Press)
George MacKay Brown, *Island of the Children* (Orchard)
Anne Harvey, *Six of the Best* and *Poets in Hand* (Puffin)
Seamus Heaney and Ted Hughes, *The Rattle Bag* (Faber)
David MacKay, *A Flock of Words* (Bodley Head)
Fred Sedgwick, *This Way That Way* (Mary Glasgow)
Geoffrey Summerfield, *Junior Voices* and *Voices* (Penguin)

Chapter 4

Primary science
Starting from children's ideas
Pamela Wadsworth

One of the most important factors influencing children's learning is the knowledge and understanding which they bring to any new task. From their experiences children build up a set of explanations and beliefs which enable them to make sense of what happens around them. The recognition that children have their own ideas about phenomena, and that they may be very different from their teacher's ideas, has important implications for teaching and learning. In this chapter Pamela Wadsworth discusses some of the ideas that primary children hold about natural events and processes and how these influence their learning in school. The chapter is based on the work of the SPACE (Science Processes and Concept Exploration) Project. She describes the strategies the project used to explore children's ideas and some of the findings. She ends by considering how teachers can create a classroom climate in which children can make use of and extend their own ideas.

1 INTRODUCTION

To begin, I shall consider some brief examples which illustrate the range of ideas about natural phenomena that children may hold, and their potential significance for teaching. Children interpret new phenomena in terms of their existing concepts and beliefs. Unless teachers are sensitive to these, what children learn may be very different from what their teacher intends they should learn.

Rusting

Children observed different metal objects (a nail, a tin can, wire wool and a copper pipe) which were left outside on a plastic tray. They recorded their thoughts in a daily diary:

> I think they'll stay the same. (5 year old)
>
> It's [wire wool] not going rusty. The brown isn't the same as on the tin can. It's ordinary brown – not rusty. (6 year old)
>
> I think that the rust is metal inside the other metal. I think that the rain makes it come and the paint wears off and you can see it. (10 year old)

The first comment may mean that the child has no experience of seeing rusted metal, or she may have seen rusty objects but not connected them in any way with exposure to air and moisture. Or she might know about rusting and have other reasons for believing that these particular pieces of metal would not rust. The second child has already developed some idea of what rust is and is not. Rust seems to be a particular kind of brown. The third child gives an explanation which is far removed from the truth. Rust is inside the metal all the time and only shows when the 'silver' is worn off. Yet this is a perfectly logical explanation from the child's point of view. It accounts for the observations made.

Evaporation

A tank of water was left in a classroom for several weeks. As children noticed the falling water level they noted down their observations in a class log book.

> Mrs Stewart [the caretaker] drank it.
>
> I think the water in the jug's gone down because it was hot. It came up and spilt by the fish tank.
>
> I don't know how it went down because I was at home in bed asleep at night.

The first child offers a possible explanation which reasonably draws on his knowledge of how water levels in containers can go down. It is a testable hypothesis. What does the second comment indicate? This child has linked the lowering of the water level with heat. This might connect with experiences of seeing liquids boiling away on a cooker. The assumption in the third comment may be that if a change occurs and you don't see it happen, then it must happen when you are not there. Evaporation is not usually directly observable. To understand it, children need to understand that such changes are possible.

Many children had a partial understanding of the process of evaporation and were aware that the decrease in water level was in some way connected to the sun and heat.

> The sun is hot and the water is cold and the water sticks to the sun and then it goes down.
>
> The sun sucks up the water into the sun.
>
> When the water evaporates it goes on a cloud and then the cloud goes in any place and later it goes out as rain. It will keep going until it is all gone and then it will go to another place with water and do the same. The cloud is like a magnet so the water goes through the cracks and goes up. That is what I think.

These ideas, which children work out for themselves, may differ from accepted scientific explanations, but they are not random or irrational. They are based on observations of everyday experience and language use. They make sense to the children and they permit them to make sense of their world.

Much research on children's explanations of scientific events has been carried out since the 1970s. This has been mainly related to physical aspects of science. It has shown consistently that many ideas held by children about natural phenomena differ from standard scientific accounts (for useful reviews of some of this work, see Driver *et al.* 1985 and Osborne and Freyberg 1985). The examples above are drawn from research recently conducted into primary children's ideas of natural phenomena in the SPACE Project. The work was carried out in ordinary classrooms with the full involvement of teachers. The project did not just aim to find out children's existing ideas. It also aimed to develop strategies which would help children reconsider and reshape their ideas in the light of new evidence, moving them towards more scientific explanations.

2 STRATEGIES TO ENABLE CHILDREN TO EXPRESS THEIR IDEAS

The idea that science teaching can be more effective if you start by eliciting the ideas which children already have was new to many of the teachers participating in the SPACE Project. Teachers had to learn to accept children's idiosyncratic ideas, even those which appeared to them to be wholly misconceived or ridiculous. In many primary classrooms, teachers introduce a new topic by means of a discussion with the whole class. This generally allows only the more vocal children to put forward their views. During the work with the project, teachers and researchers attempted to find out about the views held by every child in the class. No child was excluded. To do this, class discussion was only one of the techniques we used. Nor was it always practical or effective to talk to children individually. We used a number of other complementary methods.

Drawings

We found these extremely useful for many reasons. First, they do not depend on children's literacy or oracy skills. This is particularly important for young children who may find it difficult to explain their ideas and for children whose mother tongue is not English and who may not have the necessary English vocabulary to explain their ideas to their teacher. Drawing gives children thinking time. Children who answer 'I don't know' when asked a direct question are often capable of drawing a picture to illustrate their ideas. For example, when asked to explain what a shadow is, many young children responded with 'I don't know'. Yet all of the children could draw a picture of themselves and their shadow.

Sometimes we asked children to complete a picture. For example, we gave some a picture showing some batteries and a light bulb and asked them to show how they would connect them up to make the light bulb glow. We asked others to add to a picture of a room to show where the light was. By completing pictures children can demonstrate their ideas visually without spending a lot of time producing a complicated drawing. The drawings can then be used as the starting point for the children to test their ideas. For example, children can try out their ideas about electrical circuits practically.

Annotated drawings

If children do their own drawing, it can form the basis of a useful discussion between the teacher and the child, with the teacher helping to articulate his or her ideas. Older children can annotate their drawings to explain their views in more detail. Teachers can also annotate children's drawings for them, writing down what the children say. The annotated drawing can then be kept as a record of the child's ideas, and it can form a useful part of teacher assessment.

Group discussions

One way to encourage children to work together as a group is to ask them to discuss their explanations of a particular event. For example, the following extract comes from a discussion of rusting with a group of 5 and 6 year olds. They are looking at some wire wool that has rusted.

A: It's gone brown at the sides.
B: It's gone brown from the dust.
C: It's gone brown on the top. Underneath it's brown.
D: It's gone brown because of the rain.
C: Wire is metal. Maybe wire wool is metal.
C: }
D: } It might be rusty.

In this conversation, the children have a chance to reveal their own ideas. They are also exposed to each other's ideas. The group have begun to connect four ideas: the wire wool has gone brown; it has gone brown because of the rain; it might be metal; it might be rusty. Each idea is an important element of the explanation they are moving towards. The children's ideas are more powerful collectively than they might be individually. Each child provides a stimulus to the others, and gains from the place their own contributions play in the joint explanation.

Children can also be given statements to discuss. The statements can be from other children in the class or they might be standard scientific explanations. For instance, when trying to arrive at an understanding of the Earth in space, children discussed some of the following statements in groups.

The sun goes to bed at night.
Some people think that the sun goes round the Earth.
The sun hides behind the cloud at night.
Some people think that the Earth is flat.
The Earth is a sphere.
Some people think that the Earth goes round the sun.

Discussing statements like these and saying whether they agree with them or not gives children an opportunity to consider views which conflict with their own and to modify their existing views. They may become dissatisfied with the view that they hold so they are motivated to enquire further and test out their ideas with new evidence. This might involve them in consulting books and other sources, or it might involve practical investigations.

Practical investigations

Practical investigations are central to helping children to express and develop their ideas. The conversation between group members often reveals ideas that might not be expressed in other circumstances. What appear as passing comments can be revealing. For example, the idea that a toy car rolls down a ramp until it runs out of push is discussed as a group of children play with toys. If children are fully involved in planning an investigation, then further evidence of their existing ideas can be gained from their suggestions as to what should be tested and how.

Using databases

Collecting data in different forms so that results can be collated and compared can be done in several ways and can form the basis of much useful discussion. Children can present data in simple block graphs, pictograms or sets, or can enter it into a computer, using suitable software, to compile their own database. In these forms the information can provide a direct test for children's ideas. For instance, children comparing one habitat with another might ask questions about the colour of the animal living in different locations. To compare mini-beasts living in leaf litter with those living in bushes, children could search on one colour at a time to see if there was a pattern.

Children can also conduct investigations and form databases about their own ideas. Children comparing ideas about keeping healthy could make a class graph showing what they consider contributes to health. Do most children think that keeping healthy is to do with what they eat? How many attribute health to exercise, rest, going to the doctor? If children record and graph each other's ideas comparisons are easier and can lead to fruitful discussions about where the ideas came from.

3 THE POWER OF EVERYDAY LANGUAGE

The science that children encounter in school sometimes introduces domains of which children have little or no everyday experience. At other times it involves them in working with familiar phenomena. In some areas, such as vision, what happens to the food they eat, explanations of day and night, shadows and plant growth, many children had well-established views which they had little difficulty in expressing. Often their ideas show the influence of common sense and everyday ways of talking. We asked some children what they thought happened to food inside their bodies. Ideas included these:

It goes to my legs.
It disappears.
It goes to my muscles to make them strong.

These theories may be strongly influenced by colloquial expressions like:

You must have hollow legs.
That disappeared quickly.
If you eat it all up it will make you big and strong.

The children's views are not random. They are reasonable interpretations of the language they hear about them. Everyday language does not carry labels to distinguish scientific talk from other forms of talk. Most adults are well aware when they use expressions like 'you must have hollow legs' that they are not speaking literally. Children have to discover this.

Sometimes, an apparently unambiguous question may turn out to have alternative scientific meanings. In exploring children's ideas about vision, we asked: 'Can you explain how you see the book?' A large number of children thought of vision as an active process, more to do with our eyes than with light:

I just look with my eyes.
By using our eyes.

Few children interpreted the question as a physicist might, involving the way light is scattered from objects into our eyes. Their replies were closer to the way a psychologist or a physiologist might interpret the question, though none of the children would understand the way visual perception works. Here again, everyday language may have contributed to the way the children understood the question, since we have many expressions which represent vision as an active process:

Use your eyes!
She stared right through me.
He's got X-ray vision.

Words used in scientific contexts often have a very different meaning from their everyday meaning. The word 'light' is one example. We asked some children to add to a picture to show where the light in a room was coming from. For most children 'light' in this task means 'light bulb' as in 'Switch on the light'. It may mean the same for many adults as well. However, in one scientific sense, it means 'light wherever it occurs'. This could be light radiating from a light source, or reflected light. We found another example in asking children about the circulation of the blood. When asked how the blood moves round the body, some 5 or 6 year old children swayed from side to side to show how they could make their blood move. This is a reasonable response, since our blood does move relative to our environment when we move. However, the movement to which the question referred was movement relative to the body: the flow through the veins and arteries. This assumption behind the question was not explicit.

Unless these differences in meaning are addressed, children can become very confused. One way to avoid confusion is to build language work into science sessions. Children can be asked to write around words such as 'light', 'shadow' or 'circuit' to show what kind of meaning the word has for them. Another approach is to let children think of all the words and expressions involving a particular word, such as 'seeing' or 'looking'. A third option is to give the children a collection of expressions in common usage and ask them to discuss them, saying what they think they mean.

4 EXPERIENCE AND EXPLANATION

Experience provides the basis for all scientific ideas. But the depth of experience on which children can rely when they encounter a new topic varies from one topic to another. Equally, the depth and directness of experience which we can supply practically in the classroom varies.

In almost all cases children have some relevant experience to draw on which can account for otherwise surprising ideas. For instance, some children were asked to produce a drawing to show what is inside their bodies. They drew blood as spots. When they cut themselves, they see spots of blood and they had assumed that blood looks like that inside our bodies.

In some areas of science we want to ask questions about phenomena of which children already have experience. But this does not mean that the children think they are in need of explanation and they may not have any detailed ideas about them. For example, children may have heard musical instruments but may not have considered how the sounds are produced or transmitted through the air. Children may know that clothes dry on a washing line or in a tumble dryer, but may not have asked how or why. We seek explanations when something puzzles or surprises us. Everyday experience is generally highly predictable and so rarely offers such surprises. Yet one of the conditions for any scientific enquiry is to realise that something is in need of explanation. With many of our everyday experiences of natural events it is difficult to envisage how they could be other than they are. How could a musical instrument *not* make a noise? How could clothes *not* dry out on a warm sunny day?

Children need direct experiences of such phenomena on which to draw in formulating and extending their ideas. The growth of plants is a good example. Many children will have come across plants growing in houses and gardens. Not until they start to grow plants for themselves in different conditions may they come to see that plant growth needs explaining. By comparing growth in various conditions they can see the circumstances in which they grow, and those in which they do not. The children carrying out the work about evaporation were given the opportunity to watch the tank of water over several weeks, noting their thoughts and observations in a class log book. This gave them a new experience of evaporation, as well as time to draw on their prior experiences.

There are some phenomena of which it is very difficult to give children direct experience in the classroom. Many primary children think that the Sun moves round the Earth. This is reasonable in many ways. We are aware of the apparent movement of the Sun across the sky each day, and we are unaware that the Earth is moving at all. Our language supports our direct experience: we talk about the Sun rising, setting and moving behind clouds and buildings. It is difficult in this case to offer children the direct practical experience that will challenge their ideas and lead them to modify them. But they can discuss a range of ideas which include their own thinking, scientists' ideas and those held by earlier generations. They might find that until the sixteenth century everyone believed that the Sun went round the Earth. Then when children turn to secondary sources it will not be in a passive way, but with the purpose of checking ideas about which they have already talked.

Even when children encounter facts in books or are told the 'correct' explanation, it does not mean that they will necessarily believe them. One 11 year old who was asked about the shape of the Earth replied that he knew he was supposed to say that it was shaped like a sphere, but that he thought people only say that so that it would fit easily on a globe:

> Really, the Earth is flat because people would fall off a round Earth. When people set off in a boat to prove whether the Earth was round, they did not fall off so that proves that the Earth is flat, but people just say it is round.

Despite the fact that the conclusions are wrong, we can interpret this as the product of a scientific mind at work. Like professional scientists, he is very cautious about rejecting an explanation that accounts for what he knows, and he will not simply submit to authority. He will demand convincing evidence before he adopts a new theory. But alternatively it may be that his understanding is less certain than his comment suggests, and that further discussion would reveal doubts!

Teachers can help to develop the ideas of any child by providing them with a new range of experiences. This may mean setting up materials for children to investigate, setting up discussions between children to explore each other's views and in some cases referring children to secondary sources to compare their beliefs with the information provided there. In all cases, the experiences will be more powerful if they relate directly to children's current theories, and offer them the opportunity to test them and consider alternative accounts.

5 CREATING AN APPROPRIATE CLASSROOM CLIMATE

The techniques for eliciting and extending children's ideas which I have described will not be entirely successful unless the teacher adopts a role which is supportive and non-threatening. Children are often reluctant to express their ideas for fear of being wrong. The climate in the classroom must be one where children feel that their ideas are valued so that they are willing to commit themselves in public. We have found that creating this climate involves a number of factors. Teachers need to take children's ideas seriously, and avoid making them feel that they have to search for the right answer, hidden somewhere in the teacher's head. Open questions might start with phrases such as:

What do you think . . .?
Can you explain why you think that . . .?
Can you tell me about . . .?

This does not mean that children are led to believe they are always right. But they are unlikely to make real progress unless they are helped to formulate their own ideas explicitly and then look for evidence and compare their views to those of others. The alternative may be the public compliance combined with private doubt of the boy who could not accept that the Earth was round.

Children also need meaningful contexts for their work in science. They need to see a purpose to the activities. Science can be embedded in many other activities. For example, children planning to tell a story might decide to use shadow puppets. This could give rise to questions such as:

How can shadows be made?
Can shadows be coloured?
Where will we have to put the screen, the light and the shadow puppets?
How can we produce sharp shadows?

The questions can come equally from the teacher and the children. At every stage children's ideas can be included, so that they give rise to many opportunities for scientific investigations. The teacher's interactions with the children will be vital if the opportunities are not to be missed.

The classroom should also be one in which all children's ideas are valued. All the children in the classes we worked in were included. Teachers commented that children of all abilities benefited. Indeed they felt that in many cases children who experienced difficulties in learning responded particularly well. They felt that their contributions were accepted and valued. One result of being open to children's ideas in science is that all pupils in a class are taken seriously as learners and thinkers.

REFERENCES

Driver, R., Guesne, E. and Tiberghien, A. (1985) *Children's Ideas in Science*, Milton Keynes: Open University Press.
Osborne, R. and Freyberg, P. (1985) *Learning in Science*, London: Heinemann.

FURTHER READING

The research carried out in the SPACE Project has been written up as a series of reports, each covering a different area of science. These reports include *Evaporation and Condensation, Sound, Light, Growth, Electricity* and *Materials.* All are published by Liverpool University Press. These are being followed up with a series of curriculum materials for primary teachers based on the research findings, which will offer teachers strategies for building on the thinking which children bring with them to the classroom.

Chapter 5

What will happen if . . .?

An active approach to mathematics teaching

Adrienne Bennett with Honor Williams

This chapter describes the way that one teacher has made mathematics accessible to 14 and 15 year olds in a special school for pupils described as having 'moderate learning difficulties'. The principles underlying Adrienne Bennett's work have been developed during the Low Attainers in Mathematics Project and the Raising Achievement in Mathematics Project. In Adrienne Bennett's classroom pupils work on mathematical activities which enable them to respond in a variety of ways and at a range of levels. These activities provide meaningful challenges which give pupils reasons to practise and extend their mathematical skills. The class are encouraged to find their own solutions to problems and they can choose their own methods of working; they are encouraged to be active, independent learners. As a result of this approach to mathematics, Adrienne Bennett has found that her pupils have confounded many stereotypes about children with 'moderate learning difficulties'.

In the past two years my own views of mathematics, how people learn it, and how it should be taught, have changed. The stimulus for these changes has been a combination of my own experiences of doing mathematics and the discovery that my pupils could do mathematics in ways that I had not appreciated before. As I have altered the way I teach mathematics, I have found pupils have been more highly motivated and have demonstrated skills I had not suspected they possessed. I hope that my own account will encourage other people to reflect on their own perceptions of mathematics and the way it is taught, especially to pupils with learning difficulties.

1 MATHEMATICS AS A TEACHER AND A LEARNER

There is a close link between my own experience as a learner and the experience of my pupils. I loved maths when I was at school, but I had been taught in a very formal way. Getting work ticked was my main motivation. I was lucky: I succeeded in getting ticks. I could learn procedures and facts for a short time and I knew how to regurgitate them for examinations. Whether I understood them was another matter. Although I sailed through O-Level I never took maths any further and I never engaged creatively in the process of doing mathematics. With this background, as a teacher I saw the subject as a collection of facts and skills that I had to impart to my pupils in a well-defined sequence. If they had difficulties then I broke each stage down into small steps and gave them repeated practice. Since progress was slow – sometimes nonexistent – much of the time was spent on basic arithmetic.

In these respects, my teaching was similar to that of many other teachers working with low-attaining pupils. The Low Attainers in Mathematics Project (LAMP) and the Raising Achievement in Mathematics Project (RAMP)[1] found that the mathematical diet for low-attaining pupils often consisted of little more than basic arithmetic presented in simple step by step learning sequences and repeated frequently. Skills were often practised in isolation from any meaningful context. Pupils could not see the relevance of what they were asked to do and so lost motivation. Many teachers found that this diet did not enable their pupils to succeed. Although pupils met the same topic over and over again, they still did not understand. Pupils experienced difficulties in applying skills in new contexts, and in understanding what skills were needed to solve new problems.

The change in my approach to mathematics began when I joined an in-service Diploma in Mathematics Education.[2] In the first week I was given the task of making a $3 \times 3 \times 3$ wooden cube made up of three different pentacubes and three different tetracubes. A version of the problem is shown in Figure 5.1.

Figure 5.1 How do you make a $3 \times 3 \times 3$ cube?

With help from a tutor I finally put them together and fitted them into the cubic box I was given. One evening, some weeks later, I took the cube apart and could not get it back together again.

The following morning I put the loose pieces in my bag and took them to school. John, a 14 year old, often came to school early. He asked if he could help. I said that he could try to put the cube together and I left him with the pieces while I went to fetch some paper. I returned a few minutes later to find the cube assembled. I looked in disbelief. John assured me that it was easy and I watched, amazed, as his hands turned the pieces to assemble it again.

Then I gave John the task of making his own $3 \times 3 \times 3$ cube using multilink cubes. I stipulated that it had to be different from mine. He did this with very little effort, and I gave him small wooden cubes so that he could make a cube to keep. Would making a box for it cause a problem? Without any help he drew a net onto squared paper and copied it onto card. I didn't have to mention the flaps for sticking it together. He had already drawn them. He ended by drawing his individual pieces in perspective on isometric paper. Figure 5.1 also shows John's cube.

John obviously had considerable spatial skills. Comments on his mathematical development from other teachers made no reference to this strength.

1985 His number work has made progress and he is beginning to add, subtract and divide using HTUs.

1986 He copes with addition and subtraction to 100.

1987 Can add, subtract and multiply HTU. Some understanding of division. Can use money up to £1.00 in shopping situations.

1988 Mathematics: steady understanding of basic concepts if taken singly. Cannot apply one concept to another in problem-solving situations.

The records made no mention of John's practical work, spatial awareness, work on shape or measuring, or his skills in using and applying mathematics, save the brief reference in 1988. (Why do so many comments made on children described as having special needs concentrate on their retention of arithmetic facts and algorithms?)

John had a long history of academic failure. At that stage he was a virtual non-reader and was unable to write a coherent sentence. I began to see that mathematics might offer John and others the opportunities and challenges through which they could begin to succeed. But if that was to happen, then my practice would need to change.

In the past I had encountered statements in books and official reports that encouraged me to think of mathematics in a positive way:

> Mathematics must be an experience from which pupils derive pleasure and enjoyment . . .
>
> The aim of mathematics teaching should be to show mathematics as a

process, as a creative activity in which pupils can be fully involved, and not as an imposed body of knowledge immune from any change or development.

(DES 1985)

It was only when I was involved in learning which allowed me to be creative and to develop without feeling threatened, that statements like this became meaningful. One of the most powerful forms of learning to which I was exposed on my course was active collaborative work. We were encouraged to try many different activities. My first problem was to overcome my sense of inadequacy at my own mathematical understanding. But this steadily dissolved as we shared ideas, asked questions of one another and gave each other leads. When someone discovered something, they had to explain it to the others, and this reinforced their own understanding. We were supported by the way in which tutors worked with us. We were given tasks and problems, but we controlled how we tackled them. Tutors posed questions which refocused our attention on relevant information in our work. We were given open-ended leads such as:

Where does your answer fit in?
What do you think will happen if . . .?
What does that tell you?
Is there a connection between . . .?
Try 1.5.

We were not swamped with facts and procedures which, without our understanding them, we would soon forget and be unable to apply to new problems. While we worked together, our mathematical language was very basic, limited and tentative. Our working was often untidy. At this point worrying about the language we used would have inhibited us. Yet it was from our jottings and provisional attempts to express and solve problems that we became able to formalise our thoughts and write coherently about our work.

As I developed in understanding and confidence, my feelings about mathematics changed. I started to find great relaxation in playing with mathematical problems and puzzles. I began to see my environment in a new light as I connected the shapes and patterns I found in it with mathematics. I experienced the joy and excitement of the subject as I discovered something for the first time.

My experience as a learner has markedly affected the way I teach mathematics. The modes of learning that helped me are those that I now use with my pupils. My aims include encouraging pupils to think for themselves and to choose their own methods of working. Individual work at their own pace from workbooks is not likely to be an effective means to achieve these goals. Not only is there tremendous pressure on teacher time with this approach, but the amount of time that can be offered to each pupil is of limited value. The opportunities for pupils to share, compare and contrast ideas are limited, and children are constrained to work in the way the workbook dictates. The result is that many have to rely heavily on rote learning and memory, with limited understanding.

I have seen pupils gaining satisfaction and stimulation from actively working together, but it would be a mistake to require pupils to work exclusively in one way. They do not only work in small groups. I often set a problem and allow them to choose their own method of working. Some will choose to work alone, others will work in pairs or groups. As I notice various strategies I frequently draw the class together and encourage them to share ideas. This might give vital stimulation to others and set them on new lines of discovery.

Pupils in schools designated for those with moderate learning difficulties have often met failure throughout their schooling. It was very important that they start to succeed in some way. I wanted them to feel valued. In the rest of this chapter I shall describe how I tried to do this, drawing on my own experience and developing mathematical interests and understanding.

2 JOINT EXPLORATION

I have often found that I can share problems with them as both teacher and learner. I have explained to pupils that I do not know 'the answer' and so I can share the excitement of working out a problem with them. One example is the 'sheep pen problem':

> How many different arrangements of fences could a farmer make with eight one-metre fences to enclose his sheep? Which has the greatest area? What about ten fences, twelve fences?

I set limits by saying that the farmer only had straight and right-angled brackets with which to join the fences. I now wonder if I was right to do this. What if a pupil made a hexagonal arrangement? Could she have found a strategy for comparing the areas?

I wanted the pupils to understand the idea of a square metre and so we began practically as a class with blank metre sticks on the floor to represent the fences. They were invited to make different arrangements. This idea immediately gave rise to the question: are shapes that are rotated and reflected the same or different? The pupils decided that they were the same in that context and were satisfied that there were only three different shapes if they did not allow fences in the middle or squares just touching at the corners.

At first the pupils confused the perimeter of the shape with the area, but with the help of a metre-square quadrant they developed the idea of square metres covering the inside of the shape. They discovered that they had one area of 4 m^2 and two of 3 m^2. Now I asked them to work in pairs or individually to find the arrangements of ten fences. As there were not enough metre sticks to go round, I gave out matchsticks to represent the fences. Toward the end of the lesson we started to pool our ideas. We had five different shapes on the board by the end of the lesson. Three arrangements with eight fences; five with ten fences ... odd numbers ... Was there a pattern? I decided to work on the problem at home.

Had we found all the arrangements for ten fences? No – I found another. I also worked on twelve fences, trying very hard to find some sort of pattern.

The following day, the class started work on twelve fences. As I walked round observing the work I spotted one arrangement that I had not drawn. This was a lesson for me. I had become so interested in a nice neat pattern that I hadn't checked if I had found all the shapes. I told them how I had worked on the problem and now one of them had ruined my theory! This proved to be very motivating. We began to work cooperatively. I sat down with them and began to play with matchsticks too. I now had no idea how many arrangements we would find. We began sorting them into different area sizes as we were getting confused with those we had and didn't have.

Through such activities, where the teacher is a fellow learner, the pupils have developed the confidence to advance their provisional, partially formed ideas in the knowledge that they would be accepted and built on. My dialogue with them has been an important part of the process of valuing their own contributions. Their replies to my questions may not be those that I had in mind, but by telling them that they were incorrect I would probably have ensured that they would not be so willing to answer again. I have tried to avoid this danger by responding with words such as:

> That's interesting, what does anyone else think?
> Can you explain how you got the idea?
> I hadn't thought of that . . . can you explain?

With such support, pupils have often sorted out ideas and ended by convincing each other, rather than depending on their teacher's ideas. They have been able to work on problems not in order to satisfy an authoritative teacher, but because the problems are intrinsically interesting and challenging. In this way they have developed their capacity to be autonomous learners.

3 BUILDING ON PUPILS' INTERESTS

On various occasions I have been able to exploit pupils' own interests for mathematical ends, however transient the interest might have seemed. At a school fete, John had brought a combination-coded padlock. It had ten buttons, to be pressed in a certain order. The following week he was fiddling with it in his lap at the start of the lesson. He said he didn't know the code but was trying to work it out. He asked me to do it, as I was 'good at maths'! This was the opening: 'Have you any idea how many ways there might be?', I asked.

The four boys on the table began working with John on the problem. At first they wrote various numbers, apparently haphazardly, on a large sheet of paper. After watching them for a while I suggested that they might try to keep most numbers constant and change just one. At the end of the lesson, John asked if he could take their working home. 'There are going to be a lot, aren't there?', he remarked.

The following day we took up the problem again. I suggested that they might look at smaller numbers of buttons, and see if they could spot how the number of ways of pressing them was growing. This time the whole class shared the problem. Assuming all buttons were pressed, they could see that there was one way with one button and two ways with two buttons. They went off in groups or individually to try three buttons. It wasn't long before they found six ways.

Four buttons was more difficult. To help, we numbered the buttons 1–4. At the end of the lesson no one had found all the possible orderings of four buttons. I asked how many they had – 8, 11, 16. One boy said he had found six ways with 1 at the front. In the next lesson, I asked him to share his six ways with 1 in front, and I wrote them on the blackboard. What about 2 in front? Someone called out 'six ways'. 3 at the front? 'Six ways'. 4 at the front? 'Six ways!' We now had on the board:

1 number	1 way
2 numbers	2 ways
3 numbers	6 ways
4 numbers	24 ways

Could anyone see how the pattern was growing? Most of the class were happy to write out the 24 ways for themselves or start on five buttons. Suddenly John, the owner of the padlock, shouted in true Eureka style, 'I've got it!' I knew exactly how he felt. I went over to him and he whispered, 'Look. You times the last 6 ways by 4 to get 24. Five numbers will be 24 × 5.' And so he went on through the calculator to get the number of ways for ten buttons – 3,628,800.

The motivation and enjoyment from this activity had been pupil centred. The activity was sustained for quite a long time by pupils who, according to their label, have difficulty sustaining anything. I know that in the past I would not have had the confidence to let children work on the problem. John would probably have been reprimanded for playing with something in lesson time. As my own confidence in working investigatively has grown I have begun to see the potential of chance events like the appearance of the padlock. If our work with pupils is based on valuing what they bring to their lessons, and using this as a basis for development, then the element of chance can be minimised. Once pupils begin to see how activities can build from ideas and objects others bring in, they gain the confidence to bring in things that interest them.

4 RICH MATHEMATICAL ACTIVITIES

An important feature of the work of the LAMP and RAMP has been the role of 'rich mathematical activities'. These are activities that offer everyone in a varied class the chance to share a common mathematical experience, yet to work at a level appropriate to each individual. *Better Mathematics* (Ahmed 1987) is an account of some of the work of these two projects. It describes the necessary ingredients of a rich mathematical activity:

- It must be accessible to everyone at the start.
- It needs to allow further challenges and be extendable.
- It should invite children to make decisions.
- It should involve children in speculating, hypothesis-making and testing, proving or explaining, reflecting, interpreting.
- It should not restrict pupils from searching in other directions.
- It should promote discussion and communication.
- It should encourage originality and invention.
- It should encourage 'what if' and 'what if not' questions.
- It should have an element of surprise.
- It should be enjoyable.

(Ahmed 1987)

Many of these principles are illustrated by the work my class did on the Fibonacci sequence. This number sequence is frequently used in mathematical investigations in ordinary schools. I found it equally useful with my pupils. The sequence was discovered by the Italian mathematician Leonardo of Pisa, also known as Fibonacci (*c.* 1170–1240). It arose from a problem about rabbits. We start with one new born pair of rabbits: one male and one female. Baby rabbits take one month to grow to adulthood. At the end of each month, a pair of rabbits produces a pair of baby rabbits, again, one male and one female. No rabbits die. How does the number of pairs of rabbits grow? The sequence begins 1, 1, 2, 3, 5, 8 . . . Each number is the sum of the two preceding numbers. It is full of surprising mathematics.

My first objective was to get pupils to spot how the sequence was built up. I told them briefly about Fibonacci and I wrote the sequence up to 8 on the blackboard. Soon several children spotted the rule. There was no hesitation in working out the next number in the sequence – 13. Could anyone predict the 24th number? Ideas were recorded on the blackboard. I had predicted that no one would be anywhere near it. Most replies were in the hundreds: 123, 128, 140, 89 . . . At the end there was a murmur of question and hesitation from Daniel, who said that he wanted to say 500. The others looked at him almost in disbelief, but I could see that he had been thinking very carefully. This change of mind persuaded Stephen to change his mind. 'I'll say 1000', and then 'No, 5000'. I took this seriously, although I suspect he said it just to make the others laugh. Now they had to work out the 24th number. They started to work out the answers mentally, but soon resorted to calculators. Suddenly, from the front row, Stephen said, 'I think I'm going to be the nearest. I'm already at one thousand and something and I haven't finished yet.' There was tremendous surprise when they reached the 24th number. At the end of the lesson I explained how Fibonacci had worked on the rabbit problem, and that we would look at this in the next lesson.

For the second lesson, I thought that the class needed experience at working at a problem systematically. Chairs and tables pushed back, we used the rows of tiles on the floor to represent months, two tin cans to represent the original pair of rabbits and coloured wooden discs for the babies. Through discussion, with chalk lines and discs all over the floor, a pattern began to emerge. After the fourth month Lisa said: 'It's going to be five new pairs next month.' She had linked the numbers chalked on the floor to the sequence we had worked on the day before. By the end of the lesson we had completed the sixth month.

In the third lesson, pupils worked in pairs to produce their own diagram to show the rabbits. How to do so was their decision. The diagrams turned out to be very different. Working together on the floor had not constrained them to produce similar representations. I was thrilled at the results.

Later lessons extended our investigations. Some pupils explored the sequence with questions such as:

Which numbers are even?
Which numbers are multiples of 3, 5 . . .
Could they describe any patterns in these numbers?

As Carmel finished the 3s, she came to me and whispered: 'I think I can see what the 5s are going to be before I do it', and she explained her prediction. James, meanwhile, was trying to predict what number he would get by adding the squares of two consecutive numbers in the sequence. Was there a pattern?

$$\left.\begin{array}{l} 1^2 + 1^2 = 2 \\ 1^2 + 2^2 = 5 \\ 2^2 + 3^2 = 13 \\ 3^2 + 5^2 = 34 \end{array}\right\} \text{All the results are in the sequence}$$

When he had explored the problem, I asked him if he could write down a number in the sequence and say which numbers were squared and added together to make it. He wrote '14th', looked at his work and then said to me, 'I can't do the 14th.' He explained that all the answers he had found were in odd numbered positions in the sequence. Of course . . . except that I hadn't noticed this.

In working on these activities the class had worked systematically and persistently; they had collaborated in pairs and groups; they had identified patterns and structures in the sequences; they had made predictions and tested them; they had explained and justified their reasoning to me and to each other; they had worked practically to understand the sequence and how it could model a real life situation. They had exercised some control over how they worked and what aspects of the investigation they pursued. Finally, they had, throughout, been using and practising their 'basic skills' in a meaningful context. They were adding, multiplying and dividing, mentally, on paper and with a calculator.

In developing activities such as this, *Better Mathematics* offers some useful leads. These suggest a range of exploratory starting points:

START WITH EXPLORATORY TYPE QUESTIONS LIKE:

HOW MANY DIFFERENT

........ways to work out 21 × 13?........ ways to satisfy c = a + 2b?..... ...ways to draw an equilateral triangle?

WHAT HAPPENS WHEN........? CAN YOU FIND A BETTER WAY........?

IS IT TRUE THAT

........12% of £40 is the same as 40% of £12?

GET PUPILS TO SET THEIR OWN QUESTIONS

........pass them around.

ASK THEM TO FIND OUT HOW TO DO SOMETHING

........find the area of a triangle........construct a 30 degree angle.

START WITH A PROBLEM OR DILEMMA

........explore........sort out the contradictions or confusions.

START WITH AN ANSWER

........explore........how did they get it?........what was the question/ problem?........what's gone wrong?

USE AN OUTSIDE STIMULUS

........radio/TV/newspaper puzzles........advertisements........familiar everyday anomalies.

GET PUPILS TO MAKE OR INVENT SOMETHING

........to measure turn........to measure time........to carry a certain weight.

USE GAMES

........can they make them harder?........can they understand each others' rules?

(Ahmed 1987)

5 ENCOURAGING PUPILS TO DEVELOP THEIR OWN STRATEGIES

I have found it important to allow pupils to find and develop their own methods of calculation, rather than require them to use standard methods. Indeed we may inhibit their development if we force them to use unfamiliar approaches which slow down their thinking in the cause of a mistaken view of what it is to work systematically. Even though I now encourage my class to use any methods they like, there are still times when I wished I had not said something which could inhibit a pupil's thinking. When World Cup fever was on us in 1990, Lisa was working on a combination problem with different football strips. She had various coloured shorts, shirts and socks. She had calculated that with orange shirts there would be nine possible combinations.

Me: If you have shirts of five colours can you make a prediction at this point?
Lisa: Yes, there will be nine for each colour.
Me: Can you work it out then? What is 9 × 5?

I regretted the last statement as soon as I had said it. Perhaps I am so preconditioned by tables that I could not reflect quickly enough that there are other ways of getting the answer. Lisa had grown in confidence. She refused to take my lead.

> I don't want to do it like that. I'm going to call each 10 ... 10, 20, 30, 40, 50 ... There will be 45.

By pursuing her own method, Lisa not only gained control over her work but also showed her grasp of the nature of the problem and of the nature of multiplication. She exercised valuable mental arithmetic skills.

On another occasion, I had asked a group to work out the 'best buy' between a 25 cl can of wine at £1.19 and a 150 cl bottle at £4.59. These were real objects at real prices. Practical work showed them that they could put six canfuls into the bottle. Then, by pouring a canful of water into the empty bottle, they saw where £1.19's worth came in the bottle (see Figure 5.2). As they poured in further canfuls, I encouraged them to work out the amounts mentally by rounding off £1.19 to £1.20, and taking away 1p. Suddenly one boy said, 'I know what one is next ... £4.76.' I asked him to explain, expecting to hear a version of

Figure 5.2 Assessing the best buy: measuring canfuls in the bottle

$$4 \times £1.20 = £4.80;$$
$$£4.80 - 4p = £4.76.$$

I heard, 'Well, the pennies are going down 9, 8, 7 so the next will be 6. The next column is going up 1, 3, 5 so the next will be 7 and the £s are going up in ones. £4.76.' I hadn't noticed this.

Another boy, whilst working out a problem, had to find 28 × 8. This is what he did, working quickly.

$$\begin{array}{rrr} 28 & & \\ 28 & 16 & \\ 28 & \underline{16} & \\ \underline{28} & 32 & \\ \underline{112} & & 112 \\ 3 & & \underline{112} \\ & & \underline{224} \end{array}$$

Although a standard approach to this calculation might appear more efficient, this pupil's own method works well and reveals a lot of knowledge. He could double and halve small numbers, decompose the calculation into components and recombine them to find the solution.

6 CONCLUSION

Through the approaches I have described I have aimed to give my pupils access to a broad and balanced mathematical curriculum. I have attempted to provide situations in which pupils are encouraged to:

- take initiatives and thus work creatively;
- respond to and create their own challenges;
- find and use their own methods;
- have their own ideas valued and built upon;
- work for the intrinsic interest of the subject, not just for their teacher;
- discuss and share ideas;
- explore and use their skills through mathematically rich activities.

My own experience of doing mathematics has been vital. It is important that we continue to put ourselves into all sorts of learning situations so that we recognise what we need to do or stop doing with our pupils. Experiences that inhibit us as learners can be just as important in this respect as experiences that help.

I have found that the pupils designated as having moderate learning difficulties that I have worked with can: concentrate for long periods of time; sustain protracted investigations; be systematic; reason logically; find patterns and relationships; make and test predictions; generalise; record and explain their findings. I have found them working in ways I had never expected them to be able to. What they couldn't do was perform meaningless calculations and relate them to situations which were equally meaningless to them. But then who can?

NOTES

1 LAMP (1983–6) and RAMP (1986–9) were curriculum development projects funded jointly by the Department of Education and Science and local education authorities in England, and directed by Afzal Ahmed at the West Sussex Institute of Higher Education. RAMP operated through five regional centres.
2 Diploma in Mathematics Education, West Sussex Institute of Higher Education.

REFERENCES

Ahmed, A. G. (1987) *Better Mathematics: A Curriculum Development Study Based on the Low Attainers in Mathematics Project*, London: HMSO.
Department of Education and Science (DES) (1985) *Mathematics from 5 to 16* (Curriculum Matters 3), London: HMSO.

FURTHER READING

Ahmed, A. and Williams, H. (1989) 'A maths curriculum for all?', *Support for Learning*, 4 (4), 221–6.
Buxton, L. (1981) *Do You Panic About Maths?*, London: Heinemann Educational.
Donaldson, M. (1978) *Children's Minds*, London: Fontana.
Holt, J. (1969) *How Children Fail*, Harmondsworth: Penguin.
Pinel, A. and Boorman, P. (1989) 'Making sense of mathematics', *Special Children*, no. 31, June/July.
Trickett, L. and Sulke, F. (1988) 'Low attainers can do mathematics', in D. Pimm (ed.), *Mathematics, Teachers and Pupils*, London: Hodder & Stoughton.
Williams, H. I. M. (ed.) (1989) 'Teacher expectation: pupil achievement', unpublished RAMP Report, Bognor Regis: The Mathematics Centre, West Sussex Institute of Higher Education.

Chapter 6

Setting the agenda

Student participation on a multi-media learning scheme

Stuart Olesker

In this chapter Stuart Olesker describes the multi-media scheme at Portsmouth College of Art, Design and Further Education, where he works. He presents the scheme through the eyes of a potential student, 'Michael', who has arrived as the student-chaired monthly meeting is about to begin. 'Michael' and the deaf student (who eventually storms out of the meeting) are created from an amalgam of several students who have attended the scheme. All other references are to existing students, although names have been changed.

Michael is nervous. It is his first visit to the multi-media scheme. His social worker recommended the scheme to him but Michael has his doubts. To him the term 'multi-media' suggests some vast and streamlined emporium of screens, projectors, TVs and sound systems all linked to computers operated by high-powered technicians. The extent of Michael's 'multi-media' experience has been to take some Polaroid shots of drawings of his dog. Would he not be a trifle out of his depth here?

The 'nerve centre' of the scheme is an old building about five minutes 'push' away from the Art and Design School in the very centre of the city. As he wheels through the door he relaxes slightly. He enters a cramped and cluttered space. Exhibition displays, files, portfolios and furniture seem to be scattered around with an air of sudden improvisation. While he discerns a bank of computers by the wall (one student is typing up minutes of the monthly group meeting now in progress), Michael begins to feel a little more at home in this rather ramshackle world. He glances round at the seventeen people – who are they?: students?, support-workers?, staff? – squeezed around the two tables. The room should only hold ten people, but somehow a space is found for Michael.

He is introduced to the group by Jane, this month's student chairperson and is handed an agenda (collected from items submitted by students, support workers and staff), minutes and notes. New fears present themselves. He looks around and studies the confident performances. Soon he discovers that of the seventeen people present, thirteen are students (representing about a quarter of those enrolled on the scheme), two are support workers and two are full-time tutors.

The support workers turn out to be volunteers and 'trainees' (often via Employment Training) on placement. They tell Michael they are looking for new ways of using or acquiring skills. They feel that working alongside disabled students gives a particular significance to their teaching and learning. Like the scheme's two part-time tutors (who are absent from the meeting because they're attending courses in Sign Language and Counselling) they train as much by 'doing and reflecting' as by attending specific courses. (Incidentally the two part-time tutors were both volunteer support workers the year before.) Several of the students, like himself, are in wheelchairs through some form of cerebral palsy. Felix and Gerald, whom he recognises from his special school, have spina bifida and hydrocephalus. For some reason there are only two females present. 'I think we're a bit insensitive at times', a nearby male whispers to Michael. 'Insensitive?' challenges an incredulous support worker, 'Bloody sexist. You scare the women away.' Michael is also informed that there are proportionately fewer females in the area with these disabilities.

'Still,' moans one of the females, 'a lot of women with disabilities aren't encouraged to apply for schemes like this ...' The chairperson quashes these interruptions, Michael looks around. Three students are gazing blankly into space – bored? cogitating? – but what engages Michael's attention is the urgency and animation with which a core of the group are debating issues: advocacy, access, next term's curriculum, the conduct of group meetings, international exchanges with the USA and Hungary and 'designing for need' projects with students from other areas of the college.

He reflects on his own diffidence and awkwardness in large groups. Were these students once like him? Felix and Gerald certainly were. Felix has been on the scheme for nine months, Gerald for two years. Michael compares their histories with his own: eleven years of special schooling, the assessment by training officers for 'employability' (they, like he, were told they were 'unemployable'), the static, containing world of the activity centre. Yet they do not appear to have been cowed by systems or professionals. Whatever resentments they have stacked up they seem to have transformed into energy, driving them to learn, campaign, debate, organise and design. They seem to be on the way to finding what they need. And what does Michael need? Prospective students tend to consider the multi-media scheme after eliminating other possibilities. If they do not know what they want, they know what they do not want: not school, not set college syllabus, not residential home, not training scheme, not assessment, not sheltered employment, not activity centre. Michael decides he needs time, time to explore at his own pace projects involving the art of photography, video, tape slide, drama, art and design, computing, creative writing, music ... All these according to some notes before him, are offered by the scheme. In these notes I described the aims and origins of the scheme:

> The Multi-Media Scheme is one aspect of the Portsmouth College of Art, Design and Further Education's support for learning (another is the Bridging

> Course, offering opportunities to school leavers with 'moderate learning difficulties'). It is part of the College's general policy of encouraging students who might, for whatever reason, consider themselves excluded from Further or Higher Education to make full use of the College's – and their own – resources.
>
> The Scheme originally began in 1982 when it was funded through City Planning as a training programme for young adults with disabilities. Trainees would attend for forty weeks and in the second half of their training they would pass on skills acquired (e.g. in computing or photography) to the new intake of trainees. Before leaving the Scheme they would apply their acquired learning and confidence to work experience or to a commissioned project.
>
> The accent now is much more on education than 'training', on 'students' rather than 'trainees'. 'Training' or 'course' implies a predicted outcome with little opportunity to explore, take risks or experience 'error permitted learning'. Timetables for students have become much more flexible and there is long term support for students 'spiralling out' to employment, independent living or learning opportunities offered through Learning Links, Open Learning, Adult Education, W.E.A. and other agencies within the College's network. Students also give support to one another in self created, tutor supported groups that offer services to the community ...
>
> (Olesker 1989: 3)

What, Michael wonders, are these 'self created, tutor supported groups'? Things are made clear when the discussion turns to the progress of the Access Group. These are students who have organised themselves to undertake surveys of buildings requiring modification for full public access. They are producing reports with photographs and word-processed texts. At the moment they are being commissioned by the city to look at access to hotels and guest houses. For all this they are being paid a fee. Michael wonders if he would ever gain sufficient skills in photography or desk top publishing to form part of a cooperative or enterprise.

The next three items cover different facets of designing for need. Martin, a student from another part of the college, a Higher Diploma course, reports back on the progress of the Garden Project (designing an accessible garden). The collaboration between the Design School and the multi-media group is, he says, working out quite well. There are some problems of communication and continuity (some multi-media students are full-time, some are part-time). However, there has been an interesting development. After initial experiments with raised beds, ramps and customised tools some lateral thinkers from both groups came up with the idea of a wheelchair with a seat which could be lowered to the plants at ground level. Models of the chair have already been built. Members of the group agree to document the project with photographs and notes and to continue it after the Design students graduate.

Now Matthew from the First Diploma course reports back on the progress of another project. His brief was to design an item of cutlery *with* and not *for* a disabled student. Marjorie, a part-time student on the scheme, warms to this idea especially as the accent is as much on the aesthetic as the functional possibilities. Matthew and Marjorie have already worked together to create the initial design.

The debate now broadens to consider the overall impact of students who move or learn in a manner markedly different from the majority, on the general curriculum of the college. One tutor reports that the Principal, who has wholeheartedly supported the scheme from the beginning, would very much welcome this development. Students follow this up:

> We need more projects that bring us together.
>
> We need to learn more about other students – and they about us. Otherwise we're out of sight and out of mind – or just extras to give the appearance of integration.
>
> Some of the courses are about Environmental Design. Students learning to be future professional designers will need to think about designing with everyone's needs in mind. And they'll need to learn that now. Once they're qualified it might be too late!

The group agree to develop more collaborative projects. Ironically, as several students observe, there are real problems about wheelchair access to much of the Art and Design building – but why couldn't such problems be solved jointly between the multi-media group, Design School and county architects?

The next item particularly captures Michael's attention. Throughout the meeting he has been observing one student, possibly in his thirties, who sits in a long wheelchair with his legs straight, parallel with the floor. He is almost immobile though his eyes express a thousand shades of mood. His only sounds are occasional bass guffaws that rock the chair or whimpers of frustration when he is uncomfortable or cannot communicate. His name is Henry. Michael also has problems with speech but these are nothing compared with Henry's. What, Michael wonders, does Henry get from the scheme? Or give to it? Jane, who is not only chairing the meeting but also closely involved with 'Project Henry' enlightens him.

Henry, it transpires, is very much the protégé of Jane whose negative experiences of residential living have combined with a complex of personal problems and have generated an anger that she has tempered to a cause. She believes strongly that residents of Social Services or private homes can only too easily become the victims of systems organised for the smooth running of inadequately staffed homes. For her the multi-media scheme has been not only a counter to depression but also a means of exercising aspects of her intellect and imagination. Could the scheme not do as much for other underestimated residents?

Jane took the initiative and with encouragement from other students and tutors on the scheme she set up the Achievement Group, a 'students supporting students' programme. From her period of residential living she had developed a particular rapport with Henry. She was convinced that he was being undervalued and underestimated. Why couldn't he attend the scheme? She negotiated with Henry and the Residential Centre and fixed up for him to attend the scheme for three days a week.

After a few sessions it was becoming clear that Henry's impact on the scheme was reciprocal. Many students looked at Henry – and then at themselves and saw their individual concerns from a new perspective. For some – especially Jane – Henry's presence had given them a new role, a new meaning! They could be, by turn, feeders, interpreters, lifters, entertainers, inventors . . . One morning, several students and a support worker decided to create with Henry a word-board comprising letters and phrases (e.g. 'p--s off') that he might need to use. The result was a clear, useful, personalised word-board created on the computer, printed, laminated and attached to Henry by a spontaneously formed self-help group. Meanwhile, tutors and volunteers were scurrying about devising elaborate electronic communication devices that would supersede word-boards operated by the pointing of a nose or 'unicorn' headpiece. With the new device Henry could contribute far more to group meetings and to his own learning and development. Yet even with the primitive word-board Henry could compile an inventory of his preoccupations. This, plus a variety of photographs of him featuring a range of his involvements and achievements would eventually find a place in his portrait portfolio.

Michael finally plucks up courage to ask a question. 'Excuse me, what are portrait portfolios?' He is answered by Joseph who proudly unzips a handsomely bound, black leather, loose-leaf portfolio featuring photos (taken by his friends on the scheme and selected, developed and printed by Joseph), text and cartoons all illustrating Joseph working, playing and learning.

The resultant graphic CV was instrumental in convincing an employer (who had difficulty in understanding Joseph's curious, staccato speech) that he was capable of responsible work. He is now on full-time (subsidised) employment at the college. A similar portfolio had enabled another 'unemployable' student to obtain freelance work as one of the few fashion models in a wheelchair. Now all students on the scheme are creating portrait portfolios for one another.

Henry's portfolio would, said Jane, prove to his 'carers' what his real potentialities are. He could be photographed using the concept keyboard (and outgrowing the available programmes), being squeezed half-way into a hotel loo (as part of the Access Group) or simply having a laugh with friends on the scheme who treat him as an equal.

Michael has difficulty in following the rest of the meeting. The issues are contentious – but they are not yet *his* issues:

> Why do we take on too much? We must learn to say 'No' to some commissions . . .
>
> We need more space for Art . . . Photography . . . Drama . . . Computing . . .

More links with students and staff on the Bridging Course . . .

Fewer meetings . . .

More meetings . . .

Communication sessions! . . .

Counselling sessions! . . .

Support for support workers . . .

The last point leads on to a discussion of how staff, volunteers and students are 'selected' for the scheme. Couldn't some students be more directly involved in interviewing the people who will be working alongside them? Can the scheme really accommodate the current range of applicants (e.g. from 'half-way homes' for the mentally ill, from people with severe learning difficulties)? What criteria are being applied? If we do take on such students what about improved links with hospital and psychiatric services? More training? More staff?

New items follow in rapid succession:

- members of the group setting up a 'Survival International' branch in the city. At present there is no local branch of this organisation which campaigns for the rights of threatened tribes and cultures;
- student representation on regional SKILL (the National Bureau of Students with Disabilities) and on the local Disability Forum which is now encouraging disabled students to take a more active part in issues relating to access, employment, education and housing;
- a more structured induction day for prospective students with some longer-serving students introducing them to the scheme.

Michael is just becoming interested in this last point when, for no discernible reason, the signing student becomes deeply agitated, screams abuse and storms out of the room. Michael is surprised at how calmly this is accepted by the group.

> Don't worry. He'll return – today or tomorrow. You can't reason with him when he's like this. We don't know just what triggers them off. He is getting better. Now they're roughly once a month – they used to be every day. At least now he only attacks the wall rather than other students.

Within seconds the door opens. It is not the student returning but a flood of visitors – a lady coming to teach Hungarian to students about to visit Budapest, a social worker sorting out a student with severe memory loss whose phone is about to be cut off, a personnel officer from the Civic Offices to recruit potential employees from students on the scheme and one or two others who just seem to have wandered in off the streets.

Amidst this hubbub Jane almost shouts 'Any Other Business?' She is determined to steer the meeting through till the end. Michael applauds her tenacity. Like the rest of the group she is working against considerable odds – yet these odds are in part created by the nature of the scheme itself. It aims to be 'open', 'accessible', and to encourage a 'celebration of differences'. Inevitably, this will attract problems of security, focus and organisation. But somewhere amidst all the energy and confusion, there are clues for Michael. Something in all this might be for him. Someone suggests that he might have skills to offer others on the scheme. Would he like to come back on a quieter 'induction day'? He is not certain. Part of him wants to get back to the security of home but he knows that after a few weeks there he might long for the contacts, communication and craziness of the multi-media scheme.

REFERENCE

Olesker, S. (1989) 'A mirror for observers', Dissertation for Diploma in Individual Approaches to Learning, London University Institute of Education.

Chapter 7

Hardening the hierarchies

The National Curriculum as a system of classification

Will Swann

In this chapter, Will Swann examines the impact of some aspects of the National Curriculum on children who experience difficulties in learning. His particular concern is the organisation of the National Curriculum into ten levels of attainment. He argues that this structure makes false assumptions about the nature of learning, and disregards the diversity of learners. The subsequent assignment of levels of attainment to certain age groups introduces a further layer of control on the ability of schools to respond to diversity. Moreover, some attempts to adapt the National Curriculum to meet the needs of children who experience difficulties in learning render the system even more rigid. These features of the National Curriculum framework offer a powerful resource with which to classify children according to their level of attainment in ways that do not help teachers to overcome their difficulties.

1 INTRODUCTION: A CURRICULUM FOR ALL?

In this chapter I shall consider some of the consequences of the National Curriculum for children who experience difficulties in learning at school. There is a contradiction which has pervaded responses to the National Curriculum in special education. It is promoted as a curriculum for all children. Yet it is condemned by some as inflexible to the point where it cannot be a curriculum for all children. People who work in special education have taken views at either extreme, and at many points in between. Consider these two comments, written a year after the Reform Act:

> The ERA should be viewed as an entitlement curriculum for all pupils with a widening of curriculum opportunities for pupils with SENs.
>
> (Bailey 1989: 78)

> How will young people, no matter what their attainment, ability or background, be able to derive a sense of equal value and worth in an education system which clearly articulates delineation according to attainment and the increasing compartmentalisation of fact and knowledge? A system based on discrimination – not equality and integration.
>
> (Spalding and Florek 1989: 10)

The reasons for this level of disagreement are complex. These writers are not only giving varying assessments of the likely impact of the Reform Act. What they write can also make a difference to the way the legal plans for the curriculum are translated into classroom practice. The first comment is from a report on an in-service education of teachers (INSET) course on the National Curriculum run by the author, who is a local education authority (LEA) special education adviser. He reports on the feedback from the members of the course:

> Teachers seem to appreciate an attempt to be positive about the Education Reform Act. So much of what has been written is of the doom and gloom variety.
>
> (Bailey 1989: 82)

His stance is as much an attempt to influence the outcomes as it is a prediction of the likely consequences of the Act. If teachers believe that the National Curriculum can widen curriculum opportunities for all, and commit themselves to this cause, then it may turn out to be so. Much of the writing that followed the Act has borne this 'make the best of it' message, alongside attempts to muster the collective will to the task ahead:

> Before resigning ourselves to permanent depression and a feeling that special needs have slipped from the political agenda, it may be useful to look again at some of the implications for change for the better . . . We have to be optimistic but we must also accept that the price of educational reform for all children will be vigilance, constant restating of priorities and a powerful advocacy for children with special needs.
>
> (Russell 1990: 207–8, 222)

The National Curriculum Council's own guidance: *A Curriculum for All* (NCC 1989a), not only presents the National Curriculum as a common entitlment, but also gives it an ideological pedigree. It is represented as the final step in the progressive widening of rights of access to the full curriculum for children with special educational needs. The NCC lines up the National Curriculum with the inclusion of children with severe learning difficulties in the education system in 1970, with the Warnock Report's claim that the goals of education are the same for all pupils (DES 1978) and with the 1981 Education Act's integration clause. The Reform Act is the triumphant conclusion to the march of progress:

> The principle [that pupils with special educational needs share a common entitlement to a broad and balanced curriculum] has gained ground. Pressure for equal opportunities has encouraged its wider acceptance. It finally achieves statutory recognition in the Education Reform Act.
>
> (NCC 1989a: 1)

This bears little relationship to the diverse political motivations for the Act. Whilst the government claimed in its first consultation paper on the National Curriculum that it wished to ensure a broad and balanced curriculum for 'all pupils', pupils with learning difficulties and disabilities were not specifically mentioned (DES 1987). It later turned out that 'all' did not mean 'all'. Under pressure from professional and voluntary organisations during the debates on the Bill, the government was forced to tackle the question of whether every child could indeed follow the National Curriculum. Their legislative response was to include in the Act ways to allow some children to be exempted from the full curriculum. None of the disapplications and modifications now permissible under Sections 17, 18 and 19 of the Act were in the Bill when first presented to Parliament.

The notion that curricular breadth and balance was in any case the government's chief policy goal deserves to be treated with scepticism. This goal could have been achieved by much simpler means which do not involve detailed control of the substance of attainment targets and programmes of study. An analysis of the antecedents of the government's decision to assume power over the school curriculum suggests a range of other motives, including the wresting of control from teachers and the 'educational establishment', the elimination of perceived leftist influence in the classroom and the wish to give greater prominence to the needs of the national economy in shaping the curriculum (Demaine 1988, Quicke 1988, Whitty 1989).

If the NCC's account falls short of plausible history, then it might be explained in two ways. The first is that it turned out, political intentions notwithstanding, that the officers of the NCC saw in the National Curriculum a way to ensure that all pupils would share a common curriculum, a goal they already espoused, and that the DES found it unexceptionable to present the National Curriculum in this way. The second is that both the DES and the NCC perceived that the best way to gain acceptance for the innovation amongst teachers responsible for children with special educational needs was through the language and ideological overtones of entitlement. We do not need to envisage systematic and conspiratorial marketing plans here. The process of recruiting support may be much more subtle and less consciously planned than this. As Peter (1992) shows the negotiations during the preparation of the document were long and tortuous and involved the reconciliation of many partially competing views.

I shall not try to choose between these two theories. Both may be involved. Nevertheless I shall argue that the idea that the National Curriculum ensures a common entitlement for all should be seen as persuasive rhetoric, rather than as an indisputable truth. This rhetoric offers both a *post hoc* justification for the changes, and a rallying cry for implementation. It is not a viable account of the government's policy goals, nor of the detailed elaboration of the curriculum through subject working group reports and Orders by the Secretary of State. In arguing this I shall limit myself to the internal characteristics of the National Curriculum. Much of the critical attention paid to its implications for special education has centred on the procedures by which children can be excluded from the 'common entitlement' through the disapplications and modifications permitted by the Act (Norwich 1989, Tomlinson 1990). I recognise the importance of these processes, but if we wish to assess how exclusions might happen we must understand how the structure of the National Curriculum generates cases for exclusion. I shall argue that it creates a system of classification of children which is not defensible in terms of the facts of learning nor desirable if the goal is a common curriculum. The object of my attention will be the organisation of the National Curriculum into levels of attainment. I shall claim that this system involves the arbitrary assignment of attainments to hierarchies of knowledge, understanding and skill, and the equally arbitrary assignment of levels to ages, leading to the arbitrary classification of children. I shall also argue that some attempts to adapt and interpret the National Curriculum for use with children who experience difficulties in learning compound these problems.

I have organised my argument into five main sections following this introduction. First, I shall discuss the way in which the system of 'levels of attainment' emerged from the Report of the Task Group on Assessment and Testing (TGAT) and the purposes it was to serve. Second, I shall consider how this framework was used by the subject working parties whose job it was to produce the detailed lists of statements of attainment. Third, I shall examine how certain levels of attainment became associated with certain age groups, and what consequences this had. Fourth, I will describe how the organisation of the curriculum into arbitrary hierarchies is compounded by some attempts to make the National Curriculum accessible to all pupils. Finally, I will review the way in which the system of levels of attainment encourages the arbitrary classification of children into groups of varying educational value.

I do not wish to claim that the National Curriculum brings no benefits for special education. It is likely to widen the content of the curriculum and inject recent mainstream curriculum thinking into many special schools (Bovair *et al.* 1990). I also recognise that a common curricular entitlement depends on a degree of equity in the distribution of human and material resources. The operation of local management of schools (LMS) may ensure that resources are inequitably distributed between and within schools. Lee (1992) discusses the ways in which this might happen. In the end, the failure to offer an entitlement curriculum may not be a failure of the National Curriculum, but of the market-led sections of the Reform Act. There may even yet be reason, as Whitty (1989) claims, to be 'thankful that the National Curriculum is there as the one remaining symbol of a common education system and specifiable entitlement which people can struggle collectively to improve'.

2 THE ORIGIN AND NATURE OF LEVELS OF ATTAINMENT

In the National Curriculum, all learning between the ages of 5 and 16 is divided into attainment targets,[1] which are in turn divided into ten levels, each of which contains one or more statements of attainment.[2] The structure assumes that the sequence of levels has two characteristics. First, it is progressive: in some sense, each succeeding level must be more advanced or more difficult than its predecessors. Second, it is universal: it defines the sequence of learning for all children aged 5 to 16 in England and Wales, unless they are legally excluded under Sections 17 to 19 of the Reform Act. Thus all attainments for which the government believes it important enough to legislate are arranged into hierarchies of knowledge, understanding and skill through which all children will progress. This structure is the foundation on which the national assessment system rests. It describes a model of learning that affects all schools, teachers and children. Its consequences are profound.

In the wake of the Reform Act, the extent of a child's learning difficulties will be increasingly measured in terms of this model. As the NCC insists, the system offers a 'curricular language which all pupils and parents can share' (NCC 1989a: 2). When a Statement of Special Educational Needs is prepared for a child, a process which may entail segregation into a special school, the child's level of attainment will often be a critical element in the decision-making process. When a child is excluded from the 'common entitlement' of the National Curriculum, failure to reach a certain level of attainment will often be both the immediate cause and the justification for exclusion.

The structure of levels was an essential part of the National Curriculum from its inception . In directing subject working groups and TGAT, the Secretary of State at the time, Kenneth Baker, demanded advice on 'the measurement and recording at a range of levels of positive achievement in reasonably discrete elements' (DES 1988a: Appendix B). TGAT had the job of rationalising and elaborating this instruction so that subject working groups would operate to a common format. It held that any system of assessment should 'relate to expected routes of development' (DES 1988a: para. 91). Thus the group conceived of a set of hierarchies of learning for all National Curriculum subjects.

In a learning hierarchy, lower levels should be acquired by children earlier in their development than higher levels. There are grounds for arguing that learning hierarchies like this which are both progressive and universal are extremely difficult to find. Research which has investigated performance hierarchies in the school years has generally done so in terms of the performance of groups of learners. Relative difficulty is defined by the percentage of children who succeed in each task. We know from many studies that quite subtle changes in tasks can significantly alter their difficulty level. For example, the Assessment of Performance Unit (APU) study of the mathematical performance of 11 year olds varied the context and other details of problems and obtained significant variations in success rates. Consider these two examples:

Example 1	*Success rate (11 year olds)*
2.7 ÷ 2 =	21%
2.7 m of cloth in 2 equal pieces	27%
£2.70 divided equally for 2 children	73%

Example 2

18 potatoes for 12 people, how many for 6? 75%
18 potatoes for 12 people, how many for 8? 34%

(APU 1985)

The situation is further complicated by the fact that relative difficulty for the group is not the same as relative difficulty for individuals. Some individuals reverse the order of difficulty found in the group as a whole. Neither does varying the task necessarily affect the group success rate in the same way that it affects individual performance. What makes a task easier for some may make it more difficult for others. Murphy (1989) discusses the impact of task variations in Science on the performance of boys and girls. Changing the content of a problem from a stereotypically 'female' setting such as nutrition to a 'male' setting such as building can reverse the rank order of the success rates of groups of boys and girls.

In the TGAT Report, the nature of learning hierarchies was vague from the start.

> It is not necessary to presume that the progression defined indicates some inescapable order in the way children learn, or some sequence of difficulty inherent in the material to be learnt. Both these factors may apply, but the sequence of learning may also be the result of choices *for whatever reason*, which those formulating and operating the curriculum may recommend in the light of teaching experience.
>
> (DES 1988a: para. 93; my italics)

What is so remarkable about this extract are the words 'for whatever reason'. The group appeared willing to accept anything that experience might throw up. The message can be paraphrased as: 'Experience shows it can be taught in this order. This is not the way children necessarily learn it, nor is this order an inevitable progression from less to more difficult. But it will be taught in this order.' The Report failed to specify the conditions under which the past experience of the few might be safe ground on which to shape the future experience of every child and teacher in the country. This left subject working parties free to justify their ordering of statements of attainment into levels with appeals to the personal wisdom of their members:

> Because progress in learning a language is continuous but uneven, the definition of the different levels of attainment must in certain respects be a matter of judgement.
>
> (Modern Languages Report; DES 1990a: 11)

> We have relied mainly on our collective experience and knowledge of good teaching practice and on available research evidence [not subsequently detailed].
>
> (Mathematics Report; DES 1988b: 1)

The Geography Working Group (DES 1990b) admitted the difficulty presented by the requirement to divide attainment targets into ten levels, mentioned six aspects of geography in which progression could occur, but did not attempt to justify its detailed ordering of levels. Instead, the Report 'took heart from' and quoted the extract from the TGAT Report given above.

Although the arrangement of statements of attainment into levels is implicitly a model of learning, it would be misleading to argue that developing this model was TGAT's principal interest. Its job was to produce a system of assessment, 'including the marking scale or scales' (DES 1988a: Terms of Reference). The Group justified the development of 'marking scales' for progress in the National Curriculum in two ways:

> Most straightforwardly one could simply describe what a pupil understands, knows and can do ... We believe that it would be right for much of the communication between teachers and parents to take that form at the reporting ages and between them. However, two considerations make it advantageous also to convert the descriptions into a marking scale. One is to convey some sense of where a child is in the process of learning; the other is to make easier the analysis of results from groups of children. The last is of interest to parents who wish to know where their child stands in relation to others of about the same age and also, at various levels of aggregation, to teachers, heads, LEAs, the Government and the wider community.
>
> (DES 1988a: para. 96)

Of the two reasons given here the first is unconvincing in the light of the Group's proposals on the amount of learning progress that each level would encompasss. Each level should cover roughly two years of work. This would normally produce five or six levels. At both ends of the age range there would be variations in progress, so a total of ten levels would be needed. While the number of levels has endured, the rationale turned out to be unsustainable. Later changes left ten as an even more arbitrary figure than it was in the TGAT Report. This is most obvious in Modern Languages, where there are ten levels for Key Stages 3 and 4 only, and where pupils are expected to make 'swift progress through the early levels' (DES 1990a: 12). In many subjects, statements of attainment cannot sensibly be seen as achievements that take two years of work. For example, one of the statements of attainment in Science, AT11, Level 2, reads: 'know that some materials conduct electricity while others do not'. Whether this attainment takes two years to acquire depends on what else is to be covered in Science, not its own intrinsic difficulty or depth. In any event, few parents and teachers would be satisfied with a system with such weak powers of discrimination that it could detect nothing more detailed than changes that take two years to occur.

TGAT's second reason for a marking scale – 'establishing where the child stands in relation to others' – is at the root of the matter. Comparison and discrimination between children and schools is the essential motive for ranking children. This demands a common system of levels of attainment against which all children can be measured. It makes no allowance for individual progression which does not follow this ordering. The structure of the 'curriculum for all' rests fundamentally on the Conservative government's intention to locate children in standardised hierarchies of achievement in each subject throughout their school career, so that they could be compared to each other, their teachers' performance compared to that of other teachers and their schools' standards set against their competitors in the marketplace.

3 WHAT TGAT BEGAT: THE CREATION OF SUBJECT HIERARCHIES

In constructing subject hierarchies, the subject working groups faced conflicting demands. On the one hand there was the need to allow individual divergences from the hierarchy and to leave teachers some freedom to make their own contribution to the curriculum – a goal often repeated by all Secretaries of State as they sought to limit that freedom. On the other hand, statements of attainment had to be precise enough to guide the developers of standard assessment tasks (SATs), and teachers, in their own contribution to national assessment. This produces a stark and irresolvable dilemma. Statements of attainment could be set out in very general terms, permitting a great variety of learning routes and greater autonomy for teachers in the classroom, but they would run the risk of being uninterpretable by SAT developers and teachers, or, given the political imperative to produce national assessments, interpretable in an arbitrary fashion. Alternatively, they could be precise, leaving less doubt as to what tasks would correspond to the attainments described, but reducing the scope for teachers and pupils to vary the order and manner in which things are taught and learnt. Either way the working groups exposed themselves to criticism for failing to produce universal and progressive learning hierarchies. One can criticise the ordering of most sets of statements of attainment into levels. Whilst this may look like easy fun for those who did not have to cope with the impossible timetables and endless pressures, the reason for criticism is not to deride the working groups but to understand in concrete terms the limitations of the system now in operation. I shall take only two examples.

Most of the English statements were written at a level of generality that allows for extremely wide interpretation. Statements of attainment at levels 1 to 3 for AT1 Speaking and Listening are a case in point:

Level 1 Respond appropriately to simple instructions given by a teacher. (e.g. Follow two consecutive instructions such as 'choose some shells from the box and draw pictures of them'.)

Level 2 Respond appropriately to a range of more complex instructions given by the teacher, and give simple instructions. (e.g. Follow three consecutive actions such as 'Write down the place in the classroom where you think your plant will grow best, find out what the others on your table think and try to agree on which is likely to be the best place'.)

Level 3 Give, and receive and follow accurately, precise instructions when pursuing a task individually or as a member of a group. (e.g. Plan a wall display or arrange an outing together.)

Here hierarchy is attempted by distinguishing between 'simple', 'complex' and 'precise' instructions, and by the addition at Levels 2 and 3 of the giving of instructions. It is not obvious what counts as 'simple', 'complex' and 'precise'; indeed, the example for Level 3 is less precise than the example for Level 2. Surface grammatical complexity does not define the complexity of an instruction. Contrast 'Explain the special theory of relativity' with 'Crack two eggs into a bowl, add milk, salt and pepper to taste, whisk lightly, pour into a pan and heat, stirring all the time until well cooked and fluffy'. And there is no reason why giving instructions should be more difficult than receiving them. Most preschool children are well able to issue instructions.

Most Science statements of attainment are more precise, since they relate to specific areas of scientific knowledge. Statements of attainment for AT4: Genetics and Evolution, Levels 1 to 4, give some indication of their nature:

Level 1 Know that human beings vary from one individual to the next.
Level 2 Be able to measure simple differences between each other.
Level 3 Know that some life forms became extinct a long time ago and others more recently.
Level 4 Be able to measure variations in living organisms.

In assessing the ordering of these statements, the first problem is their level of generality. Though more specific than the earlier English example, they are not unambiguous. What are 'simple differences'? What is it to know that human beings vary? Most babies distinguish reliably between their parents and others during the first six months of life, and so already know that human beings vary. But it is not likely that the Working Group had this in mind. What it *did* have in mind is not clear. We might argue for a logical ordering between Levels 1 and 2 on the grounds that it is not possible to measure differences between people if you do not realise that they vary. Yet the relationship between the two statements is better described as recursive, rather than hierarchical. Measurement provides a deeper understanding of variation, and the observation of variation gives a reason to measure. Between Levels 1 and 2 there is at least a logical association that would support their inclusion in some form in the same hierarchy. Between Levels 2 and 3, and 3 and 4, the grounds for any form of ordering are unclear. There is no reason why a child has to know that some life forms became extinct in order to be able to measure variations between living organisms, nor is there any clear difference in difficulty between these two statements.

More thorough critical exercises have been effectively conducted by others (see for example Dowling and Noss (1990) on the Mathematics curriculum). Such analyses demonstrate that many of the orderings between one level and the next, now imposed by law on all children, lack justification in the logic of the subject or the facts of learning. They are at best the pragmatic product of the preferences of the individuals given the power to define the curriculum. Those that are so general as to encompass many alternative learning paths are at the mercy of the pragmatic needs and preferences of SAT developers and the uncertainties of interpretation by teachers during classroom assessment.

Assigning children to levels within attainment targets is only the first stage in the ranking of children and schools which the government sought to establish. The process demands simpler information than a collection of attainment target scores. This simplification is achieved through the aggregation of attainment target assessments into profile components,[3] and into results on each subject. This imposes an additional demand on the system of levels. It cannot be supposed without evidence that a given level on one attainment target is equivalent in difficulty to the same level on another attainment target. Why, for example, should these statements of attainment be thought of as equivalent?:

- Be able to vary the flow of electricity in a simple circuit and observe the effects. (Science, AT11, Level 5)
- Understand predator–prey relationships. (Science, AT2, Level 5)
- Make written statements of the patterns derived from data obtained from various sources. (Science, AT1, Level 5)

And why should these *not* be equivalent?:

- Be able to evaluate the methods used to reduce energy consumption in the home. (Science, AT13, Level 7)
- Be able to recognise that weight is a force, and know that it is measured in newtons. (Science, AT10, Level 4)
- Make written statements of the patterns derived from data obtained from various sources. (Science, AT1, Level 5)

Equivalence across levels is a fundamental assumption of the process of aggregating scores. Otherwise fixing a subject level is an arbitrary business. Yet if the *only* sense in which two statements of attainment from different attainment targets are equivalent is the number of the level to which they have been assigned, then the production of a combined score is a calculation devoid of meaning.

4 LEGISLATING FOR LEARNING PROGRESS: LEVELS AND AGES

The TGAT Report insisted that their framework for assessment was criterion referenced, that is, pupils' achievements would be measured against specific targets, not against the average performance of the age group:

> The overall national purpose is to work for achievement of the attainment targets of the curriculum. Assessment, whether for feedback to pupils or overall reporting and monitoring, should therefore be related to this attainment, i.e. it should be criterion referenced. Given this, it follows that different

> pupils may satisfy a given criterion at different ages: to tie the criteria to particular ages only would risk either limiting the very able, or giving the least able no reward, or both.
>
> (DES 1988a: para. 99)

Two pages later the Report proceeded to do exactly what it said it would not do: it coupled levels of attainment to ages, by defining the expected range of levels at which pupils aged 7, 11, 14 and 16 would perform.[4] This represented 'a rough speculation about the limits within which about 80% of pupils may be found to lie' (DES 1988a: para. 104). It could be nothing more than a speculation, since at that point levels of attainment had no meaning other than their definition in the Report. It is a moot point whether TGAT's 'rough speculation' should be seen as an empirical prediction, or a design criterion for the system.

Rough speculation was rapidly converted to law. In the Mathematics and Science Orders, the government set down ranges of levels for each key stage. The minimum levels for Key Stages 1 to 4 were to be, respectively, levels 1, 2, 3 and 4. Whilst admitting that some children would fall outside these levels, the government required teachers to 'teach with a view to pupils achieving levels of attainment within the ranges specified' (DES 1989: 7).

What then would happen to children falling below these levels, who as a result of this restriction might be denied appropriate teaching? Assuming that the 20 per cent of pupils outside the TGAT's expectations were equally divided above and below the 'normal' range, then 10 per cent of 5 to 16 year olds might fall below the required levels. This is approximately 600,000 children. Having created this problem, the government suggested three possible solutions:

> (i) provided the pupil is mainly taught programme of study material within the range of levels appropriate to his or her key stage, schools may teach the pupil for part of the time at a level falling outside the key stage . . .
> (ii) where it makes sense and is practicable, the pupil may be moved up or down a key stage for the subject in question by placing him or her in a teaching group in which the majority of pupils are older or younger . . .
> (iii) a statement of special educational needs may specify some modification in the ranges of levels appropriate at different key stages for the individual child.
>
> (DES 1989: 8)

The first option is limited flexibility. At the time of writing it is impossible to say how far schools will take the government's instructions literally. Some will find creative ways of stretching the meaning of statements of attainment to include a wide range of pupils, with some encouragement from the NCC in its guidance on pupils with special educational needs (NCC 1989a).

The second option is to hold children back in a younger class. This is common practice in other education systems, including many of the states in the USA and in France and Germany. It has been widely opposed in the UK as likely to stigmatise and isolate pupils. None the less, a number of children with severe learning difficulties are integrated into mainstream schools in groups younger than their own age.

The third option is to change the National Curriculum as it applies to a pupil. The Education Reform Act permits the modification of the National Curriculum for individual children. Section 17 allows the Secretary of State to specify 'cases and circumstances' under which the National Curriculum will not apply, or will be modified for a child. At the time of writing, this section had not been used to exclude any children with learning difficulties or disabilities. Section 18 allows LEAs to rewrite Statements of Special Educational Needs so that they modify or exempt children from part or all of the National Curriculum. There was a series of press reports following the implementation of the Act hinting at large increases in referrals for statements.[5] We cannot say how many of these are primarily curricular in nature, and how many were motivated by the prospects of additional money which might be attached to a statement under local formula funding arrangements. The NCC tried to discourage the practice: 'planning for participation by pupils with special educational needs will minimise the need for detailed statutory modification or exemption to be written into statements' (NCC 1989b: para. 10). Whether this amounts to gentle incitement to disregard the government's restrictions on age, or flexible interpretation, must be left to the reader.

5 EXTENDING THE SYSTEM

Special education has for a long time been fertile ground for curricula based on linear models of learning, guided and assessed through hierarchies of objectives. For this reason, some teachers in special schools have seen the structure of the National Curriculum, with its detailed demands for recording progress, as well matched to their traditions (Sebba 1990). Yet the statements of attainment are in most cases much less detailed than the sequences of behavioural objectives in use in many special schools. Commentators have argued that the movement from one level to the next would be too great to show teachers and children that learning is taking place (McNicholas 1989, Reason 1989). The proposed remedy is more detailed: 'Statements of attainment are best regarded as long term objectives which provide the framework, allowing teachers and pupils freedom to choose short term objectives and related activities, materials instructions and criteria' (Reason 1989: 150). Yet this is not a problem peculiar to special education. The initial design of the system assumed that levels of attainment were two years of learning apart, so it is unlikely that most statements of attainment will be usable by any teacher without more detailed teaching plans. However, we need to distinguish between elaborations of statements of attainment which permit a diversity of learning routes and those which do not. It has been assumed by some writers that statements of attainment should be adapted for children with learning difficulties by producing more detailed learning hierarchies than the statutory orders provide. The creation of these 'intermediate steps' between statements of attainment compounds the arbitrary constraints already imposed by the 'levelling' of the curriculum.

Several examples of subdividing statements of attainment have appeared (see for example Archer 1989, Miller and Portsmouth 1990). I shall examine one recently published set of materials to illustrate the difficulties that arise with this approach. *Profiles of Development* (Webster and Webster 1990) is a package designed to assist teachers to assess, teach and monitor the progress of children in relation to the National Curriculum. Although it is intended for all ages and abilities, in practice it is limited to Levels 1, 2 and 3. It is built around a large number of lists of attainments, some of which subdivide attainment targets in English, Mathematics and Science. By no means all statements of attainment in these subjects are included. For instance, there are only 17 out of the 69 Mathematics statements of attainment for Levels 1 to 3. The structure reflects traditional curricular preoccupations in special education. There is a separate list of attainments for 'number'; the rest of the Mathematics curriculum is covered by one other list: 'maths concepts'.

The authors have added their own glosses on and redefinitions of some statements of attainment. Material listed as examples in National Curriculum Orders is sometimes incorporated into statements of attainment. Each statement of attainment is separated by one or more statements devised by the authors, and all statements are numbered. These 'developmental sequences' are intended to be hierarchical: 'each sequence of steps in different domains of development progresses towards and overlaps with National Curriculum Attainment Targets' (Webster and Webster 1990: 9). In assessing whether a child has satisfied a statement, teachers are asked to record attainments as 'emerging' or 'mastered'. The authors suggest that the lists can contribute towards decisions on disapplications and modifications: 'These should help to decide whether a child is capable of reaching ATs in the areas covered by the scales' (Webster and Webster 1990: 9). So a concern with the validity of these scales is not trivial. They are advanced as a means to adjudicate curricular entitlements.

The difficulties faced by subject working groups in 'levelling' the subject matter are magnified in the task of building up smaller steps towards the statements of attainment. Webster and Webster say that the sequences are based on research findings (which are not detailed) or where these are not available, they follow a logical order. Some examples will demonstrate that there are grounds to question the composition of the scales. Not all items are the more precise statements we might expect. Writing Item 30 is 'Expresses own feelings and opinions in writing'. Maths Item 18 is 'Makes observations about objects handled and sorts consistently by selected criteria'. The ordering of statements often looks arbitrary. Writing Item 20 reads 'Uses question marks appropriately' and Item 22 reads 'Sequences a simple picture series to make a story'. Spelling Item 28 is 'Spells common vowel digraphs' and Item 32 is 'Names all letters of the alphabet'. There is no logical or necessary developmental sequence involved in either case, nor is it easy to see what research might support such orderings. Studies of the development of children's writing and spelling suggest that whilst certain broad principles of development can be discerned, children follow a wide variety of individual developmental paths within these principles (Bissex 1980, Read 1986). This research challenges the sense of prescribing detailed sequences of development, though not the importance of understanding the nature of the tasks that children face in becoming literate, nor the broad routes that children take in doing so.

Just as the statements of attainment reflect the experience and predilections of subject working groups, so the sequences in *Profiles of Development* depend on the authors' underlying theory of teaching rather than any inexorable path of learning. Writing Items 6 to 15 read:

6 Pretend-writes messages for others
7 Uses pictures, symbols or isolated letters, words or phrases to communicate meaning (English AT3/1)
8 Traces over name to label drawing
9 Copies names to label picture
10 Labels drawings with own name, without model
11 Can use word cards or word bank/folder to construct and then copy out simple sentences
12 Can complete a simple stem sentence/cloze task appropriately, given a choice of key vocabulary
13 Copies adult captions to drawings
14 Dictates writing to adult and then copies adult's model
15 Copies accurately from work card, captions or blackboard

This sequence places accurate copying later in development than 'pretend writing'. Children are seen as learning to write by direct imitation of adult models, and accurate imitation is implicitly regarded as a more advanced achievement than the child's own attempts to represent the writing system through 'pretend writing'. Underlying the sequence is a view of the learner as a relatively passive recipient of instruction. Yet much of the research of the last fifteen years in writing has challenged this view. Studies which have observed children's independent attempts at writing stress the active role children take in decoding and recreating the adult writing system. In learning to write, children are seen as developing and testing a number of progressively useful theories about how spoken language is represented on the page, and what functions the written form can serve (Bissex 1980, Ferreiro and Teberosky 1982). Both the representation of learning to write as a universal performance hierarchy, and the ordering of the specific items in *Profiles of Development* are at odds with such studies.

Competing models entail different classroom practices: 'A classroom where children spend considerable time copying letters beneath the teacher's clear print runs on assumptions about learning which are very different from those of a classroom where children write independently, inventing letter shapes and spellings' (National Writing Project 1989). The lists of attainments in *Profiles of Development* are not only a means to record learning, they are also an intervention in teaching – an attempt by the authors to define in more detail the National Curriculum as it applies to 'individuals for whom there is concern over progress'. They are said to provide:

> an effective means of looking forward to the next appropriate teaching steps. In this sense they also help to pin-point gaps in experience or competence, when a child is considered to have some areas of developmental concern . . .
>
> (Webster and Webster 1990: 2)

Profiles of Development and other material based on the same principles can be seen as redefinitions of the National Curriculum. They raise questions about the notion that it guarantees a common curricular entitlement in so far as they yield teaching stategies which are applied to children classified as having learning difficulties, but not to others. As important as the planned content of teaching – the knowledge, skills and understandings of the National Curriculum – are the messages conveyed to children about their status as learners, about the value of the ideas and understandings they bring to teaching encounters, about the control they have over their own learning, about what it is to be a successful learner. The extension of the TGAT linear model of learning to greater levels of detail for certain children may serve to foster distinctions of classroom experience between children identified as having special needs and others. *Profiles of Development* presupposes a common developmental path, and thus encourages the control of pupils' learning experience so that it conforms to that path. Alternative responses to the early stages of the National Curriculum build not from rigid hierarchies of tasks, but from pedagogical principles flexibly applied to respond to different individuals and groups, and based on an understanding of broad developmental principles and their diverse expression in individual children's work.[6]

It was characteristic of many teaching methods used with children experiencing learning difficulties during the 1970s and 1980s that they entailed more control by the teacher over children's learning than was typical in mainstream classrooms (Wood and Shears 1986). Several former advocates of behaviourist approaches have since changed their stance significantly, and begun to argue that all pupils, including those who experience difficulties in learning, should have a greater degree of control over their own learning (Ainscow 1989). The NCC's own guidance on special educational needs endorsed the use of task analysis into 'discrete learning steps' with some caution. It should not lead to a restricted curriculum, and its use was set in the context of a range of other methods which 'use pupils' own talk, interests and writing as the starting point for further work' (NCC 1989a: 33). It might be needed regularly with 'only a very small minority of pupils with s.e.n. [special educational needs]' (NCC 1989a: 38). The membership of this minority was never defined, nor was its need for a fundamentally different kind of teaching explained or justified.

6 LEVELS OF ATTAINMENT AS A SYSTEM OF CLASSIFICATION

We should not underestimate the power of official systems of classification of children, even when they are generally held to be inadequate by those that work with them. Between 1945 and 1983, all children ascertained as 'handicapped' were classified into ten statutory categories of handicap.[7] By the 1970s there was widespread dissatisfaction with this system as a means to guide the form of education that should be provided for categorised children. The arguments were effectively collected and summarised in the Warnock Report (DES 1978), and the system was abolished by the 1981 Education Act. Intellectual disenchantment did not prevent the continued widespread use of terms such as ESN (educationally subnormal) to refer to certain children and schools in the 1970s. Nor did it prevent the preservation of this category in the language of special education many years after its legal obliteration, in the acronym MLD (moderate learning difficulties), used in many of the same contexts for many of the same purposes, but without, as yet, the abusive tone that came to be associated with its predecessor. One of the reasons for the survival of the category is the survival of educational institutions defined by it: special schools and units whose purpose is to cater for MLD/ESN pupils.

By contrast, the DES's attempt to reclassify children with 'special educational needs' following the 1981 Education Act met with more limited success. Despite the rhetorical insistence that there was now a continuum of special educational needs, in 1984 the DES proposed that children's curricular needs could be classified under three headings: 'mainstream plus support', 'modified' and 'developmental'.[8] Not backed by law, these categories infiltrated policy and practice to a more limited degree. For some years the DES collected statistics from LEAs in which children had to be classified into these three headings. The terms were used in some LEAs to identify children on Statements of Special Educational Needs, and they were adopted by some authors to talk about the curriculum (Gulliford 1985). But they did not give rise to new grouping systems within or between schools. Their legacy may not survive the new system of classification now available in the National Curriculum.

The opportunities for classification afforded by the National Curriculum are more pervasive and more deeply institutionalised than any previous system. The 'common language' of the National Curriculum is presented by the NCC as one of the means by which the participation of all children in a common curriculum can be promoted (NCC 1989a: 2). The same language is also a means to identify and segregate by level. And if the allocation of statements of attainment to levels, and levels to ages, is arbitrary in part, then the allocation of pupils to levels must also be arbitrary in part, even if scrupulous care is taken to ensure that assessments are based on the best available evidence. And so decisions to exclude children from the National Curriculum must in turn be arbitrary in part.

How much this matters in practice depends on the significance that levels of attainment come to acquire in the grouping of children within and between schools, and in the perceptions of pupils by their teachers. It is hard to imagine circumstances in the 1990s in which they will have no significance. Encouragement to view children through the filtering lens of levels of attainment reached its peak in the School Examinations and Assessment Council's (SEAC) *A Guide to Teacher Assessment.* Here the National Curriculum was held to answer the question: 'of all the things which happen in the classroom, which are noteworthy?' (SEAC 1989: 21). There was positive support for treating as less relevant anything a child might do that challenged the preset structure of the curriculum: 'Sometimes children will not respond as planned ... In no sense are the responses unwelcome or unimportant; however, if the assessment is to be formative, it is important to emphasise features relating to the requirements of the task' (SEAC 1989: 22). Later, in its guidance to primary schools on Key Stage 1 assessment, SEAC claimed that the level of attainment assigned to a child 'is capable of communicating a reasonably precise meaning ... about what the child knows, understands and is able to do' (SEAC 1990: 2).

If teachers are able to resist the force of such wholly misleading claims as this from such powerful sources it will be a remarkable victory for sense over folly. But just as a deeply flawed system of classification was operated for many years before the 1981 Education Act by professionals who openly disavowed it, so it is probable that levels of attainment will be used in most decisions about children who experience difficulties. The opportunities to do so will depend on the extent to which there are formal decisions to be taken which involve the transfer of children from one bureaucratic status to another: from non-statemented to statemented; from the register of a mainstream to a special school, or vice versa; from full application of the National Curriculum to temporary or long-term disapplication. Rather than being a classification system in their own right, levels of attainment provide a resource for classification, and an invitation to classify. The use made of this resource by teachers, schools and LEAs is to a degree unpredictable, and conditional on other factors, including teachers' own ideologies. It is in this sense that there will always be something to play for.

NOTES

1 Attainment targets are legally defined as 'the knowledge, skills and understanding which pupils of different abilities and maturities are expected to have by the end of each key stage' (1988 Education Reform Act, S.2(2)). In practice, they are not this. They are areas of content and skills which the curriculum is divided into, such as 'Speaking and Listening' and 'Genetics and Evolution'.

2 Statements of attainment are descriptions of particular items of knowledge, understanding or skill. These have been reduced by some to 'stoats'. This would save me space, but I would not long resist the temptation to call them 'weasels'.

3 Profile components are combinations of attainment targets, although in some cases a profile component covers only one attainment target. Scores on profile components are based on scores on the relevant attainment targets.

4 They were: at age 7: levels 1–3; at age 11: levels 3–5; at age 14: levels 4–7; at age 16: levels 4–9.

5 For example, Bury and Sefton are reported as experiencing increases in demands for statements (*Times Educational Supplement*, 15 February 1991).

6 A contrast to the *Profiles of Development* writing checklist are the guidelines for teaching the initial stages of writing developed by the National Writing Project, summarised as a list of seventy-one practical principles and activities (National Writing Project 1989). The chapter by Bennett and Williams in this volume provided an alternative approach to mathematics with children who experience difficulties to the 'checklist mentality'.

7 Handicapped Pupils and Special Schools Regulations 1945, amended 1959.

8 These categories were defined as follows:
Mainstream plus support: 'A curriculum comparable with that of the ordinary schools . . . while providing appropriate support to meet a range of individual special needs.'
Modified: 'A curriculum similar to that provided in ordinary schools which, while not restricted in its expectations, has objectives more appropriate to children whose special educational needs would not properly be met by a mainstream curriculum.'
Developmental: 'A curriculum covering selected and sharply focussed educational, social and other experiences with precisely defined objectives and designed to encourage a measure of personal autonomy.'
(DES 1984)

REFERENCES

Ainscow, M. (1989) 'Developing the special school curriculum: where next?', in D. Baker and K. Bovair (eds), *Making the Special Schools Ordinary? Volume 1: Models for the Developing Special School*, London: Falmer Press.

Archer, M. (1989) 'Targeting change', *Special Children*, no. 33, 14–16.

Assessment of Performance Unit (APU) (1985) *A Review of Monitoring in Mathematics, 1978–1982*, London: APU.

Bailey, T. (1989) 'A positive approach to the Education Reform Act', *Support for Learning* 4 (2), 75–82.

Bissex, G. L. (1980) *Gnys at Wrk: A Child Learns to Write and Read*, Cambridge, Mass.: Harvard University Press.

Bovair, K., Carpenter, B. and Ashdown, R. (eds) (1990) *The Curriculum Challenge: Pupils With Severe Learning Difficulties and the National Curriculum*, London: Falmer Press.

Demaine, J. (1988) 'Teachers' work, curriculum and the New Right', *British Journal of Sociology of Education* 9 (3), 247–64.

Department of Education and Science (DES) (1978) *Special Educational Needs* (The Warnock Report), London: HMSO.

—— (1984) *The Organisation and Content of the Curriculum in Special Schools*, London: DES.

—— (1987) *The National Curriculum 5–16: A Consultation Document*, London: DES/Welsh Office.

—— (1988a) *National Curriculum Task Group on Assessment and Testing: A Report*, London: DES/Welsh Office.

—— (1988b) *Mathematics for Ages 5 to 16*, London: DES/Welsh Office.

—— (1989) *The Education Reform Act 1988: National Curriculum: Mathematics and Science Orders Under Section 4*, Circular 6/89, London: DES.

—— (1990a) *Modern Foreign Languages for Ages 11 to 16*, London: DES/Welsh Office.

—— (1990b) *Geography for Ages 5 to 16*, London: DES/Welsh Office.

Dowling, P. and Noss, R. (eds) (1990) *Mathematics Versus the National Curriculum*, London: Falmer Press.

Ferreiro, E. and Teberosky, A. (1982) *Literacy Before Schooling*, London: Heinemann Educational.
Gulliford, R. (1985) *Teaching Children with Learning Difficulties*, Windsor: NFER-Nelson.
Lee, T. (1992) 'Local management of schools and special education', in T. Booth, W. Swann, M. Masterton and P. Potts (eds), *Policies for Diversity in Education*, London: Routledge.
McNicholas, J. (1989) 'Curriculum implications of ERA', *Support for Learning* 4 (3), 130–5.
Miller, S. and Portsmouth, R. (1990) 'It's a SNIPP', *Special Children*, no. 42, 7–10.
Murphy, P. (1989) 'Assessment and gender', *NUT Education Review* 3 (2), 37–41.
National Curriculum Council (NCC) (1989a) *A Curriculum for All: Special Educational Needs in the National Curriculum*, York: NCC.
—— (1989b) *Circular Number 5: Implementing the National Curriculum – Participation by Pupils with Special Educational Needs*, York: NCC.
National Writing Project (1989) *Becoming a Writer*, London: Nelson
Norwich, B. (1989) 'How should we define exceptions?', *British Journal of Special Education* 16 (3), 94–7.
Peter, M. (1992) 'A curricula for all: a hard task for some' in T. Booth, W. Swann, M. Masterton and P. Potts (eds), *Policies for Diversity in Education*, London: Routledge.
Quicke, J. (1988) 'The "New Right" and education', *British Journal of Education Studies* 26 (1), 5–20.
Read, C. (1986) *Children's Creative Spelling*, London: Routledge & Kegan Paul.
Reason, R. (1989) 'Evidence of progress?', *British Journal of Special Education* 16 (4), 149–52.
Russell, P. (1990) 'The Education Reform Act – the implications for special educational needs', in M. Flude and M. Hammer (eds), *The Education Reform Act 1988: Its Origins and Implications*, London: Falmer Press.
School Examinations and Assessment Council (SEAC) (1989) *A Guide to Teacher Assessment, Pack C: A Source Book of Teacher Assessment*, London: SEAC.
—— (1990) *School Assessment Folder, Key Stage 1*, London: SEAC.
Sebba, J. (1990) 'Navigating the route', *Times Educational Supplement*, 28 September.
Spalding, B. and Florek, A. (1989) 'Narrower focus, narrowed chances?', *British Journal of Special Education* 16 (1), 10.
Tomlinson, S. (1990) 'The National Curriculum and special education needs', *Educare*, no. 37, 19–22.
Webster, A. and Webster, V. (1990) *Profiles of Development: Recording Children's Progress Within the National Curriculum*, Bristol: Avec Designs.
Whitty, G. (1989) 'The New Right and the National Curriculum: state control or market forces?', *Journal of Education Policy* 4 (4), 329–42.
Wood, S. and Shears, B. (1986) *Teaching Children with Severe Learning Difficulties: A Radical Reappraisal*, London: Croom Helm.

Part 2

Support for learning

Chapter 8

Evaluating support teaching

Susan Hart

Source: Gnosis, no. 9, pp. 26–31, 1986.

Susan Hart compares and contrasts two approaches to support teaching: one which focuses on improving the learning of individual pupils who experience difficulties and one which attempts to adapt the curriculum so as to enhance the learning of all pupils. These two approaches entail different rationales, practices and criteria of success. She argues against the individual approach on the grounds that it retains the segregation of pupils with learning difficulties which support teaching was intended to diminish. Moreover, the conditions for effective individual support are often not met: support teachers can find themselves supporting unsatisfactory lessons. Support teaching should be directed to more fundamental curriculum reform alongside working with individual pupils.

One of the main developments in special educational provision following the Warnock Report and the 1981 Education Act has been the widespread introduction of in-class support teaching in secondary schools as an alternative to offering help in withdrawal groups and special 'remedial' classes. The report *Educational Opportunities for All* (ILEA 1985) remarks upon the enthusiasm expressed by London teachers for this method of working and recommends that an evaluation of support teaching be carried out as a matter of urgency.

The problem with trying to make any general evaluation of support teaching at this stage, however, is that no generally agreed definition of support teaching actually exists. Leaving aside the growing use of the term 'support teacher' in a much wider sense (i.e. to apply to any work undertaken by the non-school-based LEA support staff), even in its original sense (I.E. providing support in the classroom rather than withdrawing children), the support teaching role has been open to a whole range of different interpretations. With their emphasis more on the location of the work than on its precise nature, support teachers have evolved their own solutions to the many questions about support teaching for which there are as yet no generally accepted answers. Our first priority must therefore be to work towards achieving a common understanding about the aims of in-class support teaching, and then draw up clear guidelines about the implications of those aims in terms of our classroom practice. The purpose of this chapter is to contribute to this task.

I shall suggest that caught up in those practices are in fact two different answers to this central question, each with its own implications for support work and criteria for evaluation, with the result that support teachers often feel themselves pulled in two directions at once. I shall then draw on my own experience to explore which of these two approaches seems to offer the best way forward, and consider what the implications might be for any future evaluation.

The question we have to decide is to do with the limits of our responsibilities in the work we undertake to meet special educational needs. It has given rise to two different approaches which I shall call the 'individual' and the 'whole curriculum' approach. Both represent such a considerable departure from previous practice, however, and share so many features in common, that it has taken a while for the dust to settle after the major upheavals of recent years and for the difference between them to emerge. For example:

- both offer grounds to favour support teaching methods in preference to withdrawal where possible;
- both favour consultation and joint problem-solving approaches with class teachers;
- both emphasise the need for curricular adaptation on behalf of children with special educational needs;
- both argue the need for preventative measures to be taken;
- both urge schools to adopt a whole-school approach to meeting special educational needs.

Both therefore see special educational provision as having an essential role to play in bringing about changes in mainstream education. The difference between them is to do with the starting point which they adopt and the nature and scope of the changes that are envisaged. The question is: are we by definition confined to making changes to the curriculum on a purely individual basis to ensure that the teaching individual children receive is appropriate to their needs? Or, is it legitimate for us to become involved in general curriculum development work which will be of benefit to all children, but especially those with special educational needs?

The 'individual' approach adopts the former stance, always starting from the individually assessed needs of each child and trying to produce a 'match' between child and task (albeit recognising that the modifications made may well have a beneficial spin-off effect for other children in the class). The 'whole curriculum' approach adopts the latter position, starting from the learning activity intended for the class as a whole and seeking ways of effecting change so that individual pupils can participate without being singled out for 'different' treatment.

Looking more closely at some of the ideas associated with each approach may help to clarify further the differences between them (see Table 8.1).

The choice between those two approaches underlies what, to seasoned

Table 8.1 Ideas associated with the individual approach and the whole curriculum approach

Individual approach	*Whole curriculum approach*
Definition: To investigate the nature of each child's difficulties, intervene to ensure that they receive teaching appropriate to their needs and facilitate access to learning in all areas of the curriculum.	Definition: To assist in finding ways to adapt the curriculum so that all children (including those with special educational needs) can participate in and derive benefit from all areas of learning.
Associated ideas	*Associated ideas*
1 Special educational needs are the result of a unique combination of physical, social, psychological and educational factors which have affected a child's development.	1 Schools can do much to prevent special educational needs from arising by adapting aspects of lesson presentation and classroom organisation to facilitate learning for all children.
2 Children with special educational needs by definition need something different from other children if they are to make good progress.	2 There is a need to question the appropriateness of the curriculum itself, not just for children with special educational needs but for all children.
3 The provision required is some variant to the general curriculum in the form of additional or different arrangements for a particular child.	3 Children with special educational needs don't need anything different in kind from other children. They need good teaching that takes individual needs into account.
4 Each child's needs must be individually assessed and programmes planned and monitored on an individual basis.	4 Working out how to meet the needs of an individual child can provide opportunities for enhancing the curriculum for all.

support teachers, must be a familiar dilemma. Many of us will have had the experience at some time or other of finding ourselves in classrooms ostensibly to help individual children overcome their difficulties, but realising that in fact the problems are more to do with the way the lesson is being presented, with the resources and teaching strategies being used or with the demands being made, than with any specific problems our pupils may have. It occurs to us that by concentrating all special educational resources on individual children we may actually be missing the point. We then have to ask ourselves what right we have, as special needs teachers, to use our time to work with teachers on aspects of classroom practice in general. And if it is beyond the scope of our work, then who can be relied upon to undertake it?

Different answers to these questions lead, of course, to different interpretations of the support teacher's role (see Table 8.2).

The difference in focus between these two models of support inevitably generates a different set of criteria with which to evaluate them, since it is the aim of the work that determines the criteria required. In the case of the 'individual' approach, therefore, the emphasis is going to be mainly on the progress of the

Table 8.2 Implications for support teaching

Individual approach	*Whole curriculum approach*
Justification	*Justification*
1 It enables child to receive any specialist support required as an integrated part of normal teaching programmes.	1 It enables support teacher to experience curriculum from the children's point of view, determine the nature of difficulties as they arise, and so be in a position to help develop methods and materials which can cater for all needs in the class.
2 It enables child to have access to full range of curriculum activities.	
3 It enables class teacher and support teacher to work in partnership.	
Implications for support teaching in practice	*Implications for support teaching in practice*
1 The support teacher's role is to help individual children in consultation with the class teacher.	1 The support teacher's role is to take part in planning for and teaching the whole class.
2 The purpose of the support is to try to produce a match between the individual child and the curriculum activity presented.	2 The purpose of the support is to help teachers adapt their classroom practice to take account of all children in the class.
3 The support teacher provides whatever additional or different arrangements may be needed for each child, e.g. one-to-one specialist support, supplementary materials, specialist equipment, etc.	3 Support teachers see the difficulties experienced by children with special needs as potentially highlighting problem areas of the curriculum which could be developed to the benefit of all.
4 The support teacher explores with the class teacher ways in which procedures to meet individual needs can become part of normal practice.	4 Support teachers seek to reinforce and promote good teaching for all children; they explore with the class teacher ways of organising learning so that all children can participate fully.

individual child, whereas with the 'whole curriculum' approach, it will be more on development of teacher awareness and skills, and progress in curriculum development. That is why it is so important for us to be exactly clear what we mean by support teaching, and which 'model' of support teaching is under investigation, before we can select our criteria for evaluation appropriately (see Table 8.3).

These criteria are only intended to give a very general indication of the range of aspects of the work that would need to feature in any future evaluation. Appropriate means would have to be found, of course, to determine progress made in each area. My purpose here is simply to draw attention to two things: first, the danger of oversimplifying the task of evaluation by using a single measure (for example reading test scores – themselves of dubious validity) to measure the effectiveness of a practice with much more complex aims; and second, to emphasise how the evaluation task may be different according to the approach to support teaching which we adopt.

To return to the central question about how the boundaries of special educational provision and therefore of support teaching are to be defined, I shall argue in the remainder of this chapter that although the 'individual' approach represents what has always traditionally been accepted to be our role, to continue to define our responsibilities in these purely individual terms could have serious consequences, not only for the future of support teaching when we come to evaluate it, but for the development of comprehensive education as a whole.

My own experience has led me to the conclusion that at the present stage of development of comprehensive education, a purely individual-based approach to

Table 8.3 Criteria for evaluating support teaching

Individual approach	*Whole curriculum approach*
1 How much progress has been made by each child in each area of the curriculum and in specific areas (e.g. reading, spelling, etc.) as stated in their individual programme.	1 How much progress has been made in developing whole-class teaching strategies and resources to make learning accessible to all children in the group (including children with special needs).
2 The degree to which the child is integrated socially and functionally into the class group.	2 The degree to which children with special educational needs are integrated socially and functionally into the group.
3 The extent to which the child's teachers show increased understanding of child's needs and how to cater for them in the classroom.	3 The extent to which planning to meet special educational needs within a class has become part of the class teacher's normal planning.

support teaching is likely to prove counterproductive for a combination of three reasons:

- First, because it limits the range of options that can be considered in trying to meet special educational needs.
- Second, because its hidden curriculum can be just as undermining to our real intentions as that of the former withdrawal system.
- Third, because the sort of classroom conditions required for it to be effective are simply not widely enough available in most secondary schools (and maybe some primary schools) at the present time.

First of all, if support teachers always take individual needs as their starting point it may be assumed that any modifications to the curriculum for a particular child relate uniquely to that child's difficulties. Adapting the curriculum just for children with special educational needs may lead to their becoming increasingly isolated and segregated within the classroom. Individualised programmes, alternative activities and simplified worksheets, when they are directed at certain children can cut them off from their peers as effectively as if they had been withdrawn. The concept of integration as a process implies teaching strategies which will enable children with special needs to learn not only alongside but together with their classmates.

Second, the presence of a support teacher in the classroom can convey unintended messages to children and teachers. The sense of inadequacy felt by children who are failing may be reinforced by having a 'special' teacher assigned to them. Class teachers too may feel justified in leaving children with special educational needs to the resident 'expert', instead of developing confidence in being able to meet those needs themselves. Support teachers sole brief is to support specific children may find that they have little room for manoeuvre to combat these likely problems.

Third, if support teachers are to use their time constructively working with individual pupils throughout lessons, then a number of basic conditions need to be met:

- Alternative ways of organising teaching and learning must have been introduced to replace the standard didactic pattern.
- The support teacher must have detailed knowledge of the lesson in advance and have prepared any necessary support materials.
- The demands being made on the child must be appropriate to his/her level of cognitive development/literacy difficulties.
- The class teacher's general class management and discipline must be good so that the support teacher does not have to work in an atmosphere of excessive noise, nor for that matter in one of silence.

Of course, these conditions do exist in some schools and in some classrooms already. But my experience, that of my colleagues in other schools and research evidence based on early attempts at widespread support teaching in Scotland

(Ferguson and Adams 1982), lead me to conclude that much groundwork usually needs to be done with teachers in terms of planning lessons jointly, and revising and adapting curriculum materials and teaching methods before any effective support work with individual children can begin. The paradox is, of course, that were this groundwork to be done there would be much less need for additional classroom support in the first place!

If support teaching gets under way, therefore, without adequate preparation, then support teachers may find themselves caught up in any of the following situations:

- Standing on the sidelines for lengthy periods while class teachers address the class.
- Helping children complete tasks which the support teacher considers to be of little educational value.
- Providing support generally in a class where most children are struggling with the work, discouraged or disaffected.
- Having nothing much to do while children are engaged in undemanding tasks that offer little opportunity for the support teacher's intervention.

Faced with this situation, but without any brief to involve themselves in working with the teacher to modify aspects of the curriculum for the class as a whole, nor indeed with any time in which to do it, support teachers are powerless to take action to improve the effectiveness of their work. Support teaching falls into disrepute with senior management, who wonder, with some reason, if scarce resources are indeed being used effectively. It also falls into disrepute with the support teachers themselves who become frustrated and disillusioned at the obstacles they face and fear that the children are losing out.

Under these circumstances, there is little doubt in my mind that the supposed advantages of support teaching are more than outweighed by the disadvantages which it presents. If we are not to be disillusioned, therefore, and retreat back into the relative safety and tranquillity of the withdrawal unit, part of our responsibility as teachers of children with special educational needs must be to tackle with class teachers ways to improve the curriculum at the level of general classroom practice. To do so will not, of course, make any of the problems go away; what it will do, however, is to shift the emphasis of our work so that the problems no longer undermine its effectiveness, indeed they become part of the raw material of our work.

Adopting a whole curriculum approach means, too, that support teachers can legitimately respond to requests from class teachers for help that are unrelated to the support teacher's responsibility for specific pupils. They can, as part of their normal teaching commitment, have timetabled sessions to help teachers develop their own skills in coping with special educational needs, or help them evaluate the effectiveness of new curriculum materials or teaching strategies for meeting special educational needs. It would help turn the call for 'all teachers to be special needs teachers' from a slogan into a practical reality. In sum, the whole curriculum approach opens up the possibility for special educational provision to become an integral part of the process of developing comprehensive education as a whole.

That is not to suggest, however, that we should adopt a whole curriculum approach to the exclusion of work supporting particular children. Neither approach by itself is adequate to take account of the complexities involved in meeting the needs of our children and our schools at the present time. Of course it is true that some children have specific needs which it would be inappropriate to attempt to deal with at the level of the curriculum as a whole. But it is equally true that there are general principles for successful teaching and learning which apply to all children. As Holdaway (1979) points out in relation to the teaching of reading, there is a set of universal conditions which facilitate success, and these need to be applied even more meticulously in the case of children who are experiencing difficulties. Our support can only be effective to the extent that these universals obtain; it certainly cannot substitute for them.

What is required, therefore, is a combination of the two approaches, and it is through support teaching that this combination can be most effectively achieved. If support teachers are alert to the possibilities within their role, and allowed the flexibility to operate at the individual or whole-class level, then support for individual children can offer a way through to improving the quality of learning for all (see, for example, Hodgson *et al.* (1984) on cooperative working groups).

In practice, this would mean that even when assigned to work with specific individual children, support teachers should:

- always look beyond the needs of the individual child to see what the implications may be for the learning needs of other children in the class;
- be aware of the need to provide not just on-the-spot support but, where possible, support that will have a lasting effect on classroom practice;
- look out for the opportunities arising from meeting children's special needs, to open up discussions about ways to improve the curricular experiences for all children in the future.

Furthermore, it need not be just specially trained 'support teachers' involved in work of this nature. Schools might be encouraged to use INSET resources to enable subject teachers to teach together and review the curriculum in their own subject areas. In this way, curriculum improvement to meet special educational needs could be combined with in-service staff development.

As far as any future evaluation is concerned, if we adopt this definition of support teaching, it is obvious that more than just the traditional concerns with pupil progress in specific skills areas will need to be taken into account. The effectiveness of pupil learning in all curriculum areas, changes in teachers' attitudes and awareness of the needs of children with learning difficulties, and long-term modifications to curriculum materials and teaching strategies will all be equally, if not more, relevant. It is important to ensure, therefore, that when we evaluate support teaching, the full complexity of what we are trying to achieve is properly appreciated, and is reflected both in the criteria we adopt and the methods we use to apply them.

However, the first step must be for us to achieve recognition at the level of official LEA policy that special educational provision begins with what the regular class teacher is doing in the classroom, and that the first responsibility of special needs teachers is to help class teachers meet special needs themselves. That means helping them not only to make any additional or different arrangements to what is 'normally available for all' to meet the needs of particular children, but also to review and develop the general curriculum, so that 'what is normally available for all' can itself be gradually transformed to provide better learning opportunities for all children in the future.

I have argued that if we allow our concept of special educational provision, and hence of the support teacher's role, to be limited to the 'individual' approach then the danger is that, not only will our own sights be limited in the measures we adopt to meet special educational needs, but our work may act as a substitute for more fundamental changes that are required. It may ensure that, beneath the new uniform, our function remains in effect little different from the former 'ambulance service' (Golby and Gulliver 1979) instead of increasingly becoming that of 'consultants in road-safety'.

Widening our concept of special educational provision to include the 'whole curriculum' approach will free us from such limitations. It will allow the sense of frustration many of us have felt for a number of years to be replaced by a new sense of purpose. The problems of the here and now can be accepted, not as obstacles to our task but as the task itself, and what previously appeared to be massive impediments to effective support work can simply become our new challenge.

REFERENCES

Ferguson, N. and Adams, M. (1982) 'Assessing the advantages of team teaching in remedial education', *Remedial Education* 17 (1), 24–31.

Golby, M. and Gulliver, J. (1979) 'Whose remedies, whose ills? A critical review of remedial education', *Journal of Curriculum Studies* 11, 137–47.

Hodgson, A., Clunies-Ross, L. and Hegarty, S. (1984) *Learning Together*, Windsor: NFER-Nelson.

Holdaway, D. (1979) *The Foundations of Literacy*, Sydney: Ashton Scholastic.

ILEA (1985) *Educational Opportunities for All?* (The Fish Report), London: ILEA.

Chapter 9

A new role for a support service

Linda Harland

Support services for children with learning difficulties changed in many LEAs during the 1980s in response to changing conceptions of learning difficulties and learning support. Many support teachers took on wider responsibilities. They worked with a wider range of pupils; they increasingly provided support in mainstream classes; they became involved in making the whole curriculum accessible to pupils; they became consultants to class and subject teachers. In this chapter, Linda Harland gives an account of the way in which these changes were made in one LEA's support service. She describes how three support teachers dealt with the changes in some of the schools in which they worked. She highlights some of the difficulties and dilemmas they faced and the solutions they found to them. The final part of the chapter looks at some of the wider consequences of the change and raises questions for the future.

1 BEFORE THE POLICY CHANGE

In common with many local education authorities throughout England and Wales in the mid-1980s (Gipps *et al.* 1987), the LEA I shall be concerned with – called 'A county' for the purposes of this chapter – had several remedial reading centres in each division. These were bases for groups of reading teachers, most of whom taught in the centres, the children being transported at the expense of the county. The centres also contained a growing collection of resources which, as well as being used for centre teaching purposes, were sometimes lent to visiting teachers, or taken to the occasional in-service sessions requested by the school.

The children taught for one or two sessions a week in these centres were described by the assessing educational psychologist as having 'specific reading difficulties', which meant, in this authority, that although judged to be of average intelligence, their achievements in reading and language were below average. It was accepted policy for children who were considered to have more general learning difficulties to be taught by the remedial teacher within their own school.

The programmes within the centre were devised by the remedial teachers; there was little correspondence with the school, apart from twice-yearly reports and discussion about transport arrangements. Often a strong relationship was built up between the reading teachers and parents, who were strongly supportive of their children receiving this small group help.

This traditional model of providing remedial teaching, prevalent until the last five or so years, was based on the view that children's reading difficulties were caused by some learning or psychological disorder, or perhaps the effects of a troubled home background – the 'child deficit' model that began to come under attack in the late 1970s (SED 1978). In the policies of this authority no causal connection was seen between children's learning problems and how they were taught. But by 1988 many of the remedial centre teachers had been influenced by courses, reading and their own experiences, and were questioning the validity of separating the pupils' learning in the centres from their learning at school. The teachers also found that they were being increasingly asked for advice by their classroom colleagues. Thus the role of the remedial reading teachers had started to change informally before the county's Inspectorate drew up policy documents which, after passing through the education committee, created a major shift in the philosophy and the practice of supporting children with special educational needs in the county.

The consultative document which was circulated by the Inspector for Special Educational Needs in 1988 included the following statement:

> The main objective of the reorganised Support Teams would be to offer an appropriate level of support, mainly to ordinary primary schools, but with the flexibility to offer a degree of support/advice in the secondary sector also, and mainly to children experiencing various learning and other associated difficulties.

The document went on to stipulate four levels of support provision within schools. Level 1 was support from the school's own resources. Level 2 involved the support teacher in an advisory capacity within school. The third level offered possible withdrawal from the class for a short period of specialised teaching, and Level 4 was reintegration into the mainstream setting.

2 AFTER THE POLICY CHANGE

Again, in common with many local education authorities (Gipps *et al.* 1987), the remedial teachers in this county changed their name and role description – and in many cases their working base and colleagues – very rapidly. In this case, the change happened in the two-week period of the Easter holiday, 1989. Now they were called support teachers. Their role was entirely peripatetic, attached to a cluster of primary schools. It was curriculum focused with no 'categories' of children excluded. They had a particular brief to ensure access to the National Curriculum for all children. It was also their role to decide, in collaboration with classroom teachers, how many children with special needs there were in a school, and thus how much money the school would get through this part of the local management of schools (LMS) formula.

Despite the gradual change of role already under way on their own initiative, there was a great deal of trepidation shown by the support teachers. A five-day, residential preparatory course did little to dispel this. Teachers in several different centres expressed similar worries. They felt that the support service was being held accountable for the successful adaptation by primary schools of the National Curriculum in order to include children with learning difficulties. Indeed, there was also a feeling by some support teachers that they were being held responsible for more widespread curriculum improvement in a primary system judged to be inadequate in many areas. This increased responsibility necessitated a much wider expertise than their previous specialised prowess in reading and language. The importance given to Science in many schools revealed gaps where the support teachers felt ill-prepared to offer advice until they had undergone further training themselves.

The support teachers did not only express concern over their future role, they also expressed regret over aspects of their work which would now disappear. The close involvement with individual children, and often with their families, would be impossible to maintain. Apart from a personal sense of loss, they were concerned that no one would now be focusing on these children if the attention was to be given to the curriculum and the classroom.

As we saw throughout the education system at the end of the 1980s, change can create worry and discomfiture, especially if effective personal support is missing. Here was a major, authority-wide change in response to special educational needs. Both class teachers and support teachers were being asked to alter their concepts of appropriate provision for children with learning difficulties. It was not surprising that the support teachers considered their new roles with some qualms.

3 THE NEW ROLE: SUCCESSES AND PROBLEMS

I shall now describe how three support teachers dealt with problems which arose during the first year of their new role, and give an account of some of their ventures. I spent some time with these teachers, accompanying them at work during their first complete year after the change.

Angela

Angela was an experienced, confident teacher, had worked in the remedial centre for eight years, and did not appear to be too worried about the changes. Her support team had adopted what they termed a rolling programme whereby each teacher worked in two schools each half-term – mornings in one school and afternoons in the other. Not all head teachers were enthusiastic about this approach, especially the ones who had to wait for their turn. One of the strategies used to overcome potential hostility to the rolling programme was a newsletter sent to all primary schools in the division. The newsletter outlined the intention behind this method of support:

> Our aim is to support schools in differentiating the curriculum according to the individual needs of children, the starting point for this enterprise being: *the school's development plan; *its schemes of work; *the learning environment; *the teaching needs of the children.

This statement implied that the traditional model of focusing on individual children had been left behind. During my first morning with Angela, however, she spent almost the whole time with individuals or groups of children outside the classroom, either in the library or the music room. She was assessing one child in response to parental concern and her own observations in class. Angela said the 'special needs net had failed' and thought it best to do an informal assessment, although this was deemed difficult without a WISC test. This intelligence test, the Wechsler Intelligence Scale for Children, is limited to use by educational psychologists. The other children were being withdrawn from the classroom because Angela felt that she had not yet convinced the teachers of the value of in-class support. She hoped that this transitional phase would not last for too long, and that the constant breaktime discussions and after-school in-service sessions would change minds.

Angela was not convinced that it was sensible to stop withdrawing children from their classrooms. She had discussed this at length with her line manager, who shared her wariness, and she felt confident about continuing to teach children separately from their peers. The school also had the services of a support ancillary helper who worked for two mornings a week, and a volunteer mother/dinner lady who worked for two whole days a week. Angela organised this work, which mostly consisted of supervising small groups of children in the library, catching up with class schemes of work in language and maths.

During the time I was with Angela, mainly in the school she visited in the morning, she fulfilled a variety of roles. As well as teaching, assessing and supervising the work of ancillaries, she spent time discussing individual children with their class teachers, deciding how much support would be appropriate. Time was spent counselling parents. At regular weekly meetings with the infant department's special needs coordinator she discussed individual children. Telephone liaison took place with the educational psychologist, who asked Angela to do preliminary assessments and gather together family and school data on some children. In the staff room at mid-morning and lunchtime she was frequently consulted about appropriate work for certain children. There was one after-school in-service session on books for early reading, which endorsed the wish by most of the teachers to move from the current 'Ginn 360' reading scheme. In addition Angela acted as a confidante to the head teacher, particularly about less-well-established members of staff. Towards the end of the half-term allocated to this school, a lot of time was spent planning for the next few weeks when there would be no support teacher. The focus of all this activity was reading, whether the reading ability of individual children or the school's approach to teaching reading.

Angela had quickly become an accepted member of the school and said how much she liked the staff and enjoyed working there, choosing to stay for lunch (an important issue for peripatetic teachers, far from base). It was a small school situated on the edge of a picturesque, wealthy town. The head teacher was popular with staff and parents, and he was very committed to and interested in provision for special educational needs. He was keen to support the new role of the support service and often took over classes so that Angela could have prolonged discussion with teachers.

At first glance, it looked as if there were few major differences between Angela's new role and her old job as a remedial reading teacher. The obvious change was the location within the school instead of the centre. During discussions with Margaret (a teacher of 7 to 8 year olds, the school's Science co-ordinator, with an admitted worry about teaching language), Angela made several suggestions, often using an almost jocular, self-deprecatory tone. They included strategies for learning spellings based on 'Look, cover, write, check'; a change from the Ginn 360 reading scheme to the Oxford Reading Tree where the books were more like 'real books', a term the class teacher did not like; and alternatives to phonics, without disagreeing with Margaret's strong adherence to letter sounds.

By half-term Angela had built up close working relationships with all the staff except the deputy head, who tended to keep apart from the rest of the school. She seemed to deal with all kinds of welfare issues and acted as mediator between the school and parents of children with learning difficulties. There were frequent comments made such as 'What will we do when you're not here? and 'Why can't you work here all the time?' Staff and parents confided quite intimate personal and family problems to Angela; even my presence as an observer did not inhibit this. Before she left, Angela spent time preparing school, children and parents for her departure, playing a role in some senses similar to a therapist.

After speaking to the teachers and the head, all of whom had the highest personal and professional regard for Angela, I was left with the puzzle of how a support teacher whose own pedagogical beliefs did not differ noticeably from those of the school, and who enjoyed such close relationships within the school, could effect the proposed move towards increased differentiation, as specified in the authority's policy document.

Deidre

I observed Deidre working for two half-days a week in a large middle school in a prosperous village on the edge of a large conurbation. She also worked for five half-days in five separate first or primary schools. Deidre had lived and worked in the area for twelve years and was the leader of the new support team of four teachers, one ancillary teacher and a part-time secretary, so she knew many of the teachers and children well, personally and professionally.

Despite an established reputation in the area as an effective support teacher, gained while breaking free from the constraints of the previous remedial teacher role before the official LEA policy changes, Deidre had to withstand hostility and wariness towards her new role from the staff of this school. During the previous term – the first one since the change of role – another support teacher in this school had encountered much resistance to the changes in supporting children with special educational needs, and had not been sufficiently skilled to deal with what became a fairly unpleasant situation.

Deidre, as the team leader, decided that it was up to her to deal with these potentially disturbing factors. One of the greatest problems was the organisation of the school. It ran on secondary lines with the day split into twenty-minute sessions, most, but not all of them, doubled up. The lessons were split into traditional secondary subject areas throughout the school. The site was large, the classrooms small and crowded and the teachers were completely unused to having another adult in the classroom. I spent time with Deidre early in the term when it was still assumed that children would be withdrawn. This assumption was quietly resisted with explanations for in-class support.

In the classroom Deidre often had to focus on pupils who had been statemented as dyslexic or as having specific learning difficulties as a result of parental persistence, while pupils with seemingly far greater learning difficulties had less help. Her work was centred around the classes of 9 to 11 year olds which contained the statemented children based in the lower half of the school. In these classes teaching approaches varied enormously. In one class Deidre found all the difficulties of being an additional body during a twenty-five minute lecture, or when a class read through a text book. In another she found the pleasure of establishing sufficient rapport in order to be able to work closely with a teacher doing stimulating work taking into account all levels of ability.

Deidre made the greatest professional break through the resistance during informal chats in the staffroom. She brought the subject of social conversations round to the curriculum and the practical approaches that teachers could adopt to encourage maximum participation. Listening to a history teacher express despair at the inability of certain children to read certain textbooks, Deidre suggested one or two ways of modifying and adapting the text and went on to indicate that she would be willing to run an in-service session where she would show them many more ways of working on textbooks.

This suggestion was taken up and within four weeks Deidre had run two after-school workshops in the school. The first session was attended by fourteen teachers, with twenty-two attending the second. This increase reflected the very favourable response. Deidre decided to approach these sessions in an entirely practical way. She felt that these teachers were not ready to listen to a theoretical exposition on curriculum change. Some success in getting them to think about materials and trying out modifications in the classroom would convince teachers of her practical credentials, as well as indirectly supporting more children than is possible in the time allocated to the school.

Deidre had attended a diploma course during the previous three years and had done a dissertation on differentiation of the curriculum. In this school she presented the concept of differentiation in terms of presenting and manipulating texts in simplified ways. The suggestions she made included photo-enlarged text, use of taped text, word searches and highlighting text, among many other methods. Where she was able to discuss plans for lessons – not easy when working with four or five teachers in a morning – Deidre would usually obtain the textbooks and work on them beforehand, thereby providing a model for the class teacher as well as supporting the children.

The following summer, after Deidre had worked for one year in the school, it was clear from talking to the head teacher and some of the class teachers that attitudes towards the new support role had changed radically. Although the head felt that an additional special needs teacher permanently attached to the school would be desirable, he was full of praise for what Deidre had accomplished over the year, and recounted the numerous complimentary remarks his teachers had been making. The teachers in whose rooms Deidre worked were very positive, admitting that none of their original worries had materialised, and acknowledging that the children had benefited from extra attention.

During Deidre's year in this school it was clear that a considerable change in teachers' attitudes had been achieved. She was now a highly regarded, welcome visitor, whose opinion was sought and respected. A practical start had been made on changing some aspects of the curriculum. However, Deidre was the first to recognise that there was a long way to go in moving the teachers from seeing all the difficulties residing in the children towards an acceptance of the unsuitability of many parts of their curriculum.

Sue

Sue had also worked for several years in the previous remedial centre role, and she remained based at the centre until the changeover. She felt that there had been insufficient consultation about the change and resented the amount of good will required from the support teachers in terms of giving up lunch times to travel, and running in-service sessions after school with no extra pay.

When I started observing Sue it was towards the end of her term in a very small rural school with two full-time teachers, one part-time teacher and a teaching head. She also worked for two half-days each in three small primary schools, and one half-day each in two infant schools. In the school where I observed her a new head teacher had started in the autumn term, having competed for the post with a long-serving member of staff. The head taught a vertically grouped top two junior years, being replaced for three half-days administrative duties by the part-time teacher who had worked in this capacity for about ten years. All the teachers apart from the head had been there for between ten and eighteen years. They had a very strong belief in their own previous work and now felt assaulted by the requirements of the 1988 Education Reform Act and the imposition of a new, young head teacher from a different authority.

On top of this they were being told that children with learning difficulties were no longer to be removed from their classroom, and that another teacher was to work in there with them occasionally, suggesting changes in practice. Conversation at mid-morning break centred around resentment of these changes. Antagonism towards the changed role of the support service was voiced openly towards Sue, who found it difficult to defend a move which she did not fully endorse. Sue did appreciate just how much change was needed in this school for access to the curriculum to be ensured for all children. There was a very traditional, whole-class approach towards subjects, despite the vertical grouping throughout. The blackboard was extensively used, and children did all their work in exercise books. Most maths and language work was done from cards or sheets, with little use of practical apparatus.

After eight weeks of working in the school, Sue still had to justify working in the classroom. She had several prolonged conversations with the head teacher. She explained that his expectation that she would work exclusively with statemented children left her no time to work collaboratively with the teachers, or to work on whole-school policies. The head teacher replied that his teachers wanted the support teacher to work with specific children, and that her job description did not fit in with what the school wanted. Yet he was not wholly opposed to her views. He was happy as a class teacher to receive suggestions and programmes to use with the children during the time Sue was not there. He did feel that certainly one of his teachers needed much more support from Sue in teaching the two or three children with learning difficulties in her class.

During this part of the term the support teachers had to carry out an audit of children with special educational needs, the results of which would contribute towards LMS funding decisions. This audit involved discussion between Sue and the class teachers, deciding where each child under consideration fell in the authority stages of intervention. Forms had to be filled in; this was unproblematic until the section entitled 'strategies implemented' came up. It was here that the class teachers' steadfast views (Sue used the word 'entrenched') were made explicit. Beth, an experienced teacher in her early 50s, was clear in her comments to Sue on what she saw as an unhelpful new role. 'This morning – the children who don't need help going with the support teacher – you know what infants are like. It would be better for me if you have the group in the corner, or outside, then it's clear to the others that that group is the special needs group for the teacher.' In reply to Sue's comments about stigmatisation, Beth said that the limited amount of time should be pinned down to the children who need extra help.

Such views from the staff were underpinned by a belief that all the problems resided within the children, and by an apparent unwavering belief in the effectiveness of their own teaching. Sue felt she could not attack their views as that would be counterproductive in many ways. First, a straightforward approach would increase the hostility already felt by the school towards the support service. Second, although the head had shown occasional signs of understanding the possibilities of the new approach, any kind of confrontation would lead him to defend his own staff and she would lose a potential ally. Third, two of the teachers were fairly intimidating women and despite her belief in an assertive approach Sue did not wish to stir up antagonisms.

Sue became increasingly uncomfortable in this school and a downward spiral of deteriorating relationships set in. It was difficult to retrieve the situation. Given the opportunity to change schools one and a half terms later, Sue moved on to what she saw as a more welcoming school. Afterwards, talking to the head and to Sue, they both recognised that there had been an unusually large amount of tension in the school at the beginning of the year. Perhaps if Sue had not been adamant about sticking to the letter of her new role, and if the head had been willing to compromise with the support service then more constructive changes could have been made to the school's methods.

4 SOME GENERAL CONSEQUENCES OF CHANGES WITHIN THIS AUTHORITY

These accounts show that an authority can invest time, money and bureaucratic procedures in a change, but there is no guarantee of immediate successful outcomes. After such a short time, final judgements cannot be made as to the effectiveness of the new support service. In two of the schools I visited the support teachers had established their credibility, were respected and listened to by the teachers and were aware of the need to introduce further changes. But nowhere was it as straightforward as the policy documents made it seem. There were many short-term difficulties which, if not dealt with, could perhaps lead to longer-term failures. There were also many short-term successes which should be built on and turned into enduring strengths.

The support teachers

On the whole the support teachers I met expressed a greater feeling of worth in their wider role and found the new approach more stimulating. They had wider boundaries and met more people: teachers, children, other staff and parents. These wider boundaries meant they had to develop interpersonal skills to deal with any initial hostility, as well as extending already established skills to deal with the whole curriculum. In one or two cases there was a feeling of lowered morale and self-confidence, and an increasing suspicion that the support service was being exploited in order to spread the financial net more thinly.

Class teachers

With one or two exceptions class teachers welcomed support teachers as people with whom to share problems, to consult with and to gain ideas from. They saw the support teacher as someone who would provide practical ideas which would enable them to fulfil National Curriculum requirements. Support teachers were also a sounding board for feelings of frustration at the perceived lack of consultation about changes in special educational provision.

Children with learning difficulties

As far as it was possible to judge from conversations and observation, children benefited from a class teacher who felt personally supported and thus was more sensitive to their needs. Pupils were often able to complete the simplified classroom tasks and thus felt as though they were keeping up with their peers. Occasionally, there was a feeling of confusion at the varying discipline and curriculum requirements of the classroom teacher and the support teacher.

5 CONCLUSION

We are now building up many accounts of support and advisory teachers whose role is to bring about change in the classroom (Gipps *et al.* 1987, Bowers 1989, Biott 1991 among many others). Although these accounts do not treat the work of support teachers as being unproblematic, they do often assume that a clear vision of the desired changes is held by someone in the LEA. We should realise that unless a great deal of consultation, discussion and training takes place, support teachers can no more undergo rapid changes in their philosophies than can classroom teachers. From the brief accounts here we can gain a sense of the complexities accompanying the change. Do we sympathise with the support teacher who feels exploited by the authority's unrealistic expectations of the support service? Do we feel any concern over the support teachers who seem to be colluding with a system that is failing so many by only changing surface details? Do we agree that change is slow in education but feel impatient with support teachers who are treading their way carefully through the minefield of innovation? It is important that local authorities, in their future evaluation of support services, do not lose touch with the intricate nature of the operation.

REFERENCES

Biott, C. (1991) *Semi-detached Teachers: Building Support and Advisory Relationships in Classrooms*, Lewes: Falmer Press.

Bowers, T. (ed.) (1989) *Managing Special Needs*, Milton Keynes: Open University Press.

Gipps, C., Gross, H. and Goldstein, H. (1987) *Warnock's Eighteen Per Cent*, Lewes: Falmer Press.

Scottish Education Department (SED) (1978) *The Education of Pupils with Learning Difficulties in Primary and Secondary Schools in Scotland: A Progress Report by Her Majesty's Inspectorate*, Edinburgh: HMSO.

Chapter 10

An extra radiator?

Teachers' views of support teaching and withdrawal in developing the English of bilingual pupils

John Williamson

Source: British Journal of Educational Studies 15(3), pp. 315–26.

This chapter explores the views of a group of secondary support teachers towards methods of learning support for pupils whose first language is not English. The teachers interviewed argue in favour of support teaching in mainstream lessons, but also see advantages in withdrawal for separate small group and individual work. They describe the ways in which effective support teaching can be hampered by poor organisation, hostile attitudes from some teachers and the sometimes low status of support teachers. Almost all the arguments and issues have close parallels in debates about support for pupils who experience difficulties in learning which do not stem from speaking English as a second language.

1 INTRODUCTION

It has long been the case that the arguments in favour of developing the English of bilingual pupils in the mainstream classroom have held sway in official pronouncements. As long ago as 1975, the Bullock Report approved of work then current in Bolton and Bradford

> where the specially appointed language specialists ... functioned both as teachers and consultants, sitting in on subject classes, analysing the linguistic demands made on immigrant [*sic*] learners in different areas of the curriculum, and offering running help to the children as the class proceeded. This is a much more effective way of working than dealing with pupils in comparative seclusion, which is bad both linguistically and socially.
>
> (DES 1975: 291)

The Swann Report came to a similar conclusion: 'We are wholly in favour of a move away from E2L provision being made on a withdrawal basis, whether in language centres or separate units within schools' and went on to point out a corollary of this, that 'in secondary schools we believe that pupils with E2L needs should be regarded as the responsibility of all teachers' (DES 1985: 392, 394). A survey of the teaching of English as a Second Language in six LEAs offered further support, noting that

> Evidence from the relatively few examples of in-class support by E2L teachers suggests that, where organisation and collaboration between the E2L and subject teacher are good, pupils are able to engage more effectively, than in withdrawal groups, with mainstream work and use English in activities relevant to the subject.
>
> (DES 1988a: 14)

This increased effectiveness arose, they suggest, because 'Pupils covered more areas of the curriculum and were encouraged to learn with their peers. The impact on other pupils of E2L work was also greater when the E2L teacher worked alongside the class teacher' (DES 1988a: 17). The Cox Report, alluding to some of the sources just cited, concludes that 'The implications are that ... where bilingual pupils need extra help, this should be given in the classroom as part of normal lessons' (DES 1988b: 58).

This is not to imply a blanket approval of support teaching at the expense of withdrawal. Swann notes that 'We recognise that in the case of pupils of secondary school age arriving in this country with no English some form of withdrawal may at first be necessary' (DES 1985: 392). HMI point out (DES 1988a: 17), with regard to support teaching, that 'such a pattern of working demands careful planning, effective oganisation, genuine co-operation, and frequent review and evaluation'.

Such caveats notwithstanding, there is a consensus, based on the soundest social, linguistic and pedagogical grounds, that the needs of the bilingual pupil are in general best met within the mainstream classroom. The impetus for the present study comes in part from teaching secondary school teachers on in-service courses in English as a Second Language (E2L) and in part from a term spent working in the E2L departments of two comprehensive schools in the North of England, when I gradually became aware that the teachers' attitudes to the debate on support and withdrawal were very complex. This was not because they were unaware of the views sketched above or of the much more elaborate reasoning and research underlying them. Of the six teachers I subsequently interviewed – whose opinions form the basis of this article – two had qualifications at higher degree level with substantial components in the teaching of English as a Second Language, and three others had undertaken at least a one year in-service course in the subject. It seemed to me that it would not only be interesting to explore in some depth the experience and attitudes of these teachers but also that such an exploration could be of great value in helping us to understand something of the forces at work here and to identify areas of practice which might need to be reconsidered if support teaching is to operate at an optimal level.

This study examines the attitudes of six teachers, three from each of two schools. The information presented here was elicited by means of a series of semi-structured interviews, an approach which seemed best suited to the task of gathering a full range of opinions. A set of questions was taken to each interview and elaborated upon as necessary, and interviewees were encouraged to develop their own points of view as extensively as they wished. The interviews, which varied in duration from about twenty to thirty minutes, took place in the interviewees' schools. Those interviewed constituted about three-quarters of the E2L staff in their schools and were all full-time members of their departments, most having specialist qualifications. All were known to me personally and the interviews were conducted in a relaxed atmosphere which, I trust, encouraged the teachers to say what they really felt rather than simply what they felt they ought to. Responses were not tape-recorded for fear that this might have an inhibiting effect; extensive written records were made at the time. For the same reason, interviewees were assured of complete confidentiality; this is a very sensitive area.

2 THE RELATIVE MERITS OF SUPPORT TEACHING AND WITHDRAWAL

The first question put to the teachers was a very broad one: 'What do you feel are the relative merits of support teaching and withdrawal?'

All of those interviewed found merits in supporting bilinguals in the mainstream setting. All bar one mentioned some of the social and personal benefits of this kind of integration, stressing the value for bilinguals of being able to mix with their peers, which was seen as valuable both in terms of enabling the bilinguals 'to be accepted more quickly' and in terms of developing their 'self-esteem' by 'being in the right setting'; the lack of this was seen by one teacher as being the main argument against withdrawal. It was the view of one of the teachers that pupils themselves prefer mainstream settings because of 'the social aspect of joining in with other children' and two others echoed this view, arguing that incorporating bilinguals into the mainstream would yield 'one less aspect in which they're seen as different'. In turn, one argued, mainstream provision has a related linguistic benefit in that it helps with the development of 'conversational language'. The second set of benefits arising from supporting children in the mainstream setting was seen to lie in affording bilinguals 'access to the curriculum which would otherwise be denied'. Further, pupils have 'access to the skills of specialist teachers' which they would not necessarily have if the same ground were covered in a withdrawal setting in which, one teacher pointed out, they would not be learning in context; just being shown the science apparatus, for instance, in the language room was, she felt, an experience of a different order. One interviewee also noted that access to the curriculum in later years was also at stake – for example, if the early stages of science were missed, it might prove impossible to fit in later. There was a general feeling in favour of learning English and working through the curriculum in tandem.

One final benefit of mainstream integration was raised by only one teacher who commented that children in that situation 'learned their way round the school much more quickly'. They came into contact with more staff and became familiar with them and with the life of the school, the timetable and so on.

The teachers were, then, in favour of support teaching for reasons very similar to those adduced in the introduction; however, by no means did they give it an unequivocal vote of approval at the expense of withdrawal.

One of the perceived drawbacks of mainstream support was summarised very succinctly by one teacher who said 'the syllabus is not available if you don't understand it'. This view was expanded on by a colleague who noted that pupils 'can get very frustrated if they're having language problems – they may sit and do nothing. Support helps with that but can be very limited. History and English can be particularly hard.' It was her view that 'everything hinges on prior consultation ... It's not enough just to have a body in the room.' Support teaching, she argued, is valuable when it is done properly but that can only be the case when it is well planned.

Nearly all of the teachers found some merit in withdrawal on linguistic, social and curricular grounds. One suggested that withdrawal provides a 'secure base to work from', lessening the trauma of having to cope with a new language, a new school and a new culture; students knew 'who to turn to for help'. A more supportive environment was provided in which pupils were 'less likely to withdraw into themselves' and in which they could be 'nursed and encouraged'. Another felt that beginning bilinguals in secondary schools cannot go totally into mainstream but need a 'halfway house'; withdrawal can provide 'a nice little nest for them' and enable them to build their self-confidence. Another teacher noted that there may be a case for help through withdrawal when a pupil is having a hard time and needs security.

Several of the interviewees commented on the linguistic benefits of withdrawal. One argued that the affective filter – 'the ... hurdles posed by the individual's emotional state and motivations' in the terms of Dulay *et al.* (1982) – should be lower because the teacher should be better qualified to teach language. Another suggested that some aspects of language (pronunciation, for example) are 'hard to teach in mainstream – small group work comes into its own'. It was also noted that 'input can be regulated and graduated to avoid confusion and bad language habits'. Perhaps this viewpoint was best summarised by one interviewee who argued that it is 'difficult in mainstream to teach a language as a language'. Teaching can be done through subjects but 'the finer points' may not be taught because, for example, the support teacher cannot intervene when the class teacher is talking.

Three of the teachers felt that there could be advantages from a curriculum point of view in withdrawing students from mainstream for at least some of the time. This view was expressed by one teacher who argued that withdrawal provided a useful back-up to mainstream lessons. She argued that subject teaching could not be thoroughly effective without follow-up and that this was so important that withdrawal was necessary. Another, while making very much the same point, qualified it by suggesting that while withdrawal offered a useful means of recapping on mainstream lessons, the need for it depended very much on the class teacher's methods – if the lesson was well taught in the first instance, there would be no need for withdrawal.

Only one of those interviewed focused on the drawbacks of withdrawal (as opposed to commenting on the complementary advantages of mainstream support). In the first place, she stressed the importance of having a policy which was clear-cut and which limited the number of lessons from which children should be withdrawn and the length of time over which withdrawal should take place. She pointed to the 'lack of stimulus in being in a language room all day' and argued that 'over-sheltering just delays the process' of integration into mainstream which she characterised as 'the shock of being put out'. There was a difficult period of readjustment but it was one which pupils had to get through and segregating them for too long was not helpful. She also had reservations about withdrawal as a means of supporting the mainstream curriculum (though she had been one of those who saw some merit in this) in that if pupils needed a whole mainstream lesson explained to them perhaps they were being faced with too much and it would be too much for them even in a withdrawal group, from which they might 'just get a handful of words which they'd have got in mainstream anyway'. The children might simply not be ready for a particular section of the curriculum and what they got from withdrawal would not outweigh the benefits of being with their peer group in the mainstream.

The teachers, on the whole, took a balanced view of the relative merits of support and withdrawal, leaning as one would hope towards the former but seeing limitations in it and expressing a feeling that withdrawal is not an option which they would like to see closed to them.

3 THE BALANCE BETWEEN SUPPORT AND WITHDRAWAL

Somewhat surprisingly, the support for withdrawal was brought out even more clearly by the second question, which asked what should be the balance between support and withdrawal. All of the teachers seemed to interpret this as a request to say what withdrawal should be used for.

Four of the group perceived withdrawal as providing, in various senses, a shelter for their pupils. One talked of providing 'a safe place where they're out of the public eye and don't need to keep pretending they've understood ... They need somewhere they can say they don't know what a beach is.' A colleague spoke of the greater confidence the children feel in smaller groups and of their having 'a better chance to relate to the teacher'. She noted that her pupils 'often don't speak in mainstream classes' whereas in withdrawal groups they were 'not afraid to experiment with language and risk making fools of themselves'. Further, there was a better opportunity than in mainstream classes to diagnose errors. Finally, one teacher felt that withdrawal met the pupils' need for 'a base to go to with problems'. Set against this, one teacher who mentioned the value of a 'shelter' also felt that there was a danger that children could be made too dependent and that reintegration could be made more difficult; accordingly, in her view, children should never be withdrawn from more than two of the five periods in the school day.

Three of those interviewed discussed the value of withdrawal for pupils newly arrived in an English-speaking environment, although interestingly their views on what should be done differed significantly. One argued that new arrivals should be totally withdrawn for an initial period of four weeks, not being assigned to a class at all. They should cover 'the practicalities – writing, intensive language work – through the subjects of the curriculum'. They should then be gradually fed into lessons over the rest of a term 'as they can cope with each subject'. In her view, practical lessons, if supported, are the best for feeding pupils into. 'The last to go are English, History and RE.' On the other hand, another teacher would hesitate to withdraw even children totally new to this country for more than two out of the five daily periods in her school. More, she would try to limit withdrawal to one period a day unless the pupil was so timid and unconfident that it would do him or her a disservice to be 'pushed out' – but even then two periods a day would be the limit.

Three of the teachers emphasised the value of withdrawal as a means of recapping material which had been covered in a mainstream class. One argued that it was 'much more valuable if you can have a follow-up withdrawal lesson – especially at GCSE level'. In the mainstream lesson, the situation could be unsatisfactory because 'you are swept along by the pace of the class – you have to keep up with the teacher's pace, the whole class doesn't necessarily stop when you want to'. A further advantage of withdrawal, she felt, was that some subjects 'uncover remarkable gaps in children's knowledge of the world' and 'it could be embarrassing to have them filled in public – you need some privacy with them'. One of her colleagues noted that one withdrawal lesson can cover, and reinforce, two or three class lessons. It was also suggested that withdrawal could be valuable in helping students of English as a Second Language who were working for formal examination qualifications.

One teacher saw the need for withdrawal primarily in relation to literacy skills rather than for the development of oracy, which should take place in mainstream lessons. Children would probably (in this region, at any rate) be learning a new script, some may indeed be illiterate in their first language and there was, in her view, no provision for meeting this need in secondary schools.

Two of the teachers, one from each school, explicitly stated that the balance between support and withdrawal should 'depend on the children's needs and the stage they're at', one of them stressing the need for flexibility: 'there should be no set policy'.

4 FEEDING INTO MAINSTREAM

One question which I considered to be quite crucial was that of the basis for feeding children who have been withdrawn back into mainstream.

Four of the teachers felt that this was a matter in which decisions should be made on an individual basis; indeed, one felt that the problems were created in this respect by the fact that 'the hierarchy want to know in advance, for practical reasons', when transfer to the mainstream would take place. She added, 'We resist being pinned down.' The same teacher felt that children (typically new arrivals to this country) should join the mainstream 'as soon as they can cope socially rather than academically', so they would pick up 'appropriate language and ways of working' and become familiar with the ways in which 'a particular subject is communicated'. Ideally, this would be done with support (a widely expressed view). A teacher from the other school agreed that the decision should rest largely on social needs (although she also considered academic needs and ability to be important). She argued that if pupils are 'happy to be in a class' that was 'one of the best reasons for putting them out more'. She was the only one explicitly to mention linguistic criteria here but put little emphasis on them: 'It's easier as they acquire more English – but if we waited for that alone, we could wait for two years.' One of her colleagues felt that introducing children into mainstream 'depends on the nature of the subject and how much support there is'. Essentially, the process underlying all these views is a subjective one; in the words of one teacher, it's a matter of a 'gut feeling'.

This subjectivity worried one of the interviewees, who felt that there 'has to be a time limit'. She took the view that it was dangerous to use 'readiness' as the sole criterion although even she agreed that the time limit should be applied 'in accordance with the specific needs of the child' and recognised that it might be necessary to withdraw a child again if mainstream entry had been initiated too soon.

The remaining teacher saw the advantages in a particular form of long-term withdrawal. She referred to the situation in which bilingual pupils were withdrawn from French (on the grounds that there is no point in them studying French if they are having problems with English). That decision having been taken, the bilinguals have three lessons a week for the first three years in which they can be withdrawn. This teacher felt that even if pupils' English problems were not too severe, this time was still not wasted as it could be used to revise mainstream work and do extra reading.

5 IMPROVING SUPPORT TEACHING

My next question, on how support teaching might be improved, obviously touched on a fairly raw nerve. These six teachers raised over a dozen separate issues, some of them expanded on at considerable length. These teachers clearly feel that there is scope for improvement in the way support teaching operates in their schools.

The issue most frequently mentioned was the need for consultation with colleagues if support teaching is to be effective. Put at its most negative, one teacher complained 'often we don't know what we're going in to, so we can't prepare'. Another noted that it's 'unsatisfactory grabbing fifteen minutes at lunchtime'. More positively, one argued for the need for a contract between the teachers concerned, which would fix aims and objectives and would involve negotiating the scheme of work for the period to be supported. The support teacher should have equal responsibility for presentation, marking and writing reports. Ground rules on such issues as discipline should be agreed beforehand to guarantee consistency and equality of status. She argued that the relationship should be such that the class would see itself as having two teachers for the subject in question. In general, it was felt that there was a 'need to identify exactly the role of each teacher in the process'. Clearly, these teachers felt that there was a major difficulty here and one which could only be resolved by developing enough resources to free staff for consultation.

There was a related cluster of opinions which centred on the relationship between support and mainstream teachers. One interviewee noted a lack of awareness of the support teachers' role, some mainstream teachers seeing themselves as being supported rather than the children and feeling resentful because of this. She also observed that some specialist teachers believe that only other specialists can give support in their subject; she commented that it is 'hard to build up a relationship unless both teachers know what their role is going to be'. A colleague stressed the importance of the support teacher being introduced to the class so that all the children know her name and see that she is there to help everyone; otherwise, she will not have 'proper standing' in the classroom. Another said that she felt 'uncomfortable' when her presence in the classroom was not acknowledged and commented also on the personality factors involved – some teachers were 'welcoming, friendly and open, others difficult'.

Two interviewees commented on the importance of the teaching styles adopted by the mainstream teachers, one going so far as to say that 'success depends on teaching method – for example, if the teacher talks to the class a lot rather than setting tasks, it's very difficult for the support teacher to participate. More project work, where children research and work in small groups would help.' A colleague recommended that class teachers look at ways of teaching which would involve every child – 'not just "hands up" questions'. It was also suggested that more cross-curricular approaches would be beneficial, in that language acquisition would take place in a context in which there would be more prospect of reinforcement; the example given was that of dealing with 'The Normans' in History, Art, Geography and Drama. Another teacher shifted some of the onus onto the support teacher, who needs, in her view, 'a really intimate knowledge of the curriculum' so that she would

> not spend so much time standing around waiting for relevant moments where she can step in and give help. We would know that if a particular topic was

> being dealt with that at a particular time we could do something more constructive with individual pupils.

The quality of support staff was a point developed at some length by one of the teachers who argued that they should be experienced teachers so that they would have the background and confidence to make suggestions to class teachers, and that they should have some experience of primary school methods and a wide range of subject expertise as well as linguistic knowledge. She also argued for in-service provision to help teachers know what to look for and to recognise problems.

The final major point was made by one head of department, who suggested that support teaching could be more structured from the departmental point of view, with more monitoring of children, a chance to comment on their reports and time to discuss progress with parents so that they would be apprised of their children's position.

6 DRAWBACKS AND ADVANTAGES OF SUPPORT TEACHING

On the face of it, this question might seem to overlap rather with some of the previous ones. In fact, the teachers tended to interpret it on a more personal level and their answers yielded some new insights.

Perhaps because I framed the question with the negative aspect placed first, and perhaps to avoid repeating themselves too much, the teachers here tended to concentrate on the drawbacks of support teaching. In terms of negative impact on the teachers themselves, the general position was stated by one interviewee who noted that some of them 'feel they're not seen as proper teachers' (although she added that this was something which didn't 'bother' her). In the words of another, 'I miss not having a classroom and doing what other teachers do, even though I value what I do do.' Sharing someone else's classroom, one teacher noted, was mainly disadvantageous on those occasions when the support teacher didn't know 'her position in the room. Often there's not time to sort this out in advance.' A colleague disliked 'having practically no autonomy in the classroom – you don't feel you belong anywhere in particular'. She went on to stress the importance of making 'your role clear to the rest of the class' and to other members of staff who very often only begin to appreciate the support teacher's value when they see her in operation. Even then, it can be 'very hard to co-operate with other staff', some of whom give all the information needed, but some of whom don't. This was seen by another interviewee as being particularly troublesome when there were 'personality clashes – which is inevitable'. On the other hand, one suggested that 'once you build up relationships there's no problem'.

One specific difficulty raised was that of discipline: 'It can be hard to assert your discipline levels in classes where the class teacher has a different level. It can be hard when the children see you in different situations. It can affect your morale when you are never properly in control, never have your own classroom.'

One teacher felt 'It might help if I always did the same subject areas, built up relationships with staff, had a file of work and knew the syllabus well – but I cover for everything. At times I feel a jack of all trades and master of none.' One of the implications of this view was spelt out by another teacher who suggested that a 'huge staff' would be required to do support teaching 'properly'. One teacher, I suspect, summarised a general fear in saying that the support teacher could suffer 'a lack of self-esteem as a bona fide teacher'. That these difficulties are not entirely one-sided was suggested by one interviewee who noted that the situation can also be difficult for mainstream teachers: 'sometimes the subject teacher can't accept support teaching – it can be inhibiting'.

Only one teacher commented on the drawbacks of support teaching for pupils; she touched on the danger of jealousy on the part of monolingual pupils, the risk of bilinguals becoming too dependent on the support teacher and the possibility that, in a mainstream lesson, too much information might be delivered, the teacher might go too fast or that texts might be used which were too long. Pupils, she suggested, were 'often bewildered by the plethora of things going on'. Further, bilingual pupils often had to do different work from the others because they were lacking in the necessary background.

Set against this, one teacher said how she appreciated the variety offered by the support role: 'It's much more interesting – I meet more staff than normal, help all the children and learn about things I knew nothing about.' This view was echoed by a second teacher. A third focused on the advantages for the pupils: the bilinguals 'learn appropriate English more quickly' and find social benefits; for the monolinguals, there is the possibility of promoting understanding between races, they can see that a bilingual peer 'might be very bright and the situation helps to promote friendships'. I suspect that the general view was summed up by one teacher who felt she had little new to say in answer to this question but did assert her belief that 'the advantages to the pupils outweigh the disadvantages'.

7 THE ATTITUDES OF MAINSTREAM TEACHERS

The unanimous view was that the attitudes of mainstream teachers varied: 'Some positively welcome you, some are suspicious and antagonistic.' Mainstream teachers are 'often apprehensive at first' but the consensus was that once they had experienced support work they were 'happy and pleased to have us'. As one interviewee said, 'Once they realise you're an extra body, not there to interfere in lessons, things get better.' Some value the presence of a support teacher because she 'helps with discipline and class management' and helps 'relieve pressure in the classroom'.

However, the position may be more complex than it seems at first sight if we accept the view of one interviewee that 'Some agree to support teaching to seem to be doing the right thing, but they don't really want it.' Certainly, a progression towards acceptance is by no means automatic in these schools – 'Some can't function with another adult in the room, with the best will in the world.' Another felt that a minority (probably a small one) of mainstream teachers

> won't have any support teaching – they tend to feel children should be withdrawn; it makes you wonder what they're doing for them. They don't see language acquisition in context is more meaningful and that there are things other than academic gain that children get from mainstream. They show a lack of understanding of children's needs and will say that new children are not getting anything.

This view was complemented by that of a colleague who held that

> The biggest danger is that the teacher thinks that support teaching clears them of responsibility to the bilinguals – so there is no compromise in the lesson, they don't worry about the bilinguals not getting anything, because the support teacher is there and that limits their responsibility.

In her opinion, this situation was 'pretty general'.

One teacher, reinforcing a point made elsewhere by others, noted that some mainstream teachers 'won't let me know what the lesson will be about' so that she was unsure about what they wanted her to do. She had also found that some class teachers would not let her help monolinguals because she was not a specialist.

Finally, one discerned a certain resentment among class teachers, a feeling that support teachers had 'an easy number' and treated them 'like a radiator at the back of the room'.

8 THE ATTITUDES OF PUPILS

To some extent there were mixed feelings about pupils' attitudes to support teaching but in general the teachers seemed to take a positive view and felt that their contributions were welcomed on the whole both by bilingual pupils and their monolingual peers.

It must be said, however, that their perception of the attitude of the bilinguals was somewhat equivocal: 'the more sensible appreciate having someone there who'll give extra help'; 'most bilinguals like it'; 'they really appreciate help in the main'; 'once they start becoming proficient, they like to shake it off'.

Several points were raised which might help to explain some of the reservations implicit in those statements: 'some are embarrassed by the thought you might be there for them – they don't want to feel they need extra help'; 'no child wants a minder'; 'they don't like to be highlighted – often the colour of their skin makes them stand out enough'; 'other children get at them if you help and they do well'; 'a few don't like it because it draws attention to them'; 'we often create a situation that is too intense for one or two children'.

The same equivocation was expressed about the attitudes of the monolingual children. All of these teachers were aware that they ought to be helping all the children and most noted that extra help was often welcomed by the monolingual children but the teachers were very sensitive to the dangers of resentment being felt towards the bilingual pupils.

The most pessimistic view was expressed by one teacher who claimed that 'the children generally don't see you as a proper teacher'. Another said that 'ideally' children should see the support teacher 'as another bona fide teacher working with the whole class. They don't always – perhaps the fault of support teachers themselves.' This last comment would seem perhaps too hard a line to be taken by a teacher working under the kind of difficulties outlined here.

9 CONCLUSION

The views of teachers such as those interviewed here are important for several reasons. These teachers are very much aware of, and at least broadly sympathetic to, arguments of the kind sketched in the introduction in favour of mainstream support as a means of helping bilingual pupils in the secondary school. However, the nature of their experience gives rise to insights about the specific value of the two approaches to teaching bilinguals which we have been considering, about the problems of working with colleagues and about some of the organisational implications of support teaching.

One thing we can learn from these interviews is that we can envisage an ideal situation as follows: an experienced, relevantly qualified teacher supports pupils in a subject in which she is knowledgeable; she has a clear view of the whole syllabus, a welcoming class teacher and time for consultation; she has a secure place within the structure of the classroom and a role with the class as a whole.

These teachers have shown many ways in which the teaching of bilinguals in their schools could be improved. This in itself may be of value to others in similar situations, for there is no reason to believe that the schools in which they work are unique. Certainly, the reservations they have expressed about the drawbacks of restricting provision to mainstream support are worthy of consideration.

The most worrying issue raised by this study, however, relates to the possibility of bringing about the kind of improvements we have been discussing. If changes cannot be made in respect of some of the problems we have seen, are we in a position in which we have to drastically rethink our provision for bilinguals in the secondary sector? Or are we in danger of condemning these teachers – and their pupils – to an endless struggle which cannot be won?

REFERENCES

Department of Education and Science (DES) (1975) *A Language for Life* (The Bullock Report), London: HMSO.

—— (1985) *Education for All* (The Swann Report), London: HMSO.

—— (1988a) *A Survey by Her Majesty's Inspectorate of the Teaching of English as a Second Language in Six LEAs*, London: DES.

—— (1988b) *English for Ages 5 to 11* (The Cox Report), London: DES.

Dulay, H., Burt, M. and Krashen, S. (1982) *Language Two*, Oxford: Oxford University Press.

Chapter 11

In the driving seat?
Supporting the education of traveller children

Chris Mills

In this chapter Chris Mills describes her work as a peripatetic support teacher for traveller children. She made the transition to this work after supporting children who experience difficulties in learning in the mainstream and was surprised by the extent and depth of the prejudice towards the children that she encountered. She provides an example of practice where the contribution of the children to school life was welcomed but indicates the negative attitudes and misunderstandings which she found in the schools on her patch. She argues that progress towards recognising the curricular needs of this minority group has been pitifully slow despite the attention given to them in a series of government reports.

1 INTRODUCTION

It is just over a year since I was appointed as Curriculum Support Teacher for Traveller Children. It was a new post, in line with national trends in traveller education. Local education authorities have a statutory duty to provide education for all children who reside in their area, whether permanent or temporary, and many authorities are setting up services to meet the needs of travellers. In order to make meaningful provision, a count of gypsy caravans takes place nationally in January and July each year. At the last count there were 11,544 caravans in England, with 753 in my local authority.

I was interested in the post because at the time I was working as a special needs teacher in a school with many children from army families. After eighteen months, most of these families were re-posted and so the problems associated with enforced mobility were not completely new to me. I felt, therefore, that I would be working in a role which was familiar to me, but supporting a very different group of people.

My experience in special needs had given me a strong sense of direction. Soon after starting my present job I attended a 'Sharing with Colleagues' course. One of our tasks was to assemble a collage from magazine cuttings to represent feelings about our present post. My collage featured a car on a long road, with myself very much in the driving seat. I have since reflected that as a result of courses, books, circulars, policy guidelines and recent legislation in special needs, as a special needs teacher I was following a well-worn path. I didn't realise at that early stage that there were few prescriptions to follow in the education of traveller children.

2 THE SCOPE OF THE JOB

There are approximately 400 traveller children attending school in my county. I belong to a team of six teachers and two education welfare officers, each with responsibility for a geographical area. Mine is a large, sparsely populated agricultural area containing small village primary schools, with larger primary schools and a secondary school in each of the three main towns. Although my brief is to support traveller children throughout their education in mainstream schools, in practice this mainly covers the primary phase, as most travellers do not go on to secondary education.

There are three permanent sites for travellers, one transit site and many tolerated unofficial sites in my 'patch'. Most traveller families in this area spend the winter on site, then follow the seasonal work on farms in the summer. Some travellers move into the area in the summer-time to find employment in the seasonal farm work. As a result of this movement, many children are away from school for much of the summer. In a year when the weather is good, this can be from March until October. Some teachers from neighbouring authorities have given 'Distance Learning Packs' to the children in order to bridge this gap. It has had limited success, and their feelings are that children should attend local schools whenever possible.

Before starting this work, I assumed that all children attended school and received some formal education. I have learnt that this is not so, but it is difficult to estimate how many children are not in school. A Department of Education and Science report estimated that, nationally, in 1983 about 50 per cent of primary and traveller children and 15 per cent of secondary aged pupils attended school (DES 1983). In my patch only a handful attend at secondary age, certainly less than 10 per cent. Recently, an adult literacy bus, funded by Community Education, drew onto a permanent traveller site within the LEA. The bus had previously been used as a playgroup bus and was decorated on the outside with pictures of zoo animals. An unforeseen event was that children of school age appeared, attracted by the brightly coloured decorations. It had been assumed, as this is a permanent site, that most of the children would attend school. I found it an interesting exercise to consider why the parents of these children do not value school enough to send them there.

I spend approximately 60 per cent of my time in schools, working in a variety of ways. I support individual children in class, many of whom have had little formal education. Where possible, I liaise with special needs teachers within these schools to discuss programmes of work for individual children and to share resources. Sometimes I accompany parents and children in their first visit to school, after negotiating this with the head teacher, parent and educational welfare officer. I attend staff meetings in primary and secondary schools to join discussions on issues relating to travellers. Recently I have spent some time planning and attending meetings with a view to setting up adult literacy classes for travellers in a secondary school.

When the need arises I obtain information about travellers in this area from the travellers' liaison officer, the Save the Children Fund development worker, social workers, probation officers and site wardens. I liaise with teams of teachers for travellers from other counties, and advisory teachers from this county since multicultural issues are fundamental to every subject.

I meet other members of my team regularly, to plan in-service training and to work on an information book about travellers, for schools. One section of this booklet is about traveller lifestyle. We felt that it was necessary to question some of the commonly held views about travellers. Contrary to the general stereotype, most travellers strive for personal cleanliness, often in adverse conditions. Many use different bowls for washing clothes and themselves. Generally, they live in a close-knit supportive community. Travellers who live on permanent sites have always paid rates like the housed community, and all travellers are liable for the community charge. If they move around they are generally directed to move on at very short notice, and do not have time to clear up all of their belongings. They would prefer it if they were given more advance warning so that they could dispose of everything properly. They recognise that if that were the case, they would be more welcome if they returned to the same spot at a later date. Of course, these are generalisations, and, like any group, travellers are made up of individuals.

3 COUNTERING NEGATIVE ATTITUDES

I am very fortunate within this area: there is a primary school which is noted for its good practice with traveller children. The head teacher of this large primary school holds the view that children from the nearby traveller site are just as much a part of the catchment area as other children. He encourages the parents to go into school, and staff visit families on site. These policies have been pursued for several years, although they have not always been favourably received. The head teacher told me that in the early years, his school was known as 'The Gypsy School' by local residents, and this wasn't meant in a kindly way. He had experienced ill-feeling towards travellers from other parents. His response to these parents – that there were other schools in the area if they didn't like his – resulted in a strongly worded rebuke from the local education authority. It is interesting that this school is now held as a model of good practice, and that he and his deputy are now involved in leading in-service training regarding travellers in other schools.

However, I am concerned about the prejudice against travellers which I encounter in other schools. The most worrying aspect of this is that it is present in teaching staff rather than children. I sense that, in general, it is considered to be an acceptable prejudice. I have heard comments made against travellers, which I feel sure would not have been made against other ethnic minorities. In one school staffroom, a teacher of infants with traveller children in her class, said of traveller parents, 'I have no time for them myself. If they can't be bothered to send their children to school, then why should we make any effort for them.' It concerned me that she didn't take into account the nature of the travellers' way of life.

A further example of prejudice amongst teaching staff occurred in a secondary school. A Personal and Social Education module was planned for pupils, to tackle prejudice against travellers. Two teachers in school told the head of year that they felt unable to teach the module because of their own prejudices. I find it disturbing that this went unchallenged in spite of the LEA's multicultural policy, which states that the County Council 'welcomes the multicultural nature of its schools and will ensure that all teachers receive a copy of the statement on Multicultural Education'.

I attended a case conference in another secondary school which was arranged to decide the fate of a 'difficult' traveller family. Five boys from one family were being threatened with expulsion from school. The parents had not been informed that the case conference was due to take place and were therefore not able to make their views known. The meeting took place away from school and was attended by various support staff and other professionals within education. There were no members of the school staff present, and thus the placement of five boys was decided by professionals who had no direct dealings with, or knowledge of, the boys. A very negative report, in which the family were said to have 'an instinct for violence', was prepared by the school staff and this formed the only basis of decisions made. The report did not make reference to the fact that one of the boys was suffering from a severe kidney disorder which made him incontinent. A decision was reached that the most suitable placement for the five boys was within their present school, with modifications to the timetable and support from a teacher for behaviourally difficult pupils. This proved to be very unpopular with the school staff. None of the recommendations were taken up, and some of these boys are now indefinitely excluded from school with no plans to reinstate them.

One traveller family had led a very isolated life in a remote area of the Fens. They came to be housed when their trailer blew over in high winds and most of their possessions were destroyed. The Education Welfare Officer and I negotiated the children's entry into school, and, as a result, the children were separated from their parents for the first time. To ensure that all ran smoothly, their mother accompanied the children to the classroom and continued to do so for the first few weeks. The class teacher stated that, in his opinion, no 11-year-old girl needed to be brought to the classroom door by her mother. It is surprising how often teachers expect a child to make any necessary changes to fit into a school, rather than being prepared to make some changes themselves.

I am aware that prejudice which travellers encounter does not only come from schools. At a day conference about traveller education, attended by a variety of professionals, a librarian stated that it was the policy in that area not to allow travellers to join the library service. This included travellers from the permanent site, who might never leave the area, and who paid rates like housed families. I know of at least two pubs in this area which display the sign 'No van dwellers' on their door. As recently as two years ago there were frequent raids by police on some permanent sites in this area. These often took place in the middle of the night, with one search warrant for the entire site. I learned recently that this is still taking place in neighbouring authorities. As teachers, there is very little that we can do about this, but we need to be aware that the traveller children in school may have had similar experiences.

One of my early concerns when I began this work was that I was moving further and further away from mainstream education. I am now firmly convinced that my role is to operate within the framework of mainstream education. I have witnessed the sense of panic within teachers and head teachers when traveller children arrive in school. When one considers that these children are English-speaking, have no specific learning problems, are motivated to learn and are generally well-behaved, it is difficult to understand why. I feel sure that a little flexibility in the school's organisation would meet the needs of these children.

4 PARENTAL EXPECTATIONS

For a variety of reasons, many traveller parents have had little experience of formal education themselves. Many perceive the need for basic literacy and numeracy, but there can be differences in the schools' aims and the travellers' perception of education. An Irish family I know simply want the school to teach their daughter how to write a letter. I often wonder how traveller children make sense of this situation. Alice, 10-year-old girl, told the head teacher of her school that she did not want to learn to read. The head teacher was very surprised because the class teacher and other staff in the school had made a great effort to teach Alice to read. When he asked why, Alice replied that her mother had told her that she had to leave school when she was able to read, and Alice enjoyed going to school. It is increasingly recognised that parents play an important role in their child's education. When it is a traveller child, the relationship between school and parent is a vital one. Travellers need more knowledge about particular schools and education in the broadest sense as, often, they have very little experience to draw upon.

One deputy head of a primary school stated that, 'Most parents regard you as a professional who can be trusted with the care of their children. To traveller parents you are just a stranger.' In her reception class, there was one occasion when an entire traveller family watched in the corridor next to her classroom all morning when their child attended school for the first time.

5 FINDING APPROPRIATE MATERIALS

At the end of my first year in post, I feel that there are several issues which need to be addressed. A major area of concern is the lack of resources in schools which reflect traveller lifestyle, for both children and teachers. Many teachers are unaware of issues which may be sensitive to traveller children in their class, and find it difficult to gain access to this information. In addition to this, most resources in schools are aimed at children from the housed population. I am not aware of any reading scheme which features a family who live in a trailer, or any materials from other areas of the curriculum which reflect the traveller way of life. I suspect that this gives a very powerful message to the travellers that school is not for them; and to other children in the school, that travellers are not valued. In order to overcome this problem I visited the Annual Special Needs Exhibition in London, and went to the multicultural exhibition stands. My request for resources which reflected traveller culture resulted in blank stares and genuine bewilderment. There were resources to support many ethnic minorities within our society, but none for travellers. It brought to mind the Plowden Report which had described the children of travellers as 'probably the most severely deprived children in the country' (DES 1967). The Swann Report argued that 'the situation in which travellers' children find themselves illustrates to an extreme degree the experience of prejudice and alienation which faces many other ethnic minority children' (DES 1985: 740). It is, perhaps, hardly surprising that so many traveller children underachieve in school.

6 THE FUTURE

For the future, I have some fears for travellers in the many changes which are taking place within education. I wonder how they will fare in the National Curriculum, given that many are absent from school in the summer months. Distance learning is not sophisticated enough to meet the demands of the National Curriculum, and Standard Assessment Tasks are due to take place in the summer term. I see distinct stages in the work which needs to be done. The short-term aims would be to ensure that all traveller children were on a school register, and attended school regularly, in the primary and secondary phase. The medium-term aim would be to ensure that they received a relevant curriculum and meaningful experiences when they were in school, with the long-term aim being for travellers to take on professional roles themselves and be more involved in the planning and implementation of this work.

The last twelve months have been a very enjoyable and valuable learning experience for me. It has been necessary to question many of my own beliefs and attitudes. My own awareness of many issues within multicultural education has been raised. It has been interesting to observe the different reactions from teachers and head teachers when a child who is a little bit different arrives in school. It is encouraging to note that many schools are very welcoming and value the new dimension which a traveller child can bring into the classroom. I know of one school secretary who writes letters for a traveller family and reads the replies to them. I have also learnt a great deal about the richness and diversity to be found within local history and traditions, linked to travellers, fairs, circuses and the Showmen's Guild. I would hope that others who are fortunate enough to work with travellers can share this and value these children.

REFERENCES

Department of Education and Science (DES) (1967) *Children and Their Primary Schools* (The Plowden Report), London: HMSO.
—— (1983) *The Education of Travellers' Children*, London: HMSO.
—— (1985) *Education for All* (The Swann Report), London: HMSO.

Chapter 12

Chris Raine's progress

An achievement to be proud of

Alyson Clare

In this chapter Alyson Clare describes the progress made by Chris Raine, a pupil at the small rural primary school of which she is head teacher. Chris is a child with Down's syndrome and despite the misgivings of some within the local education authority, but with the ready support of his community, he began school in a nearby village rather than the special school over twenty miles away. Alyson recorded the way professionals and pupils combined forces to provide Chris with an education.

1 INTRODUCTION AND BACKGROUND

In September 1987 we at Ravenstonedale School admitted seven reception children. One of them, Chris Raine, had Down's syndrome. Despite the wishes of his parents, the recommendations of various people who had monitored Chris's development since birth and our willingness to try to integrate and educate him at Ravenstonedale, the authority had decided to send Chris to Sandgate School in Kendal, over twenty miles from his home.

Everyone concerned appealed against this decision and eventually it was decided that Chris should be educated within a day special school or special education unit. However, Chris should initially be admitted to the local primary school with individual support, transferring to a special school at a later date. We admitted Chris in September 1987 and with him came Rana Coleman, our newly appointed Special Attachment Welfare Assistant (SAWA).

With Julia Holloway, the infants' teacher, I spent a great deal of time discussing and planning for the day Chris started school. I had had a little experience working with children with disabilities but Julia had had none and although very willing to try, was initially and quite understandably apprehensive. We had many positive things on our side, not the least of which were parental and community support. Ravenstonedale and Newbiggin-on-Lune (the village one mile away where Chris lives) are very rural. Consequently everyone knows everyone else. Mr and Mrs Raine had purposely strived to make Chris a part of this community from an early age. He had attended chapel and the parent-run playgroup regularly. All thirty-three children at school knew Chris and, having talked to them, we anticipated that they would be protective towards Chris and make allowances for the fact that he was different.

Another positive factor was the SAWA. Initially the authority had offered us help for fifteen hours per week but Chris was still in nappies and we did not think him capable of restricting his need for clean nappies to coincide with the fifteen hours a SAWA would be present! Rana was consequently appointed full-time for thirty hours per week.

The local speech therapist, a physiotherapist and a pre-school teacher for children with learning difficulties, would all be available to help us on what felt like a journey into the unknown. Even the school bus drivers were willing to take care of Chris on the school bus, enabling him to be as much like the other children as possible. It seemed like a very tall order at the outset, but our philosophy was that if Chris was to be educated at Ravenstonedale, he was to be treated as much like the other children as we could. If concessions were to be made they must be for a specific purpose and for as short a time as possible. We would, of course, have back-up from the educational psychologist and from the experienced staff at Sandgate Special School.

So, with all this ready to support us, Chris started school. With him he brought his dinner money, his PE bag and just four distinguishable words – 'mummy', 'daddy', 'car', 'bus' and within a week, a fifth one, 'school'.

2 EARLY LANGUAGE DEVELOPMENT

Initially, our primary concern was to get Chris settled into school. For the first two sessions Mrs Raine stayed with him. It was clear from the start that there would not be a problem integrating Chris socially. He joined in classroom activities quite happily and ran to children he knew in the playground; they were only too pleased to play with him. We wondered what would happen when the 'honeymoon' period was over but the children settled into what we consider to be a healthy, caring, no-fuss relationship with Chris. They will play with him and give him the extra time he needs to take part but they are also fair and firm and do not make too many concessions or allow unacceptable behaviour.

One of the oldest girls, Nicki, became a firm favourite with Chris. She spent a great deal of time during playtimes and before school playing with him, talking to him, encouraging him and teaching him new skills. The period before school started had been a worry to us. The school bus would arrive over twenty minutes before school started, at which time Rana would arrive. The children had always been encouraged to use this time constructively with toys, sand, drawing, writing, reading, etc. Chris fell into this pattern quite easily. It was useful to us for two reasons: first, we became aware of Chris's quite extraordinary powers of concentration when looking at books, and second, it became obvious just how much he could learn from other children.

Nicki and some other children spent the first few weeks teaching Chris to draw faces. He was keen to please and to copy what the others were doing. The one big problem Chris encountered was real communication with the rest of us. The pre-school teacher for children with learning difficulties, Mrs Tipping, and her replacement, Maureen Ellis, had told us that Chris's understanding of language far outstripped his spoken language. We found that Chris could follow even quite complicated instructions easily, especially if you made certain you had his full attention in the first place. Situations arose, however, where Chris could not make himself understood. We would try various suggestions but if they were wrong Chris would become frustrated or even resign himself to the fact that he could not make us understand. On reflection, the children coped better with this situation than we did. Perhaps they did not expect to be able to meet all his needs or wants. They would simply distract him and do something else with him. As adults, we found the situation upsetting, frustrating and unacceptable.

The speech therapists, Pauline Smithson and Tara Winterton, offered a possible solution: they would teach us, along with Chris, to use Makaton sign language. Initially, we did not really see Makaton as a solution, more as a means of attacking the problem. We were worried that Chris would come to rely on Makaton at the expense of developing speech. Julia, Rana and I discussed the matter and felt it was worth trying, so we approached Mrs Raine. If this were really to be beneficial to Chris, she would have to learn it too – and so, we decided, would all the other children in school.

Pauline agreed to come to school about once a week, for about twenty minutes, to teach us all in stages. The adults admitted to feeling a little nervous about learning this new skill. The children took to it like ducks to water, including Chris! From the youngest infants to the oldest juniors the children picked up the signs very easily, often recalling them more readily than the adults. After four or five sessions and lots of practice we had all mastered the first four stages. This enabled us to sign many of the words one would need in simple conversation with a 4 or 5 year old. Signs like 'egg', 'biscuit' and 'jam' were not so important for us in school but 'play', 'ball', 'book' and 'crayon' were. Throughout the learning period, Pauline repeatedly stressed that we must always say the words as we used the signs. Makaton was not only to help Chris communicate, it was to encourage him to speak too.

We still recall with pleasure the times when Chris used a new sign spontaneously for the first time. He could now sign 'ball' and one of the children would get him one. But this did not last for long. The children began to demand 'ball please' of him and Chris obliged. And then it was 'play ball please'. We had a slight worry that parents might object to their children learning Makaton but we had some very positive feedback and know that more than a few parents learned a new skill from their children during those weeks!

Then spoken language began to appear with the signs, slowly and sometimes indistinctly at first, often in a whisper until he gained in confidence. We knew Chris had difficulty in making some sounds but he could make reasonable approximations. At this stage, staff and children were quite firm about encouraging Chris to verbalise as well as sign. To encourage him to speak out and not just whisper, Pauline brought us a new gadget. It was a large, red plastic apple. If Chris held it close to his mouth and said a word loudly, a worm would pop out of the top of the apple. Whisper a word and the worm would not appear. This helped a great deal. Like all 5 year olds, there were times when he would try to get away with as little effort as possible but on the whole he was cooperative and keen to imitate the others.

By the time Christmas came around we were all in full flow with Makaton. To the children it seemed a natural progression to incorporate it into our Christmas production. We were performing a Nativity Play with the infants acting, the juniors reading from the Bible and everyone singing. It wasn't long before the infants were signing as they acted so we wrote them a very simple script which was a compromise between the Authorised Version and the range of Makaton signs they knew. Chris was a shepherd boy and with a few others had to say 'Where's the baby?' and 'Let's go to see the baby'. Despite the fact that he wouldn't wear his head-dress, he was excellent at the dress rehearsal. In the actual performance he was too tired and simply lay down. Nevertheless, we were very proud of him.

One set of signs we all learned was the set for letter names. The infants learned them as the sounds the letters make and developed a little game with them. When it was time to go somewhere – to dinner, to the playground or to put coats on – one child would say, 'If your name begins with "a" you can go.' At the same time they would make the sign. Chris loved to be the one in control and very soon could look at each child quite pointedly and make the sign for the sound their name began with, thereby allowing them to go. For this game, Chris did not verbalise the sounds, we encouraged him to say the child's name. Some of them, especially the long ones, were very indistinct at first. Many sounds were difficult for him, thus 'Laura' sounded more like 'orrs'. We encouraged him to say the longer names syllabically so that 'Al' eventually grew to be Alexander. Each time we had to make sure that Chris was watching our mouths and trying to copy. Occasionally this syllabic method backfired; Chris now calls James, Jamers with two very distinct syllables. No one seems to mind.

In one-to-one situations with Rana, Chris was now being encouraged to use two words together, e.g. 'pink pig' or 'black cat'. His one-to-one correspondence was very good and his number words quite distinct so 'three dogs' or 'ten apples' was fairly distinguishable and within his capabilities. Chris was quite happy to repeat these phrases after somebody else. However, with a picture of two pink pigs before him, Chris would only say 'pigs'. He was unable to use more than one word spontaneously, with the exception of the phrase 'play ball'.

It is, perhaps, appropriate to mention here some of Chris's other achievements apart from those in the area of oral language development. His gross motor control and general coordination were vastly improved; he was well-adjusted socially; he could trace or draw recognisable pictures; he could copy-write and write his name unaided; he had learned to take his turn; he had begun a toilet-training programme and was making slow but steady progress; and he was happy.

3 FURTHER INITIATIVES

Chris's lack of spontaneous oral language to communicate with the rest of us was the next obstacle to be overcome. We knew he could say strings of words but we were unsure how meaningful they were to him. We needed to devise further strategies to develop this aspect of his language. Our close monitoring of his development to date meant we knew exactly where he was at. Two possible lines of attack seemed open to us: these were his obvious love of books and his ability with numbers. Add to this his strong desire to do what the others could do, and we had the beginnings of a new programme of work for Chris.

The overall plan was to saturate Chris with language. He needed to hear lots of meaningful sentences spoken directly to him and to be encouraged to repeat phrases and sentences in a specific context. Apart from doing this through games, speech therapy exercises, normal conversation, etc., the main areas of attack were to be through the reading scheme (Ginn 360), other books and the maths scheme (Peak). As his drawing improved and became more recognisable another line of attack was to get him to write sentences with his picture and read them to anyone with the time to listen!

Chris's love of books is quite remarkable for a child of his age. It is not unusual for him to look at books on his own for more than twenty minutes. He often takes a book to Rana for her to read to him. His visual memory is excellent but it still surprised us all when he began to assimilate the sight vocabulary for Level One of the reading scheme. In some of the books the sentences are actually questions requiring a one word answer. When Chris answered these spontaneously it indicated to us that he understood at least some of the strings of words he was verbalising. Rana asked Mrs Raine for some photographs of Chris when he was younger and made a book out of them with spaces for Chris to write about himself. Chris had already learned the word 'me', but the book was useful to reinforce this and to encourage the use of 'I' and 'mine'. It also encouraged him to talk about events in the past, something he had found difficult. He also enjoyed acting out events so Rana could guess what he was doing.

4 EVALUATION: JANUARY 1989

It is now seventeen months since Chris started at Ravenstonedale School. Occasionally when we find it difficult to understand something he is desperate to communicate to us we recall the early days when this happened many times a day. It is a much rarer occurrence now and that in itself means we have made progress. But how much? What has happened to the Makaton? Have we been able to achieve our aim of getting Chris to communicate in sentences? Although Chris's expressive language is now largely limited to three or four word phrases the elements of a sentence, subject–verb–object, are often there. He communicates spontaneously with adults and other children far more frequently and he can expand on what he has said more readily now when prompted. The speech therapist tells us that 'flaccid oral musculature' contributes to his difficulty in articulating certain sounds and we are working on exercises to improve this.

Two weeks ago, just after the school bus arrived, I heard someone crying in the cloakroom. It was Chris; two top-infant girls were trying to find out what was wrong. They said they thought he wanted to play with the football he had brought to school that morning. Chris is difficult to understand when he is crying so I aimed for some one word responses. The conversation went like this:

Me: Did you bring a ball to school this morning, Chris?
Chris: Yes.
Me: Do you want to play with it?
Chris: Yes.

At this point I wasn't going to let him get away with two one-word answers so I asked, 'Where do you want to play with it?', hoping for 'In the playground' but the response came after a very deep breath and it was: 'Please I play Chris's ball?' The girls were so excited they rushed off to tell Mrs Holloway.

It has always been our philosophy to treat Chris as much like the other children as possible. Over the time he has been with us we have become increasingly aware of the very tiny steps we must take with Chris's development, whether it be in his physical development, toilet-training or communication skills. Over seventeen months, our achievements with Chris, or perhaps we should say Chris's own achievements, have been remarkable. Makaton became a thing of the past months ago. One tiny vestige of it remains – Chris still uses the sign for thank you. On most occasions Chris can make himself understood using words and gestures though it is easier to follow what he says in context rather than out of context. It is getting easier all the time but sometimes we seem to make little progress. 'Hasten slowly' is perhaps a good motto to bear in mind. Chris is contributing to his class and is, in turn, benefiting from the contact with his peers. Just like any other child, Chris can be demanding, exasperating and frustrating but he has added a new dimension to the lives of everyone at Ravenstonedale School and it is a joy to have him with us.

5 UPDATE: JANUARY 1991

Chris has now been at Ravenstonedale School for nearly three and a half years and he continues to make steady progress. There have been three intakes of 4 year olds while Chris has been with us and they have easily fallen into the general air of acceptance of Chris's differences. Socially Chris gravitates towards younger children who are engaged in activities more appropriate to him. Now that he is a Year 3 child, officially a 'junior', he spends part of each day in the junior classroom. He could probably cope in a class of Year 3 children but a village school class of Year 3 to Year 6 children cannot offer all the play activities Chris still needs.

Chris's oral language continues to improve and one aim at the moment is to encourage the use of more complex sentences of six words or more. Another is to use, where appropriate, 'I' and 'my' instead of 'Chris'.

After an absence of more than six months I returned to school recently and was staggered by the improvement in the clarity of his speech. His willingness to contribute comments to the discussion of a story was also notable.

There is still a long road ahead and we are unsure how long Chris will be able to remain at our school with support. We will continue to be proud of all his achievements and to feel privileged to have been witness to them.

ACKNOWLEDGEMENT

Credit for Chris's development to date must be given to his class teacher, Mrs Julia Holloway; the SAWA, Mrs Rana Coleman; the support services; the children at his school; and his parents who have supported all our efforts with Chris.

Chapter 13

Signing and talking in a Leeds primary school

Beate Schmidt-Rohlfing

Source: Case study 2.11 from *Talk and Learning 5–16: An Inservice Pack on Oracy for Teachers*, Milton Keynes: Open University Press, 1991.

This chapter considers some features of support for deaf children in mainstream schools. In Leeds, deaf children are integrated into the mainstream as bilingual pupils, using British Sign Language and English. Beate Schmidt-Rohlfing, a teacher of the deaf based in a Leeds primary school, outlines the policy in Leeds and examines how it works to support one deaf girl from a Punjabi-speaking family. She describes the support provided for this girl and some aspects of her learning experience in school. In this chapter 'deaf children' refers to all children who have a hearing loss, regardless of degree.

1 THE LEEDS POLICY

Until 1987 Leeds had a school for the deaf and the education policy was to teach deaf children to communicate orally. In 1987 deaf education in Leeds experienced a major change of policy. Prior developments within the deaf school led up to that change. Falling rolls made it increasingly difficult to provide a broad curriculum and staff became dissatisfied. There was growing pressure for change from the deaf community and from parents. Some parents acted under the 1981 Education Act and had their children individually integrated into mainstream schools with a personal teacher who was to compensate for communication difficulties.

Leeds' new policy saw the integration of all deaf children into mainstream provision. This coincided with a more general change of policy which prepared for the integration of all special needs children.

But more important was the Leeds bilingual policy for the education of deaf children. Underlying this policy was a belief in 'total communication'. The Leeds policy defines this as an 'umbrella term': it includes the use of speech, lip-reading, reading and writing in English – but also, crucially, the use of signing. Implicit in the policy is the recognition of BSL as a legitimate language of education, and as the first language of most deaf children.

British Sign Language (BSL) is the language of the deaf community in Britain.

It is a visual-gestural language: whereas spoken languages rely upon combinations of sounds to produce words, BSL uses combinations of handshapes, hand positions and movements, body positions and facial expressions to produce signs. BSL has its own grammar. This is not the same as the grammar of English, but makes full use of the spatial nature of the medium. It is not possible to speak English and use BSL completely simultaneously, but it is possible to switch between one language and the other as between two spoken languages.

It is significant that the driving force behind this bilingual policy was the deaf community, who argued that deaf children should have BSL as their first language with English taught as a second language.

In their mainstream schools, younger deaf pupils are supported by Deaf Instructors who communicate with them in BSL, ensuring children learn the language from native signers and also providing adult role models. Older pupils have Educational Interpreters, who use BSL to relay information from the class teacher. Deaf pupils also have access to a Teacher of the Deaf, who teaches English as a second language and also facilitates access to the curriculum. These staff are referred to collectively as 'support staff'.

In implementing the new policy, a conscious attempt has been made to involve parents. Family support groups have been set up and parents meet to learn BSL (taught by Deaf Instructors) and to talk to each other. There is an evening sign language class for parents who work during the day.

Some deaf children come from Asian families (mainly Punjabi-speaking) and an Asian family support group has been established. This employs a bilingual (Punjabi–English) interpreter to work with the Deaf Instructor. Some parents are effectively learning English and BSl at the same time. The parents of one child have asked that he be exposed to Pakistani Sign Language to gain an insight into, and an understanding of, his own culture. So far, there has been no move by parents of younger (primary school) children to have them taught Punjabi.

There has recently been a proposal to employ two bilingual family support workers. The Leeds hearing-impaired service hopes to develop liaison with parents further: so far, this has not been geared sufficiently towards ethnic minority parents.

2 ASIMA

I shall show how the bilingual policy works in practice by focusing on the experiences of one child, whom I shall call Asima.

Asima is a 9-year-old profoundly deaf Asian girl. She is the second eldest of five children. The oldest child, a boy, is also deaf. Asima's family speak Punjabi at home. Her father also speaks English; her mother speaks very little English. Both Asima and her brother use sign or mime to communicate with members of the family. Asima's parents have attended classes in signing with the Asian family support group.

Asima began her education in a partially hearing unit in which Sign Supported

English was used. Sign Supported English (SSE) is the use of spoken English, using English word order but accompanied by signing. Sometimes the English is 'spoken' without any voice. Normally only keywords are signed. Asima joined her present primary school in September 1989. It caters for about 250 children aged from 5 to 9 years, plus a nursery. Of these, 75 per cent are Asian, most of whom have Punjabi as a home language, and 25 per cent are either monolingual English-speaking children or come from different ethnic minority groups. When Asima joined the school, there were already five deaf children on roll, all boys from Asian families. The school employs Asian bilingual staff to promote the first language of many of the children, but as yet employs no deaf Asian people who could promote an Asian sign language and culture to the Asian deaf children.

The deaf children (in a group of four and a group of two) are attached to mainstream classes chosen for matching academic ability rather than age. They also have some lessons as a separate group in a specially equipped 'base'. They have integrated very smoothly into the school. Initial contacts with hearing peers were quickly established. Asima made a hearing friend shortly after her arrival – the sister of one of the deaf boys, who is familiar with signing and confident to use this as a means of communication. Nevertheless, various problems have arisen between deaf and hearing children.

Sometimes there are problems in the playground. Some of the deaf boys, occasionally with one or two hearing children, have formed a 'gang' and there is a lot of 'gang-warfare' going on. 'The deafies are fighting us again' is a complaint often heard. The hearing children's view of deaf children changed a little after Asima joined the group as the only girl. Assemblies have also been used to promote a positive image of deaf children.

The mainstream staff and all the hearing children I have spoken to agree they would like the opportunity to learn more sign language. Hearing children have not, so far, been taught any sign language. The mainstream staff regret that a weekly lunchtime course in BSL ended after one year due to staff shortage. Some have since attended night classes to learn more BSL.

Asima's day

I recently spent a day observing Asima in school. Her day began in 'base' in a group with other deaf children. The Deaf Instructor used this session to promote communication skills in BSL. Asima then joined the mainstream class until playtime. The teacher explained to the class what work they had to do and Asima used the interpreter to follow. With help from support staff, Asima then worked in a group with hearing children and one other deaf child. After play she worked in 'base', on English language – taught in 'base' because it needs modification to present it in an appropriate form. At lunch Asima sat with her hearing friend, but was nevertheless 'alone' for some of the time because she missed a lot of the conversation around her. (I sat and chatted to her for some of the time and she has begged me ever since to come again.) In the afternoon she joined her mainstream class again. The children were given a problem to discuss in their groups and Asima joined a group with hearing and deaf children. She rarely attempted to contribute to the discussion, although support staff were available to interpret for her. Sometimes hearing and deaf children do communicate more freely, e.g. when sharing felt-tip pens with deaf children the hearing children quickly picked up the signs for the different colours, and asked me how to sign 'Can I have the yellow/red/blue . . .' Both hearing and deaf children enjoyed this exchange. The session after play was in 'base'. The group of deaf children had a story signed to them by the Deaf Instructor; on another occasion they might 'retell' in BSL a familiar story and so learn about story-signing skills.

I recorded on a chart Asima's communication with deaf peers, hearing peers, mainstream teachers and support staff. This chart shows how often Asima initiated contact with others, and how often others initiated contact with her (see Figure 13.1).

The conclusions I drew from these observations are that Asima feels confident and happy to 'chat' to her deaf peers but will not often initiate conversation with hearing peers although they are keen to communicate with her. She also lacks confidence, and perhaps the necessary communication skills, to contribute to group discussions. She is well accepted in her class and certain children try hard to be friendly, showing this sometimes in physical closeness. Asima also freely communicates with the Deaf Instructor and other support staff but very rarely with her mainstream teacher. I observed her showing completed work to her teacher but never asking her anything or trying to communicate with her. Asima does not yet seem to be able to watch the interpreter consistently and often has to be briefed twice. Other deaf children find it equally hard to make good use of the Educational Interpreter – some work on how to use an interpreter might be helpful here. Asima rarely tries to contribute during a class lesson. In the playground she is keen to be with her hearing friend but often just follows her along without getting involved herself.

The Deaf Instructor believes Asima's signing skills are not yet up to the standard of the other deaf children close to her age. She does not always understand questions in BSL and has to be encouraged to ask more questions herself. Some important features of BSL, such as handshapes and placement of the hands, are not yet sufficiently developed. She needs more practice at retelling a familiar story in BSL to avoid unconnected presentation. Some of her difficulties could be explained by the lack of a role model (native BSL user) which other deaf children of the same age have had consistently for three years.

3 CONCLUSIONS

Hearing people in Asima's school (staff and children) are keen to learn BSL and are prepared to attempt communication with deaf children. But in spite of these positive attitudes deaf children are excluded in many situations every day. The support staff mentioned some integrated situations where it becomes impossible

	'A' to deaf peers	deaf peers to 'A'	'A' to hearing peers	hearing peers to 'A'	'A' to deaf Instructor	deaf Instructor to 'A'	'A' to support staff	Support staff to 'A'	'A' to class teacher	class teacher to 'A'
1. session base 9 – 9.40	26	24			17	12				
2. session classroom 9.40 – 10.30	14	15	3	6			18	21	0	1
playground	8	5	4	3						
3. session base 10.50 - 11.55	21	23					16	22		
lunch 12.00 - 12.20	12	12	4	6						
4. session classroom 1.05 – 2.25	25	26	4	7			23	15	2	2
playground	5	7	2	5						
5. session base 2.45 - 3.15	9	8			10	10				

Figure 13.1 Asima's communication with deaf peers, hearing peers, mainstream teachers and support staff in one school day

to do justice to deaf children: when spoken and visual information are presented simultaneously and also when a group of hearing children needs more specific teaching and it becomes impossible to teach both hearing and deaf children at the same time.

Communication between deaf and hearing children via the Educational Interpreter or Teacher of the Deaf is rare. I have only observed it in unavoidable situations, i.e. 'trouble in the playground'. Maybe hearing as well as deaf children should learn more about an interpreter's functions and how to best use her/him.

Some of the deaf children's communication problems may be due to their lack of security in their first language (BSL). An example illustrates this: One of the deaf children (7 years old) could be described as a partially hearing child. He had never been to a deaf school but spoke very little and in a very quiet voice when I first met him. He gained confidence with the input of BSL and at the same time refused to talk altogether. He preferred BSL. Now, two years later, he is ready to use English fluently and with a much stronger voice.

Ways of communicating successfully with a deaf child have included learning more BSL or using an interpreter adequately. But what about using 'dialogue journals' to communicate through writing? This could be an answer for successful communication between deaf and hearing people. The support staff in this school have started a project using the written form for interpersonal communication. The deaf child uses a 'secret' book to communicate in writing/drawing to a member of the support team. Nothing is corrected. The receiver responds and, where appropriate, elaborates. Nobody else has access to this book. The deaf children enjoy this activity greatly and learn to value the written word which will facilitate access to English for them.

Chapter 14

Expanding horizons

Microtechnology and access to the National Curriculum

Christopher and Rowena Onions

Microtechnology is an indispensable tool for many children and young people with disabilities in school, further and higher education. In this chapter Christopher and Rowena Onions examine the ways in which microtechnology can give learners access to the curriculum, enhancing their ability to acquire, record, manipulate and communicate information. They focus on the three National Curriculum core subjects: English, Mathematics, Science and Technology. To be used effectively in widening the choices available to learners with disabilities, there need to be well organised support systems to provide training and practical advice. Later in the chapter, the authors discuss problems of equity, participation and control raised by the use of microtechnology to give people with disabilities access to the mainstream. Schools and colleges need to deal with attitudes which see microtechnology as conveying an unfair advantage to its users, and need to ensure that it does not serve to isolate rather than integrate children and young people.

The pace of change in the field of microtechnology is phenomenal. Twenty years ago the latest computer occupied a whole floor of one of the university buildings where we were students, required a sophisticated air conditioning and temperature control system, a team of technicians and operators, and cost over £1 million. Yet it was not capable of doing some of the things that the computer on which we are currently writing this chapter can do, and ours is by no means the most sophisticated of the microcomputers now available. We have therefore deliberately refrained from referring to specific equipment and programs as whatever we write about these will rapidly be out of date, some of it by the time this is published. We have tried to indicate how microtechnology can give children with disabilities more control over their lives and greater access to education.

1 POSSIBILITIES AND PROBLEMS

Microtechnology has already had an enormous impact on many schools and on the lives of many children with disabilities and learning difficulties. The last decade has seen a revolution in the ways in which children with disabilities can be assisted to communicate, to learn and to control their environments. This revolution has been brought about, in part, by the rapid and widespread deployment of microcomputers throughout the education system. Less than ten years ago, although there were a few highly publicised cases of children with disabilities being helped by microtechnology, these were few and far between. The technology was available but for the majority there was neither the support necessary to set up and maintain the use of such equipment nor the acceptance on the part of many teachers that work produced via technology was *real* work.

In the not too distant past, we found it was a major battle getting teachers in a primary school to allow a child with minimal cerebral palsy to use a portable, electronic typewriter for written work; it was thought of as almost 'cheating'. At secondary level the resistance tended to be even greater. One of us (Christopher) spent many futile hours with staff at a secondary school questioning why a child who had major difficulties with handwriting was not allowed to demonstrate his knowledge of History, Geography, Science, etc. by submitting oral answers on tape. The strongest objections were not based on the practical problems of listening to and marking orally produced work but on whether it was fair to other children and on the belief that unless you have actually written with a pen on paper you haven't worked. The exasperated suggestion that on the basis of that argument we really ought to return to stone tablets and chisels didn't win a great many friends! We suspect that the widespread introduction of microtechnology into schools has gone some way to help to change attitudes like these, although the strange insistence of some teachers that children should produce a reasonable written copy before being allowed to type it out on the word processor suggests that there are still some problems.

For children in special schools, where specialised aids and individualised learning programmes were far more common, there tended to be fewer problems of this kind. It could still be amazingly difficult to obtain, set up and maintain microtechnological solutions for children who could obviously benefit from them, although by and large obtaining the equipment was not the major part of the problem. At about the same time that we were trying to convince mainstream schools that portable typewriters were not educationally subversive, we were both involved with a child in the Special Care Unit of a school for children with severe learning difficulties. Sarah had severe cerebral palsy. She was the first child with whom we worked to provide microtechnological support. She was unable to speak but those who knew her well were convinced that she understood a lot of what was said; more distant (and more powerful) professionals were more sceptical. The only action over which she had some very limited control was in the movement of her head, down to the right and back to the left. Her tendency to go into spasm meant that even control of this action was not always reliable. We were lucky enough to receive a charitable gift which enabled us to buy one of the first BBC B microcomputers complete with disc drive, colour monitor and printer, specifically for this child.

One of the first problems we encountered was how to provide the staff, who worked with the child on a day-to-day basis, with a basic level of competence and confidence with the technology, at a time when computers in classrooms were still a novel idea. Having spent time setting up equipment and going through its use, and having left a telephone number where we could be contacted, we often returned a week later to find that nothing had been used because some simple and easily remedied, unpredicted snag had occurred. Without technological self-confidence the staff involved had not liked to ask for help because they thought they might be making fools of themselves. On the other hand, this same lack of confidence prevented them from trying to solve the problem for themselves. Had they attempted to do so they would probably have been successful and would have developed both their knowledge and self-confidence in the process. The 'technophobia' of the teachers concerned gradually reduced, but it was really only fully overcome when the school appointed its own member of staff with responsibility for computers and microtechnology and the LEA arranged for her to go on a specialised course.

We soon discovered that it is often not the large or obvious things that hinder the use of microtechnology with children with disabilities, it is small everyday things. How do you fit switches to a child's wheelchair when the wheelchair is totally unsuitable for this purpose? We also discovered that microtechnology cannot be seen in isolation from other aspects of the child's needs. Who has the responsibility for carrying out any modifications and who pays? Who will be responsible for providing a more appropriate wheelchair if the existing one cannot be adapted? How can all the different agencies involved with their different budgets and priorities coordinate their efforts to provide for the child's overall needs? These problems are not new. They will undoubtedly be depressingly familiar to anyone who has worked in the area of special needs, but they become even more crucial when one considers the fundamental difference that microtechnology can make to the lives of some children with very severe difficulties.

Sarah was labelled as 'mentally handicapped' by professionals who considered that if you could not speak or write in response to a question then you did not know the answer. At school-leaving age she would certainly have been destined for occupational day care at the local centre for those with severe learning difficulties. The provision of a microcomputer, with adapted switches to control it and software to cater for a variety of needs, enabled her to communicate with those about her in a way that had been impossible before. She rapidly demonstrated her ability to learn and within weeks of starting to communicate, by selecting from an array of simple picture symbols on the monitor screen, she had begun to read the words (which were mainly there for the benefit of the others around her) that had been paired with the symbols, rather than the symbols. Sarah went on to attend an FE college with specialist facilities for physically disabled people.

The rapid pace of development in the field of microtechnology, and the fact that it probably has more than its fair share of dedicated fanatics who love nothing better than having a problem to get their teeth into, means that there is a danger of a set of technologies in search of problems to solve. This sometimes leads to some very unsatisfactory arrangements. We have come across a number of examples of children using technology just for the sake of it when some simpler and better solution has been available. But if teachers, parents and disabled people can express clearly their needs for access then it may well be that microtechnology has a solution, if not immediately, then in the near future. We will illustrate this by looking at how microtechnology can provide or enhance access to the National Curriculum.

2 ACCESS TO THE NATIONAL CURRICULUM

The implementation of the National Curriculum has left many parents and educationists anxious about its implications for children with special needs. There are those who argue that large parts of the National Curriculum are not appropriate for children with disabilities and that therefore they should be exempted. Others, ourselves included, are worried that the temptation to exempt these children from the National Curriculum will result in restricted educational opportunities. It is rather like saying that because access to shops is difficult for many people with disabilities we will exempt them from using shops and will organise special means of shopping for them, using mail order catalogues or getting others to shop for them. This approach restricts the freedom of the person with a disability. We argue that we should ask how we can give people with disabilities better access to as many aspects and areas of life as possible. The same approach should be taken with the National Curriculum. How can we make as many areas as possible accessible to those with disabilities? What can microtechnology contribute to this process?

English

Speaking and listening

A physical disability may make it impossible for some children to speak orally but there are now a variety of computer-based systems which can give these children an electronic voice which they can use by operating a keyboard, adapted keyboard, touch-sensitive keyboard, head-controlled light wand or whatever system of switches suits their particular physical abilities. These systems are based around a word processor linked to a voice synthesiser. Switch-operated systems rely on the user selecting a word or phrase from a screen display which is scanned manually or automatically, depending upon the ability of the user. Once selected, the word or phrase can be 'spoken'. Both male and female voices can be generated. These systems may be a little slow at present but already increasingly sophisticated predictive word processing programs are becoming available. These analyse the sentence being constructed and on the basis of past experience display the words most likely to be required by the user for the next word after each word has been typed. The most advanced systems have now reached a level of sophistication that enable them to 'learn' the linguistic style of individual users or the style and vocabulary likely to be required for a particular subject or topic.

Advances in microtechnology have also increased access to this area of the curriculum for children with hearing impairments. Hearing aids are one piece of microtechnology that has been around for many years, so many in fact that today we almost take them for granted and forget what a difference they have made to the lives of many people. Technological development has already made major improvements to the quality of the sound produced by hearing aids and has drastically reduced their size and intrusiveness. The phonic ear allows a teacher to wear a radio microphone which enables him or her to communicate directly with the child without any intervening background noise. The same system can allow the wearer to hear a radio, TV or telephone without distraction. The electronic signal produced by these devices is received directly by the hearing aid rather than being converted to sound waves and then amplified. Speech decoders will soon be generally available that will convert speech into print on a screen. This will provide even greater access to the spoken word for those with hearing difficulties.

Reading

Reading presents obvious problems to people with a visual impairment. Not very long ago they had to rely upon strong magnifiers and good lighting or Braille translations of printed books. More recently, talking books – books prerecorded on cassette tapes – have proved to be a tremendous asset. Text can be magnified using special video cameras to produce an enhanced image; foreground and background colours can be changed and their contrast adjusted to suit individual eye conditions. It is relatively simple to have a Brailler connected to a computer so that anything appearing on the computer screen can be printed out in Braille to be read by a visually impaired person, or the information on the screen can be 'read' aloud by the computer if connected to a speech synthesiser. There is now a device that can be used by a visually impaired person which will 'read' aloud any printed word over which it is passed.

Physically disabled people may be quite capable of reading but may have problems in turning over pages of books. A page turner is a sophisticated book stand that allows the user to turn the pages of any book placed on it at the touch of a button. Obviously, this does not overcome the problem a physically disabled person may have with scanning reference books, but there are computer programs now available that store whole books on disc and allow a physically disabled person to scan and search through the material electronically using only one switch. There are electronic data storage systems, based on video discs and compact discs, with the potential to store massive amounts of information, both text and pictures. These can make whole libraries of reference materials available to those with disabilities. Unfortunately, at present these systems are very expensive and not widely available. The question might be asked, 'How much real difference will these systems make to children in schools in the next twenty years?' This is difficult to answer. It was only ten years ago that many sceptical teachers were claiming that microcomputers were far too expensive ever to be used widely in schools in this century and that there certainly would not be more than one per school. Today, it is not uncommon to have one micro per class. Personal computers that cost over £3,000 only three years ago are now available for less than £1,000 and in some cases they are being given away free with the software!

Writing

Perhaps the word processor has done most to reduce the handicap that many people with disabilities experience when called upon to write. In the past, people who are blind could learn to touch type but they could not check their work and had to rely upon a sighted person to correct any errors. Some people with physical disabilities were able to use adapted typewriters but for many this was a very slow and laborious process; for some, correcting work was impossible without assistance. The adapted computer-based word processors, which we mentioned above when discussing alternatives to speech, have also revolutionised the task of writing, putting this attainment target well within the reach of many more children. Spelling check features enable corrections to be made easily and ensure that the work of a child with a disability is as presentable as that of any other child.

Mathematics

While the word processor has become quite sophisticated and is now familiar to many people, the maths processor is not, as yet, nearly as sophisticated or as well known. A maths processor enables the user to produce mathematical drawings, such as graphs, nets, set diagrams, as well as giving the user the ability to use indices, carrying figures, etc. The user can move around the screen to position numbers, symbols and signs exactly where they are required. A scratch pad enables rough working to be carried out on the screen and a calculator is also available that can be programmed to carry out regularly used numerical operations. As with word processors, adaptations can be made to enable the program to be operated by one switch if that is all that the user can manage to control. The maths processor clearly provides access for physically disabled children to the attainment targets in number and algebra.

Data handling is another element of the Mathematics curriculum. Here, too, the maths processor can be a great help to physically disabled children. All children are required to have a knowledge of simple, computer-based, data-handling packages and how to categorise, organise and retrieve specific facts and information. Adapting these for use by children with physical disabilities or for use by children who are blind is relatively easy. Programs and systems exist that will allow a user with a disability to control almost any computer program. Keyboards can be by-passed with individually tailored switch systems and any words printed on a screen can be made audible via a speech synthesiser.

The early levels of the Mathematics National Curriculum require children to have first-hand experience of shape and space. Providing this experience for those with disabilities has been greatly assisted by the development of programs which allow children to control the movement of an object about the floor of a classroom or around a monitor screen. The non-ambulant child can explore the properties of space. Other programs enable anyone who can use a switch to move and manipulate different shapes on a computer screen, an operation that would previously have been very tedious, if not impossible, for many children with physical disabilities.

Practical experience of measurement is also required. In everyday life many mechanical measuring devices are rapidly being replaced with electronic ones. There are now generally available electronic scales, electronic thermometers, electronic tape measures. Any device that produces a visual reading via an electronic signal can be fitted with a speech chip to convert the electronic signal into an audible as well as visual reading, so benefiting those with a visual impairment. 'Point and read' electronic tape measures may enable some children with physical disabilities to carry out measuring tasks that otherwise would be impossible.

Science and Technology

The maths processor and electronic measuring devices also make the Technology curriculum more accessible. There is a wide range of art and design packages from the simple to the complex that have been developed to run on microcomputers. Computer-aided design is a major use for computers in industry and a significant part of the Technology curriculum. These programs too can be operated by switch users allowing them to engage actively in design work and to produce the same kind of work as other children. Given the current shortage of computer facilities for Technology in some schools, it is quite possible that a child with a disability, equipped with his or her own computer could be the 'expert' computer user when it comes to computer-aided design. At present, it is not possible to give children with more severe physical disabilities access to the production side of the Technology curriculum. But if one considers the advances in robotics that have allowed cars to be produced without human hands, other than on control buttons, one realises that it is only a matter of time before such systems become a possibility for people with disabilities.

In Science, the same systems will allow greater access to practical activities. Much of the Science curriculum is concerned with the learning of information and concepts. All the necessary information can be stored electronically and in this form can be more easily accessed and used by those with special needs. Information processing and data handling are required skills in all these areas of the curriculum and therefore anyone who can operate a computer can engage in these activities on an equal footing with their peers.

3 SUPPORT NETWORKS

If technology is to be successfully used to help a child within a school it is essential that the staff should feel at home with the equipment. They don't need to be experts, in the same way as one does not need to be a TV engineer to operate a VTR successfully. But some basic knowledge is required, a willingness to have a go and someone to turn to for advice if one really gets stuck. In practice, teachers need the time and opportunity to play with the equipment so that they become familiar with it and see it as no different from any other equipment that they may use in the classroom. It is perhaps at the classroom level that support is most crucial. On more than one occasion we have come across a child who has been expertly assessed at a nationally recognised centre and provided with all manner of special programs and adapted equipment which have remained in the boxes, unused, because the necessary support at classroom level has not been available.

A network and hierarchy of support is required, first within the school for day-to-day problems and then from outside at the LEA level for the more complex difficulties – equipment failure, major adaptations, etc. In this rapidly moving field, the LEA support should offer a wide knowledge of just what is possible and available. Finally, an expert level is required. This will be provided at regional and national levels for the very complex individual cases that require very specific tailoring of equipment and programs to suit individual needs.

Such a system of support is now in existence, more or less. Like Topsie, 'it growed' and consequently, like much in education, some areas are far better served than others. Some LEAs offer considerable support to their schools with trained advisory teachers for microtechnology and special needs backed by technicians and electronic engineers; others are not so well served. As microtechnology becomes more and more important in minimising the handicapping effects of disability, so good technical back-up to ensure the speedy repair of faulty equipment becomes essential.

Expert assessment and advice on individual children is provided at regional level by the Aids to Communication in Education (ACE) centres in Oxford and Oldham to which children can be referred by their LEAs. Each of these government-funded centres is staffed by a multidisciplinary team of professionals, including speech therapists, teachers and computer technicians. They have access to and information about the very latest equipment. There are also some NHS-run facilities offering a similar service. The level of expertise that such centres can offer is invaluable. Problems can arise when children are assessed away from the environment in which they normally live and when there cannot be regular contact between the experts and the people who have to work with the children on a day-to-day basis. Therefore, some of these centres are now trying to ensure that assessment is usually carried out in a child's home and school.

The Special Education Microelectronic Resource Centres (SEMERCs) were originally envisaged as providing regional advice for LEAs on developments in the field of microelectronics and special needs and providing a more local level of expert help and advice. Never established as comprehensively as originally envisaged, these centres have been further hit by government spending cuts. The effects of these cut-backs are already being felt. Some LEAs have taken up the challenge and have sought to provide their own support bases and resource centres to take on the role previously undertaken by the SEMERCs. Others have not, and in these there are examples of expensive equipment that is not being fully used or which is not being used at all. In a field as rapidly moving as microtechnology, specialist advisory centres are essential if relevant information is to be made available in accessible form. It is quite possible that in one LEA children may be appropriately assessed and equipped with communication aids that will enable them to follow the National Curriculum in a mainstream school, while in another children with very similar disabilities may be regarded as 'mentally handicapped' and may continue to receive their education in a school for children with severe learning difficulties, all for the want of some basic expertise.

While expert support is essential, it is not without its problems. There is a well-documented history of the deskilling effects that experts can have on classroom practitioners. How can this be avoided? First, anyone who is going to be involved in using a computer with a child with special needs, must be happy using it themselves. They need to have that general level of technical 'know how' that we mentioned above which only comes about through practical 'hands on' experience. Second, it needs to be made quite clear that any support from outside is there to help overcome problems of access to a subject or major technical difficulties and that the responsibility for what is to be taught remains, at all times, with the class or subject teachers. The class or subject teachers need to be encouraged to say what it is they wish to achieve educationally and what are the practical difficulties; support should be 'need'-driven rather than 'resource'-driven.

4 ISSUES OF EQUITY

There are a number of issues that we have touched on in this chapter that remain unresolved. One is the question of fairness. In essence this is no different to the old question about the use of calculators in maths (which has still not been fully resolved to the satisfaction of all). The power and potential of microtechnology make the issues much more complex and the implications more far reaching. Examination boards are only just coming to terms with allowing 'severely dyslexic candidates' to use word processors to write their answers. In school, how reasonable is it that a child should make use of a spell check facility on a word processor? Is it all right if she or he uses it for all subjects except English? Is it all right if it is used in English providing it is not the ability to spell that is being assessed? What about predictive word processors? Are these educationally acceptable, since in a way the task of writing is being made easier by a machine?

In Modern Languages, it is already possible for a word processor and speech synthesiser to enable a child with limited speech to 'speak' in a foreign language by typing in what he or she wants to say. Given the way in which oral and written skills in a foreign language are currently separately assessed, how will teachers assess the performance of a child with a disability who is using such a system? It is even possible to make computers translate aloud in a foreign language words typed in English!

If we look at what has been achieved in the past few years and at the research developments that are currently taking place it is clear that these issues will become even more complex. We already have the technology to enable disabled people to extend their control over the environment through switch-operated control systems. In a very short space of time advances in robotics are going to extend these possibilities still further and at some stage, in the next twenty years or so, we will see a partnership between the 'intelligent' machine and a human being. Will this be seen as acceptable in our competitive education system? No one argues that a child with a hearing impairment should be denied a hearing aid or that a child with a physical disability should not be allowed a wheelchair. Are more sophisticated machines designed to overcome disabilities any different?

So far we have talked mainly about children with physical and sensory disabilities but the issues extend to children with learning difficulties. If a child with a physical disability is allowed to use an intelligent word processor with spell check facilities to minimise the handicapping effects of his or her disability, why should the child with a learning difficulty not also be allowed the same assistance? It seems to us that these issues only become problems because of the competitive nature of our education system. If we are genuinely concerned that each child should be able to function as independently as possible within our society then any assistance that can be provided to a child, no matter what the nature or cause of disability, is surely allowable. If a person with a disability or a person with learning difficulties is able, with the assistance of microtechnology, to work after leaving school at a level comparable to that of other individuals, is this in some way unfair? One of us (Christopher) has very poor handwriting and writes rather slowly. The microcomputer allows him to work with far greater speed and flexibility than would otherwise be the case. Is this cheating?

Computer technology is still not cheap in proportion to the size of school budgets and so decisions have to be made about who should be provided with the technology. Often it seems that those decisions are made on the basis of intellectual ability or academic potential. An obviously bright child with a physical disability is far more likely to be provided with a computer than a child in a special care unit. The first child with whom we worked would have been very unlikely to have been provided with equipment by the LEA because the other professionals involved doubted her 'intellectual potential'. Given that we have got a competitive educational system, there are no easy solutions. If we were to decide that computer resources should be allocated on the basis that the greatest share of resources should go to those with the greatest disabilities how would we deal with the situation, which could arise in the future, where a slow-learning child is enabled through microtechnology to produce work of a better standard than a child without a recognised learning difficulty who does not have the same access to microtechnological support?

5 ISSUES OF PARTICIPATION AND CONTROL

We have concentrated on the ways in which technology can improve the access to the curriculum of children with disabilities and can increase their integration and participation in the life of mainstream schools and classrooms. Microtechnology can provide people with disabilities with real choices. But there are dangers that the very equipment that has made greater access, integration and choice possible may be used to limit it. A good example is a case recounted by Stuart Rees from UMIST (University of Manchester Institute of Science and Technology). Rees was closely involved in pioneering the use of microcomputers with children with disabilities in this country. He had equipped one boy, who had a severe physical disability, with a microcomputer and a set of programs, some of which were educational and some of which were purely for fun. Not long after the boy had begun to use his computer in school, an anxious teacher approached Stuart Rees and asked him if he would mind removing the games programs from the discs containing educational programs as she had caught him playing 'Pacman' with another child when he should have been doing maths. To his credit, Stuart Rees refused to do so, pointing out that the child no longer had to sacrifice his right to be naughty just because he had a physical disability. This anecdote serves to remind us just how much freedom may be lost by people with a disability, how great is the potential of microtechnology to liberate them and how much this still depends on the attitudes of other people.

An exclusive stress on technological solutions to the problems faced by people with disabilities can be oppressive if it leads us to impose solutions on unwilling recipients. Some people find some technologies threatening and dehumanising. It is important that in seeking to help people with special needs to obtain greater independence we do not devalue those who choose not to make use of technological solutions for whatever reasons. If the reason for developing microtechnology for people with disabilities is to enable them to have greater control over their lives, then they must be free to reject it. Microtechnology, combined with new surgical techniques, has made it possible to enhance the hearing of some deaf people through the use of cochlear implants. This is a minute electronic 'amplifier' which is surgically implanted in the inner ear and which can improve the quality of the auditory information being transmitted along the nerves from the ear to the brain. Some deaf people contend that cochlear implants do not liberate them. Rather, this technology forces them to aspire to the normality of hearing people. They argue that their own deaf culture, based on sign language, is devalued and controlled in the process.

Financial constraints, combined with a stress on technological solutions, have the potential to exclude rather than include people with disabilities from the mainstream. Despite the incredible miniaturisation that has taken place, computers, monitors and printers, together with specialised access equipment, are still very cumbersome and are not always moved easily from one location to another. It is all too easy to start suggesting that children might be better off remaining in a special resource room or even a special school where they can have full and straightforward access to all the equipment that they need. It might, for example, be argued that very expensive equipment such as video disc- and compact disc-based data storage systems can only currently be provided at special centres. Is integration to be sacrificed for the sake of more sophisticated technology? The argument that this is a far easier and more cost-effective way of providing expensive equipment and the support services needed to maintain its use can be a very persuasive one. Yet it is really no different to the arguments used to support segregated education in the past.

The National Curriculum has placed considerable emphasis on speaking as an attainment target in English but it has also emphasised talk as a medium for learning and collaborative work in other areas. Communication via word processor and speech synthesiser is not a simple and fluent process. How patient will teachers and other children be towards a child with a disability who is trying to communicate in this way? Will they feel that the child might be better occupied working on her or his own with a computer while the rest of the class engage in activities involving talk? Some children experience difficulties in making social relationships with adults and other children. They have found their computers so much more rewarding than other people that they have virtually ceased communicating except with their computer. May not the same thing happen to children with disabilities if they are not made to feel that they are a part of the class and school? The technology alone will not automatically increase the participation of children with disabilities in the life of the classroom and school. But combined with the right attitudes on the part of those without obvious disabilities it can make participation far easier.

Attitudes: the conditions for access

In this chapter we have tried to show what is possible and what is likely to be possible in the near future. Microtechnology is not a panacea, but it can significantly reduce the handicapping effects of disability in a wide range of areas if people's attitudes will allow it to do so. Attitudes will undoubtedly prove to be far more important than the technological possibilities. Unless society sees disabled people as valued human beings it is unlikely that the use of this technology to improve access and performance in school will be seen as legitimate. Equally important, it is unlikely that the money to fund it will be found.

FURTHER READING

Behrmann, M. M. (1985) *Handbook of Microcomputers in Special Education*, Windsor: NFER-Nelson.

Goldenberg, E. P. (1984) *Computers, Education, and Special Needs*, London: Addison-Wesley.

Hawkridge, D., Vincent, T. and Hales, G. (1985) *New Information Technology in the Education of Disabled Children and Adults*, London: Croom Helm.

Hope, M. (ed.) (1987) *Micros for Children with Special Needs*, London: Souvenir Press.

Rostron, A. and Sewell, D. (1984) *Microtechnology in Special Education*, London: Croom Helm.

Vincent, T. (ed.) (1990) *New Technology, Disability and Special Educational Needs: Some Case Studies*, Coventry: Empathy Ltd.

SOURCES OF FURTHER INFORMATION

The following organisations maintain up-to-date information on equipment and software likely to be of use to children with a wide range of disabilities and learning difficulties:

NCET (National Council for Educational Technology), Special Needs Manager, Sir William Lyons Road, Science Park, Coventry CV4 7EZ.

ACE (Aids to Communication in Education) Centre, Ormerod School, Wayneflete Road, Headington, Oxford OX3 8DD.

Northern ACE Centre, Park Dean School, St Martins Road, Fitton Hill, Oldham OL8 2PY.

Bristol SEMERC (Special Education Microelectronics Resource centre), Redland Hill, Bristol Polytechnic, Bristol BS6 6UZ.

North-West SEMERC, Fitton Hill CDC, Rosary Road, Oldham OL8 2QE.

Redbridge SERC (Special Education Resource Centre), Dane Centre, Melbourne Road, Ilford, Essex IG1 4HT.

IT in NAFE Regional Centre (Special Needs in FE), Trowbridge College, College Road, Trowbridge, Wiltshire BA14 0ES.

The National Access Centre, Hereward College of Further Education, Bramston Crescent, Tile Hill Lane, Coventry CV4 9SW.

Part 3

Changing special curricula

Chapter 15

Becoming a reflective teacher

Mel Ainscow

In this chapter Mel Ainscow reflects on the ideas he has had, at various stages in his career, about how to tackle difficulties in learning in schools. He discusses the perspectives he acquired as a head of a special school for pupils categorised as having moderate learning difficulties, as a local authority adviser on special needs and in his present job involved in the in-service training of teachers.

1 INTRODUCTION

Somebody said to me not so long ago, 'There are three kinds of people – people who make things happen; people who watch things happen; and people who wonder what the hell did happen!' If I look over the last few years of my career in education I sense that I have at various stages been each of these.

My main professional interests are with the difficulties that some children experience in school – and the attempt to find ways in which we as teachers can help all children to experience success in learning. Having worked in secondary and special schools I became a head teacher where my main role was to make things happen; I then worked as a local education authority adviser where I was able to spend more time observing practice in schools; and more recently, working in higher education, I have found myself looking back, reflecting on what I have learned from these experiences.

It is with this attitude of reflection that I have written this chapter. I will provide accounts of the two most significant projects in which I have been involved. The first of these took the form of a curriculum development initiative in a special school; the other was an authority-wide staff development project related to special needs in ordinary schools. I will then go on to discuss how these experiences led me to reflect on, and change, my approach.

2 CURRICULUM DEVELOPMENT IN A SPECIAL SCHOOL

During the 1970s I spent six years as head teacher of a special school for what were then referred to as ESN(M) (educationally subnormal – moderate) pupils (now designated as pupils with moderate learning difficulties). The population of the school consisted of pupils aged 5 to 16, most of whom were from very poor families.

In collaboration with my colleagues in the school I attempted to develop an approach that would provide an educational experience suited to the needs of the pupils as we perceived them. We assumed that the children were in the school as a result of experiencing difficulties in ordinary schools and that in many instances these educational difficulties had come about, at least in part, as a result of social deprivation. Consequently, a strong influence on our thinking was a desire to compensate for the inadequacy of the children's experience. We were also keen to provide forms of intensive help that would accelerate their progress. Indeed, wherever possible our aim was to bring the pupils to a level of achievement that would enable them to return successfully to ordinary schools.

Informed by these perspectives, I saw it as my task to coordinate a team of people in developing and providing a curriculum that emphasised consistency and continuity. Our view was that the best way to help our pupils to learn successfully was to provide teaching that was carefully planned and which coordinated the efforts of each member of staff.

This work was going on during a period when the world of special and remedial education was subject to some criticism, particularly with respect to curriculum thinking and practice. This was an element of a wider concern about the purposes and quality of schooling, leading to demands for greater accountability. There were, in addition, other more specific pressures that seemed to draw attention to the need for an examination of what happened in special schools. The Warnock Report suggested that the quality of education offered to pupils in special provision was unsatisfactory, particularly with respect to the curriculum opportunities provided, and that many special schools underestimated their pupils' capabilities (DES 1978). A number of other publications were also critical of existing practice (e.g. Brennan 1979, Tomlinson 1982).

Teachers in many special schools reacted to this new focus of attention on their work by taking a greater interest in the theoretical basis of their practice. Many became interested in curriculum theory, and in their search for guidance the staff in some special schools were influenced by the literature on planning with behavioural objectives, sometimes referred to as rational curriculum planning. This approach to planning, which was by no means new in the field of curriculum studies, had become popular in special education in North America, probably because of the strong influence of behavioural psychologists. Many of us working in special schools in the UK found the approach helpful as we sought ways of planning our teaching in a more systematic manner.

Initially this interest grew as a result of our own discussions, building upon the previous experience of the staff. Gradually this became affected by ideas from elsewhere. David Tweddle, who at that time was the educational psychologist attached to the school, was one such influence.

Planning the curriculum

Over a period of years the staff established a pattern of meeting together on a regular basis to plan the curriculum for the whole school. Recently this sort of approach has become quite familiar in many schools, particularly with the introduction of staff development days, but at that time it was not that common.

To provide a framework within which these discussions could take place we adopted a simple curriculum model which consisted of the following two aspects:

1 The closed curriculum: This was an attempt to define those areas of skill and knowledge that were regarded as essential learning for all pupils in the school.
2 The open curriculum: This was viewed as being more open-ended, allowing content to be modified to take account of the needs of individual pupils. pupils.

It is important to note that within the school there was considerable commitment to the idea of providing a broad and enriching programme for all pupils. Indeed, there was very good work in areas such as creativity, personal and social development, environmental studies and outdoor pursuits – an orientation rooted in our desire to provide compensatory education.

It is also important to recognise that while the open/closed framework was seen as a useful basis for planning, it was not the intention to use this distinction in planning actual classroom activities. In other words, it was acknowledged that pupils might well be engaged in tasks and activities related to closed and open curriculum intentions at the same time.

Our detailed planning was based on agreed objectives. This involved taking broad goals and expressing them in terms of intended learning outcomes as a basis for planning and evaluating the teaching that was provided. It was also seen as a means of establishing the consistency and continuity to which we aspired. So, for example, a goal to do with teaching pupils to tell the time might lead to objectives such as

1 Reads aloud hours from the clock.
2 Reads aloud minutes from the clock.
3 States that 60 minutes equals one hour.
4 Reads aloud time by half and quarter hours.

Within the closed curriculum, objectives were stated as relatively precise statements of observable behaviour that could then be used as a means of observing and recording pupil progress. Furthermore, these objectives were arranged in hierarchies of learning steps in the belief that progress would be accelerated by teaching the pupils in a step-by-step manner. Figure 15.1 is an example of how this approach was used as a basis for planning and recording progress. Further examples of this format, based on the work carried out in the school, can be found in Ainscow and Tweddle (1979, 1984).

Name: David Date commenced: 25th September

Teaching goal: To develop the use of some basic sentence structures

Objective	*Working on*	*Mastered*	*Checked*	*Comments*
1 Uses an identity statement of the form 'This is a tree' in response to the question 'What is this?'		25th Sept (assessed)	10th Oct	
2 Uses the negation of objective (1), i.e. 'This is *not* a tree'.	25th Sept	10th Oct		Lang Mast cards introduced 2nd Oct David is responding v. well
3 Uses the identity statement 'The dog is black' in response to the question 'What colour is the dog?'		25th Sept (assessed)	10th Oct	
4 Uses the negation of objective (3), i.e. 'The dog is *not* black'.	12th Oct	18th Oct		Lang Mast cards used - prefers this to group puppet sessions.
5 Uses an action statement of the form 'The boy is running' in response to the question 'What is the boy doing?'		25th Sept (assessed)	19th Oct	
6 Uses the negation of objective (5), i.e. 'The boy is *not* running'.	19th Oct			Expect rapid progress (ie. 26th Oct.)

Figure 15.1 Format for recording progress using an objectives approach
Source: Ainscow and Tweddle (1979)

In the open curriculum, planning was carried out in a less precise way, thus allowing individual teachers to provide opportunities that took account of the interests and experiences of their pupils. Consequently a more flexible use of the objectives approach was encouraged, including the use of objectives that stated more general intentions and others which described experiences without predicting intended outcomes.

An area support centre

A further development of the work of the school grew out of the then novel idea of the special school establishing a role as area support centre. This involved the creation of links with local primary and secondary schools in order to provide advice and support on dealing with learning difficulties. One element of this initiative was a series of in-service workshops, held in the special school for teachers from primary schools, with a main focus on developing individual learning programmes based on objectives and task analysis.

Further publicity for the work at the school was provided by a range of publications written by members of staff, including the book *Preventing Classroom Failure* (Ainscow and Tweddle 1979), and the participation of colleagues in various conferences and courses. This publicity had an impact on teachers in special and ordinary schools around the country. It also influenced the work of many educational psychologists and support services. I believe this influence was a positive one in many ways. It gave many teachers a means of talking about their work in ways that seemed practical and purposeful. It also had the effect of raising expectations about what certain pupils might achieve. The emphasis placed on observing pupil progress within the classroom as opposed to the previous over-use of norm-referenced tests was also a significant step forward in many schools.

On the other hand, the approach had a number of limitations and, indeed, potential dangers, particularly if used inflexibly. These concerns can be summarised as follows:

1 Planning educational experiences based on sequences of predetermined objectives tends to encourage a narrowing of the curriculum, thus reducing opportunities for learning.
2 Whilst the idea of individual programmes of objectives may be seen as a strategy for encouraging integration of pupils, it tends, in practice, to encourage segregation.
3 Where the approach has been presented as a 'science of instruction' it tends to make teachers feel inadequate since it appears to give no value to their previous professional experience and expertise.
4 The idea of planning leaves little or no room for pupils to participate in decisions about their own learning. Consequently they are encouraged to adopt a passive role.

5 Programmes of objectives can become static, leading to them being used even when they are found to be inadequate or even redundant as a result of unexpected circumstances occurring.

In reflecting upon the work that was carried out by my colleagues in this particular special school I have come to the view that the successes that undoubtedly occurred were less to do with the idea of planning with objectives and more to do with group processes. In particular, I believe that the emphasis on staff discussion and collaboration influenced the outlooks of individuals by raising their expectations and by providing a supportive social and professional environment. It also led to a strong sense of common purpose throughout the school, a factor which may be a common feature of all effective schools (see for example Mortimore *et al.* 1988). I should add that I have also witnessed similar positive effects in other schools that have adopted this way of working.

3 A LOCAL AUTHORITY STAFF DEVELOPMENT PROGRAMME

In 1979 I became Adviser for Special Educational Needs in Coventry. As part of my duties there I instigated and helped coordinate a major staff development initiative, 'The Special Needs Action Programme' (SNAP). This project had arisen as a result of a review of the authority's special education provision which led to a recognition of the need for significant change. Detailed accounts of the development of SNAP are provided in Muncey and Ainscow (1986) and Ainscow and Muncey (1989). In general terms the aim was to redirect special education provision and services away from ways of working that encouraged segregation of pupils towards a much more integrated range of responses. It was not seen as a revolutionary strategy but as an attempt to bring about gradual change in ways that would limit the risk of damaging existing good practice.

The development of the project was influenced by a number of significant factors. As part of a wider movement aimed at protecting the rights of minority groups in the community, there had been an increased recognition that the rights of children are significantly reduced if they are excluded from all or part of the programme of experiences generally offered in schools. There was also the impact of government legislation, particularly the 1981 Education Act. Whilst this had not come into effect at the outset of SNAP, the various consultative processes associated with its formulation helped to encourage the debate about special educational needs that had been fostered by the Warnock Report.

In addition, the influence of parental opinion was having an increasing impact upon the education service. In the special needs field in particular, the idea of 'parents as partners', as promoted in the Warnock Report, had become widely accepted if not implemented.

Finally, developments in educational thinking generally were also influential. New ideas about curriculum, teaching and learning styles, forms of assessment and recording and staff development had all enriched the discussion about how schools might respond to pupils experiencing difficulty.

The aims of SNAP were to encourage head teachers of ordinary schools to develop procedures for the identification of pupils with special needs; to assist teachers in ordinary schools to provide an appropriate curriculum for such pupils; and to coordinate the work of the various special education support services and facilities in ordinary schools.

We did not attempt to use SNAP to impose one model of achieving these aims. We felt that each school should develop policies and practices compatible with its situation and usual ways of working. We attempted to disseminate examples of good practice that schools could use as vehicles for reviewing and, where necessary, extending existing procedures. This last point is important since some of the publicity given to SNAP nationally was based upon a misunderstanding of the ways in which the project operated in Coventry. For example, groups in some local authorities took some of the SNAP materials and used them as a means of imposing a particular way of working on teachers. Our emphasis was placed on helping schools to develop approaches that were consistent with their traditions and philosophies.

Initially the project focused solely on primary schools, but subsequently it had an impact in the secondary phase. The central strategy in both sectors was the introduction of in-service courses related to special needs in ordinary schools which were developed by teams within the authority. These were presented initially to representatives from each school in the authority at the teachers' centre and then as part of school-based staff development programmes.

The early courses tended to be concerned with helping teachers to devise individualised teaching programmes. So, for example, the course for primary schools 'Teaching Children with Learning Difficulties' was based upon a workshop guide, 'Small Steps'. This introduced procedures for developing individual programmes based upon planning with behavioural objectives. However, as SNAP developed, the courses gradually took on a much broader perspective. The course 'Problem Behaviour in Primary Schools', for example, examined issues related to school management and organisation as well as examining principles of classroom organisation. Similarly, the course 'Special Needs in the Secondary School' attempted to get schools to review all aspects of policy and practice as a means of finding ways of meeting the individual needs of all pupils.

From starting in a small way as just another in-service initiative SNAP gradually grew until it became effectively the coordinating mechanism for the whole of the authority's policy on special needs. As such it was a remarkable example of how change can be facilitated provided the efforts of those involved are coordinated and supported over a period of years. Unfortunately, too often sound initiatives aimed at bringing improvements in educational contexts are less successful because this long-term commitment is not sustained.

Evaluating SNAP

Since the main purpose of SNAP was to help schools to review and develop their policies and practice this had to be the main focus of its evaluation. Extensive evidence from a number of sources, including intensive case studies of the work in schools and follow up evaluations of particular courses (e.g. Ainscow and Muncey 1989, Arthur 1989, Gipps *et al.* 1987, Moses 1988), indicated that a series of features incorporated in the various courses developed as part of SNAP were particularly effective in encouraging staff development and change.

We found, for example, that the self-contained format of the course materials appeared to provide a relatively neutral stimulus that staff could use for reviewing existing practice. They did not imply that a school's existing approaches were redundant, but rather sought to build upon good practice. In addition the emphasis on active learning approaches and group problem-solving, as opposed to the traditional didactic teaching style of so much in-service education, encouraged participation and seemed to help overcome fear of change. Furthermore, involving all staff within a school in a process of review and development of policy helped facilitate a commitment to implement any changes that were agreed.

The courses attempted to present practical ideas and, in some cases, materials that could be used in the classroom. They also aimed to provide teachers with early success by getting them to try out strategies in their own classrooms. This was much appreciated by participants who suggested that too many in-service experiences provide theory without any attention to practical implications. The credibility of courses seemed to be enhanced by the fact that they were tutored by practising teachers. Furthermore, considerable efforts were made to support teachers as they tried out new approaches in their classrooms. This was provided by members of the various advisory and support services. A further source of help was created by emphasising the importance of within-school support between teachers.

In reflecting upon the success of SNAP in Coventry it seems to me that once again the major lesson to be learned relates to the importance of group processes. Whilst the in-service materials that developed were often impressive the greatest impact may have resulted from the collaboration that they stimulated. This collaboration seemed to occur at different levels within the service. First of all, the teams of people who came together to develop materials gained much from the professional dialogues that this process demanded. Then, those who acted as tutors gained in terms of their own confidence and expertise as a result of working together with representatives from the schools. Finally, where schools were able to use the project materials to facilitate review and development of policy and practice, this seemed to be an effective strategy for encouraging more coordinated whole-school approaches.

4 ENCOURAGING CLASSROOM SUCCESS

The period I spent in Coventry led me to change my views in a number of ways, particularly as a result of the many opportunities I had to observe teachers at work in primary and secondary schools. This gave me a much better understanding of the issues involved in attempting to respond to the needs of individual pupils in classes larger than those in the special schools in which I had taught.

My perspective was further widened by my involvement in the planning of various other authority staff development initiatives (e.g. management, personal and social education). Consequently I was able to review my ideas about the nature of educational difficulties. I began to recognise that much of my earlier work had been based on the assumption that, to a large extent, these difficulties were a result of within-child factors. I had tended to reject causal explanations that might lie in larger social, political and organisational processes that are external to the individual child. Furthermore, this is a perspective that leaves the organisation and practice of ordinary schools untouched since they are assumed to be appropriate for the great majority of children. In other words, the provision of special education tends to confirm the assumption that difficulties occur in schools because certain children are special and becomes a justification for the maintenance of the *status quo* of schooling.

I have therefore come to the view that traditional special education responses, despite good intentions, often have the effect of limiting opportunities for children. I believe that the segregation processes and the inevitable labelling with which they are associated have negative effects upon the attitudes and expectations of pupils, teachers and parents. Furthermore, the presence of designated specialists encourages teachers to pass on to others responsibility for children they regard as being special. Resources that might otherwise be used to help make all schools more flexible and responsive to the needs of individual pupils are channelled into separate provision and services. The nature of the educational experiences provided is often narrow. Consequently it was necessary to find better ways to conceptualise and respond to educational difficulties.

It seems reasonable to assume that when children experience significant difficulties in school these arise as a result of the interaction of a complex range of factors. These may involve, for example, factors to do with a child's previous schooling, those that arise as a result of the presence of a disability or others to do with wider environmental influences. In practice, however, the problem becomes a curriculum one: the inability of a teacher or group of teachers to provide classroom experiences that are meaningful and relevant given the interests, experiences and existing skills and knowledge of particular children. In making this statement I am not seeking to replace child-blaming with teacher-blaming. The capacity of teachers to provide appropriate learning opportunities for their pupils is constrained by wider school structures and systems, some of which may be imposed from outside the school.

In attempting to conceptualise educational difficulties in a more constructive way we can most usefully see pupils experiencing difficulties as indicators of the need for reform. It is worth adding that in my view such reforms are likely to benefit all pupils. In other words, the aim should be effective education for all.

How, then, might this be achieved? First and foremost it requires the school system to give up the search for special teaching methods for special children and concentrate available resources on attempting to provide forms of teaching that take account of the individual needs of all children. More specifically we have to find ways of developing schools as *problem-solving* organisations and teachers as *reflective* practitioners. Let us consider the implications of these two interrelated ideas.

Problems and problem-solving are a central part of the process of education. Consequently schools should be places where teachers and pupils are engaged in activities that help them to become more successful at understanding and dealing with the problems they meet. In this sense problems can be seen as opportunities for learning. Consequently my first strategy in seeking to make schools more responsive to the needs of all children is to find ways of gearing them to problem-solving. This means that schools need to be organisations within which both pupils and teachers are engaged cooperatively in the task of learning. Classrooms become places where pupils and teachers see one another as resources and there is an emphasis on strategies such as cooperative group work, peer coaching, pupil choice and negotiated records of achievement.

Schools that are able to develop such a cooperative ethos make use of the expertise of all personnel, provide sources of stimulation and enrichment that foster professional development and encourage positive attitudes to the introduction of new ways of working. They provide the context that is necessary for helping teachers to take responsibility for the learning of all their pupils. There is evidence from a number of different parts of the world of schools and school districts that are attempting to use this orientation as a basis for school improvement (Ainscow 1991). Furthermore, it is interesting to note that these initiatives see special needs not as a separate issue but as an essential element of their activities. In other words, school improvement is regarded as a search for strategies for meeting the needs of an increasingly diverse pupil population in the mainstream.

Schools that are organised to provide support for teachers to collaborate in solving problems encourage teachers to adopt a reflective attitude towards their own practice: to learn from experience and experiment with new ways of working alongside and with their pupils and colleagues.

This approach to the development of professional practice represents a very different orientation from the usual pattern of teacher education. Traditionally, teacher education, particularly in the field of special needs, has been seen as a search for better solutions to solve a technical task. Consequently teachers have attended courses and workshops to learn about theories and techniques derived from research in order that they can use these to improve their teaching.

However, the perspective on educational difficulties that I wish to encourage points to the need for a very different approach to the improvement of practice.

My aim is to find approaches that encourage us as teachers to learn from our own experience. While it would be foolish not to take note of evidence from elsewhere as to how teaching can be improved, I believe that the most important forms of knowledge can only be developed through reflecting on practical experience. Furthermore, this form of professional learning can be encouraged and supported by greater collaboration in schools.

These two ideas – schools as problem-solving organisations and teachers as reflective practitioners – are, therefore, the outcomes of my experience particularly with respect to the two projects that I have described.

Almost ten years after completing the book *Preventing Classroom Failure*, David Tweddle and I met up again with a view to writing a revised second edition. After a series of meetings we came to the view that this was now impossible. Our thinking had moved on so far as a result of our experiences, and our assumptions had changed so fundamentally, that we decided that it would be wiser to write a new book, *Encouraging Classroom Success* (Ainscow and Tweddle 1988).

In this book we provide a framework for reviewing practice as a means of finding ways of helping all pupils to experience success. It is an approach that replaces the rather closed prescriptions of our earlier work with a more open agenda that is intended to encourage teachers to take responsibility for their own learning. Our aim is to help all teachers to become what Donald Schon refers to as 'reflective practitioners' (Schon 1987). Classroom evaluation is central. This is a process of gathering information about how pupils respond to the curriculum as it is enacted. The focus is on areas of decision-making over which teachers have a significant influence. Broadly speaking these areas are:

Objectives: Are objectives being achieved?
Tasks and activities: Are tasks and activities being completed?
Classroom arrangements: Do classroom arrangements make effective use of available resources?

Because of the complexity of classroom life and the importance of unintended outcomes, there is also a need to keep a further question in mind. This is:

What else is happening?: Are there other significant factors that need to be considered?

We recommend, therefore, that the framework provided by these four broad questions be used by teachers and pupils to reflect upon the encounters in which they are engaged. In other words, the framework becomes an agenda for reflection. This approach is based upon our belief that success in the classroom is more likely to occur if objectives, tasks and activities and classroom arrangements take account of individual pupils and are understood by all those involved. Classroom evaluation is seen as a continuous process, built into the normal life of the classroom. Furthermore, it requires collaboration and negotiation if it is to be effective.

Proposing this wider perspective has major implications for the ways in which the education service provides support to youngsters experiencing difficulties in learning. It requires that the focus of assessment and recording should be children in their normal classroom environment; that information should be collected on a continuous basis; that pupils should have a key role in reflecting upon their own learning; and that the overall aim should be to improve the quality of teaching and learning provided for all pupils. It is perhaps worth adding that it is a perspective that does not lend itself to the provision of 'quick-fix' solutions to educational difficulties.

5 POSTSCRIPT

Occasionally when I give lectures, members of the audience charge me with having changed my mind. They quote things that I wrote years ago, suggesting that I now seem to have different views. Some even feel let down that I no longer support ideas that they have adopted as a result of my influence.

I hope that the arguments presented in this chapter will help readers to make sense of my changing ideas. I also hope that they will encourage others to 'wonder what the hell did happen'!

REFERENCES

Ainscow, M. (ed.) (1991) *Effective Schools for All*, London: Fulton.

—— and Muncey, J. (1989) *Meeting Individual Needs in the Primary School*, London: Fulton.

—— and Tweddle, D. A. (1979) *Preventing Classroom Failure: An Objectives Approach*, London: Fulton.

—— —— (1984) *Early Learning Skills Analysis*, London: Fulton.

—— —— (1988) *Encouraging Classroom Success*, London: Fulton.

Arthur, H. (1989) 'Inset issues and whole school policies', in M. Ainscow and A. Florek (eds), *Special Educational Needs: Towards a Whole School Approach*, London: Fulton.

Brennan, W.K. (1979) *Curricular Needs of Slow Learners*, Milton Keynes: Open University.

Department of Education and Science (DES) (1978) *Special Educational Needs* (The Warnock Report), London: HMSO.

Gipps, C., Gross, H. and Goldstein, H. (1987) *Warnock's 18 Per Cent: Children with Special Needs in the Primary School*, London: Falmer.

Mortimore, P., Sammons, P., Stoll, L., Lewis, D. and Ecob, R. (1988) *School Matters: The Junior Years*, Wells: Open Books.

Moses, D. (1988) 'The Special Needs Action Programme', in S. Hegarty and D. Moses (eds), *Developing Expertise*, Windsor: NFER-Nelson.

Muncey, J. and Ainscow, M. (1986) 'Meeting special needs in mainstream schools: a transatlantic perspective', *International Journal of Special Education* 1, 161–71.

Schon, D. A. (1987) *Educating the Reflective Practitioner*, New York: Jossey Bass.

Tomlinson, S. (1982) *A Sociology of Special Education*, London: Routledge & Kegan Paul.

Chapter 16

Conductive education

Contrasting perspectives

Mike Oliver and Virginia Beardshaw, with an introduction by Will Swann

Sources: Oliver, M. (1989) 'Conductive education: if it wasn't so sad it would be funny', *Disability, Handicap and Society* 4(2), pp. 197–200.
Beardshaw, V. (1989) 'Conductive education: a rejoinder', *Disability, Handicap and Society* 4(3), pp. 297–9.

Conductive education is an approach to the teaching of children and adults with physical disabilities. It has generated a great deal of controversy in the UK in recent years. Some of this controversy is reflected in this chapter. After a brief introduction to the approach by Will Swann, Mike Oliver, who is himself disabled, attacks conductive education as deeply oppressive. He argues that it is based on forcing people with disabilities to conform to able-bodied norms, whereas the problems that people with disabilities face are not generated by their disabilities, but by the refusal of the able-bodied world to take account of them. In the second part of the chapter, Virginia Beardshaw, whose daughter has attended the Institute in Hungary, defends conductive education against Oliver's critique, arguing that it exceeds in quality anything customarily available in the UK. By contrast, she castigates most rehabilitation methods in use in this country as 'slipshod, ineffective and oppressive'.

1 INTRODUCTION

Will Swann

Conductive education originated in Hungary and was the creation of András Petö, a Hungarian physician. After the Second World War, Petö set up a service in Budapest for children with disabilities. By 1952 he had opened a National Movement Therapy Institute which later became the Institute for Conductive Education of the Motor Disabled. Petö died in 1967. Since then the Institute has been directed by Dr Mária Hári. It is now generally agreed that in Hungary the system has achieved remarkable results. Children with severe disabilities have been taught to move independently in ways which go beyond common professional expectations in this country.

The system has been known about in the UK since the 1960s. The first British account of the approach was published in 1965 by Esther Cotton, a physiotherapist working for the Spastics Society (Cotton 1965). During the remainder of the 1960s and the 1970s, Cotton worked to introduce the approach into British special schools for children who have physical disabilities, especially those run by the Spastics Society. By the mid-1980s, some twenty special schools had adopted features of the approach. However, a survey reported by Sutton (1987) showed that there were significant differences between conductive education as practised in these schools and as practised in Budapest. It appeared that most schools were selective in the features of the approach they adopted. The results achieved did not compare with the achievements claimed by Budapest. In summarising developments up to the mid-1980s, Sutton (1987) commented:

> Conductive education aims at qualitative change in its pupils, CEUKS [Conductive Education UK Style] merely quantitative changes, which, desirable though they might be, are at best an improvement on current British practices, not the breakthrough that appears to have been achieved in Budapest.
>
> (Sutton 1987: 126)

In the mid-1980s interest in the method grew rapidly amongst some parents and professionals. In 1986, following a BBC documentary about conductive education, a pressure group – Rapid Action for Conductive Education (RACE) – was established, and there was a great deal of political activity aimed at securing funds to set up a British equivalent to the Institute in Budapest. In the same year, the Foundation for Conductive Education was established in Birmingham with the support of the Budapest Institute. The Foundation's aim was to establish a programme of conductive education as close as possible to Hungarian practice. It established the first British school attempting to implement full-scale conductive education in 1988, with staff trained in Budapest.

What are the principles of conductive education? The language of the approach is, in places, rather technical. Its central aim is *orthofunction.* This refers to the ability to master independently the demands of daily life, despite disability. At its most abstract, orthofunction is 'that protean capacity involving the entire personality enabling an individual to satisfy the biological (and social) demands made on him' (Hári and Akos 1988: 140). The opposite of orthofunction is referred to as dysfunction. This is what conductive education aims to overcome: an inability to adapt to the demands of life without external assistance of some form. In conductive education aids, equipment and prosthetics are at an absolute minimum, to avoid children 'becoming slaves' to them. The objective is that children should eventually learn to do tasks through their own efforts:

> it is always what he learns to do that counts as an achievement and that is why it would be quite wrong [for example] to correct the way he sits by holding him or fixing him on the chair with some kind of appliance.
>
> (Hári and Akos 1988: 193)

Although orthofunction is an idea that is biological in conception, practitioners of conductive education argue strongly that a child's whole personality is involved in learning, indeed children are seen as having orthofunctional or dysfunctional *personalities*: 'lack of successful achievement, failure and frustration affect our general capacity for adaptation and when repeated several times eventually cause adaptive development to slow down or stop altogether. This is exactly what creates a dysfunctional personality' (Hári and Akos 1988: 143). Conductive education rejects the idea that treatment and education should be directed to the disability in isolation. It should be aimed at developing the whole personality.

The approach is based on the view that despite damage, the nervous system remains flexible and has a 'residual capacity' which can be brought into use by teaching children to overcome the limitations imposed by their disabilities: 'recovery is conditional both on the imposition of all those demands appropriate to his age and on the dysfunctional's [sic] being directed towards carrying out independently the tasks set by those demands' (Hári and Akos 1988: 145).

All teaching is done by 'conductors', who train for four years before qualifying. Each group has two to three conductors attached to them, working in shifts. Conductors are responsible for all aspects of the children's learning. The Institute is strongly opposed to the division of labour into specialisms such as 'teaching' and 'therapy'. It is argued that the same people should teach children at all ages in the acquisition of new skills: from early practice through to using skills in a variety of everyday tasks.

Conductive education in Budapest is an intensive, full-time residential system. It demands a daily schedule during which all activities are carefully planned from getting up at 6.30 a.m. to going to sleep at 9.00 p.m. No opportunity for teaching is lost. Ordinary tasks such as dressing, using the toilet, washing, moving from one room to the next, eating and drinking, writing, playing, are all organised to provide opportunities for children to tackle a problem that is within their reach. The minimum necessary support – 'facilitation' – is provided by the conductor to enable the child to achieve each task, and support is progressively withdrawn as the child begins to be able to do the task independently. This means that routine self-care tasks can take a long time.

In between morning, midday and evening self-care routines, children work on 'task-series' devised for them by their conductors. Task-series constitute the core of the learning day – up to six hours for some children. Each one consists of about twenty to thirty separate tasks. Children learn to perform actions that they are able to do with a minimum of intervention. As each new movement is learnt, the demands steadily rise and children become able to perform actions in more flexible and variable ways.

It is worth giving an extended example of part of a task-series to give an indication of what teaching and learning in a conductive education can involve:

> For instance, a diplegic[1] child learns as a general aim to keep his outstretched legs abducted[2] in every position. In the following detail taken from his task-series he has to achieve it during and after turning over on his stomach. At this

point the entire group is lying supine, legs stretched out and abducted. The children intend verbally:

'I stretch my right hand back.'

The conductor is teaching this particular child that he has done this correctly only when his arm is stretched back beside his ear, his elbow and fingers staying straight and his legs which he has previously stretched and parted, remain in that position.

After this the children's next partial task is:

'I stretch it down again', then:
'I stretch my left hand back.'
'I stretch both my hands back.'
'I clap my hands.'

Before the handclapping, the conductor shows them how to clap hands behind the head by demonstrating that the hands must be held apart behind the head before bringing them together to clap. While these partial tasks are being done, it is essential to ensure all the way through that legs and feet are stretched and maintaining an abducted position.

The sequence of tasks continues by raising first the right foot, then the left, introducing with verbal intending and rhythmic counting. The child we have chosen as an example is not yet able to keep his raised leg stretched out and so, by way of facilitation, the Conductor places a small chair on the slat-bed. The child puts his heel on this, now intending, 'I stretch it out'. His knee straightens out…

This task-series includes many other partial tasks, such as gripping, hand coordination, sitting, and ultimately standing. And from all these the general goal is that they all in any circumstances shall be able to put into practice the intention of stretching and abducting the legs. With this the way opens up to a whole series of goals which had been blocked previously from their lack of these particular orthofunctions.

(Hári and Akos 1988: 163–4)

A large part of the day's work in the Institute is taken up with task-series, but formal education is not neglected. School-aged children follow a normal primary curriculum in the afternoon, during which all activities are also planned to give the child tasks which support and extend the rest of the day's programme.

Although the learning programme is rigorously planned and executed, there is a great emphasis on ensuring children's commitment and attention to tasks in a positive fashion. This involves frequent variation in tasks, aiming to ensure regular success in meaningful tasks, and by means that any teacher would use to make learning an enjoyable experience: songs, games and so on. Spontaneous activities from the children are built into programmes, which are reviewed and developed daily. If children are losing attention, this is taken as a sign that the conductor has to rethink the teaching. The Institute staff take an obvious pride in the 'indefatigability' and commitment of the children to their learning.

Children learn in groups of twenty to thirty. They can cover a wide age range, and several different disabilities. They are selected to have broadly similar 'dysfunctions'. This is not simply an organisational convenience. The group is seen as an essential part of the child's learning environment; its collective responsibility and achievement are seen as providing motivation for each child to learn. Task-series are planned for the group as a whole, but there are individual variations in the way tasks are accomplished. There is a common goal, but individual solutions to it. Children are arranged in the group for each task-series so that those who are less able at that task can observe and learn from the more able. Conductors encourage an atmosphere in which children encourage each other.

2 CONDUCTIVE EDUCATION: IF IT WASN'T SO SAD IT WOULD BE FUNNY

Mike Oliver

The current fashion for conductive education has created a furore in the world of education. If it wasn't so sad, it would be funny. We have seen the creation of three new organisations aimed at furthering it, television programmes extolling its virtues, demonstrations at the House of Commons, picketing of the Spastics Society and the alleged poaching of conductors. To understand why all this is sad rather than funny, it is necessary to look at what conductive education claims to be and some of the wider issues that it raises.

So what is this conductive education that the furore is all about? Well, it isn't a medical treatment and it does not claim to cure the 'motor impaired' as its recipients are usually insensitively called. Rather it claims to be a method of enabling the motor impaired 'to function in society without requiring special apparatus such as wheelchairs, ramps or other artificial aids'. Well yes, but don't we all use artificial aids of one kind or another; try eating your dinner without a knife and fork or going to Australia without an aeroplane.

Its claims are built upon two underpinnings, one theoretical and one practical. Its theoretical underpinning is that under the right conditions 'the central nervous system will restructure itself'. Its practical underpinning is 'orthofunction': a teaching method which involves the whole person physically and mentally and which instils 'the ability to function as members of society, to participate in normal social settings appropriate to their age'. The word 'normal' crops up a lot in the writings of Dr Mária Hári, the leading proponent of conductive education, and her ever growing band of disciples.

Unfortunately for them, the theory remains unproven for there is no evidence that the central nervous system of any human being has ever restructured itself in the manner suggested. But does that really matter if orthofunction as practical activity actually works? The evidence here, is, perhaps, stronger; published studies indicate significant improvements in functioning in many motor-impaired children, as do personal accounts provided by the ever-increasing number of visitors to the Petö Institute in Hungary.

But, as any competent undergraduate social scientist will tell you, correlation does not prove causation. In other words, the relationship between the application of orthofunction and functional improvements may not be a causal one. It may well be that factors other than orthofunction are producing these improvements; factors such as better resourcing, a purposeful environment, the amount of time spent in active learning each day or the one-to-one relationship with conductors, may be equally or more important than the specific application of the technique of orthofunction itself.

So, not only is conductive education theoretically unproven but also practically unsubstantiated. I would go further and suggest that it is also ideologically unsound. Its constant, uncritical use of the concept of 'normality' and its insistence on adapting individuals rather than environments flies in the face of much social scientific and educational wisdom, and, more importantly, the expressed wishes of many disabled people who want society to change, not themselves.

Unsound ideology can quickly turn into oppression and Dr Hári's views are certainly oppressive to a large number of disabled people. In one example, she endorses orthofunction as a way of teaching people with a spinal injury to walk and adds that 'teaching must restore the will of the individual to do so'. As a person with a spinal injury, this view is oppressive to me, and to other people with a spinal injury, in two ways. First, how dare she assume that our main goal is to walk, without consulting us in the first place. And second, how dare she imply that those hundreds of thousands of people with a spinal injury throughout the world are not walking because they lack the will to do so.

It is also interesting to note that Dr Andrew Sutton, Director of the recently established Foundation for Conductive Education, can endorse these remarks as 'endearingly characteristic'. They are grossly offensive to me and many other disabled people, and it is symptomatic of the gap that usually exists between the consciousness of the able-bodied staff of many disability organisations and the disabled people they are supposed to serve.

Given that conductive education is theoretically unproven, practically unsubstantiated and ideologically unsound, why are we currently seeing many local education authorities and, indeed, the Spastics Society itself, besieged by angry parents demanding the provision of conductive education almost overnight?

To begin with, conductive education does offer a positive approach to a clear set of goals, whether you agree with them or not. That is something that special educators have, so far, lamentably failed to offer disabled children and their families. For far too long disabled children have been put away in special schools and been made to feel that there is something wrong with them, their disabilities are a burden and a thing of shame. While conductive education does offer an alternative vision, it is unfortunate that this vision implies the removal of burden and shame through the achievement of normality.

In addition, conductive education does offer higher expectations than those to which special education has aspired. Thus Andrew Sutton can comment that conductive education can produce results 'which seem quite beyond the expectations of children growing up with cerebral palsy and spina bifida elsewhere'. Given that the expectations of professionals about what disabled people can actually achieve has always been pathetically low, almost any intervention system which raises expectations is likely to produce similar results.

Throughout human history, disabled people have constantly confounded the low expectations of others, and how much better it would be for special educators to raise the expectations of disabled children and their families by giving them an understanding of this, by helping them to accept their disabled identities with pride, by helping them to understand their place in the world and their rights as well as giving them the practical skills to deal with these issues. Of course, in order to do this, special educators would need to understand these issues themselves.

Finally, it is sad but understandable that the parents of disabled children should clutch at the straw of conductive education as a means of resolving their own problems. To have a handicapped child in a society which has developed a fetishism for normality and which fails to even acknowledge the needs of those parents, let alone make any provision to meet them, is clearly a profoundly disturbing experience. But accepting the fetishism of normality can never even address these problems, let alone resolve them.

Those of us who were privileged to hear Paddy Ladd's moving account of the struggles and pride of the deaf community at last year's International Conference in Bristol, England, will long remember his response to a challenge from the floor that many parents regarded the birth of their deaf children as tragedies. He said that he understood this and was sorry, but could only add that the deaf community regarded the birth of each and every deaf child as a precious gift. We, as a society, could learn from that, and, if we regarded the birth of every disabled child as a precious gift and were prepared to provide the necessary resources to the children and their parents to allow these gifts to develop, then perhaps we would be spared the distressing sight of individual and groups of parents pursuing the latest fashionable cure for their child's blindness, deafness or other disability at whatever cost to themselves, their families and friends.

So, to what kind of a world does conductive education envisage we are moving? One in which we are all exhorted to approximate to the walkie-talkie model of living, where physical and social environments remain unchanged and unchanging. I have an alternative vision where difference is not just tolerated, but valued and even celebrated, and where physical and social environments are constantly changing to accommodate and welcome these differences. What's more, I think my vision is an achievable dream, that of conductive education an unachievable nightmare.

My dream is achievable because all we have to do is to stop doing some of the things we are already doing: stop using the productive forces we have developed to create disabilities through warfare, environmental pollution and industrial accidents; stop creating disabilities through poverty by using our vast wealth not in pursuit of capital accumulation and profit, but in ensuring that we all have the necessities to sustain material life; and stop judging and treating people on the basis of the contribution they can or cannot make to the development and operation of these productive forces.

The nightmare of conductive education is unachievable because nowhere in human history have the *different* been turned into the *normal* and neither medical science nor other rehabilitative techniques or educational interventions can assist in this process. The reason is simple: normality does not exist. Someone else, not very long ago, had a vision of normality associated with blond hair and blue eyes, and look where such a vision got him.

3 CONDUCTIVE EDUCATION: A REJOINDER

Virginia Beardshaw

According to Mike Oliver, I am a 'straw clutcher'. By deciding in late 1987 to take my daughter to Budapest's Petö Institute for a spell of conductive education I contributed to 'the distressing sight of individuals and groups of parents pursuing the latest fashionable cure for their child's ... disability' – in her case, cerebral palsy.

Of course, Dr Oliver is partly right. Learning to treasure my daughter's uniqueness in a world obsessed with 'normality' was – and still is sometimes – a very painful thing. Search for alleviation and cure is a very basic human reaction, as shrines from Lourdes to high-tech oncology clinics testify.

But by portraying those of us who have sought conductive education for our children as unthinking lemmings dashing off for a dose of Hungarian miracle water, Dr Oliver's polemic does us – and conductive education – less than justice. More importantly, by castigating conductive education he obscures some very important implications that the method has for the West.

The irony is that Dr Oliver has done more than most to document the real reasons why conductive education is attractive to parents from Britain and many other Western countries. He and other writers from the disabled people's movement have dissected the inadequacy of current approaches to disability. Together, they have criticised the slipshod, ineffective and oppressive rehabilitation methods, and called for higher standards for the education of young people with disabilities. They have analysed the way that children with disabilities are encouraged to be passive recipients of care in our society, and have fought against this. Above all, they have emphasised the need for higher expectations from society as a whole about what disabled people can achieve, and have argued for the necessary resources to be devoted to helping them achieve them.

Conductive education is about high expectations. It is about motivating people with neurological damage to achieve things for themselves, and, in so doing, get more control over their lives. For children with cerebral palsy it involves a focused yet wholistic approach designed to stimulate them to move themselves out of the passivity lack of control over their bodies has encouraged since birth. Doing so allows them to experience and interact with their environment and other people. That encourages experiential learning and socialisation in a way that few Western special education or therapeutic settings do.

Conductive education is also about setting ambitious goals, and then getting children to achieve them *because they want to for themselves*. Doing so requires great skill, and an integrated and wholly dedicated application of the techniques we know separately as physiotherapy, occupational therapy, educational psychology, speech therapy and teaching. For Dr Oliver to dismiss the knowledge and skill base of the method – which is breathtakingly more advanced than anything we have in the West – by claiming that conductive education is successful simply because it is an 'intervention system which raises expectations' is to ignore a number of important points.

But parents like me cannot afford to ignore them, even to permit Dr Oliver to find a totally ideologically sound approach to alleviating disability. Like him, and his many fellows in the disabled people's movement, we have had direct experience of the unfocused and frequently inept workings of rehabilitation professionals in this country. We know that, even given half-way decent funding, rehabilitation approaches and much of special education could never work well for our children because they start with low expectations, and are very unclear about what they are trying to achieve. What is worse still, they start from a wholly inadequate skill base which hinders more than it helps by carving up approaches which should be integrated into arbitrary professional divisions called 'occupational therapy', 'physiotherapy' and so on. In other words, we have already learnt the painful lesson that, despite all the kind words and good intentions, for most practical purposes society has already written our children off. It is unprepared to offer them the skilled attention that they need.

That is not good enough for some of us. And so – in my case very reluctantly, in a slow process of decision-making that took two years – we have taken the road to Budapest. There we have found not miracles but dedication, hard work, love and – the phrase repeatedly used by parents at the Petö – 'a lot of common sense'. I do not think that any one of us expects our children to walk out of the place 'normal', but we do know that it is the best place in the world for them to achieve their fullest potential. With its emphasis on self-motivation, active participation and problem-solving, the Petö method is their best chance of doing the best they can with what they have got.

To change tack slightly, I am not equipped to comment on Dr Oliver's critique of conductive education's theoretical base. All I will say is that in attempting to develop theories about the alleviation of neurological dysfunction as she has, Dr Hári has been one of very few medical scientists to address an important 'black hole' in the research agenda. Few others have been interested to devote resources and research talent to it, despite the fact that an estimated 1 in 500 children are born with cerebral palsy and that neurological disorders are one of the largest group of disabling conditions for adults. I think that this neglect is another part of the 'writing off' process that disabled people are still subject to.

I also think that before sitting in judgement on Dr Hári's 'uncritical use of the concept of "normality"', a social scientist of Dr Oliver's calibre might stop to think for a moment about the social context in which those remarks were made. Hungary is a much poorer country than Britain. Few of the flats in which most urban Hungarians live have lifts. Whole sections of Budapest, with its steep hills, have no pavements at all. Ramped access to public buildings is all but unknown. The public transport on which ordinary people depend is inaccessible to wheelchairs. During the 1980s, social security arrangements of all kinds have broken down. Hungary is a tough environment for all its citizens – able-bodied and disabled. Understanding this may make Dr Hári's remarks – delivered as they were in a foreign language – less 'oppressive'.

NOTES

1 Diplegia is a form of cerebral palsy in which both legs are affected, and the arms to a lesser extent.

2 Spread out away from the midline.

REFERENCES

Cotton, E. (1965) 'The Institute for Movement Therapy and School of Conductors, Budapest', *Developmental Medicine and Child Neurology* 7 (4), 110–14.

Hári, M. and Akos, K. (1988) *Conductive Education*, translated by N. Horton-Smith and J. Stevens, London: Tavistock/Routledge.

Sutton, A. (1987) 'The challenge of conductive education', in T. Booth and W. Swann (eds), *Including Pupils with Disabilities*, Milton Keynes: Open University Press.

Chapter 17

'Totally impractical!' Integrating 'special care' within a special school

Jenny Corbett

In this chapter Jenny Corbett describes the changes in approach from 1971 to 1991 at a school for children and young people aged 2 to 19 who are categorised as having severe learning difficulties. She worked as head of special care at the school between 1977 and 1982 and draws on the recollections of staff at the school as well as further visits to document the school's development. She focuses on one particular issue: the suggestion that those pupils classified as in need of 'special care' because of their frailty, lack of development or 'challenging' behaviour might be integrated with the other pupils. The proposal from the head met with a diverse set of responses, including the view of a member of her own department that it was 'totally impractical'.

1 INTRODUCTION

The 'special care' department at my school consisted of four classes of pupils, totalling about thirty-five out of the 100 or so on the school roll. I taught one of the classes and had responsibility for supporting three other teachers and nine welfare assistants. Children were placed in 'special care' because they were considered to be very frail and in delicate health, thus requiring nursing care, or because they were severely physically disabled and therefore had no means of mobility, or because they were extremely disruptive to teachers and other children. Once in 'special care' they either received intensive physiotherapy and nursing care or individual behaviour modification programmes, depending on their perceived need. Most teachers in this school regarded 'special care' as a non-teaching area and avoided it. It was a part of the school in which toileting, feeding and physical caring was seen to predominate and in which horrible sights and sounds occurred. It was the area of the school which welfare staff dreaded working in and which stigmatised teachers. When I applied for this post in 1977, I was the only candidate who stayed around for the interview: two dropped out and two looked around and declined.

2 'JUST A MATTER OF CONTAINING THE CHILDREN'

In order for me to understand why colleagues behaved as they did and how institutional practice can prove resistant to change, it was essential to learn of what came before. I was fortunate in this school to have access to two teachers who had worked with the 'special care' pupils from the early days, when the school was born from a junior training centre in 1971. The asylum ethos was still present in those early years: out of sight and out of mind. They, like most staff working with the 'special care' group then, were not trained teachers. They were carers, who had been employed by Social Services, working under conditions which most teachers in today's special schools would consider absolutely intolerable. As one of these teachers, reflecting on her 'caring' role in 1971, explained:

> We had fourteen to eighteen immobile or hyperactive children to two staff. It was just a matter of containing the children, looking after them for their safety. Literally, taking their coats off in the morning, getting them all changed and feeding them. There were only two of us for feeding: trying to get them to eat their food, clear it away, get them changed again, get them their milk and then get them ready to go home. All day, that's all we were doing, constantly going around changing them or trying to make them comfortable. Because we were both new to the children we hadn't the faintest idea how to feed them or how much to feed. We started at 9 and, at 11, had a coffee in the room. I stood on a chair, so I could drink my coffee while my assistant kept the children away. Then she stood on a chair to drink hers. We had half an hour for lunch and no break or cup of tea in the afternoon. So it was a very long day. When qualified teachers came into the school they demanded proper lunch breaks and coffee breaks.

She recognised the support which the schools were offering to parents, formerly expected to manage on their own:

> It was thought of in terms of 'taking the burden from the homes' and caring, keeping them clean and feeding them.

Yet staff were left to cope as best they could, with no resources:

> We had no equipment, down to things like toilet tissue or floor cloths. We were forking out of our own purses. There was no physiotherapist or occupational therapist. There was no one to tell us what was best for these children, whether to support them or lay them down. We were completely frustrated. We used to try to make them comfortable and do a lot of talking, playing, laughing. We didn't have any expectations of them. We treated them much like babies.

In 1972, change was created by the separation of the disruptive from the immobile children. This accentuated the role of containment. This teacher recalls her responsibility for the disruptive group:

> From 1972 to 1977 I was in the same small room with the most difficult children – up to sixteen at one stage. We were always locked in. If a teacher found a child to be a disturbance in the class, distracting other children, they were shunted into special care. I had only one assistant. There was no programme for us to go anywhere or do anything but remain locked from 9 to 4 in that room.

This, then, was the legacy which greeted the new head teacher who arrived in the mid-1970s. 'Special care' had gained a reputation within the school for being synonymous with changing nappies, feeding for hours on end or enduring violent and difficult behaviours. Nothing productive was expected to happen there.

3 GAINING CONTROL

It is not surprising, therefore, that when behaviour modification techniques were introduced into the school in the late 1970s, they were seen by many staff as a means of raising professional status. Young staff working in the special care department were particularly enthusiastic to find individual programmes designed to teach the children they were working with. Rather than retain the feeling that they were no more than glorified child-minders, they could see the opportunity to build a curriculum around apparently scientific methods.

This was ostensibly a change from the role of a low status carer to that of a skilled professional. However, these teachers were very much under the influence of psychologists who visited the school regularly from the local hospital to teach behaviour modification methods. They would observe children in the classroom and then leave teachers with elaborate programmes which they were expected to implement over a two-week period until the next visit. Sometimes these programmes worked well. Often there were problems, yet teachers would still adhere rigidly to clearly faulty approaches, as though, in the adoption of behaviour modification, they had lost their imagination.

What many teachers appreciated was the feeling that they had control. Rather than become overwhelmed by a disruptive child, they could use a programme to manage behaviour. It was comforting.

4 THE IMPACT OF LABELS

Among the invidious effects of labelling is the confining of identity and narrowing of horizons. For the pupils in special care this meant that they were seen as having a distinct and different nature (neatly termed 'need') and, therefore, were best kept quite separate. For the staff in special care, we too were seen as different and rather strange. I had an additional label in that I did not conform to my special care colleagues' commitment to the merits of behaviour modification. Not only was I strange but I was reactionary to boot.

The story of the head teacher's changing perception of labels is interesting.

She became most concerned about the adverse effect of labelling after her experience with a new pupil. An adolescent girl arrived from another borough and her notes had not yet been forwarded. The head teacher placed the girl in the group which was appropriate for her age. Although she proved to be sometimes awkward and ill-tempered, the class teacher was able to cope. After a short period of settling-in, she started to develop rapidly, showing an interest in many tasks. It was only when her notes arrived some months later that the head teacher discovered that this girl had been in the special care unit of her previous school, where she had been regarded as a behaviour problem.

This caused the head teacher to reflect on how far children become behaviour problems once they have been labelled as such and have been placed with a separate group of children, all of whom are considered behaviour problems. She felt that, once children had been so labelled and segregated, expectations which teachers had of them became diminished and their behaviour was likely to be adversely influenced by other children with behaviour problems.

Prompted by this chance experience, she decided to embark on a project throughout the school to integrate as many of the special care pupils as were felt to benefit, starting on a modest scale of three afternoons a week, for an hour at a time. I was enthusiastic to support her plan but asked that, if she were planning eventually to disband special care as I felt she should, she would find me another role within the school, related perhaps to curriculum design. She looked at me in disbelief. 'But you're special care!' she said, as though that was my chosen role for life. While I am grateful that her attitude spurred me into moving on and finding a series of new labels for myself, I find it ironic that she expressed such concern about labelling pupils while emphatically labelling her staff.

5 INTEGRATING SPECIAL CARE

The head teacher sent a note around to all staff in the school to outline her plan. She asked for feedback before calling a staff meeting to discuss the issue. I called this chapter 'Totally impractical!' because it is what one young member of staff said and subsequently wrote on the feedback form when asked if the segregated 'special care' section could be integrated into the main body of the special school. It is a familiar expression when the subject of integration arises, in whatever context.

In addition to the 'Totally impractical!', the following were staff responses to proposals for integration in 1982:

> I disagree with the whole idea [member of special care staff].
>
> Fine with me.
>
> I think a tremendous amount of thought has to be put into any integration, considering the benefits/disadvantages to everyone [member of special care staff].

I am very unsure about the idea.

I don't agree with the idea.

As my children are on behaviour programmes which need complete consistency, I would not agree with them being put in other classrooms [member of special care staff].

We need more integration with normal nursery and primary schools.

What is expected to happen when these children are in the class?

The general mood of caution probably reflects a mixture of fear, lethargy and lack of imagination, common features of resistance to change. However, it was the three members of my special care staff who were among the most overtly hostile to the scheme. It is not surprising, in relation to their roles in the school. Any credibility they had gained was from the smooth operation of their individual behaviour programmes. The more they suspected my desire to temper this approach with a diffusion of learning experiences in integrated groups, the more they would hold out against it.

The outcome of this débâcle was that a one-hour exchange occurred on just one afternoon a week, with staff exchanging groups so that special care staff got a break. A few pupils were to be moved from special care into a new 'language' group, which would be absorbed into the main body of the school, leaving the remaining special care department further segregated.

6 PROVING INTEGRATION WORKS

I did manage to establish an 'integrated' provision for a further pupil by negotiation with a sympathetic and flexible teacher. The pupil was 17, had cerebral palsy and possessed a most engaging and sociable personality. I was able to keep a diary record of how well he played with other children in musical games, even though one of them had to help him catch the ball, and how they liked to push him around in his chair and generally enjoyed his company.

At the time, I recorded this as an example of successful integration, proving that integration works. The other pupils were able to display caring qualities and he shared their enjoyment. I would now regard my view of this integration as something of a 'cop-out'. It was such an easy example to choose. It could hardly fail. He was agreeable and alert, eager to please. What would have happened if I had chosen a much more typical pupil from special care who was either racing around the classroom hitting out at other children or was fast asleep for much of the day? Could I have 'proved', then, that integration works?

It is very difficult to persuade teachers of the benefits of integration if they have become disciples of specialist doctrines. If teachers feel that they have created order out of chaos, then the very suggestion of experimentation appears foolhardy. Yet I cannot help but reflect that I have been lucky enough to be able to break out of my label. Many people are not so fortunate.

7 POSTSCRIPT

As the developments which I have described took place between 1971 and 1982, I would like to come up to date with curricular changes in this school. In January 1991 I visited the school again, to speak to the current head teacher who took up her post in 1985. It was interesting to me that, although none of the teachers I had worked with were still there, many of the welfare assistants were. Also, those children who had been in the nursery when I was at the school were now adolescents, several of them being in the senior class for those with 'challenging behaviours'. This aspect of change alone reflects the chemistry of institutions in which – for many practical reasons – some people remain *in situ* whilst others move on, and the way in which behaviours which were 'cute' at 4 years old become 'challenging' at 17.

The nature of the 'special care' section of the school has changed. The policy in the school now is to keep children with their peer group as much as possible, regardless of disability. Toilet facilities have been adjusted throughout the school to cater for pupils with a range of disabilities. The total number of pupils in the school has shrunk from about 120 when I went there in 1977 to only seventy in 1991. This means far more space and a much-improved staffing ratio. Clearly, both these factors have helped teachers to cope with the integration of children who would formerly have been placed in 'special care'.

The number of children receiving physiotherapy is about twenty, which is a high proportion among seventy pupils. The school has been influenced by the growth of conductive education and has adapted this method to suit their resources. They regard it as sensory stimulus and have adopted much of the equipment required, with the support of the physiotherapists.

The one group which is still taught separately for at least some of the day is the senior class for students with 'challenging' behaviours. The teachers concerned with this group have developed a programme adapted to their needs and also work in collaboration with other teachers in supporting them when integrated through the school.

One of the most significant curricular changes has been the move towards team teaching and working collaboratively across the curriculum which has developed steadily over the last two to three years. This may have been particularly influenced by the influx of new teachers coming into the school from the mainstream sector. However, despite her enthusiasm for this approach, the head teacher has some reservations about abandoning all that came before:

> We've relaxed a little bit on the very tight behaviourist model of programme planning but we've got to be very careful that it doesn't go totally out of the window.

The National Curriculum is another influence which is changing practice gradually. The head teacher welcomes the broader context it offers in taking children beyond individual programmes and in including special schools in a national initiative:

We are no longer on the edge of what is happening.

Yet, it is proving hard to get the National Curriculum initiatives off the ground when there are so many staff changes at the school. In 1990 there were five out of nine classes covered by supply teachers, reflecting a common pattern in inner-city schools.

The perennial tension between practical and theoretical issues continues. At one level, there are the daily problems of keeping the school up and running (on the cold day I visited the heating had broken down!); at the other, there are the implications of responding to changing influences.

Chapter 18

Returning to the basics

A curriculum at Harperbury Hospital School

Dave Hewett and Melanie Nind

In this chapter the authors give an account of their approach to the teaching of young adults at Harperbury Hospital School. They describe how they came to question the relevance of a traditional behavioural curriculum for their students who experience very severe difficulties in learning. They indicate, in detail, the approach of 'intensive interaction' which they developed as an alternative and explain their theoretical rationale for it. They discuss the ethical implications of the close personal contact which their new practice entails and consider the possibilities for its use in other settings.

1 DEVELOPING A CURRICULUM CRITIQUE

The teachers at Harperbury work with a diverse group of students who have in common their residence in a long-stay hospital for people with learning disabilities. In many cases, the students have been unable to communicate either formally or informally and have difficulty in forming relationships with others. Characteristically, they have not developed beyond the earliest understandings of the immediate environment. They may behave in ways which disturb the people around them; they may roam the room rapidly and persistently, rock continuously and clap their hands; they may have an obsession with excreta, be preoccupied with seemingly purposeless, repetitive activity, with sexual self-stimulation, self-aggression and aggression to others. Such ways of behaving have considerable implications for the level and quality of staffing and for what teaching approaches are feasible. In addition many of the students have sensory and/or physical disabilities. Some of their eccentric-seeming behaviour has been exacerbated by their stay in a long-term hospital.

In 1985 the curriculum for our students was typical of schools for students with severe learning difficulties. The written curriculum was based on the skills analysis model (see Crawford 1980, Gardner *et al.* 1983), with core areas of development subdivided into components, and each component having a list of target behaviours. For every pupil there were written aims and objectives for each component and a written programme specifying how she/he would be taught and where the objective fitted against a checklist of skills. Core areas included motor development, social skills, self-help, language, number, play/leisure skills and behaviour. This type of curriculum dictated intricate, highly structured teaching methods based on behavioural techniques including shaping, fading, prompting and chaining (see Kiernan *et al.* 1978, Gardner *et al.* 1983).

Classroom practice was founded on such structured programmes and there was an uneasy adherence to superficially purposeful table-top activities such as inset puzzles, posting boxes and stacking toys, where the teacher could physically prompt the student. Students were helped to complete a few set tasks before being rewarded by a return to their own free choice of activity or perhaps a sweet. The teaching of discrimination skills, self-help skills and socially appropriate or manageable behaviour was given priority largely because the subject of the teaching activity was tangible and lent itself to skills analysis. Behaviour modification techniques were employed, primarily involving use of extrinsic rewards and time-out rooms as punishment, which were a feature of every classroom.

The growth of reservations

Gradually we allowed ourselves to recognise that the activities of the structured curriculum had little relevance to the needs of students. The role of the teacher tended to be rigidly prescribed and lacked warmth towards students. The classroom atmosphere came to be recognised as stressful, tense and authoritarian. We questioned whether learning could readily take place in such an environment (see also Wood and Shears 1986, Billinge 1989).

The curriculum seemed to produce regular failure for both teacher and student Many of the students had to be physically compelled to sit at the table to carry out tasks, though for some even physical domination could not achieve compliance. Some students continued to be expert at undressing themselves at inopportune moments though they had failed to learn the first step in the backward chain or incremental tasks in doing up a zip.

There was growing discomfort with the inflexibility of a curriculum structure which gave little scope for following up the students' own interests and strengths or for capitalising on instances of calm or tolerance. The student was seen as a passive recipient of the teaching activity.

We began to recognise much of the behaviour of our students as a response to situations which they did not understand; as demonstrating communication difficulties rather than behavioural difficulties, and this enabled us to look afresh at their learning needs. We came to see the development of communication and relationships as priorities, paramount over the teaching of self-help skills and discrimination abilities. We felt that if we could communicate, and begin to relate to one another, teaching and learning in all other spheres would become easier and more meaningful.

We concluded that our behavioural techniques were inadequate when addressing the complexities of communication and sociability. For instance, we could use gestural and physical prompts to get students to use the Makaton sign for 'biscuit' in a certain situation, but this would not help them to express their emotions and preferences. We might be able to eradicate play with saliva, but we did not have anything in our tool box with which to teach a positive and meaningful alternative.

We felt frustrated by the lack of formal knowledge about the teaching of the fundamentals of sociability and communication, and began to seek a theoretical foundation and a new teaching practice for ourselves. A period of practical experimentation in the classroom and theoretical inquiry complemented and informed each other.

2 THE EMERGENCE OF A NEW CURRICULUM

We were aware that successful communications and social exchanges with our students had tended to happen incidentally, outside of the formal teaching situation. We learned to value these moments as the most valuable learning experiences taking place across a whole week of supposed education. When, intuitively, we synchronised our walk and our sounds with those of a student as we escorted her to the door, and knew from her signals that she was aware of this shared behaviour, we recognised the implicit educational potential. We began to develop such play-like activity by use of dramatic exaggeration and by incorporating some friendly commentary about what was happening. We sought to make this happen more frequently and to find other ways of blending our behaviour with hers to make her aware of our mutuality. This early, naïve experimentation brought responses from the students which we had not formerly seen, and the reward to us of such success prompted the cumulative developments which followed. Without rationalising what we were doing, we built humorous tension and expectancy into the process of helping a student to get his arm in the sleeve of his coat, and playfulness on the part of the teacher rather than stark aloofness started to underpin such daily routine. Quickly, we learned that such an approach to the day's tasks was more enjoyable and effective for both students and staff. Thus, interactive play experiences were gradually brought from the periphery to the core of the curriculum.

We began to use other playful approaches to bring students to the table to perform a task, but the task soon diminished in importance in favour of the play itself. Formal teaching of set activities gradually gave way to such purposeful play with the students. With different expectations we freed ourselves to go and sit on the floor in the corner with someone rather than insist that this safe place be left. Here, over time, we achieved eye contact and enjoyed a willingness of the student to share his previously aggressively defended personal space.

Without fully realising it we stopped dominating the classroom with our rules, our language and our activity, and began negotiating the curriculum. We allowed ourselves to employ our natural teaching styles which meant that we adjusted ourselves to become interesting and accessible people for our students. Confrontations with students became rare since, now, we were willing to negotiate different routes to the same end. As we tuned in to the signals of our students we were able to respond to them and avoid violent outbursts.

The atmosphere in the classrooms changed dramatically. Pleasure and good humour pervaded and the more anxious students began to relax. The more active students slowed down; as they spent greater periods of time sharing warm physical contact with staff they seemed to adopt a different tempo.

As teachers, aware of the demands of accountability, we began to formalise these interactive activities into a new curriculum. It was pleasing to blend our rule of thumb practical work with the rationale of theoretical inquiry which centred on recent research into the growth of communication in early infancy.

3 DESCRIBING OUR PRACTICE

'Intensive Interaction' teaching is concerned with the development of pre-verbal communication. We include learning to tolerate and then enjoy the proximity of another person, accepting physical contact, making meaningful, communicative eye contact, developing and using facial expressions, taking turns and successfully exchanging the signals which facilitate this. We aim for the students to evolve a full, purposeful knowledge of their immediate environment, particularly, of course, the people in that environment.

We are concerned with the same processes that assist learning commonly, in early infancy. All of us have a tacit awareness, at least, of the extent to which pleasure, playfulness and games are part of interactions with infants. The willingness of adults to employ playfulness seems to be very important in cognitive development at this stage – it is a powerful motivator for the infant to take part in social interactions, and social interactions based on play are an essential, natural learning situation. Very frequently, especially in the early months, the play may have no particular focus other than pleasure; objects are often not present, the 'subject matter' of the learning is that which is occurring between the two people.

We behave in a similar way in our teaching with students who are older, even adult. Teachers negotiate their presence and their activity by being sensitive towards, that is by 'tuning in' to, the signals of the student in order to attract and sustain his or her attention with games. This sensitivity to the reactions of the student enable her/him to become an active participant and decision-maker at the earliest stage. The pleasure of participation and the knowledge that one may exercise some effect and control over the behaviour of another person are regarded as important achievements in their own right.

The nature and intensity of activity in Intensive Interaction varies between for instance, noisy rough and tumble, intense face-to-face mutual studying or simply sitting together in physical contact. We have recognised that even the most passive-seeming of interactions has purpose, and indeed for many students the mere sharing of space is a major achievement. Whatever the intensity, the teaching situation is highly informal and the activity is free-flowing. The interaction sequences take place in the usual everyday classroom environment and an atmosphere of playful purposefulness pervades when other staff and students are similarly engaged in various parts of the room.

We work with each student to make these games more frequent, varied and of longer duration, and to allow the activities to become progressively more complex and sophisticated. For most young children these sequences constitute rehearsal for later intentional communication.

This general style of interaction with students has become the most natural way for staff to carry out all other activities. Thus staff use 'interactivity' rather than dominance or compulsion to organise the movements of students around the school, or to lead an activity such as food preparation.

Patricia and Steve

Patricia is an athletic-looking woman of 20. She does not speak or communicate in any formal sense. She is extremely energetic and may spend whole days rushing around, running from wall to wall knocking down anyone or anything in her path. She will sometimes slap, scratch or bite others and will frequently vomit and smear faeces. Sometimes she withdraws completely and sleeps.

Patricia and Steve sit face to face having been involved in a gentle hand pat game. Then, with playful drama, Steve pulls Patricia's face to his and makes a prolonged 'wowowow' sound in her ear. Patricia laughs and leans back. Steve repeats but makes the sound even longer. Patricia again leans back, laughing loudly, this time with her eyes fixed on Steve's face. Steve is reciprocating, transmitting warmth and pleasure in return. There is a pause, then even more dramatically and deliberately, Steve pulls Patricia towards him, keeping his facial expression wide-eyed in her line of sight, at the same time intoning in rising expectancy, 'ah ... ah ... ah...'. This build up culminates in the anticipated sound in the ear. Patricia laughs uproariously, attention still fixed on Steve. This sequence is repeated five times, but each time the build up becomes slower and more deliberate, and Steve and Patricia wait a successively longer interval for the climax. Patricia alternates between prolonged laughter after the climax and still, patient expectancy before it. Most of the time her full attention, her gaze and her body language, is fixed on Steve. At one stage she moves away for about thirty seconds. Steve remains where he is, his body language signalling availability. Soon Patricia returns and sits expectantly opposite Steve.

Stelios and Sarah

Stelios is a small man of 26 who has visual and hearing impairments. When we first knew him he did not look at faces, perhaps did not know that faces existed. Moreover, he did not seem to distinguish between objects and people, and if he found another person's hand he mostly employed it in rhythmic patting, banging and mouthing which, together with rocking, characterised most of his activity.

Stelios sits spread-legged on the floor. Sarah sits opposite him and gently pulls him closer, her legs overlapping his. Stelios is rhythmically vocalising 'mumu-mumum'. Sarah starts imitating, falling into his rhythm, smiling. She raises the volume of her vocalisation, exaggerating her mouth movements and carefully bringing her face into line with his. Stelios stares at Sarah's mouth, which is in synchrony with his own. Sarah places her forehead and nose directly against Stelios's. He starts to smile as he looks directly into Sarah's eyes. She slowly draws back, keeping his gaze and with evident build up moves her head to one side before closing in to make a loud 'boo' close to his cheek. Stelios laughs and takes hold of her face, framing it with his hands. Sarah returns to face-to-face synchronous movement. Stelios starts to move Sarah's head from side to side in rhythm with his vocalisations. Sarah smiles broadly, increasing the volume of her vocalisations again. Stelios is still staring at her face. He pauses in his movements for a moment and Sarah seizes on the opportunity to tickle his ribs, joining in with the resultant laughter. Sarah holds Stelios's attention for about five minutes with these activities. Throughout she is studying his responses and making variations in the game accordingly. She waits patiently during moments of waning engagement and signals availability until he indicates readiness for more. She works all the time from what he does and from what she already knows about the types of play he enjoys and the kind of mood he is in.

4 OUR THEORETICAL RATIONALE

Teachers organise their activity within interactive sequences by employing a judicious combination of intuition and intellectualisation. By intuition we mean the sort of specific and natural-seeming actions we may use to facilitate social development with infants. We rarely give conscious thought to how we use these actions to help infants through the complex and important learning achievements of early life. In Intensive Interaction teaching, we wish to retain the power of such intuitive responding and to supplement this with the benefits of careful analysis.

One way we have intellectualised our teaching technique is through knowledge of the elements of the interactive process in infancy. The knowledge that in interaction with caregivers the infant is a full and active participant in her/his own development, even at the earliest of stages, has emerged in the psychological literature of the last two decades or so (Carlson and Bricker 1982, Hogg and Sebba 1986). From the late 1960s onwards there was an increasing understanding of the interactive nature of infant development (Schaffer 1971a, 1971b, 1977a, 1977b; Brazelton *et al.* 1974; Brazelton and Heidelise 1979; Trevarthen 1974; Field 1978a). This research has shown that while the caregivers are the responsive mediators of experiences, the activity and involvement of the infant is crucial: 'The child's response is more than a simple reaction to its environment; it should be seen in the light of its power to affect and restructure that environment' (Kysela and Marfo 1983: 206).

The elements of the interactive process are derived from such studies for instance, the role of mutual enjoyment (Stern 1974, Hoddapp and Goldfield 1983) and games (Field 1979, Bruner 1983), the importance of physical contact (Montagu 1986), the significance of imitation (Pawlby 1977, Field 1978b), the growth of turn-taking behaviours (Kaye 1977, 1982), the need to behave as if infant behaviour has meaning (Brazelton *et al.* 1974, Field 1977, Warren and Rogers-Warren 1984, Langley and Lombardino 1987), caregivers' modifications of their face and voice (Stern 1974, Snow 1977), caregivers using infant behaviours as the starting point of an interaction (Schaffer 1977a) and the need for caregivers to watch, wait and use careful timing (Brazelton *et al.* 1974, Stern 1974, Arco and McClusky 1981, Clark and Seifer 1983).

We have adopted the points on this list as guiding principles for our teaching and think of them in the following way:

1. Mutual enjoyment – we have already indicated the need for the learning activity to be enjoyable and hence motivating.
2. Starting with the students' own actions as the focus for the activity so that the starting point is familiar and comfortable.
3. Playful imitation of the students' actions.
4. Burst–pause sequences – where the teacher leaves pauses after her/his utterances or actions as if the student is going to fill the gap with a response.
5. Tension/expectancy games – which seem to have importance in their ability to attract and maintain attention and to develop anticipation. These games characteristically feature the teacher using playful, repetitive build-up to a pleasing climax (as in the Patricia example).
6. Physical contact – a fundamental form of communication inherent in infancy. In our teaching we readily use touch as an irreplaceable form of communication.
7. Intentionality – where the teacher behaves as if an utterance or behaviour by the student is communicative, even if this is not the case. It is thought that this is one of the ways in which true intentional communication is developed.
8. Gentle running commentary – given in a naturally simplified and/or repetitive speech pattern.
9. Rhythm, repetition and timing – naturally used to maintain the learner's attention and involvement in the activity.
10. Simplification – face/voice/body modification which change the teacher from an oversophisticated, probably incomprehensible communicator into someone who is attractive, stimulating and meaningful.

Although we think about and employ all the above elements our activities with our students are seamless, with these elements blending and blurring.

We believe that Ephraim (1979) first postulated and explored the applications ot a teaching model for people with severe learning difficulties derived from the work on early infant interaction. It was some time however, before educational literature reflected developments in practice, as may now be seen in our work (Nind and Hewett 1988, Hewett and Nind 1989, Hewett 1989) and in the work of Miller and Ephraim (1988), Coupe and Goldbart (1988) and Knight and Watson (1990). A similar approach has been developed by Burford (1986), though couched in the language of her profession as a movement therapist.

Some ethical considerations

When we give workshops on our teaching approach we are often asked about sexual arousal. Other teachers are concerned that such free use of physical contact with students who have very limited understandings, but are none the less sexually mature, may be sexually arousing. This is an issue which we have kept in the forefront of our minds from the very earliest stages of this work. We have found however, that sexual arousal virtually never occurs during the type of interaction sequences which we are promoting. The reason for this may not be immediately obvious, but increasingly we have come to believe and accept that it is simply to do with the nature and quality of the human interaction taking place. We think that teachers are transmitting loud and clear something like: 'Hey this is going to be fun. We are going to touch and romp, have a great time, *but it isn't sex.*' In any event, one of the foremost attributes of the teacher activity is responsiveness to the signals of the student. Sexual signalling, should it occur, is treated as negative signalling and not responded to as part of the interaction sequence being promoted. Thus sexuality can be appropriately met at the very earliest age of its occurrence.

Also, some practitioners who are used to working with students for whom there are very strong expectations about age-appropriate curricula and behaviour comment that our teaching activity may be inappropriate for adult students, or even to one advanced beyond the toddler stage. We cannot deal at length with this important issue in this chapter. However, we feel that the teaching activity is most definitely intellectually and emotionally appropriate to the students, and that if a concept of age-appropriateness prevents a practitioner from doing that which is clearly beneficial then a reconsideration of the concept may be advisable. We very much concur with the worries of Ephraim (1986) and of Jackson (1988) about the Wolfensberger (1980) concept of 'normalisation'. We are more concerned with accepting our students as they are than with making them like ourselves.

5 THE FUTURE

We see potential in using Intensive Interaction teaching with young, even very young children, who have learning difficulties. This potential lies, we believe, both in its use as an effective general teaching approach and as a way of helping to minimise additional or secondary handicaps. Sources of 'additional handicap' may be various, but here we mean the effects that may occur because an original handicap acts as a barrier to early interactive experiences, demotivating both infant and carer with possible long-term effects on all subsequent learning. Intervention programmes for developmentally delayed infants in the United States often reflect an awareness of the early interactive processes and address the need for a responsive, child-oriented style of interacting (Bromwich 1981, Calhoun and Rose 1988, Mahoney and Powell 1988, Odom *et al.* 1988).

Here in Britain, other schools for pupils experiencing severe learning difficulties have become interested in our work, and investigation and adoption of the approach is taking place in a number of areas, most notably Edinburgh (Knight and Watson 1990). We have found, also, that there is a considerable interest within social services provision for people with severe learning difficulties. We stress to social services practitioners in residential work that the style of relating brought about by a knowledge of early interactive processes is well suited to the informal periods of life in residential schools and group homes.

We hope to continue our own research and development, though now in settings other than Harperbury Hospital School. We look to other practitioners (not just teachers) to do similarly, for we feel we are only at the start of an exploration of these methods. We are intrigued by the potential of the application of our principles to students who have already achieved use of language. In particular, we are thinking about work with young people who may have a full command of vocabulary and grammar, but who may experience difficulty, in various degrees, in making human contact.

We have developed an approach in which we negotiate the pace and content of the curriculum with our students and which gives them a right of veto over whether or not to engage in any particular activity. We suspect that it may be this principle which will provoke the greatest resistance in other teachers to learning from our practice.

REFERENCES

Arco, C. M. B. and McClusky, K. A. (1981) 'Change of pace: an investigation of the salience of maternal temporal style in mother–infant play', *Child Development* 52, 941–9.

Billinge, R. (1989) 'The objectives model of curriculum development – a creaking bandwagon', *Mental Handicap* 16, 26–9.

Brazelton, T. B., Koslowski, B. and Main, M. (1974) 'The origins of reciprocity: the early mother–infant interaction', in M. Lewis and L. Rosenblum (eds), *The Effect of the Infant on its Caregiver*, London: John Wiley & Sons.

—— and Heidelise, A. L. S. (1979) 'Four early stages in the development of mother–infant interaction', *Psychoanalytic Study of the Child* 34, 349–69.

Bromwich, R. M. (1981) *Working with Parents and Infants: An Interactional Approach*, Baltimore: University Park Press.

Bruner, J. (1983) *Child's Talk: Learning to Use Language*, Oxford: Oxford University Press.

Burford, B. (1986) 'Communication through movement', in E. Shanley (ed.), *Mental Handicap – A Handbook of Care*, Edinburgh: Churchill Livingstone.

Calhoun, M. L. and Rose, T. L. (1988) 'Early social reciprocity interventions for infants with severe retardation: current findings and implications for the future', *Education and Training in Mutual Retardation* 23, 340–3.

Carlson, L. and Bricker, D. D. (1982) 'Dyadic and contingent aspects of early communicative intervention', in D. D. Bricker (ed.), *Intervention with At-Risk and Handicapped Infants*, Baltimore: University Park Press.

Clark, G. N. and Seifer, R. (1983) 'Facilitating mother–infant communication: a treatment model for high-risk and developmentally delayed infants', *Infant Mental Health Journal* 4, 67–81.

Coupe, J. A. and Goldbart, J. (1988) *Communication Before Speech*, London: Croom Helm.

Crawford, N. B. (ed.) (1980) *Curriculum Planning for the ESN(S) Child*, Kidderminster: British Institute of Mental Handicap.

Ephraim, G. (1979) 'Developmental processes in mental handicap: a generative structure approach', unpublished Ph.D. thesis, Brunel University, Department of Psychology.

—— (1986) 'Is normalization normal?', *Talking Sense* 32 (1), 13–14.

Field, T. (1977) 'Maternal stimulation during feeding', *Developmental Psychology* 14, 539–40.

—— (1978a) 'The three Rs of infant–adult interactions: rhythms, repertoires and responsivity', *Journal of Paediatric Psychology* 3, 131–6.

—— (1978b) 'Interaction behaviours of primary versus secondary caretaker fathers', *Developmental Psychology* 14, 183–4.

—— (1979) 'Games parents play with normal and high-risk infants', *Child Psychiatry and Infant Development* 10, 41–8.

Gardner, J., Murphy, J. and Crawford, N. (1983) *The Skills Analysis Model*, Kidderminster: British Institute of Mental Handicap.

Hewett, D. (1989) 'The most severe learning difficulties: does your curriculum "go back far enough"?', in M. Ainscow (ed.), *Special Education in Change*, London: Fulton.

—— and Nind, M. (1989) 'Developing an interactive curriculum for pupils with severe and complex learning difficulties', in B. Smith (ed.), *Interactive Approaches to the Education of Children with Severe Learning Difficulties*, Birmingham: Westhill College (available from Westhill College).

Hoddapp, R. M. and Goldfield, E. C. (1983) 'The use of mother–infant games with delayed children', *Early Child Development and Care* 13, 17–32.

Hogg, J. and Sebba, J. (1986) *Profound Retardation and Multiple Impairment, Volume 1: Development and Learning*, London: Croom Helm.

Jackson, R. N. (1988) 'Perils of "pseudo-normalisation"', *Mental Handicap* 18, 148–51.

Kaye, K. (1977) 'Toward the origin of dialogue', in H. R. Schaffer (ed.), *Studies in Mother–Infant Interaction*, London: Academic Press.

—— (1982) *The Mental and Social Life of Babies: How Parents Create Persons*, London: Methuen.

Kiernan, C., Jordan, R. and Saunders, C. (1978) *Starting Off: Establishing Play and Communication in the Handicapped Child*, London: Souvenir Press.

Knight, C. and Watson, J. (1990) 'Intensive interaction teaching at Gogarburn School', Edinburgh: Moray House College (available from Moray House College).

Kysela, G.M. and Marfo, K. (1983) 'Mother–child interactions and early intervention programmes for handicapped infants and young children', *Educational Psychology* 3 (3 & 4), 201–10.

Langley, M. B. and Lombardino, L. J. (1987) 'Application of a normal developmental model for understanding the communicative behaviours of students with severe handicaps', *European Journal of Special Needs Education* 2, 161–76.

Mahoney, G. and Powell, A. (1988) 'Modifying parent–child interaction: enhancing the development of handicapped children', *Journal of Special Education* 22, 82–96.

Miller, J. and Ephraim, G. (1988) 'The role of "augmented mothering" in teacher education in special needs', *Mental Handicap* 16, 108–11.

Montagu, A. (1986) *Touching: the human significance of the skin*, London: Harper & Row.

Nind, M. and Hewett, D. (1988) 'Interaction as curriculum', *British Journal of Special Education* 15 (2), 55–7.

Odom, S. L., Yoder, P. and Hill, G. (1988) 'Developmental intervention for infants with handicaps: purposes and programs', *Journal of Special Education* 22 (1), 11–24.

Pawlby, S. J. (1977) 'Imitative interaction', in H. R. Schaffer (ed.), *Studies in Mother–Infant Interaction*, London: Academic Press.

Schaffer, H. R. (1971a) 'Cognitive structure and early social behaviour', in H. R. Schaffer (ed.), *The Origins of Human Social Relations*, London: Academic Press.

—— (1971b) *The Growth of Sociability*, Harmondsworth: Penguin.

—— (1977a) *Mothering*, London: Fontana/Open Books.

—— (1977b) 'Early interactive development', in H. R. Schaffer (ed.), *Studies in Mother–Infant Interaction*, London: Academic Press.

Snow, C. E. (1977) 'The development of conversation between mothers and babies', *Journal of Child Language* 4, 1–22.

Stern, D. (1974) 'The goal and structure of mother–infant play', *Journal of the American Academy of Child Psychiatry* 13, 402–21.

——, Beebe, J., Jaffe, J. and Bennett, S. L. (1977) 'The infant's stimulus world during social interaction', in H. R. Schaffer (ed.), *Studies in Mother–Infant Interaction*, London: Academic Press.

Treavarthen, C. (1974) 'Conversations with a two month old', *New Scientists*, 2 May 1974, 230–5.

Warren, S. F. and Rogers-Warren, A. (1984) 'The social basis of language and communication in severely handicapped pre-schoolers', *Topics in Early Childhood Special Education* 4, 57–72.

Wolfensberger, W. (1980) 'The definition of normalisation', in R. Flynn and K. E. Nitsch (eds), *Normalisation, Social Integration and Community Service*, Baltimore: University Park Press.

Wood, S. and Shears, B. (1986) *Teaching Children with Severe Learning Difficulties: A Radical Reappraisal*, London: Croom Helm.

Part 4

Children and young people under pressure

Chapter 19

Lassies of Leith talk about bother

Gwynedd Lloyd

In this chapter Gwynedd Lloyd gives space to a group of young girls to express their views about getting into trouble at school. They describe the common events which get them into 'bother' with teachers. They suggest that many of their problems lie in shortcomings in the way teachers relate to them. Teachers, they argue, should be able to keep control, but should also allow them to be themselves and have a laugh. Through her discussions with them, Gwynedd Lloyd rejects an image of these girls as passive victims of teacher expectations and decisions.

1 INTRODUCTION

This chapter reports the views of some adolescent girls on how girls get into trouble, or what the girls often call 'bother', at school. It is based on a series of interviews and group discussions with twenty-two girls in a youth project in a disadvantaged neighbourhood around a city port. The girls attended the youth project for different reasons, eight of them had been identified as the most disruptive pupils in their school and had been referred by the school to a social education/discussion group in the youth project. The rest came to evening activities and to a girls' group. I was known to most of the girls as someone who sometimes took part in the activities of the project but not as a teacher. This, and the open atmosphere of the project, created a climate where the girls were willing to discuss freely. What follows is an illuminative account of their experiences of 'bother' at school. I am grateful to the girls for being so open. I have, with their approval, used their real names (even though this means there are two Kellys, two Angies, two Amandas and a Mandy!).

Most of the girls with whom I spoke had been through the school disciplinary cycles of lines, detention, being sent to deputy head, put out of classroom, put out of school with a letter home. None had yet been permanently excluded, although since the interviews one of the girls has been excluded and another has been placed in a 'secure' (i.e. locked) residential school. Several, especially amongst the girls identified by their schools as disruptive, had been temporarily excluded several times and were 'on their last chance'.

Sharon: Mr J, he's always saying 'You're on your last warning'!

None of the girls spoke positively about their educational experiences as a whole though not all of them had given up completely on the value of education. There was heated debate between them about whether it was more boring to go to school or stay at home.

Jane: What's the point in going to school – it doesnae help you to get a job after.
Angie: School isnae useful, they just make you do the same work over again – it's purely boring! The only class I like is craft and design 'cause you get a laugh.
Julie: It's boring without going to school.
Rhona: You should go or how do you ken anything – your dad cannae teach you everything.

Most of the girls saw the main value of school as a place to meet your pals, have a laugh, a gossip and for about half, a smoke.

2 WHAT LASSIES GET INTO BOTHER FOR

In my discussions with the girls the most frequently mentioned examples of 'bother' began with talking in class and being cheeky to teachers.

Kelly: Being cheeky to teachers.
Jane: The same as laddies do, sometimes worse – just being cheeky to teachers.
Kelly 2, Amanda 2, Lindsey and Julie: For talking!
Vicky: Mucking about in class.
Verona: Disturbing the class.

Julie's swearing and answering back was more explicit and Angie 2 referred to the incident that had led to her most recent 'conduct sheet':

Angie 2: I walked out of a teacher's class and when she told me to come back I told her to fuck off.
Kelly 2: How? [=why]
Angie 2: 'Cause she was a pain in the arse!

Two girls mentioned make-up and five cited smoking.

Amanda: Putting on nail varnish and a' that.
Arlene: Being cheeky and bringing their hairspray out in class and make-up and chewing gum – that's about it.
Kelly [point to Lindsey]: Girls smoke in class – she smokes in class.
Lee Anne: Smoking, getting caught smoking.

Emma: Mostly it's trouble because the girls are down in the toilet having a fag, that's how most of them are late for their class, 'cause the boys dinnae bother going down the toilets – they just go outside or something.

Toilets – a source of trouble and a grievance

Toilets, and the perceived unsympathetic attitude of teachers towards their physical needs, featured strongly in many of the girls' accounts. For all the girls, access to toilets seemed to be a frequent cause of argument with teachers.

Verona: Our toilets – they're always locked.

Sharon: Ken us – you know the raj ones at school – when we go to the toilet she always takes the keys back off you and goes back in and checks! [raj = daft, crazy]

Fiona: Only some teachers will give you a permission slip.

Emma: We're different from what laddies are – like when we ask the teacher to go to the toilet we cannae wait.

Nicky: That's what Lynn got suspended for – walking out of class to go to the toilet.

Kelly 2: Mr I says you need a note from home to go to the toilet – every month!

Nicky: I says to Mr U, 'have I got to make the seat red before I can go?'

Catriona: Lassies have a harder time than laddies. We go through our periods – they don't. The teachers won't let you go.

Toilets, in the view of all these girls, had a number of functions. Apart from their explicit purpose they were also places where you had a chat with your friends, relatively free of adult supervision, and a fag. The girls did recognise that the reason that teachers didn't always 'let you go' was because of the frequent vandalising or because they thought the girls wanted a 'skive' from class or a fag.

Rhona: Mr O, he's barry, he kens what we're like, like if we go 'Can we go to the toilet sir?' he'll go 'No, if you wait till the end I'll let you out for five minutes for a smoke then.' [barry = good]

Nevertheless they still felt strongly about not being allowed to go. Several of the girls said that this was because teachers failed to understand how difficult it was to be a girl and have periods, and how sensitive the girls felt about having to mention them.

Lee Anne: Everyone felt dead sorry for Mary when she says to Mrs D she wants to go to the nurse – look the seat's red!

Prendergast talked to girls in school about menstruation and observed that the majority of girls saw it as 'mostly negative and to be endured' (Prendergast 1989:

90). They felt embarrassed about telling anyone – half of them said they didn't like to talk to teachers and they were embarrassed about having to obtain and dispose of sanitary towels in school. This situation, as for the girls I spoke with, was made worse by vandalised and often locked toilets.

Control of time and space

The girls in my study, as in Griffin (1985), used the toilets as a refuge from teachers and from boys. The young women in her study had tried to avoid teachers' control by making their own 'leisure' in school.

> This ranged from not going to school at all (i.e. 'wagging it' or 'nicking off'), 'skiving off' lessons for a smoke or a chat; through to day dreaming or 'cutting off' when teachers were present.
>
> (Griffin 1985: 19)

The girls in my study also talked about 'kipping' or 'skiving' school and the way they coped with the reactions of the teachers. 'Skiving' might be for the whole day, with or without parental consent, or might just be for individual classes or involve arriving late.

Fiona: It's OK to go up the town with your ma to get jeans or shoes or that.

Roseanne: Sometimes my mum asks me to watch the wee one for her.

Verona: I skive school – what's the point in going to school?

Mandy: Mr T, our regy teacher – he was always giving me one [a punishment] for being late, it didn't teach you a lesson – I've got about forty seven to do.

Emma: Mr U, he's exceptionally bad – oh he's mad, he's doolally – the other day I went into his class and I was late because I had lost my timetable, and then that was quite a good reason for being late and it was true as well! So he started going mental at me, it was like he was going to hit me, I was crapping myself standing there. He sent me outside, he was bawling outside the room and he got complaints and a' that, ken, for shouting. I'm getting moved out of his class.

Mr U featured frequently in the girls' accounts of teachers with whom they got into bother, and will be discussed further.

Fighting

Most of the girls mentioned fighting between girls as common – sometimes over boyfriends, to defend someone in their family like a younger sibling, or 'if somebody slags you'. They thought that fighting was quite acceptable, indeed often obligatory for girls, but at the same time there seemed to be a level of fighting that became unacceptable, that was in Vicky's words, 'too much like a laddie'.

Sharon: More lassies fight than laddies.
Jane: Lassies are always in fights.
Kelly 2: Lassies fight mostly with the laddies.
Lindsey: No they fight with each other.
Nicky: Lassies do fight as much as laddies, girls fight over their boyfriends, if they want to bag off with them.
Vicky: . . . Lynn she's always getting into trouble in class – she's too much like a laddie, fighting in class and that with a laddie! [Lynn (not her real name) did not take part in the interviews but was known to all the girls. She was excluded from school for fighting and being abusive to teachers.]
Arlene: Lynn, she goes out of her way to get into trouble, she thinks it's hard, she does it all the time. She's in one of my classes and I just ignore her.

Campbell (1981), in her study of girl delinquents, argues that girls are more willing than boys to acknowledge the relative harmlessness of fighting. The girls she interviewed had quite clear rules about fighting: 'Proscriptive rules (those that state what must not be done) are more common in this sample than prescriptive rules (which state what should be done)' (Campbell 1981: 164). They argued that you should not take on more than one person at a time, should not ask your friend to help and should not report the fight to the school or to the police. They also argued, probably contrary to popular mythology, that it was acceptable to punch and slap but not to bite, tear clothes or fight when your opponent was on the ground.

The girls with whom Wolpe (1988) spoke mentioned girls fighting as common, although their teachers did not mention this.

> Perhaps the teachers, like the girls, hold an ideological view of girls as non-aggressive and non-violent even though examples of such behaviour are far from being rare.
>
> (Wolpe 1988: 66)

Schostak (1986), argues, too, that it is 'a myth that girls must not be hard, not violent. They fight.' He sees the boys as 'supported in their hardness by the equation of hardness with manliness' (Schostak 1986: 128). The girls with whom I spoke saw 'hardness' as masculine, and therefore as inappropriate in girls, so were critical of girls like Lynn. But they also saw girls and women fighting as normal in everyday life and as something that was often a cause of getting into trouble at school.

Slagging and reputations

The girls felt that they had to guard their reputations and that while a certain amount of teasing and ribaldry was expected and was part of having a laugh, there were clear limits. To slag someone could mean either humorous, jokey, teasing, or real and offensive insults which meant a tricky boundary to be negotiated. Overreaching the limits was responded to by Nicky, for example, with 'a good slagging back or a kicking'.

The girls use the terms 'cow', 'whore' or 'prostitute' to describe a girl who supposedly sleeps around, although they know the difference between this and real prostitution which they see daily on the streets. They were critical of the way in which boys slagged girls but also did it themselves, frequently.

Laddies start it, lassies finish it

Several girls argued that it was often boys who got them into bother with teachers at school.

Vicky: The boys get you into trouble.
Nicky: Laddies start it, lassies finish it and they get caught ... Likes of say, somebody feels your tit or something and you slap the guy and you get caught.

My impression from talking to the girls and also from observations in the youth centre, was of a constant stream of sexual innuendo and minor sexual harassment towards the girls. There seems to be a constant negotiation of the boundaries of acceptability. As with slagging, attempts by the boys at physical 'touching up' are considered by the girls to be sometimes offensive and sometimes entertaining. The girls did not suggest that they would prefer to go to a single sex school – which only exist in Scotland in the private sector – and although they complained about boys getting them into trouble, they obviously spent a fair amount of time at school gossiping and laughing about who had 'bagged off' with, or was going out with, whom.

Several girls suggested that the girls who got into trouble most frequently, apart from those who were trying to be 'hard' and like 'laddies', were in Amanda's words 'the ones that have got tons of boyfriends and that, ken, like wee Helen. She gets into trouble all the time.'

Dress and appearance

None of the girls with whom I spoke said that they wore a full school uniform, despite the efforts of schools, although several compromised by wearing skirts and jumpers, sometimes in the school colours. They mentioned putting on nail varnish and bringing out hair spray in class, and the wearing of make-up and big gaudy ear-rings to school, as reasons for getting into trouble with teachers. The biggest source of trouble with teachers over uniform, they said, was wearing jeans or trousers, in particular the currently fashionable 'shell suits'.

Verona: I dinnae feel comfy in a skirt.
Jane: The only reason that they're bothered is that it gets a bad name for the school.
Kelly: See thae shell suits, some people get sent home for them and not others.

Several of the girls felt that the rules over uniform were arbitrarily and inconsistently applied, creating difficulties for those who tried to edge around on the boundaries of acceptable dress, not conforming but trying to avoid 'being got at all the time about your claes'.

3 RELATIONSHIPS WITH TEACHERS

The girls talked a lot about their teachers. For them, as for the 'wenches' in Davies (1984), 'Teachers were a source of interest, contempt, amusement, anger, affection, prestige' (Davies 1984: 28). If they got into bother in class they thought it was mainly the teachers' fault, either because they were unfair or inconsistent or because they were unable to control their classes properly. Teachers were expected to be able to control their classes, but at the same time it was considered entirely legitimate by the girls to try to have a laugh or wind them up:

> We should explore the interesting inversion of logic whereby it becomes the teachers' fault if pupils cannot resist playing them up. If a girl wins a confrontation a teacher's right to sympathy is also withdrawn.
>
> (Davies 1984: 32)

The girls I spoke to set high standards for teacher behaviour. A reasonable teacher would not only keep control but would also let you eat, have a laugh and a chat and 'would know who you were as a person'. Whether many teachers could live up to the contradictory expectations of them is open to doubt.

Mandy: Mr N, he was the best teacher, 'cause he would see it from your point of view.
Nicky: Reasonable teachers would be polite with you, let you talk for a wee while.
Emma: Like if I was a teacher I'd get to know them, have a laugh with them and that and then if you just really know them and that they just dinnae hassle you.
Lindsey: The worst teachers are the ones who dinnae let you talk and dinnae let you eat.
Kelly: The worst teachers are nippy, shouting all the time.

Kelly 2: Teachers should keep their tempers, some teachers just go off like that. [snaps fingers]

Angie 2: The best teachers give you a laugh – ken Mr O he lets you eat and everybody swears in his class.

Kelly 2: And, ken, he lets you eat your chewing gum in peace.

He picks on me for nothing

All the girls expressed the view that sometimes they got into trouble because of unfairness on the part of teachers. Many of their comments could be described in terms of what Tattum (1982) describes as 'techniques of neutralisation' – 'a partisan view of the truth used to account for one's behaviour'. Tattum says that the most frequent explanation of disruptive behaviour offered by pupils was that it resulted from teachers not being fair, from inconsistency of rule application. The girls in this study mentioned several examples of what they saw as unfairness, for example inconsistencies over the enforcement of uniform rules, e.g. the reaction to 'shell suits' or over access to the toilets. They saw some teachers as unfairly expressing their own bad temper or prejudice.

Kelly 2: Miss R is a bitch, she always picks on me, I dinnae dae nothing!

Angie 2: Mr T he picks on me for nothing – he takes out his mood on us. I asked him a question and he goes 'Are you a kind of junkie or something...?'

Sharon: I dinnae dae that much except talk to my pals and that irritates him and I goes, 'Sir why do you always shout at me?' And he goes 'I cannae help it if your face irritates me.'

Kelly: That's right, in his room you cannae even talk to your pals.

Sharon: Mrs D she slapped me for yawning.

There was one teacher, Mr U, mentioned earlier, who stood out as being particularly disliked by the girls for his 'unfair' bad-temperedness.

Lee Anne: Mr U, he takes an instant dislike to you, he picks on you.

Nicky: Mr U should get the sack. Every time I walk into his class he goes 'Right you, out!' He says 'I don't appreciate you talking in my class', I says I just walked in the door and he goes 'Don't answer me back'. In his class you can't even go – 'Meet me in the dinner hall'.

Mandy: Mr U a right pain in the arse!

A possible clue to understanding Mr U's difficulties was provided by Arlene: 'Mr U, he's always threatening us. Everyone messes him around.'

The relevance of gender

The girls had very varied views as to whether they preferred, or whether they got into bother more with, men or women teachers. They also differed as to whether teachers were more likely to 'pick on' girls or boys.

Emma: The teachers take it out more on the girls than they do on the boys.
Mandy: No they dinnae!
Arlene: Aye they do!
Vicky: The teachers dinnae expect the lassies to muck about in class – they expect the laddies to.
Amanda: Some of the teachers would rather teach the boys than the girls – like my teacher, Mr C he's really sexist, gets all the boys started first.
Lee Anne: Some men pick on you all the time. Mr Q picks on me just because I can't finish my work – it's too hard. Just because I sit beside Sharon and Lisa and we talk a lot and we dinnae do our work so just before the end of the period I scribble it all down and he says 'This is a load of rubbish, we can't put this' and he rubs it all out and says 'Do it again for homework' and you forget to do it and get two pages of punny.
Emma: It's normally men teachers – with hair spray and all that – it's guys that get the girls.
Jane: A teacher is a teacher. I get into trouble with both.

Winding up and having a laugh

Amongst the five 'techniques of neutralisation' identified by Tattum (1982) is that 'everybody messes around, it is only having a laugh'. The girls with whom I spoke felt that it was the teacher's job to control the class and that it was mainly the teacher's fault if they got into trouble. At the same time they talked with pleasure about some of the things they did to 'wind up' teachers and get a laugh.

Jane: You wind them up when you're arguing with them and you start laughing.
Kelly 2: Mr D, ken like Jonathan Ross how he cannae say his 'R's, this is how Mr D says it 'Jane and Kelly get away from that twolley'. We used to wind him up with that. We used to stand and muck about by the trolley so he'd say 'Get away from that twolley' and everyone would laugh.
Vicky: A good teacher can control a class, be strict at first until you get to know them, let you talk for a wee while.
Amanda: The saps, they cannae control you, they just let you away wi' anything, they just let you wander across the class, ken, slag them.
Vicky: Some lassies just like causing trouble more with some teachers, the softest teachers.
Julie: Mr I, he cannae control his classes.
Angie: His glasses?
Julie: No his *classes*! People speak back to him, eh Kelly?
Kelly 2: Aye, he does give you a row and all that but you can just run around the classroom and everything. Mrs N, they all speak back tae her and

take the mickey and all that. She does shout but it doesnae dae nothing.

Mandy: We had this teacher, Mrs R, she couldnae keep control – we werenae that bad – we worked, you know in home economics, and we were doing something about hooses, ben the hooses, but outside and all that and we went and grassed her off to Mr N and she was greeting and all that. [ben = in, greeting = crying]

The girls were well aware of the consequences for teachers if they lost control of their tempers and let fly:

Kelly: I got a slap in the face from my science teacher.
Sharon: Aye, cause she laughed, sniggered.
Kelly: I was going to take him to court, he was crapping his pants.

Getting personal

Several girls mentioned their dislike of being asked personal questions or of personal comments being made by teachers with whom they felt they did not have a good relationship. Sometimes these reflected the anxiety of teachers about pupils' use of drugs:

Angie: The teachers think they've got a right to ask you anything.
Sharon: Mr R says to Angie, 'Angie, what've you been on?' she says 'Nothing, I just woke up' – he keeps asking us 'Are you on drugs?'
Rhona: Me and Sharon, we were in the same science class and I goes 'I'm going to get acid and pour it over your hair and set a match to it' – ken we were just saying that, we didnae mean it. The teachers took it the other way, they thought we meant acid tablets and smoking and all that and we were all on drugs – we were all taken to Mr J and he's going 'If I find any of you with acid or that...'

Parental support?

There was resentment on the part of some girls that their mothers appeared to be on their side at home but didn't sustain this in the school.

Angie: See my mum, she'll always go 'I'll go down and get these teachers tellt' – she goes down and she's always on his side!
Jane: See Mr N when he hit me, right, and I hit him back. My mum goes 'What height is he?' and I went about that [she demonstrates about average height]. She goes 'When I see him, he's going to get it severely!' and I went 'All right' so she went to school and says to Mr J 'My daughter's just been hit by one of your raj teachers.' But then she was on his side all the time.
Kelly: My mum says 'I'll go down and get them sorted out' and they say

'You know Kelly's no angel' and she goes 'I ken Kelly's no angel' – Aye, she shouldnae be daeing that anyway!

4 CONCLUSIONS

The girls enjoyed telling of their more dramatic confrontations with teachers, putting a cake into a teacher's face, hitting teachers and fighting in class. Although about half the girls involved in this study were seen by their schools as extremely disruptive it became clear that girls saw 'bother', mainly, as a result of persistent everyday misbehaviour – talking, eating, smoking, not wearing 'suitable' clothes, lateness and some absence and generally resisting the attempts of the school to contain them.

All the girls shared a critical view of school and of teachers, a strong view of teachers failing to understand their concerns and problems. Although most of the girls were willing to identify some teachers they liked, they felt there was an issue of solidarity with their mates in classroom confrontation with teachers. They enjoyed the laughs and the excitement provided by the winding up of teachers and the diversion from work provided by the deviance of other pupils.

Like the girls in other studies, these girls describe themselves as active and initiating classroom negotiation and not as simply responsive to teacher behaviour. They did not see themselves as victims of sexism in the way girls are sometimes presented in the radical feminist tradition 'as the victims of male tyranny' (Wolpe 1988: 145). Although they complain of harassment by boys and by male teachers they described themselves as resisting this. The girls seem to be both creative and restricted in their lives, to be both powerful and powerless.

REFERENCES

Campbell, A. (1981) *Girl Delinquents*, Oxford: Basil Blackwell.
Davies, L. (1984) *Pupil Power and Deviance in School*, Lewes: Falmer Press.
Griffin, C. (1985) *Typical Girls? Young Women From School to the Job Market*, London: Routledge & Kegan Paul.
Prendergast, S. (1989) 'Girls' experience of menstruation', in L. Holly (ed.), *Girls and Sexuality*, Milton Keynes: Open University Press.
Schostak, J. (1986) *Schooling the Violent Imagination*, London: Routledge & Kegan Paul.
Tattum, D. (1982) *Disruptive Pupils in Schools and Units*, Chichester: Wiley.
Wolpe, A. (1988) *Within School Walls*, London: Routledge.

Chapter 20

Bullying in two English comprehensive schools

Colin Yates and Peter Smith

Source: Munthe, E. and Roland, E. (eds) (1989) *Bullying: An International Perspective,* London: David Fulton.

In this chapter Colin Yates and Peter Smith report on an attempt to discover the extent and nature of bullying in two English schools using a questionnaire with groups of 13 and 15 year olds. They compare their findings with reports of bullying in Norwegian schools, where attention has been directed at the problem for some years but where the reported incidence is far lower than in this and other English studies.

1 INTRODUCTION

How serious are bully/victim problems in British schools? It seems that this problem has only begun to be seriously considered. The general problem of discipline in schools was considered by the Elton Report (1989), but this focused mainly on difficulties experienced by teachers. What about bullying and victimisation of pupils by each other? Sections 65–7 of the Elton Report did specifically refer to the occurrence of bullying and racial harassment in schools and the need to take action against it. The report refers to the publication of *Bullying in Schools* (Tattum and Lane 1989) to make the point that bullying may be more extensive than previously thought. Some of the chapters in that book suggest that the problem is very serious. For example, Stephenson and Smith (1989) found that some 23 per cent of children were involved as either bullies or victims, in a survey based on teacher reports in twenty-six primary schools. Earlier, Arora and Thompson (1987) had reported that in one small comprehensive school around 20–30 per cent of all children between 12 and 14 stated that someone had threatened to hurt them, or had tried to hit them, at least once during the previous week.

These figures seem higher than the kinds of results reported in the extensive Norwegian studies of Olweus (1989). He found that in Norway some 9 per cent of schoolchildren were bullied, and some 7 per cent were bullies, 'now and then' or more frequently. These figures fell to 3 and 2 per cent respectively for 'about once a week' or more frequently. The figures for being bullied (but not for bullying) were less for Norwegian children in junior high school (aged about 13–15 years), falling to about 6 per cent for 'now and then' or more frequently.

It would seem that British figures for bullies and victims indicate a considerably more prevalent problem than in Norway. However the comparison is not exact because of the different methodologies used. The report by Stephenson and Smith (1989) is based on teachers' reports, while that by Arora and Thompson is based on a booklet given to pupils. Olweus by contrast has developed a self-report questionnaire given to pupils, specifically on bully/victim problems, which we have employed with only slight modifications in this study. The present report therefore enables clear and direct comparisons to be made with the extensive Scandinavian findings, albeit with only a limited sample size so far.

The schools

The study was carried out in two schools, A and B. Both were medium-sized comprehensive schools in a large industrial city, with between 600–1,000 pupils (School B had 20 per cent less pupils than School A). Both lay on the outskirts of the city, one in the north and one in the south, and had catchment areas which included within their boundaries large council estates which suffered from multiple deprivation. However, neither had this problem so much as some of the inner city schools. Both schools were predominantly white (less than 10 per cent of the children were from other ethnic backgrounds) and the children came from mainly working-class backgrounds.

The questionnaires

The questionnaires were given to the third year (approx. 13 years old) and the fifth year (approx. 15 years old) in each school in February 1989. There were 137 questionnaires from School A (40 boys and 40 girls in 3rd year, 29 boys and 28 girls in 5th year) and 97 questionnaires from School B (25 boys and 26 girls in 3rd year; 25 boys and 21 girls in 5th year), giving 234 sets of responses in all. Anonymity and confidentiality were stressed, and it was ensured that pupils did not confer.

The questionnaire closely followed the design of that used by Olweus, but some minor changes were made to suit the British context and current word usage. We asked pupils generally to report on the *last month* at school, this corresponded more or less to the extent of the term so far at the time of assessment. The following definition of bullying was used:

> We say a young person is *being bullied*, or picked on, when another young person, or a group of young people, say nasty and unpleasant things to him or her. It is also bullying when a young person is hit, kicked, threatened, locked inside a room, and things like that. These things may take place frequently and it is difficult for the young person being bullied to defend himself or

> herself. It is also bullying when a young person is teased repeatedly. But it is *not bullying* when two young people of about the same strength have the odd fight or quarrel.

This is the same definition as used by Olweus with a minor amendment in the last phrase.

2 OUR RESULTS

How often are children bullied?

The percentage responses to the question 'how often have you been bullied at school?' are shown in Table 20.1. Overall 22 per cent of pupils reported being bullied 'now and then' or more often, and 10 per cent 'once a week' or more often.

On an analysis of variance by age, sex and school, there were no significant sex or school differences, though there was a significant sex-by-school interaction. At School A more girls reported being bullied, while at School B more boys reported being bullied. The age difference was nearly significant, with a tendency for younger children to report being bullied more frequently (see Table 20.1).

When pupils were asked how often they had been bullied *last term*, the frequencies were 16 per cent for 'now and then' or more often, and 7 per cent for 'once a week' or more often. Of the 51 children who reported being bullied this term, 30 reported being bullied last term as well.

The question 'how often does it happen that other students don't want to spend break time with you and you end up being alone?' assesses what Olweus (1989) calls 'indirect bullying'. The incidence was similar for boys and girls, being 15 per cent for at least 'now and then' and 3 per cent for 'once a week' or more often.

Where the pupils were bullied

Rather fewer pupils, about 6 per cent, reported being bullied on the way to and from school ('now and then' or more often). Most of these were also bullied at school.

About 18 per cent of pupils reported that they had been bullied somewhere else in the last month – 5 per cent had been bullied in the street where they lived, 4 per cent in town, 3 per cent at a youth club and 8 per cent elsewhere; a variety of locations were written in here, including on the bus, at the fair (twice), at home (twice) and at the local Chinese take-away shop.

Who did the bullying?

Two of the questions asked 'in what class is the young person or young people who bully you?' and 'what sex is the young person or young people who bully you?'

Table 20.1 Percentage of pupils who reported being bullied at school

	It hasn't happened	*Only once or twice*	*Now and then*	*About once a week*	*About 2 or 3 times a week*	*About 4 or 5 times a week*	*Several times a day*
Boys (n = 119)	55	24	10	2	5	3	2
Girls (n = 115)	60	17	14	3	2	2	3
3rd yrs (n = 131)	51	24	12	2	5	2	2
5th yrs (n = 103)	65	17	12	2	1	2	2
School A (n = 137)	60	20	10	3	2	2	2
School B (n = 97)	54	22	14	1	5	2	2
Overall	57.3	20.9	12.0	2.1	3.4	2.1	2.1

In 35 per cent of the cases, the bully was reported to be in the same class as the victim, and in another 31 per cent of cases in a different class in the same year. In 24 per cent of cases the bully was in a class one or more years above, this naturally happening almost only with the third year rather than the fifth year pupils. Only 8 per cent of cases involved a bully from one or more years below, and 2 per cent involved bullies from different years.

Of the boys who reported being bullied, the great majority, 88 per cent, reported being bullied only by boys. This was not the case with girls, 48 per cent of whom reported being bullied by boys, 24 per cent by girls and 28 per cent by both boys and girls.

The sex difference in who bullies boys and girls is also reflected in the answers to 'who do you usually think are the worst bullies?' (Table 20.2). Most boys think it is other boys, but many more girls think that boys and girls are both the same.

What form does the bullying take?

When asked 'in what way have you been bullied in school?' 64 per cent of the pupils replied they had not been bullied in the last month (a slightly larger proportion than previously, cf. Table 20.1). Of the remainder, 71 per cent of the replies were that they had 'been teased only'. However 12 per cent were that they had 'been hit and kicked' and 11 per cent that they had 'been both teased, hit and kicked'. Only 2 per cent reported that 'young people demand money or belongings from me'. Rather more girls reported being teased only; rather more boys reported being hit and kicked.

Who knows about the bullying?

The pupils were asked if they had told 'any of your teachers or your form tutor' or 'anyone at home' that they had been bullied. Of those pupils who reported being bullied 'now and then' or more frequently, only 15 out of 51 said that they had told their teachers or form tutor about it, and only 21 had told someone at home about it. In answer to a separate question about whether 'any of your

Table 20.2 Whom pupils report as usually the worst bullies (percentages, n = 119 boys, 115 girls)

	I don't know	*Boys*	*Girls*	*Both the same*
Girls' replies	14	28	12	46
Boys' replies	19	56	6	19

teachers' or 'anyone at home' had talked with them about being bullied at school, 13 of these 51 said that a teacher had talked with them once or twice about their being bullied in school; only one pupil reported that the teacher had talked with them several times. Similarly, 17 said that someone at home had talked to them about it once or twice, and 4 more said this had happened several times.

When asked how often 'the teacher' or 'other young people' 'try to put a stop to it when a young person is being bullied at school', teachers were seen as more effective than other pupils, (Table 20.3). The relatively few pupils who *did* think other young people helped tended to be girls.

What are the feelings of those being bullied?

Pupils who were bullied 'now and then' or more frequently were more likely to report being alone at breaktime (15 out of 51, compared to 20 out of 183 for non-bullied children). They also more frequently reported being lonely in school 'now and then' or more often (12 out of 51, compared to 18 out of 183 for non-bullied children), and feeling less well liked than other young people in their class 'now and then' or more often (31 out of 51, compared to 43 out of 183 non-bullied children). However they did not particularly report having fewer friends, or liking breaktime less.

How frequent is bullying?

The percentage responses to the question 'how often have you taken part in bullying other young people in school?', are shown in Table 20.4. Overall 12 per cent of children reported that they bullied other children 'now and then' or more often, and 4 per cent 'once a week' or more often.

On an analysis of variance by age, sex and school, there were no significant age or school effects, or interactions. There was a highly significant sex effect. Only about 5 per cent of girls reported bullying 'now and then' or more often, but 21 per cent of boys did so (see Table 20.4).

Table 20.3 Whom pupils report as trying to put a stop to it when a young person is being bullied (percentages, n = 234)

	I don't know	*Almost never*	*Once in a while/ now and then*	*Often/almost always*
Teachers	29	13	20	38
Other young people	24	23	44	9

Table 20.4 Percentage of pupils who reported bullying other young people in school

	It hasn't happened	*Only once or twice*	*Now and then*	*About once a week*	*About 2 or 3 times a week*	*About 4 or 5 times a week*	*Several times a day*
Boys (n = 119)	51	29	13	3	2	0	3
Girls (n = 115)	66	29	3	0	1	0	1
3rd yrs (n = 131)	58	32	5	2	1	0	2
5th yrs (n = 103)	59	25	12	0	2	0	2
School A (n = 137)	62	28	7	1	1	0	2
School B (n = 97)	54	30	10	2	2	0	2
Overall	58.5	29.1	8.1	1.3	1.3	0	1.7

How consistent are reports of bullying?

When asked about how often they had bullied other young people *last term*, the frequencies were 9 per cent for 'now and then' or more often, and 3 per cent for 'once a week' or more often. Of the 29 children who reported bullying this term, 18 reported bullying last term as well.

Fewer children reported bullying other young people on their way to and from school, about 3 per cent 'now and then' or more frequently. Of these 8 children, 6 also reported bullying at school.

Who knows about the bullying?

Of the 29 self-reported bullies, 20 said that their teacher had *not* talked to them about their bullying other young people; 7 said a teacher had talked to them once or twice, and 2 said this had happened several times. Similarly, 23 of the 29 said that *no one* at home had talked to them about their bullying other young people; 5 said it had happened once or twice, and one said it had happened several times.

How do bullies feel?

When asked how they usually felt when they saw a young person being bullied in school, 12 out of the 29 bullies replied 'I don't feel much' whereas only 23 of the 205 non-bullies did so. The remaining children chose replies that they thought it 'a bit unpleasant' or 'unpleasant'.

Similarly, 16 of the 29 bullies replied that they would do 'nothing, because it's none of my business', if they saw a young person of their age being bullied in school, compared to only 54 of the 205 non-bullies. The other children chose replies that they thought they ought to help, or would try to help.

When asked 'what do you think of other young people who bully others?', bullies compared to non-bullies over-reported 'I don't know' (17/29 compared to 70/205) and were similar in 'I can understand why they're doing it' (7/29 compared to 47/205). They under-reported on 'it's hard to understand why they're doing it' (5/29 compared to 74/205) and 'it upsets me a lot that they're doing it' (0/29 compared to 14/205).

Were bullies also victims?

The cross-tabulation of being bullied and of bullying others is shown in Table 20.5. Of the 51 bullies and 29 victims, 10 were both bullies and victims. Most of these were boys.

Table 20.5 Number of reports of being bullied in school, and of bullying other young people, in the last month, for boys and girls (n = 119 boys, 115 girls)

(a) Boys

		BULLYING OTHERS			
		It hasn't happened/ only once or twice	*Now and then*	*About once a week or more*	
BEING BULLIED	*It hasn't happened/ only once or twice*	79	11	4	94
	Now and then	8	3	1	12
	About once a week or more	9	1	3	13
		96	15	8	

(b) Girls

		BULLYING OTHERS			
		It hasn't happened/ only once or twice	*Now and then*	*About once a week or more*	
BEING BULLIED	*It hasn't happened/ only once or twice*	85	3	1	89
	Now and then	15	1	0	16
	About once a week or more	9	0	1	10
		109	4	2	

3 COMPARISON WITH PREVIOUS FINDINGS

Summary of findings

- About 1 pupil in 5 reported being bullied at least 'now and then', and 1 in 10 at least 'once a week', over the last month.
- Boys were almost all bullied by other boys. Girls were bullied more by boys, but considerably by girls as well.
- Most bullies were in the same class or year as the victim.
- The majority of the bullying took the form of teasing but about a quarter involved physical violence.
- These victims of bullying were more likely to be alone at breaktime and to feel lonely and less well liked at least now and then.
- Less than half of these pupils had talked to a teacher, or anyone at home about their being bullied. This was despite a *general* perception by many pupils that teachers would try to stop bullying. Not many felt other pupils would do so.
- About 1 pupil in 8 reported bullying other young people at least 'now and then', and about 1 in 25 reported doing so at least 'once a week'.
- Boys are about four times more likely than girls to report bullying others, and for boys the previous figures rise to 1 in 5, and 1 in 12, respectively.
- Over two-thirds of the bullies reported that no one had talked them about their bullying, at school or at home.
- Bullies were generally more tolerant of bullying in others than non-bullies were.

The summary of findings above is broadly consistent with the Scandinavian research concerning the context of bullying, but differs considerably in the overall frequency of bully/victim problems, which appear to be at least *twice* those typically reported in Norway.

As regards the context of the bullying, the age and sex trends parallel those shown in other studies. Olweus (1989) has reported a decrease in age with frequency of being bullied, but not in frequency of bullying; and a predominant sex difference in the latter. Similarly, the Norwegian studies have found that in junior high school less than half of the students involved have talked to teachers or parents about bully/victim problems.

Like Olweus (1989), we found that bullying on the way to and from school was considerably less frequent than bullying at school. Olweus (1989) concluded from this that 'the school is, no doubt, where most of the bullying occurs'. However we did include an extra question on whether pupils had been bullied anywhere else, and nearly as many pupils responded to this as replied that they had been bullied in school at least 'now and then'. Of course, this extra question tapped a large number of places where bullying might happen. Thus, it probably is true that the school is the one place where bullying is most likely, as Olweus suggests; but it also seems that in aggregate, a roughly equal amount of bullying may happen outside school.

In general, the consistency of these findings with those reported in Scandinavia is impressive. However, in one respect our findings are markedly discrepant. This is in the overall incidence of bully/victim problems.

If we take at least 'now and then' as the criterion, our incidence figures for being a victim are 22 per cent, and for bullies, 12 per cent. This compares with figures from Olweus (1989) of about 6 per cent and 7 per cent, respectively, at this age level. If we take at least 'once a week' as the criterion, our incidence figures for being a victim are 10 per cent, and for bullies, 4 per cent. This compares with figures from Olweus (1989) of about 3 per cent, and 2 per cent, respectively, for all ages. Using this same criterion Roland (1989) reports an incidence of about 1–3 per cent for being bullied, and 1–3 per cent for bullies, for 13 to 15 year olds in S-W Norway.

Thus our present figures are about three times larger for victims, and twice as large for bullies, than the Norwegian data, independent of the criteria taken.

There could be a number of explanations for this. First, of course, the data are only obtained from two schools. Perhaps these schools are exceptionally troubled by this problem. However we believe them to be not untypical of large city comprehensive schools in Britain. They were not selected on the basis of any particular problems being reported. Other studies we are carrying out in middle and secondary schools also seem to be finding a comparable level of bully/victim problems. This level is also broadly consistent with that reported by Stephenson and Smith (1989) on the basis of teacher report (23 per cent involved in bully/victim problems in junior school) and to that reported by Arora and Thompson (1987) on the basis of 12- to 14-year-old pupils' replies to a booklet, given to them at a small comprehensive school.

Second, one might question the validity of questionnaire responses. However, while it is always possible that a few pupils may fake answers to the questionnaire, we have generally been impressed by the seriousness with which pupils treat it. The responses to the questionnaire are consistent, both within the questionnaire when responses are compared (for example when the incidence of being bullied is compared across a number of questions which assess this, directly or indirectly), and in the structure of the answers compared to other available data. We are currently comparing questionnaire and interview data on bully/victim problems; our provisional conclusion so far is that the questionnaire is preferable to the interview as a confidential, anonymous means of getting information on bullying.

In summary, this and other evidence is beginning to suggest quite strongly that bully/victim problems in British schools are considerable, and markedly greater in extent than in Norwegian schools. We also know that victims experience less happy and at times very distressing circumstances with peers, while bullies are experiencing a training in aggressive behaviour which may well potentiate future antisocial activities. If bullying and victimisation are at anything like the levels reported, there is no excuse for complacency in our response. A coordinated intervention strategy has been shown to be effective in the Norwegian context

(Olweus 1989). It is urgent that in Britain, too, we not only find out more about the nature of the problem, but also take active steps to remedy it.

REFERENCES

Arora, C. M. J. and Thompson, D. A. (1987) 'Defining bullying for a secondary school', *Education and Child Psychology* 4, 110–20.

Elton Report (1989) *Discipline in Schools*, London: HMSO.

Olweus, D. (1989) 'Bully/victim problems among schoolchildren: basic facts and effects of a school based intervention program', in K. Rubin and D. Pepler (eds), *The Development and Treatment of Childhood Aggression*, Hillsdale, N.J.: Erlbaum.

Roland, E. (1989) 'Bullying: the Scandinavian research tradition', in D. P. Tattum and D. A. Lane (eds), *Bullying in Schools*, Stoke-on-Trent: Trentham Books.

Stephenson, P. and Smith, D. (1989) 'Bullying in the junior school', in D. P. Tattum and D. A. Lane (eds), *Bullying in Schools*, Stoke-on-Trent: Trentham Books.

Tattum, D. P. and Lane, D. A. (1989) *Bullying in Schools*, Stoke-on-Trent: Trentham Books.

Chapter 21

From school to schemes

Out of education into training

Robert Hollands

Source: Edited version of Chapter 4 of Hollands, R.G. (1990) *The Long Transition: Class, Culture and Youth Training*, London: Macmillan.

This chapter is drawn from a study of the transition from school to work experienced by working-class young people in a large city in the West Midlands, conducted during the mid-1980s, when YTS – the Youth Training Scheme – was a route taken by large numbers of school leavers. In the first part of the chapter, Robert Hollands uses interviews with young people on training schemes to reveal their experience of the final years of compulsory schooling. It was widely seen as a negative, irrelevant experience. Hollands then contrasts the hopes and expectations young people held about work with the harsh reality of a shrinking labour market. In the final section he describes the often random way in which young people found their way into training schemes as a substitute for work.

Young people are in the midst of a new transition, delineated by an arm of the state, whereby they are no longer schoolchildren nor are they fully fledged workers entitled to proper wages and conditions. And yet, they do not easily succumb to the imposition of a new transition into work. Instead, in negotiating their way through the new vocationalism, young people actively help to produce a variety of identities and transitions into work and adulthood. Experiences of schooling provide one of the main social contexts for how they react to and negotiate their way on to training schemes.

1 EXPERIENCES OF SCHOOLING[1]

Three main experiences of schooling most often recalled by trainees were: (a) the desire to leave school and move into work; (b) a resentment of the inapplicability of the education curriculum and criticism of schooling relations and exams; and (c) making the best of a bad situation, 'muckin' about' and having a good time as they reached the end of their compulsory time in education.

A significant majority of young people interviewed were adamant that they wanted to leave school for the world of work, many at the earliest possible moment:

BH: Did you leave school early?
Jackie: I left school in May – I was 16 the day I left.

BH: When did you start thinking about leaving school?
Ben: At the end of the second year – I just used to stay at home, that was the fourth year, sit at home and write poems or go for a walk ... I eventually stopped going to school during the mock exams.

While leaving school was the wish of the majority, there was a significant gender dimension to those few who wanted to stay on in an attempt to pass some exams.[2] For example, there was a small subgroup of young women who saw exams as an essential stepping stone to a vocational career (i.e. in nursing, childcare, working with the handicapped, fashion, etc.). This is not to say they were academically oriented. However, many realised that such vocational courses offered by colleges often required some exam results. The YTS, for this group, was a second option or fall back choice when they failed to achieve satisfactory exam results. On the other side, there were very few working-class males in the sample who specifically mentioned they wished to stay on at school. The dominant desire of working-class youth as a whole social group, in this study, was to leave school to search for work.

One of the primary reasons for wanting to leave, in addition to the status gained by moving into the adult world of work, was criticism of the school curriculum and a dislike of the social relations of education. Many working-class school leavers come out of education deeply wounded by the experience. A sense of failure, frustration and powerlessness over what is taught combined to create quite negative self-images and impressions of school:

Julie: Educationally, I'm no good – on the education side I'm not that good. As thick as two short planks. But um, practically ...
BH: As what?
Julie: I'm as thick as two short planks. It's a saying. I'm thick. Um, but – I'd say educationally I'm no good, but practically I am good. I'm good with children, I'm good with handicapped, I'm good with everything – and shopwork and everything. But educationally I'm no good. I tried to go to college – I had this feeling that if I went to college to try and get this course then I'd be all right. But it just doesn't happen with me.
BH: Do you think at school they don't appreciate those other things? I mean you were saying.
Julie: You have to be educationally – if yer not educationally good, in this place they just put you in um, elementary classes. And they stick you in there and that's about it. And they help you try and build up your education but ... yuh know, more help.

BH: Were you glad to leave school then?

Julie: I wasn't, I didn't really mind leavin'. There were no tears or anything [laughs]. I just left on goodwill with everybody.

This personal confession expresses a number of broader processes at work in a class-biased education system. For example, it demonstrates how streaming and the curriculum merge to produce self-blame and evaluations that one is 'thick' or a failure. And while many young people realise that they do indeed possess real practical skills, they also recognise that these are often undervalued in relation to academic knowledge. Finally, Julie's comment hints at how young people's frustrations at school can get translated into positive evaluations of training schemes, which are often seen as relevant, practical and related to the world of work.

Other young people provided equally forceful critiques of the education system and curriculum, particularly as it relates to preparing them for life in the 'real' world:

Mick: All these things yuh learn at school – is not really genuine knowledge at all yuh need out in the world – yuh don't need nothin' of that.

BH: What was the worst thing about school? Ah, what subjects and things?

Billy: English and maths are the worst subjects you can get.

Chris: Science ... you ain't gonna be a scientist, yuh ain't gonna end up a scientist in secondary school are yuh?

BH: What about mathematics?

Billy: It's useful in some ways ... but the things they teach yuh, yuh know, logs and all that sort of stuff – simple addings and minusing and timesin' – that's all yuh really need. Yuh don't really need all these er logarithms, Pythagoras, Pythagoras' theories and all – I was at school right, got this K + A = B or somethin' like that. I thought, where did they get these letters from and what do they mean? It really got me lost that did.

If the 'real world' is defined primarily in terms of work, home and community, then school was definitely not the institution in which one expected to gain 'really useful knowledge'. Similarly, within working-class culture, purely theoretical knowledge is often viewed as totally absurd, as Billy's final comment so cogently expresses.

More specific criticisms of the school curriculum revolved around the stress on examinations and the ranking of traditional academic subjects over technical ones. The exam system continues to dominate what is meant by success in schools and differentiates 'intelligent' students from the others:

Jan: Well, the O-levels are the higher grade one and the CSEs are the lower one. And I took the O-levels which were the higher grade one for more sort of intelligent people. I didn't do very well [laughs].

Furthermore, in many cases there is still a bias towards traditional academic subjects in school and young working-class people are acutely aware that technically based subjects are somehow viewed as inferior. This should not imply that all young people readily accepted this distinction. However, they were not always in a position to challenge the situation or relate this dilemma to the outside world of work:

Ben: It's a vicious circle really 'cos they say yuh gotta work towards qualifications to get a job. Then you see the real world outside and there's no jobs around so you think I'm not doin' this anymore. So you drop out and then you do find out that if you do have qualifications it's an advantage, not much, but it is an advantage. But you can't work towards that advantage 'cos it's too late.

Clearly, the contradictions generated by the real world of work and the limited benefit of qualifications for many working-class jobs created a 'no win' situation for many young people.

If the proponents of the new vocationalism are right about anything, it is their criticism of the continuing elitism of much of the educational system. This should not imply that the insertion of work-based subjects back into schools is only a recent phenomenon or is automatically a positive thing in its own terms. Many educational theorists have argued that vocationalism is slowly coming to dominate the school curriculum (Bates *et al.* 1984). The problem has been that the rise of the new vocationalism in schools has actually been used to justify and exacerbate the distinction between 'hand' and 'head' labour.

Pupils have had their own criticism of the irrelevance of schooling for many working-class jobs before the MSC made its assault on education and these two views should not be conflated. Working-class youngsters have long seen through the value of compulsory schooling (even liberal teaching methods and career guidance) in helping them make the transition from school to work, and instead have relied on their own cultural forms and family/community contacts to make the transition.[3] A lack of real jobs for young people in the future may signal a further breakdown in the classroom, characterised by disruptive behaviour and non-cooperation from many students:

Kathy: My brother, he don't even bother in school anymore 'cos he knows that you don't need qualifications to get on YTS. So he's stopped tryin' – he's not doin' anything in school – just messin' about.

Proponents of the new vocationalism have sought to build on these dissatisfactions as justification for a work-based school curriculum. However, they fail to see that young people will similarly reject aspects of vocationalism unless a direct link to real jobs can be demonstrated and many will continue to rely on their own cultural milieu for support, rather than accept patronising life and social skills educational models.

In addition to their disdain of the school curriculum, there was a generally negative evaluation of the social relations of schooling. In other words, the desire to leave school was based partly around wanting to shed the child-like image of school and enter into the adult world of work:

BH: Did you notice a big difference in the way people treat you on YTS from school? I mean is YTS like school at all?

Julie: From school – from school to college you don't know what's, what's goin' on in the world. You don't, it sounds terrible, but you don't. And when you come on this [YTS] you find out that you've got to look after yourself – that you've got this backing, you've got like at work, you can, if anything goes wrong you can fall back on this and they push yuh back up and yuh get on your way. But yuh know after this you haven't got anybody to push you back up on a pedestal, you know.

Besides not teaching one about the real world, school relations were also viewed as 'immature':

Nigel: Well, when I was at school, I really didn't think much of school. I mean, any young person could say that, I didn't think much of school. I couldn't see the point of gettin' up every morning and coming into this building and jus' sit down – and um, school was um, a very immature place to be really. I don't think anybody in school could actually say, when I was in the fifth form, that you were mature. Because you go home and you come back and you're the same person you were the day before. And um, very childlike manner at times.

While this immaturity is often projected on to school leavers themselves, clearly the problem lies with the whole institutional structure of education. For example, many young people felt that teachers had no confidence in them and hence treated them as children. The irony is that working-class pupils may be labelled childish precisely for developing coping behaviours necessary to endure compulsory schooling, which they rightly perceive as blocking their transition into adulthood.

Compulsory schooling up to the age of 16 means that many working-class pupils have little option but to make the best of a bad situation. The third recollection trainees had of school, then, related to an endless array of stories of 'muckin' about', having fun with mates, winding up teachers and generally making do until their sixteenth birthday.

Disillusionment with formal education often took a few years to set in. Many remembered their initial entry into school as one of general conformity, followed by a transitional period whereby the last few years were viewed as a 'waste of time'. Related research on working-class transitions from school to work shows that although an overall pattern exists, there are crucial gender differences – with the male peer group structure being perhaps more organic to this transformation (Willis 1977, Griffin 1985). Billy's story, for instance, demonstrates a shift from trying to be a 'posh' student to his coming out as one of the 'lads':

Billy: [laughs] I used to be an upper-class twat. When I went to Broadhurst they changed me.
Mick: Yuh haven't changed much.
Billy: I 'ave, I used to go to Knightsbridge, that was an upper-class school ... Knightsbridge – when I was there, there was all these top notchers and everything, yuh know, ha, ha, ha [thumbs his nose].

The pattern for working-class girls takes on quite a different form. As Griffin (1985) argues, best friendships rather than collective group structures characterise female school relations. Additionally, female transitions involve preparing for marriage and the domestic sphere, and forms of deviance amongst working-class girls are often not as visible as that of the lads. This does not mean that young women as a social group were any less disruptive than young men, or equally unsatisfied with the social relations of schooling. In fact, even Julie, who had largely conformed to the ideology of the YTS, admitted she was a bit of a 'troublemaker' in school:

BH: Did you muck around in school?
Julie: Yea, a bit yea [laughs] – quite a bit. I was in the lower class anyway so it didn't make any difference to me. I could bunk off and go to the toilets [laughs].

Clearly there were varied gender reasons for disliking school and different oppositional strategies were adopted.

While schooling relations are an important social context for understanding how some youngsters relate to the various skilling regimes on the YTS, they are not the sole factor in determining school leavers' expectations of training schemes. Also crucial in preparing young people's acceptance of schemes is the massive disjuncture between their expectations upon leaving school and the brutal realities of the youth labour market.

2 LEAVING SCHOOL: EXPECTATIONS AND REALITIES

While the main option for the majority of working-class youths was to leave school in search of work, a small number also mentioned college or apprenticeships. Whatever 'choice' was eventually settled on, there was often an unbridgeable gap between what many of these young people expected and what real opportunities existed in the labour market. One of the key elements of the new transitions is the substitution of training schemes for the expectation of work – aided, in part, by the sheer monotony of unemployment.

Of course, there were some young people who left school because of lost opportunities and unforeseen events. These circumstances included having to change schools in mid-year, personal problems, a dislike of teachers and 'messing up' one's exams:

Shabaz: I wanted to go back to Broadhurst because ah, all the people I was with then, I had, they all got good marks in the exams and I was all right in school. I didn't take any exams though [at the new school] – I didn't get the chance.

In most cases these missed opportunities were seen in strictly personal terms and in the context of individual failure:

Kathy: I just messed up in school, it was my own fault. You can't get in the police force if you haven't got qualifications. It was my own fault really, I should have done more work at school.

It is far too easy to substitute a middle-class model of choices and options about staying on at school – but for many working-class youngsters life simply didn't work that way. While only a minority actually wanted to stay on, circumstances meant that even these few were often forced to leave early.

There was also a small group of young people interviewed who saw college as a possible option in a shrinking job market. Getting a place on a college course was again no simple choice. Many courses required some kind of entry qualification and there was always the problem of money:

Liz: I was going to go to college full time, but I couldn't get any help. I couldn't get a grant or anything ... You don't get any help at all from anywhere. The only place where you get decent grants is when you go to university. I went to find out about it when I got interviewed to do this part-time course I'm doing [in fashion]. I was after a full-time place at the college to do a BTEC diploma course. And I went to the grants office to find out if I could actually get a grant and I found that I could get something like £6 a week at the most, if I got a grant at all.

Some young people who started out on college courses, before going on to the YTS, mentioned that they weren't really ready for the experience:

Nigel: When I was at college, I was doing part time and I tended to slack off very much and not do much work ... I used to spend a lot of time in the canteen actually doing nothing, just wasting time. And my attitude was very carefree indeed. I didn't really put my mind to my work.

So a lack of experience, support, money and qualifications often closed off the college option for many working-class school leavers. Some of this group joined college-based schemes and used the YTS to simulate the college experience.

For the majority, however, college was not seen as a viable option. It was perceived as an extension of formal schooling and was to be avoided at all costs. Those who were effectively forced to undertake a part of their YTS off-the-job training in a local college often mentioned that they saw it as 'a doss' or 'school-like'. Absenteeism in these situations was high.

The vast majority of early leavers left school with the expectation of finding employment. However, their initial enthusiasm and optimism about obtaining work soon faded when the task proved to be much more difficult than they originally anticipated:

Mandy: I'd rather get a job, that's what I thought . . . thought I'd look around for a bit and look for things. Now I'm on YTS.

Dan: I didn't particularly want to go on a scheme, but I knew I had to do something. So, I hadn't really thought beforehand what – I thought I'd get a job as well, but that soon proved to be wrong [laughs].

In fact, six months after leaving school that year, only 9.2 per cent of fifth formers in the city were in employment. Hidden within this overall figure is the influence other factors such as race, gender and disability had upon obtaining work. For example, only 3.6 per cent of Afro-Caribbean, 4.3 per cent of Asians, 8 per cent of women and 18 out of 583 disabled fifth formers found employment over this same period.[4] The apprenticeship route into a trade had virtually collapsed. However much young school leavers expected and wanted to find a job, the reality of the youth labour market prevented them from doing so.

A final option, if it can be considered an option at all, was to become unemployed (go on the 'dole'). Legislation in force at the time meant that young people refusing a scheme could lose up to 40 per cent of their social security payment. Recent changes in benefit entitlement effectively mean the YTS is now compulsory (i.e. no payment will be made to refusers or those who leave the scheme to become unemployed). At the time of this research, there was a trend whereby early school leavers had to wait for a period before they qualified for benefit. They often viewed this initial period as a break from school and work, but many soon found they became extremely bored and fed up with having little or no money. Schoolday perceptions of the dole as a 'bit of a lark' were quickly altered:

Baz: I thought, oh, great, get outta school – on the dole now. Everybody thinks, Oh god, let's all go on the dole, doss around, just get money for dossin' around . . . yuh go out and, it's more or less boring.

Liz: I didn't want to be on the dole particularly, you know. I wasn't thinking oh this is great I'm not doin' anything, I don't have to bother gettin' up for work or anything like that.

Billy: When you first go on the dole it's great . . .
Mick: No you don't.
Billy: Yuh know, gettin' paid for dossin' about. But once yuh get used to it, it's really bad, it gets on yer nerves, it's boring and all. I've only bin on it a month or two.
Chris: I'm tellin' yuh, yuh lose, you lose the habit of gettin' up in the morning. It's crap, I tell yuh.

None of the young people I spoke to voluntarily chose to go on the dole. Most had left school with the intention of finding a job and this remained an important goal for them throughout the scheme. It was a combination of a strong desire to work and grow up and the dull experience of unemployment which led many working-class youths back to the Careers Office, only to be offered a training scheme substitute. More and more youngsters are now moving straight from school on to schemes. Part of the reason is 'compulsion' (i.e. no benefit) as well as a recognition that there are very few jobs about. It is also impossible to ignore the hyped up advertising campaigns conducted by the MSC or the importance of the Careers Service in promoting training schemes. Increasingly, the transition into work for many school leavers is now predicated upon the expectation of being placed on the YTS.

3 'CHOOSING' A SCHEME: INFORMAL KNOWLEDGE AND THE ROLE OF THE CAREERS SERVICE

In order to provide a more complete and realistic picture of how young people actually choose a particular type of training scheme, it is useful to compare and contrast young people's informal knowledge of the YTS with the information provided through the Careers Service. While Careers affords the main official mechanism for being placed on schemes young people's own focal concerns and knowledge, drawn from the wider working-class community, are not incidental to this process. What is significant here is the changing relationship and balance of forces between the official agencies and the informal culture.

With virtually no chance of finding a job and with the sour taste of unemployment in their mouths, many of these young people turned to the Careers Service for help and advice. The vast majority of school leavers interviewed gained information and were put in touch with their scheme through their local Careers Office. Some also received advice from careers teachers in schools. Interviews with Careers Officers in the area made it clear that the new vocationalism had literally transformed their entire job description. Advice about schemes, rather than jobs, has become the norm.

Earlier, I argued that many working-class school leavers became acutely aware that their chances of obtaining employment were slim. For some, this realisation began in school:

Mick: Everyone was sayin', everyone didn't think we'd get a job. Everyone thought we'd go straight on the dole ... Yuh had a career lesson, listen, yuh had a career lesson, instead of talkin' about jobs, they talk about how to sign on the dole.

In other cases, expectations of training schemes in place of work were also planted in school:

Finchy: Well, when I was, when I, yea, when I was at school that was all they [careers teachers] told me I could have, like. They didn't mention the job side, it was what training scheme do you want to go on when you leave school, right?

This was also the kind of advice many young people received when they visited their local Careers Office:

BH: Were they realistic about your chances of getting work, do you think?
Shanaz: They just try and tell us to go on a training scheme. You have to go on a training scheme now, you don't have any choice.

Only one trainee recalled that Careers actually mentioned a job. The role of Careers in helping to prepare young school leavers to accept the YTS, in place of work, cannot be overestimated.

In discussions about the role of the Careers Service, some young people volunteered additional information as to how they were treated while speaking to officers about their future prospects:

Dan: Their attitude was ah – it was the first year of YTS and it was the first term of people actually going on to YTS. And their attitude was 'at long last we've got something we can give to them to get them out of the way quickly'. And ah, like they just were good, glad to get rid of you as soon as possible and get on to the next person and get rid of them.

A good number of trainees mentioned that they felt Careers people saw the YTS as an easy answer to their problems. Schemes were talked about enthusiastically as new career opportunities, rather than as a substitute for work and a proper wage.

While Careers may have been the main venue for finding out about and getting an interview with a particular scheme, all young people had prior knowledge, alternative sources of information and culturally based dispositions towards training schemes. Much of this information was based upon appraisals of the Youth Opportunities Programme (YOP) which predated the YTS and was heavily criticised, not least by the participants themselves. These often less than favourable evaluations circulated within families, schools and neighbourhoods and came from older brothers, sisters, parents and friends:

Margaret: It's terrible this trainin' scheme wage – my dad calls it slave labour.
Mick: That's what the YOP was, that's why they scrapped the YOP. 'Cos yuh didn't go to the training centre, yuh just went straight to the firm – they'd just use yuh as slave, slave labour.

Mandy: I couldn't be bothered to go on one. All I heard was that they were bad. And ah, I met a friend that was down here on this scheme and she told me to come along.

Angus: They were sayin' like it's a bad thing – people at school were sayin' cheap an' all that.

The possession of this type of information made many young people wary of the YTS. Conversations with friends sometimes helped them to distinguish between and choose the best available scheme. Although parental opinion was important, many families did not have details about the scheme when it was first launched and, anyway, there were few alternatives to boost the family wage. Certainly, one view was that all schemes were 'slave labour'. Other parents saw the scheme virtually as a regular job and welcomed the extra income. Information gleaned at school, from teachers and other pupils, was also taken into account and influenced school leavers' views of the YTS.

With the aid of professional career counselling, one might initially expect that a young person's choice of scheme and type of training would reflect his or her interest in a particular occupational area. While this was sometimes the case, there were often multiple and conflicting factors which contoured this decision. One of the key factors influencing young people's choice was their orientation towards work and how susceptible they were to officers' suggestions. Some young people were predisposed towards abstract and more generalised forms of manual labour and were usually directed towards broad-based training schemes offering a wide range of work experience. In other words, they possessed a very real cultural knowledge that many contemporary working-class jobs do not require a specialist skill or in-depth training. On the other hand, a number of young people became influenced by certain officers' portrayal of the YTS as a career stepping-stone. They genuinely believed that schemes could be used to work one's way up in a profession and develop a career (this usually, although not always, occurred in the service sector). Suffice it to say here that the Careers Service emphasis on the YTS as a genuine 'career opportunity' is attractive to a section of the young working class.

A second element of class culture, which often overshadowed any straightforward choice of scheme, was locality. The location of a scheme in relation to the family household was an important consideration for many young people. Garnie, who desperately wanted to pursue training and possibly a career in electronics, gave up the idea because of the scheme location:

BH: Did you just come to one scheme?

Garnie: No, this scheme I came to because I don't wanna go to no scheme that's in the Isle of Wight or somethin' like that . . . you know? I prefer to just get out of my bed and just walk down this road here and come here. I don't want to go, he wanted to send me to Ashton . . . I told him no I don't wanna go out there, it's too far.

BH: So it was the location of the scheme that was . . .

Garnie: Yea, it was electronics he said, but it was too far though.

Despite the fact that most school leavers were given a number of schemes to visit, many picked one near their area, even if it did not suit their first occupational choice. Very few actually visited more than one YTS programme and there was no way to compare what different schemes were really offering.[5] Part of the reason why a training scheme is chosen on the basis of locality, I would argue, is a continuing working-class preference for familiarity, neighbourhood and easy access to the family household (Clarke *et al.* 1979).

Finally, the choice of a scheme offering training in a particular occupational area did not automatically guarantee work experience in that field. Once accepted on to a scheme, obtaining one's initial choice also depended upon whether an appropriate work placement could be found or one's interest in a certain field matched one's aptitude. This often led to some bizarre training swaps:

Dan: Well I went on to the scheme originally to do computer programming, or if I couldn't do that computer operating and that. There was no question about my ability to do that. When I went to my interview or the chat and they said 'fine, fine, we'll accept you' and ah – I did computing at school and I was quite good at it. So when it actually came to them findin' us a job they said 'well, we've had a bit of a problem tryin' to find you, tryin' to find computer placements. They're not as easy to find as we expected. So is there anything else you'd like to do?' So I ended up doing plumbing [laughs] and I wasn't very good at all.

There were quite a number of training and career changes in the movement from school to the YTS. Young women often switched from one type of traditionally female labour to another (i.e. hairdressing to office work). Many young lads who requested specific craft training in a particular field were given a broad-based training in the construction field instead. Getting on to a proper scheme and receiving training and work experience in one's chosen field upon leaving school was more a matter of luck and chance than a planned decision.

In summary, the ultimate decision to get on to a scheme must be seen in the larger context of working-class attitudes towards formal education, a lack of jobs and school leavers' aversion to the dole. The process of being accepted for a specific scheme was the product of a combination of official mechanisms (Careers), informal working-class knowledge (cultural forms drawn from family, friends, school networks) and the pull of locality and community. As the new vocationalism slowly takes hold and schemes become the norm, some of these older mechanisms used to find out about training and work may further diminish. In their place a new transition, substituting schemes for jobs and professional advice for local class knowledge, is evolving. At the moment, however, most of these training choices appear to resemble a great training lottery, rather than a service sensitive to the needs, cultures and desires of working-class youth.

NOTES

1 Class-based experiences of schooling, although not determining, are important in understanding how young people respond to going on to schemes and what they do

when they actually get there. Due to the self-imposed limitations of the study, I have relied on young people's major recollections of their school years. The point is not to provide a comprehensive presentation of these experiences (this has been conducted elsewhere), but rather use them to help comprehend young people's orientations towards the YTS. For discussions of schooling, see Hargreaves (1967), Sharp (1976), Willis (1977), Davies (1979), Ball (1981), Stanworth (1983), Griffin (1985), Lees (1986).

2 A large-scale survey of the young unemployed in a nearby town showed that, overall, 56 per cent of males compared to 47 per cent of females said they wanted to leave school 'very much'. White working-class males were the most overtly disaffected with school, with 61 per cent saying they wanted to leave 'very much'. See Willis (1985: 203).

3 For historical examinations of working-class responses to compulsory schooling see Humphries (1981) and CCCS Education Group (1981).

4 These figures are from the local Careers Service and pertain to the period in which this research was conducted.

5 While the local MSC produced a directory of the YTS in the city, it was not in a form that could be used by school leavers to choose between schemes.

REFERENCES

Ball, S. (1981) *Beachside Comprehensive: A Case Study of a Secondary School*, Cambridge: Cambridge University Press.

Bates, I., Clarke, J., Cohen, P., Finn, D., Moore, R. and Willis, P. (1984) *Schooling for the Dole*, London: Macmillan.

CCCS Education Group (1981) *Unpopular Education*, London: Hutchinson.

Clarke, J., Critcher, C. and Johnson, R. (eds) (1979) *Working Class Culture*, London: Hutchinson.

Davies, B. (1979) *In Whose Interests? From Social Education to Social and Life Skills Training*, Leicester: National Youth Bureau.

Griffin, C. (1985) *Typical Girls?*, London: Routledge & Kegan Paul.

Hargreaves, D. (1967) *Social Relations in a Secondary School*, London: Routledge & Kegan Paul.

Humphries, S. (1981) *Hooligans or Rebels?*, Oxford: Basil Blackwell.

Lees, S. (1986) *Losing Out: Sexuality and Adolescent Girls*, London: Hutchinson.

Sharp, S. (1976) *Just Like a Girl*, Harmondsworth: Penguin.

Stanworth, M. (1983) *Gender and Schooling*, London: Hutchinson.

Willis, P. (1977) *Learning to Labour*, Westmead: Saxon House.

—— (1985) *The Social Condition of Young People in Wolverhampton in 1984*, Wolverhampton: Wolverhampton Borough Council.

Chapter 22

Stressing education

Children in care

Felicity Fletcher-Campbell

In this chapter Felicity Fletcher-Campbell reviews the routes by which children arrive in care and stresses the importance of continuity in planning the education of children in care. She argues that education may be neglected when discussions take place about the needs of children taken into care, and that low expectations for educational achievement may have far-reaching consequences.

Of the current under-18 population in England and Wales who are of statutory school age, about 66,000 (only a little over 0.5 per cent) are 'in care' but, although the actual numbers may be relatively small, their associated problems are often considerable.

A child can be legally received into the care of the local authority by various routes. There have been attempts to categorise children in care but these are largely unsuccessful as boundaries are often blurred. Basically, children are either received into care by court order (the majority of these have been subject to neglect or abuse, though a proportion are deemed 'beyond parental control' or have offended) or voluntarily, when there is some degree of cooperation between families and social services (the family might be homeless, the home conditions unsatisfactory, or a parent be ill, for example). Until the 1989 Children Act, the legal situation was that education departments could initiate care proceedings for children with poor attendance. However, the Children Act no longer allows this and, instead, introduced Education Supervision Orders which local authorities may apply to take out. The intention is that the local authority will appoint someone to work with the family and advise parents as to how they might improve their children's attendance. The opportunity to receive the children into care is still there but school non-attendance is only one factor among many and there is no longer any clear route between non-attendance and being taken away from home.

Some children will move in and out of care rapidly, within a few weeks or months; others may spend the whole of their childhood in care, either regularly in and out of it, or in care permanently (if they are not adopted). Of those who remain some time in care, some may have a relatively stable career while, for others, it may be more disrupted, with a number of short stays in various placements – either foster or residential or even at home 'on trial'. Placements (or where a child actually lives after reception into the care of a local authority) can have a profound influence on social adjustment and educational careers. They are also interdependent: the care placement is liable to break down if the education placement fails. Frail relationships can reach breaking point if a 'difficult' young person is at home all day and, in any case, working foster carer(s) invariably cannot supervise the child during the day. On the annual census date for children in care (March 31) in 1987, just over half (53 per cent) of the in-care population were in foster homes, 20 per cent were in residential community homes and the remainder either with parents, relatives or in some other accommodation (older children might, for example, be in hostels).

In many ways, it is quite understandable that the educational arrangements for children in care have remained neglected. Other more urgent needs, such as finding a roof over the child's head at short notice, push education low down the social workers' list of priorities. When the total number of foster homes is permanently below the target and there is the need for 'matching', for example, temperaments and ethnicity, or removing children from their locality on the grounds of their own safety, the educational suitability of a particular care placement is far back in people's minds. It is often not possible to maintain a child at his or her previous school without incurring considerable transport costs (and long journey times for the children concerned) to which local authority officers are loath to commit themselves. There is the feeling that there are schools everywhere but foster homes are few and far between. Once in care, a child may have a series of care placements – some planned, others not (as a result of breakdowns) – which, traumatic in themselves, compound disruption to educational careers.

The education component of children in care's statutory reviews can be scanty and ill-formed, and often focuses merely on attendance and social behaviour rather than progress and achievement. At least one authority has recently redesigned its review report forms specifically to ensure that a fuller response to 'education' is prompted. In some cases it is not considered appropriate for school representatives to attend (there are various understandings of 'confidentiality' for example), but in others a representative from the child's school may attend. In the case of primary-aged children, this is usually the head teacher – which is relatively straightforward. With secondary pupils, however, it can be the tutor, head of year or pastoral deputy. The tutor may know the child best but, unless supported from above, may have insufficient 'clout' to effect desired structural change such as an independent timetable or part-time schooling for the child. On the other hand, the deputy head may have the necessary 'power' but, unless adequately briefed, be insufficiently familiar with the particular young person. With the advent of local management of schools, and the problems of providing supply cover, it may be that schools are increasingly reluctant to free staff to attend reviews. Sometimes, a full written report is adequate but it is not unknown for a social worker to phone up the school, get a verbal report on the child and then relay this at the review; the opportunities for 'reinterpretation' in such a situation, be it conscious or unconscious, are obviously rife.

One of the most salient characteristics of children in care is that their lives are fragmented: various people (foster carers, residential social workers, field social workers, natural parents) at various times have a relatively intimate knowledge of them but, often, the overview is lacking. Whereas most children have a parent who has recourse to a memory supplying continuity of knowledge, children in care lack this and 'memory' has to be replaced by files and records. But the quality of these is often inadequate: data such as where all an authority's children in care are receiving education, or a linear log of an individual child's educational career, are generally only accessible by means of a manual trawl through case files (which can amount to three bulging, largely unsystematic wallets for a 10 year old).

The problem of fragmentation is not helped by unclear management and poor liaison between, and within, education and social services departments; and, related to this, mutual misunderstanding and ignorance among teachers and social workers, and education and social services officers. Bureaucratic and professional boundaries often obscure the fact that the child is in the care of the local authority – not merely the social services department. The problem of inadequate and ineffective multi-professional cooperation is not unique to the management of children in care: uneasiness was identified by Goacher *et al.*'s (1988) study of the implementation of the 1981 Education Act. Over twenty years ago the Seebohm Report (1968) recommended that there should be a unitary department for attending to children's needs rather than responsibility being spread among Education, Health and Social Services. Flexible and responsive partnerships between professionals are vital for the welfare of the more disadvantaged groups, be the disadvantage temporary or more permanent: pathways are often clearer and straighter for the better endowed. Inadequacy as regards partnerships is not only inefficient and wasteful of resources, but it also threatens equal opportunities.

Children in care have been affected by integrationist policies. The number of Community Homes with education on the premises has declined since an adverse HMI report (DES 1980) and it is now more common for children in residential care to be educated in mainstream schools with support rather than in educational units attached to children's homes. Teachers – either employed by social services departments, originally to staff education units, or seconded from education departments – are now involved in much more support teaching in mainstream schools. The model is akin to that of special educational needs support teaching though, arguably, the role has greater complexity as more issues are involved and there are more points of contact. These teachers' functions include supporting children within the classroom, dealing with school-related problems, running homework clubs, helping find school places for children when this is necessary and acting as advocates and advisers. This practice, which had reaped dividends where it exists, is not widespread and there are few authorities which have a clear and positive policy in this area. One of the consequences of this is that in-service training to support the education of children in care may be negligible or non-existent and teachers are having to take on new and often threatening responsibilities with goodwill but little professional preparation.

A proportion of children in care also have disabilities or have been categorised as having moderate or severe learning difficulties. They may be Statemented either before coming into care or subsequently. The foster parents of children who are the subject of statements often feel vulnerable about educational issues.

A critical outcome of the social status popularly afforded children in care is the low educational expectations that are held of them. The ready acceptance of the young people going to low status jobs and assumptions regarding low ability and poor motivation are widespread and largely unchallenged; they are supported by such sentiments as 'unhappy children cannot learn' and a desire on the part of many social workers to sort out the emotional problems before giving any thought to progress at school. That this is so is particularly depressing in the light of Rutter *et al.*'s (1983) follow-up study of children in care which suggested that it was those best-qualified educationally who seemed to thrive best in life as adults. Whether or not the educational factor was cause or effect is not clear but to ignore it and not subject it to scrutiny would seem to be both unwise and a serious denial of equal opportunities.

REFERENCES

Department of Education and Science (DES) (1980) *Community Homes with Education*, London: HMSO.

Goacher, B., Evans, J., Welton, J. and Wedell, R. (1988) *Policy and Provision for Special Educational Needs*, London: Cassell.

Rutter, M., Quinton, D. and Liddle, C. (1983) 'Parenting in two generations', in N. Madge (ed.), *Families at Risk*, London: Heinemann.

Seebohm Report (1968) *Report of the Committee on Local Authority and Allied Personal Social Services*, London: HMSO.

FURTHER READING

Fisher, M., Marsh, P. and Phillips, D. (1986) *In and Out of Care*, London: Batsford/BAAF.

Fletcher-Campbell, F. J. (1991) 'Pastoral care for children in care: what can the school do?' *Pastoral Care*, March.

—— and Hall, C. (1990) *Changing Schools? Changing People? The Education of Children in Care*, Slough: NFER-Nelson.

Jackson, S. (1987) *The Education of Children in Care*, University of Bristol: School of Applied Social Studies.

—— (1989) 'Residential care and education', *Children and Society* 2 (4), 335–50.

Millham, S., Bullock, R., Hosie, K. and Haak, M. (1985) *Children Lost in Care*, London: Gower.

Packman, J., Randall, J. and Jacques, N. (1986) *Who needs Care?*, Oxford: Basil Blackwell.

Chapter 23

Adolescents, sex and injecting drug use
Risks for HIV infection

Marina Barnard and Neil McKeganey

Source: Aids Care 2 (2), 1990, pp. 103–6.

In this chapter the authors present data on the HIV-related risks for adolescents growing up in an area where injecting drug use is prevalent and HIV infection has been identified among local injecting drug users. They report on young people's knowledge, attitudes and perceptions of drug use and injectors; HIV and AIDS; sex, safer sex and condom use. These adolescents had an extensive and practically oriented knowledge of illicit drugs and drug injectors. The majority of adolescents contacted had an unsophisticated but approximate understanding of HIV transmission and how to guard against infection. The data suggest that many adolescents find issues relating to sex awkward, embarrassing and difficult to discuss. In a final section they consider some of the policy implications of their work focusing in particular on the prevention of injecting, the promotion of condom use and the necessity of avoiding a focus upon risk groups.

1 INTRODUCTION

Within Europe and North America the highest risk behaviours associated with the spread of HIV infection to date have been the shared use of injecting equipment by drug users and unprotected sexual intercourse between male homosexuals. However, the incidence of heterosexual spread of the virus is increasing. In particular, concern has been voiced that the 'real heterosexual epidemic' (Moss 1987) will originate from sexual contacts between injecting drug users and their non-drug-injecting partners. The fear is that the sexual partners of drug injectors will act as a conduit for HIV infection into the heterosexual, non-drug-injecting population (Des Jarlais *et al.* 1987, Chaisson *et al.* 1987). Additionally, in areas where drug injecting is commonplace those in social contact with drug injectors might also be judged at risk of HIV infection as there is the risk that an individual might begin injecting drug use as a consequence of that contact.

Research reports on injecting drug users from places as far apart as New York City (Des Jarlais *et al.* 1984), London (Donoghoe *et al.* 1989) and Glasgow (McKeganey *et al.* 1989) indicate the extent of the overlap between injecting drug users and others. In all three cases the majority of male injecting drug users had female partners who did not inject drugs. In New York City injecting drug users are believed to be the source of HIV infection in 87 per cent of the cases where heterosexual activity is assumed to be the only mode of transmission (Des Jarlais and Friedman 1987). Similarly in Edinburgh, Robertson and Skidmore (1989) state: 'heterosexual sex as a risk factor is now more common than exposure to needle sharing. Those most at risk are sexual partners of current or former drug users who are infected with HIV.'

An important first step in any strategy aimed at limiting the spread of HIV infection into the heterosexual population would seem to be one of looking precisely at the nature and extent of the contacts between drug injectors and those others not injecting drugs. Such information could then be used to inform the development of intervention strategies appropriate to those in sexual or social contact with drug injectors.

In this chapter we will report on data collected from non drug injectors living in an area where injecting drug use is prevalent and HIV infection has been identified among local drug injectors. This work forms part of an Economic and Social Research Council funded ethnographic study looking at risks for HIV amongst a teenage population exposed to injecting drug use and HIV infection (McKeganey 1989, McKeganey *et al.* 1989). We look at young people's knowledge, attitudes and perceptions of (1) drug use and drug injectors, (2) HIV and AIDS, (3) sex, safer sex and condom use. These findings are situated within the local context as this forms an essential backdrop to any discussion of these adolescents and their risks for HIV infection.

We will first describe the methods of data collection. This will be followed by our findings in the three subject areas. In a final section we consider the policy implications of this work.

2 METHODS

In the larger study, of which the data presented here form a part, we have attempted to contact three broad groups of people living in the study area: injecting drug users in contact with drug treatment agencies; injecting drug users not in contact with drug treatment agencies; and, finally, young people potentially at risk of drug injecting and HIV infection as a result of living in an area where injecting drug use is common and HIV infection has been identified among drug injectors. It is this latter group we are focusing upon here.

In order to contact such individuals we have employed a variety of techniques: semi-structured interviewing, group interviews, street interviews and direct observation of young people. We collected these data ourselves within a range of settings in the study area. The three main locales were two local schools (one Catholic, the other non-denominational), a community centre and an intermediate treatment (IT) social work group. This latter is a service provided by the social work department for young people (aged 13–16 years) with identifiable problems at home or in school. It combines an activities and counselling-based programme aimed at providing a constructive intervention into the adolescents' life.

The study locales were chosen because they afforded access to a large number of young people in settings which were not uniquely drugs oriented. However, in the course of our work we contacted adolescents and family members in other settings. Where apposite we have used these data to illustrate our point.

Contact with school pupils was agreed by the local authority and head teachers concerned. A total of sixty-four pupils of mixed sex and ability took part in the discussion groups. Each discussion group consisted of eight pupils chosen by the contact teacher. Four groups were seen in each school. The chosen age range was 14–16 years as it was felt that individuals at this age group were those most likely to be experimenting with drugs and/or forming sexual relationships. Classes were organised by the researchers and were unsupervised by teachers. Pupils were assured that anything they said would be held in strict confidence. The discussion groups were taken twice weekly over a period of two months in 1989.

The discussions, which lasted approximately three-quarters of an hour, were intentionally informal in tone. We sought the adolescents' opinions of their home area, asking them to note down what was negative and positive about where they lived, and what they considered was healthy or unhealthy about their lifestyles. The discussions were semi-structured in terms of the subjects that pupils raised for discussion. It is a measure of the prevalence of drug use in this area that pupils would invariably and spontaneously mention injecting drug use when discussing the negative side of living in their area. In broad terms the group discussions covered the subjects of drugs, HIV and AIDS, and sex. In addition we asked them to comment on their home area and what they felt the future held for them. Notes were taken by one of two researchers during the discussion groups, although on three occasions audio-recording equipment was used. Neither taking notes nor audio-recording appeared to have an inhibiting effect on pupils.

Our contacts with adolescents in the community centre and the IT group were more low key. In both instances participant observation was used primarily for data collection. Fieldnotes were only written once the research locale had been left.

The community centre houses a variety of community-based activities such as dancing, indoor sports, youth clubs, etc. There is also a cafe and a pool table providing an informal setting which made it possible to meet a range of people attending the centre. We attended the centre on a regular basis for a period of approximately six months in 1988–9.

Access to the IT group was negotiated through the senior social worker who ran the group. The group itself was made up of a core of five girls, their average age was 14 years. All the girls had been referred to the group by their own social workers who had identified them as being in particular need of the intervention of IT, which provided an environment conducive to confronting and/or discussing problems or anxieties in their lives. One of us (MB) attended this group on a weekly basis for its year-long duration 1988–9.

3 FINDINGS

In this section we will discuss the results of our work with adolescents contacted in the study area. Initially we describe the social and physical geography of the study area to give a context to our findings. We then report on the knowledge, attitudes and perceptions of adolescents we spoke to with respect to drug use and drug injecting, HIV and AIDS, and sex, safer sex and condom use.

The study area

The study took place within an inner city scheme (council estate) to the north-west of Glasgow. It has been designated by Strathclyde Regional Council as an area for priority treatment (APT) because of its markedly poor physical and social condition. It is a visually depressing area with many houses boarded up and derelict, walls heavily graffitied and stray dogs roaming streets bereft of cars.

In the 1981 census, unemployment among 16–24 year olds was over 50 per cent. Low income and unemployment are a common feature of households in the area. Numbers of single parent or large families are higher than is average for the region, overcrowding is endemic and housing is generally recognised to be in a state of poor repair (McKeganey and Barnard 1988). Additionally, since 1981 large numbers of young people living in the area, as indeed in other parts of Glasgow (Ditton and Speirits 1981), have begun injecting drug use.

Despite the evident signs of physical and social deterioration many locally resident people we met described the social fabric of life there in fully positive terms. It is noteworthy for instance, that in the school discussion groups a total of 34 out of 59 pupils testified unprompted to a sense of community, citing neighbours as friendly, friends being all around and family close by. Many adolescents, and indeed their parents, were born and bred in the immediate area and have long-standing, deep ties with people there. In our observational work our attention was often drawn to the practical, everyday demonstration of these social ties in the constant traffic of sharing seemingly everything and anything.

There is little in the way of service and amenity provision in the area, particularly for adolescents. The community centre and two other youth clubs tend to attract younger children and those in their early teens. Attendance of 15 year olds and upwards at these places is infrequent if at all. Adolescents stand between worlds, no longer children but not yet adults (Coffield *et al.* 1986, Glassner and Loughlin 1987). Little seems to cater to this transitional state particularly as for many adolescents money is in short supply. The majority of school pupils reported that their evenings were spent outside walking about the scheme, talking to friends and being ‘bored’. Over 50 per cent complained that there was nothing to do; in addition standing about made them vulnerable to the police who dislike the practice and do not encourage it, particularly on the main street which is also the prime drug dealing site in the area.

The preceding description of the physical and social features of the area bears importantly on our forthcoming discussion of the locally resident adolescents and their risks of HIV infection. The overall lack of amenities and general deprivation of the area make adolescents reliant on each other for providing entertainment which mostly takes place on the streets and in tenement stairwells. It is on these same streets that drugs are bought and sold and in many of these stairwells that drugs are injected. Socially there is a good deal of overlap between drug users and others in the community, many having grown up together. This is evidenced from the anxiety by one mother of two adolescent boys, one at school, the other recently made redundant from work:

> She looked out of the shop watching her sons walking up the main street 'I don't like it, them just stoatin' about aimlessly.' She then expounded 'It's no' as if they don't know people that do it [take drugs], they grew up wi' them, they were at school wi' the ones that's doin' it, so it's no' as if they're strangers.'
>
> (Chemist, 8 August 1989)

Drugs and drug users, far from being regarded as strangers, seemed to be viewed rather resignedly as part and parcel of the area. Where drug use is so prevalent it is unavoidable that adolescents should be in contact with, or have knowledge of, or be related to drug users. A sense of this can be gleaned from the account given by a boy whose elder brother died of an overdose:

> All my brother's friends and the ones that I know, the mature ones, I mean they have been junkies longer than the ones I went to school with. I see them, I know them, I know of them, 30 or 40 names that I could say that's Peter, that's Paul, or that's Mary, that's Jeannie, or Peter's sister or that's somebody you know, I know who people are ... there's always somebody that knows someone very well that's on drugs. There is always a relation or very close friend. Everybody knows about it.
>
> (Community Centre, 5 December 1988)

Experimentation with drugs in adolescence is well documented (Kandal 1980). In the next section we consider issues related to drug use in adolescence in the light of our data.

Adolescents and drugs

The adolescents we contacted displayed an extensive knowledge of drugs. It was evident from the responses of the pupils in the school discussion groups for example that their knowledge of the local drug scene was current. They could cite clinical and local names of those drugs injected, their administration and the effects:

> Neil asked if they knew what drugs were being used by drug injectors, 'smack' (heroin), 'tems' (temgesic), 'eggs' (temazepam), 'speed' (amphetamines). He then asked what terms were 'It's like a wee pill you put in water and hit it up.' Another added, 'Aye, you put it in a syringe.' Neil then asked what it was like. They shrugged their shoulders 'Dunno, never tried it,' 'Never hit up', 'Havenae got the bottle', one hazarded a guess 'Gouching, like getting a buzz out of it.'
>
> (School, 28 November 1989)

None of the adolescents we spoke to admitted to injecting drugs themselves, although it was clear that many had either used or knew of drugs administered orally or nasally or smoked. These drugs were typically hashish, amphetamines/sulphate, temazepam and the designer drug 'ecstacy' (methylenedioxymethamphetamine). The latter drug was less commonly mentioned, perhaps because of its prohibitive cost (£15–20 a tablet). This situation does not seem confined to the study locale as recently reported data from a longitudinal study of schoolchildren indicate an absolute increase in knowledge and experience of drugs amongst this age group (Wright and Pearl 1990).

Personal experience of drug injectors was very nearly unanimous amongst all the adolescents we spoke to, a typical response to the query of whether or not they knew anyone injecting drugs was 'Oh aye, everyone in ---- knows someone who's using.' Indeed it was often the case that the adolescent speaking to us had a brother or sister who was injecting drugs. Some did express a dislike of drug injectors and tried to avoid places where they were likely to come across them. The attitude more generally however was one of indifference, although some were wary of drug injectors because they felt they were unpredictable:

> All of them [the school pupils] knew people who were injecting drugs and mostly they gave them a vote of indifference 'You cannae avoid them', 'There's too many of them about.' I wondered if they felt at all threatened by them, one boy said 'They're not bothered about you, they leave you alone unless they're mad at something', another said 'They're all right when they're no full of it', i.e. if they haven't injected recently. A girl added 'Some do talk to you but when they're dying for a hit you don't know what they'll do.'
>
> (School, 4 December 1989)

From the accounts given to us it was clear that injecting drug use was viewed as being as much a feature of the landscape as the houses themselves. With one or two exceptions they had all seen discarded, used needles and associated drug-injecting paraphernalia. They knew where people went to inject drugs, some indeed had actually seen people injecting themselves:

> Tina related how she and Jackie had watched a boy injecting in front of them: 'He did it right in front of us, I couldn't move, I was just stuck there watching him.' Jackie added, 'He was standing in front of us doing this [she gestured

> him pushing the plunger in and out], he could have easily put it in her [Tina], it was horrible.'
>
> (IT, 1 March 1989)

The group discussions with school pupils were not considered a suitable forum for us to probe individuals directly on their own use of drugs. However, analysis of these discussions strongly indicates that for many personal experience of drugs informed their expressed opinions on drug use. Individualised, personal data on drug use from IT group members complements that collected from the school pupils and indicates a good deal of experimentation amongst adolescents:

> The IT group leader asked two of the group members if they had ever been offered heroin. Lena quite nonchalantly said 'Aye but I didnae take any', Cheryl said 'No, but that ---- he had to force me to take hash and acid'. Later on and out of the group leader's earshot Lena said she had taken 'hash, and acid, Tems . . . and I took they eggs an' all. They make you dead tired they do.'
>
> (IT, 15 February 1989)

> We asked if they knew if people took drugs at school 'Aye, but no heavy ones, jelly eggs, hash, one's that you swallow.' I asked if they knew people who were injecting, 'Aye, there's some that's jagging but mostly it's swallowing them.'
>
> (School, 13 December 1989)

The potential addictiveness of a drug was not obviously measured pharmacologically but in terms of the control an individual had over his or her drug use. The controlled use of drugs was clearly considered a possibility.

> 'It depends on the person, you could be taking a lot of drugs but that wouldn't necessarily mean you were a junkie.' 'There are people who take sulph and that but they're not junkies.'
>
> (School, 27 October 1989)

The tendency seemed to be one of indexing substances according to their use in different situations and their mode of administration. A drug which was swallowed and used for a specifically social purpose could be categorised differently from when it was injected by a drug user. The following fieldnote seems to endorse this indexing:

> I asked what drugs they felt it was okay to take. One boy said it was all right to take pills. 'There's lots of people that do it, for the dancing.' He said he wouldn't try and stop a friend from taking pills, that wasn't perceived by him as worrying, only injecting, then he would be concerned.
>
> (School, 13 December 1989)

These accounts can be juxtaposed against the reasons the young people gave for why they thought people took drugs. Typically they cited boredom or depression. In common with a number of other studies, social and group pressure were seen as influencing adolescents' decisions to take drugs (Swadi and Zeitlin 1988, Wright and Pearl 1990).

> We tried to get them to talk about getting involved in drugs, they suggested ways it happened 'hanging about with people who take drugs', 'your pals take it', 'people just get smart', 'some people were too daft and got right into it, to show off'.
>
> (School, 27 October 1989)

None of the adolescents we contacted defined themselves as seriously involved in drugs but it was clear that the majority had direct, personal experience of them. This is hardly surprising given the sheer volume of drugs coming into the area and their reported ease of access. Many were clearly using drugs which were potentially addictive and it was in recognition of this that they called upon self-control to prevent over-usage. However, the fragility of this notion of avoiding addiction was exposed by their own accounts of how people became involved in drug use. Essentially they saw drug use as occurring in the context of their friends and as part of their interactions with each other. It is friends who introduce each other to drugs as instanced by the fieldnote below:

> 'See, before I started coming to the IT I took these pills called .... have you heard of them? Anyway, my friend gave me them. She said "Go on they'll make you feel nice", so I did, I took 20 but they made me dead dizzy and then bang, I went out like a light.'
>
> (IT Group, 7 December 1988)

It is clearly untenable to argue that because an adolescent uses drugs recreationally, or indeed lives in an area where drug use is prevalent, he or she will inevitably go on to inject drugs at a later stage. Many simply cease with drug use altogether as they grow older and as their priorities change (Glassner and Loughlin 1987). However, other data do suggest that injecting drug use begins at about 16 or 17 years of age (Pearson 1987, McKeganey *et al.* 1989). The adolescents we contacted were at a stage where they were actually experimenting with drugs but not overinvolved in their usage. It seems highly likely that a proportion of those adolescents we contacted are prospectively at risk of beginning injecting drug use and therefore are also at high risk of HIV infection.

Adolescent knowledge and attitudes towards HIV infection

Fears of epidemic spread of HIV and AIDS amongst the heterosexual population have prompted the government to institute a series of campaigns aimed at providing health education on the disease and how to protect against it. In addition to media coverage many schools are now incorporating teaching on HIV and AIDS into their health education programmes. Given this exposure to information one might expect a relatively accurate knowledge of AIDS, how it is transmitted and how to protect against getting it. Studies on adolescent health beliefs and knowledge on HIV and AIDS indicate an approximate, imperfect knowledge amongst this age group (Price *et al.* 1985, Di Clemente *et al.* 1986). Additionally, adolescents do not appear to spend much time discussing HIV or AIDs among themselves except perhaps as an aside or as a joke (Perlmutter Bowen and Michal-Johnson 1989, Wright and Pearl 1990).

The results from the school discussion groups revealed an uncertain knowledge of medical aspects of the virus, for instance few were clear about the difference between HIV and AIDS although they understood them as related in some sense, with HIV preceding AIDS. This situation has also been reported in other studies of adolescents' knowledge of HIV and AIDS (Strunin and Hingson 1987). However, displaying a medical understanding of HIV and AIDS is arguably less important than the display of a more practically oriented knowledge of transmission dynamics and means of guarding against infection. Our data suggest that the majority of the adolescents we contacted had an unsophisticated but practical understanding of these facts such that all could name two main ways in which the virus was transmitted: through the shared use of unsterile injecting equipment and through unprotected sexual contact. The following fieldnote is fairly typical of their response to questions testing their knowledge on HIV transmission pathways:

> Sheigla, with the other four girls butting in, listed ways of getting the virus 'You can get it through sharing needles, you can get it through sexual intercourse [they sniggered at this] and you can get it from cigarettes [sharing them] and from drinking out the same can.' They debated this amongst themselves concluding with Andrina saying 'It's body contact isn't it, you know mixing body fluids.'
>
> (IT, 7 June 1989)

Clearly these young people have attributed HIV with a greater infectiousness than it possesses. The notion that social contact might be sufficient to spread infection has also been reported elsewhere (Hastings *et al.* 1987). This may be the consequence of alarmist stories in the media; it may also, in this context at least, be more indicative of knowledge of precautions appropriate for protection against hepatitis B.

The clearest perception of risk for HIV was associated with contact with drug injectors and also contact with discarded injecting paraphernalia which was generally considered to be potentially infective. Their prognosis for drug injectors was not optimistic, many felt that they would get AIDS, figures such as 50 per cent, 75 per cent or 'all of them' were not uncommonly called out.

Some in the school discussion groups expressed contamination fears, citing 'junkies spittin' on you' as being one mode of transmission. Judging from the comments made by many we spoke to, it seemed that the concern evinced by them regarding their contact with drug injectors pre-existed AIDS. Infections such as hepatitis were mentioned by many adolescents in connection with drug injectors:

> We were standing talking to a boy [non-user] he said he had noticed that neither Marina nor I had accepted the offer of a drink of Sean's ginger [Sean injects] adding 'I don't accept anything like that or a smoke if Sean had it before me. If I have ginger and Sean asks for it I just say "Sorry Sean it's no' mine".' I asked him what he was concerned about and he said 'I'm no wanting to catch hep or AIDS.'
>
> (Street, 22 June 1989)

A more extreme practice was related by a boy whose sister is a drug injector:

> 'See ma big sister, when she comes round to our house and if she has a cup of tea, my da smashes the cup.'
>
> (School, 13 December 1989)

A constantly voiced concern was the large numbers of discarded, used injecting equipment left lying around, particularly as young children could, and did, pick them up to play with them. To prevent this many said that they would try to remove them, without touching them if possible, commonly by kicking them down roadside drains.

Given that drug injecting is so widespread in the area it is perhaps unsurprising that the adolescents we spoke to were not attempting to isolate themselves from contact *per se* with drug injectors. Rather, their concern was to avoid a situation where they might come into contact with body fluids such as saliva or blood.

Whilst a quite natural desire to avoid HIV infection was evinced by the adolescents we were in contact with, they did not show an equivalent concern to avoid HIV-infected individuals. A substantial minority did know people with HIV infection. Their reaction to them was very similar to that expressed towards drug injectors. The following fieldnote is illustrative of this:

> Valerie asked me about working with drug injectors she wondered if I was afraid of them, I said I wasn't but was she? 'Aye, I'd be afraid they'd want to take my purse. I'm no afraid 'coz of AIDS or nothin' I'd be scared they'd want to rip me off.'
>
> (IT, 2 May 1989)

Their identities seemed to be defined primarily in social terms and 'so long as they're no' injecting you with it' the fact of their HIV seropositivity was not considered a problem.

There is a degree to which these adolescents seemed to hold contradictory ideas on HIV infectivity. On the one hand there was no demonstrable fear of, or aversion to, people known to be seropositive. Yet on the other hand they did seek to limit their potential contact by not drinking out of the same can, not sharing cigarettes, etc., citing a desire to avoid HIV infection as being the reason for doing so.

The prospect of being HIV-tested did not seem to present difficulties for many, although some did say that they would only be tested if they felt they were at risk of HIV infection. The expressed rationale for being HIV-tested was so that they could protect the health of others, particularly children. Despite their willingness to be tested the majority were disinclined to make public their HIV status if positive.

Adolescents and sex; heterosexual spread of HIV

HIV infection has been identified amongst injecting drug users resident in the study locale. So long as shared use of unsterile injecting equipment continues to occur (McKeganey *et al.* 1989) so it can be assumed that the virus will continue to spread amongst this group. It is unlikely that the virus will be contained, however, as it is evident from our fieldwork that there is a good deal of sexual contact between injecting drug users and others. The potential for heterosexual transmission of the virus clearly exists in such a situation.

It seemed clear from the school group discussions that they would not choose as a partner someone known to be injecting drugs. However, there was divided opinion as to what they would do if injecting drug use was discovered in the context of a relationship. In general the attitude held by the boys was hardline, comments like ‘sling ’em’, ‘out the windae’ or ‘I’d set about her’ were not unusual. By contrast the girls’ attitude was much more conciliatory often saying they would ‘gie them a chance’ to come off drugs. Some girls stated that the deciding factor on whether or not a relationship continued would not be injecting drug use *per se* but the personal attributes of the drug user. They saw themselves as first trying to help their partner stop taking drugs rather than immediately ceasing contact with them. Given this situation it seems that females are more likely to remain in relationships with males who are injecting drugs than are males in an equivalent situation with a female injecting drugs. This assertion seems borne out by the data showing the greater numbers of female non drug users in relationships with drug users than males (Des Jarlais *et al.* 1984, Donoghue *et al.* 1989). This is cause for concern in light of recent evidence indicating that male to female transmission of the virus is more likely to occur than from female to male (Brunet *et al.* 1987).

Given that the majority of adolescents claimed they would not choose a relationship with someone known to be injecting drugs we asked what strategies they employed, if any, to determine if someone was injecting. From their response it was evident that they relied on external cues based on appearance: ‘bags under the eyes’, ‘track marks’, ‘you can tell by looking at their eyes’, ‘dead skinny’, ‘dirty’, were frequent remarks. However, some felt that you could not always tell if someone was injecting drugs. This seems especially likely to be the case where an individual has only recently begun injecting drug use (reportedly most often at about 16 or 17 years of age) which may not yet be habitual (Parker *et al.* 1987, McKeganey *et al.* 1989). Unfortunately this may be a time of high risk for HIV infection as initiation into drug use is most often through use of someone else’s injecting equipment (Parker *et al.* 1988, Power 1988).

It was significant that with one or two exceptions none of the school pupils felt it would be possible to ask someone if they were injecting drugs. The following field extract is indicative of their attitude to this in general:

> Neil asked if they would ask someone if they were using drugs, the response seemed unanimously one of incredulity: you wouldn't, you couldn't do it. It was felt to be insulting to ask someone if they were, even if you were going to have sex with them. 'I think it'd be an insult if somebody said to me are you a junkie, have you got anything?' A boy responded sharply to that, 'Don't be a fool, be safe. They might be endangering your life.' One girl added she would be upset 'Aye I would, I'd think I looked like one or something.'
>
> (School, 27 October 1989)

These data are suggestive of the social difficulties encountered in the negotiation of relationships such that even while professing a reluctance to become involved with an injecting drug user it would be unacceptable to make direct enquiries of this nature.

It is not inevitable that an individual will become directly involved with an injecting drug user. However, as many adolescents are not in long-term stable sexual relationships but are none the less sexually active (Johnson *et al.* 1989, Abrams *et al.* 1990) the risk of infection remains. In the absence of a cure for HIV infection it is necessary to take adequate measures to protect against contracting and spreading the virus. Heterosexuals have been strongly advised to use condoms and to practise safer sex, particularly where there is uncertainty as to the sexual history of one's partner.

However, for many the use of condoms is socially problematic. Prior to the December 1986–March 1987 health education campaigns urging greater use of condoms as protection against HIV it is clear that they were increasingly unpopular as a means of contraception (Wellings 1988). The objections to using condoms are well known, people generally report them embarrassing to use, clumsy and messy. Notwithstanding their use as a means of avoiding becoming infected with a life-threatening disease, these same objections to their use still seem to remain:

> 'There's 15 reasons why people won't use them, at least 15 reasons, one reason and that just discourages them altogether. From things like buying them to wearing them, anything, and I don't think there is enough done by the government to promote it, maybe it's not a good thing to promote but it is good, it's not sort of the done thing.'
>
> (Community Centre, 5 December 1988)

Rather more optimistically, research from Edinburgh indicates a greater acceptance and use of condoms among those under age 25 in Edinburgh and Glasgow (McQueen 1989).

The 'negotiation of safer sex' is a term much used in HIV-related health education. However it belies the fact that while for many people the negotiation of any kind of sex is a potentially fraught and uncertain business, this may be especially the case for young sexually inexperienced adolescents. Even raising the subject of sex amongst the adolescents we contacted was sufficient to generate a good deal of embarrassment and sly laughter. In our experience sex was not a subject they felt able to discuss seriously in any detail either as a group or singly with a researcher of the same sex. The following is illustrative of an observed reticence to discuss matters related to sex:

> We asked what other ways could you get the virus other than through needle sharing. There was a long silence but they knew and were reluctant to say so. Finally they mentioned 'through sex'.
>
> (School, 7 November 1989)

If adolescents find discussing sex problematic, it is unsurprising that they report finding condoms embarrassing to buy, carry and use, despite recognising their use in protecting against HIV infection:

> The girls all said they'd be embarrassed to carry a condom and said that their friends would think they were a slag if they found out. But who should carry condoms I asked? All the boys thought it was the responsibility of the woman. I asked if they would insist on a condom being used. The girls were unanimous, boys less certain, all shaking their heads. So I asked: 'You wouldn't wear one then?' 'Nah, no' if I'd been goin' with her a while', 'Depends if she was bogging [dirty]'
>
> (School, 13 December 1989)

In tandem with other research (Abrams *et al.* 1990) it seems that females are most likely to encourage the use of condoms. However there was a noted reluctance on their part to be the ones purchasing and carrying condoms because of the negative social comment they felt attached to such behaviour.

Our findings suggest that for many adolescents the whole issue of sex is negotiated with awkwardness and embarrassment. The recommendation that condoms be used to protect against HIV infection needs to take account of these difficulties, particularly with regard to gender differences in attitudes to their use. As Weinstein and Goebel (1979) point out, contraceptive use should be viewed as more than a simple mechanical procedure because it seems invested with social meanings.

4 POLICY

Before considering the policy implications of our work it is important to stress that this chapter is based upon our contacts with a number of individuals living in one Scottish city. It should not be assumed that these individuals are representative of young people generally. The study area was chosen on the basis of having a large injecting drug-using population living alongside young people who were not yet injecting drugs themselves. It is important to stress, however, that this situation undoubtedly exists in a number of British cities, see for example, Parker *et al.* (1987) and Pearson (1987).

Our data point to the inadequacy of focusing on risk groups in HIV health education campaigns. Such a perspective assumes that the people engaging in risk behaviour form self-enclosed, socially isolated groups. On the contrary, these data are indicative of a good deal of contact between those deemed to be in high risk groups and others.

Fears of heterosexual spread of the virus have concentrated to date on the potential role played by prostitutes acting as a bridge into the heterosexual non-drug-using population. However, in an area where injecting drug use is prevalent it is not unreasonable to begin with the assumption that all those who are in contact with injecting drug users are at risk of HIV infection, whether it is through sexual contact with injecting drug users or through beginning injecting drug use themselves.

Future health education campaigns need to adopt a more broad-based perspective which rather than just focusing on those engaging in high risk behaviours also targets those they are in contact with and who by implication may be judged at risk of HIV infection. In seeking to influence and change social behaviour the evidence suggests that the more credible the source of information the greater the likelihood of its adoption (McGuire 1985). In this sense there may be value in school-based health education classes using both health professionals and ex-injecting drug users to make the case against beginning injecting drug use.

Many adolescents are likely to experiment with drug use to a degree. This is probably inevitable, particularly in an area where drugs are readily available. However, drug prevention strategies should be devised to dissuade initiation into injecting, thereby at least reducing the risk of HIV infection. One initiative might be to target adolescents at school with detailed information, not only on the health risks associated with injecting drug use but also on the financial and social costs to family and friends as well as to themselves. It has to be acknowledged, however, that in so doing one might paradoxically draw attention to the action of injecting drugs in such a way as to stimulate an interest that might previously not have been there. Health education advice on the risks of HIV infection through injecting drug use needs to be relevant and credible to adolescents. In this respect there is much to recommend the use of locally based campaigns which mirror local conditions rather than national ones which are inevitably more general in scope.

It is clear from our data as it is from others (Di Clemente *et al.* 1986, Abrams *et al.* 1990) that many adolescents hold incorrect or confused ideas of HIV and AIDS. This suggests that schools should perhaps allocate more time to providing pupils with health education. In addition, devising programmes which are reflective of local circumstances would increase the likelihood of the relevance of such information in adolescents' own lives.

It is during adolescence that many individuals have their first sexual experiences. Issues of sex and sexuality are often difficult subjects to raise and discuss among adolescents. Yet it is important to do so, not least because of the need to guard against sexual transmission of HIV infection. The advocation of safer sex needs to be set in the context of adolescent relations which seem gender differentiated, often awkward and uncertain. Encouraging adolescents to adopt safer sex techniques such as the use of condoms needs also to take account of the ways in which adolescents manage their sexual relationships and their ability to communicate within them, particularly as regards protecting against HIV infection. One suggested means of promoting the adoption of safer sex behaviours among adolescents has been to work on strengthening beliefs that peers will accept safer behaviours thereby increasing its acceptability to the individual (Joseph *et al.* 1987). The onus on health educationalists is to encourage adolescents to exploit and develop appropriate interpersonal skills which would help in the negotiation of safer sex.

Campaigns to promote wider usage of condoms are unlikely to succeed where they do not address prevailing attitudes to their use, particularly when their purchase and possession run counter to what adolescents consider as appropriate mores of behaviour. Attitudes to condom use appear gender related; it would therefore seem fitting for any health education strategy to target males and females separately. In particular, for many adolescent girls the carrying and buying of condoms makes loaded, adverse, comment on their morality.

Heterosexual transmission of the virus is a real possibility, particularly for those who are in sexual contact with injecting drug users. Lacking a cure for HIV infection our best defence is appropriate behaviour change. What seems most likely to facilitate this is an equivalent change in attitudes rendering the negotiation of safer sex an integral part of any sexual relationship. It is perhaps in this direction that policy moves should be made.

ACKNOWLEDGEMENTS

We would like to thank all of the people who agreed to take part in this research. We are especially grateful to the staff of the two schools, the IT group leader and the staff of the community centre. For reasons of confidentiality we are unable to identify these individuals, however this study would not have been possible without their help and cooperation. We should like to thank Patrick West for his advice in setting up and running the school discussion groups. We are grateful to Margaret Seaforth for her work on this manuscript. We appreciate the financial support of the Economic and Social Research Council for this study.

The Social Paediatric and Obstetric Research Unit is supported by the Chief Scientist Office, Scottish Home and Health Department and the Greater Glasgow Health Board. The opinions expressed in this chapter are not necessarily those of the Scottish Home and Health Department.

REFERENCES

Abrams, D., Abraham, C., Spears, R. and Marks, D. (1990) 'Aids vulnerability: relationships, sexual behaviour and attitudes among 16–19 year-olds', in P. Aggleton, P. Davis and G. Hart (eds), *AIDS: Individual, Cultural and Policy Dimensions*, Brighton: Falmer Press.

Brunet, J. B., Des Jarlais, D. C. and Kodi, M. A. (1987) 'Report on the European Community Workshop on epidemiology of HIV infections: spread among intravenous drug abusers and the heterosexual population', *AIDS* 1, 59–61.

Chaisson, R. E., Moss, A. R., Onishi, R., Osmond, D. and Carlson J. R. (1987) 'Human Immunodeficiency Virus Infection in heterosexual drug users in San Francisco', *American Journal of Public Health* 77, 169–72.

Coffield, E., Borrill, C. and Marshall, S. (1986) *Growing Up at the Margins*, Milton Keynes: Open University Press.

Des Jarlais, D. C., Chamberland M. E., Yancovitz, S. R., Weinberg, P. and Friedman, S. R. (1984) 'Heterosexual partners: a large risk group for AIDS' (letter), *The Lancet* 8, 1346–7.

—— and Friedman, S. R. (1987) 'HIV infection among intravenous drug users: epidemiology and risk reduction', *AIDS* 1, pp. 67–76.

——, Wish, E., Friedman, S. R., Stoneburner, R., Yancovitz, S. R., Mildvan, D., El-Sadr, W., Brady, E. and Cuadrado, M. (1987) 'Intravenous drug use and the heterosexual transmission of the human immunodeficiency virus: current trends in New York City', *New York State Journal of Medicine*, May, 283–6.

Di Clemente, R. J., Zorn, J. and Temoshok, L. (1986) 'Adolescents and AIDS: a survey of knowledge, attitudes and beliefs about AIDS in San Francisco', *American Journal of Public Health* 76, 1443–5.

Ditton, J. and Speirits, K. (1981) 'The rapid increase of heroin addiction in Glasgow during 1981', Background Paper 2, Department of Sociology, University of Glasgow.

Donoghoe, M., Stimson, G. V. and Dolan, K. A. (1989) 'Sexual behaviour of injecting drug users and associated risks of HIV infection for non-injecting sexual partners', *AIDS Care* 1, 51–8.

Glassner, B. and Loughlin, J. (1987) *Drugs in Adolescent Worlds: Burnouts to Straight*, Basingstoke: Macmillan.

Hastings, G. B., Leather, D. S. and Scott, A. C. (1987) 'AIDS publicity: some experiences for Scotland', *British Medical Journal* 294, 48–9.

Johnson, A. M., Wadsworth, J., Elliott, P., Prior, L., Wallace, P., Blower, S., Webb, N., Heald, G., Miller, D., Adler, M. and Anderson, R. (1989) 'A pilot study of sexual lifestyle in a random sample of the population of Great Britain', *AIDS* 3, 135–41.

Joseph, J. G., Montgomery, S. B., Emmons, C. A., Kessler, R. C. and Ostrow, D. G. (1987) 'Magnitude and determinants of behavioural risk reduction: longitudinal analysis of a cohort at risk for AIDS', *Psychology and Health* 1, 73–96.

Kandal, D. B. (1980) 'Drug and drinking behaviour among youth', *Annual Review of Sociology* 6, 235–85.

McGuire, W. J. (1985) 'Attitudes and attitude change', in G. Lindzey and E. Aronson (eds), *Handbook of Social Psychology*, 3rd edn, New York: Random House.

McKeganey, N. P. (1989) 'Drug abuse in the community: needle sharing and the risks of HIV infection', in S. J. Cunningham-Burley and N. P. McKeganey (eds), *Reading in Medical Sociology*, London: Routledge.

—— and Barnard, M. A. (1988) *A Statistical Comparison of Study Area and Other Neighbouring Areas*, Glasgow Social Paediatric and Obstetric Research Unit Report, August.

——, —— and Watson, H. (1989) 'HIV related risk behaviour among a non-clinic sample of injecting drug users', *British Journal of Addiction* 84, 1481–90.

McQueen, D. V. (1989) *A Study of Lifestyle and Health: Interim Report*, Research Unit for Health and Behavioural Change, Edinburgh.

Moss, A. R. (1987) 'AIDS and intravenous drug use: the real heterosexual epidemic', *British Medical Journal*, 14 February, 389–90.

Parker, H., Newcombe, R. and Bakx, K. (1987) 'The new heroin users: prevalence and characteristics in Wirral, Merseyside', *British Journal of Addiction* 82, 147–57.

——, Bakx, K. and Newcombe, R. (1988) *Living with Heroin*, Milton Keynes: Open University Press.

Pearson, G. (1987) *The New Heroin Users*, Oxford: Basil Blackwell.

Perlmutter Bowen, S. and Michal-Johnson, P. (1989) 'The crisis of communicating in relationships: confronting the threat of AIDS', *AIDS and Public Policy Journal* 4, 10–19.

Power, R. (1988) 'The influence of AIDS upon patterns of intravenous drug use: syringe and needle sharing among illicit drug users in Britain', in R. J. Baltjes and R. W. Pickens (eds), *Needle Sharing among Intravenous Drug Abusers: National and International Perspectives*, Research Monograph no. 80, pp. 75–88, Washington D.C.: NIDA.

Price, J. H., Desmong, S. and Kukulka, G. (1985) 'Perceptions and misconceptions of AIDS', *Journal of School Health* 55, 107–9.

Robertson, J. R. and Skidmore, C. (1989) 'Heterosexually acquired HIV infection, 1989', *British Medical Journal* 298, 891.

Strunin L. and Hingson, R. (1987) 'Acquired Immunodeficiency Syndrome and adolescents: knowledge, beliefs, attitudes and behaviours', *Paediatrics* 79, 825–8.

Swadi, H. and Zeitlin, H. (1988) 'Peer influence and adolescent substance abuse: a promising side?', *British Journal of Addiction* 83, 153–7.

Weinstein, S. A. and Goebel, G. (1979) 'The relationship between contraceptive sex role stereotyping and attitudes towards male contraception among males', *The Journal of Sex Research* 15, 235–42.

Wellings, K. (1988) 'Other indicators of response to the AIDS public education campaign', *Health Education Authority Report*, September, London: HMSO.

Wright, J. D. and Pearl, L. (1990) 'Knowledge and experience of young people regarding drug abuse, 1969–89', *British Medical Journal* 30, 99–103.

Chapter 24

Affected by HIV and AIDS

Cameos of children and young people

Philippa Russell, with an introduction by Tony Booth

This chapter is about the impact of HIV and AIDS on the lives of children and young people. In the introduction Tony Booth provides some basic facts about the spread of HIV and AIDS. Then in a series of cameos, Philippa Russell graphically illustrates some aspects of the impact of HIV and AIDS on young people's lives, drawing on material collected in work at the National Children's Bureau (see Honigsbaum 1991). There are inevitable omissions. Young people growing up gay and reflecting on the pressures on their identity from the stigma of misconceptions about AIDS as a 'gay disease' are one such group.

1 INTRODUCTION

Tony Booth

World-wide, it is estimated that by 1992 there will be 660,000 children with AIDS and 1,100,000 who are HIV positive (Chin 1990). Most of these children will be in parts of sub-Saharan Africa, the Caribbean and South America. It is also estimated that 4,400,000 women will be HIV positive by 1992. There are many lessons in such figures. They indicate the global scale of human misery caused by HIV, and the extent to which children will be born with the disease because they catch it from their mothers or affected by it because they are growing up with parents who may fall ill with AIDS. Finally, they dispel any lingering ideas people may have about HIV as only affecting gay men.

In the UK, 2,375 people had died of AIDS by the end of January 1991 (DHSS 1991). The great majority of those people we know to be HIV positive can be described as being in one of three groups. Of 13,335 people known to be HIV antibody positive at the end of January 1991, 2,017 were injecting drug users and had caught HIV through shared needles, 8,595 were men who had caught the virus primarily through anal sex with other men and 1,391 had been infected through blood products. In the latter category, more than a thousand were men and boys with haemophilia who had been given infected factor 8, a clotting agent. This represents about a fifth of all people with haemophilia.

In the UK, HIV has had its major impact in the past on the above groups of people and on those close to them; both those who have been at risk of sexually transmitted HIV infection and others who are affected by the possibility of a family member or friend becoming ill with AIDS. But it is clear that HIV and AIDS will touch the lives of most of us in the future.

The incidence of HIV infection contained in the monthly government figures is thought to be a gross underestimate of the extent of the problem, since there is no encouragement to widespread testing. In any case these figures give only a snapshot of the past. The pattern of HIV infection is changing fast. In Scotland one in three new cases are women and one in six are women in England (Norman *et al.* 1990). The results of a screening programme of pregnant women in Dundee led the consultant coordinating the project to estimate that the HIV infection rate amongst women in the 16–20 age group might be as high as 15 per 1,000 (*Independent*, 12 July 1990).

It is estimated that somewhere between 15 and 33 per cent of children will be born infected with the HIV virus if their mothers are infected (Norman *et al.* 1990). The rest, for an as yet unknown reason, are unaffected even though they are born with antibodies to HIV in their blood. Up to the end of January 1991 there were 201 babies known to have been infected from their mothers during pregnancy or at birth.

Some further indication of the time delay of our knowledge of who is infected has emerged as it has been increasingly realised that the transition from HIV to AIDS may take many years to occur. One mother and daughter have been documented in the USA as HIV positive but free of AIDS for twelve years (Burger *et al.* 1990).

2 CAMEOS OF CHILDREN AND YOUNG PEOPLE AFFECTED BY HIV AND AIDS

Philippa Russell

Jonathan

Jonathan had coped well with his haemophilia until he was 14 years old. He had never asked about his HIV status and his parents claimed he 'didn't know, did not even think about it'. Two of Jonathan's extended family were also HIV infected and there was enormous concern that other family members should not know anything about their condition. Jonathan, however, had several bad falls in a few months – in both cases due to deliberate risk taking. On his second spell in hospital he was angry and resentful with staff, threatened to discontinue treatment and said he did not wish to go home. A year later he was still resentful and angry. His parents were experiencing major problems in their marriage, disagreeing about how best to manage Jonathan.

At 15 Jonathan was a good-looking and popular boy at school. He began to have girl friends and his parents again quarrelled bitterly about when and how to tell him of his condition. But their worries seemed groundless. After a few weeks Jonathan ended each relationship abruptly. At 16 he was still moving rapidly through relationships, doing badly at school work and still getting on poorly with his family. Jonathan's head teacher, the only staff member in the school who understood his condition, felt that he needed counselling. She was also very worried by Jonathan's admittedly short-term relationships. Where did her duty lie, she pondered. Should the girls be given an indication that care was needed in any active sexual relationship? She felt that Jonathan *did* know about his condition. It seemed possible that ending relationships as soon as they became serious was a way of limiting any sexual relationship without having to reveal his HIV status. Eventually she was successful in persuading Jonathan's family that he *must* be told and that their own quarrels and evident unhappiness were in fact contributing to Jonathan's difficulties. Jonathan was told – with parental consent – at his local Haemophilia Centre. Although he initially cried, he quickly recovered. He said he had suspected for several years that he must be HIV infected. Otherwise, he said, they would surely have told him he was negative. He was pleased that his head teacher knew – and that she had lived with the diagnosis almost as long as he had. An intelligent and thoughtful boy, he wanted detailed information on HIV and the different management routines. He wished to meet what he called 'survivors', men who had been healthy with HIV for a number of years and who were working and leading ordinary lives. Although his medical prospects are obviously unclear he is aiming for A-levels and university. But he still feels too unsafe to tell any school friends or other teachers. Joking, he says he has switched from girls to a dog, 'love on demand'. There is still a chronic sadness about the life he might have lived – and his head teacher acknowledges that the school may have difficulty in coping well if he develops AIDS.

Sadie

Sadie, a 10 year old, is another child affected by haemophilia. She attends a primary school in South-East England with her younger brother (who has haemophilia but not HIV). Sadie's – and the school's – dilemma is that both her father (who has haemophilia) and her mother are HIV infected. Her father is well and has few problems from his haemophilia. He continues to work in a small family business, but at home is overwhelmed by the depression and anxiety of his wife. She has developed ARC (AIDS Related Complex) and has frequent periods of ill-health. AZT, a drug used to ameliorate the effects of the illness, is only marginally effective and the whole family are having to face the bleak prospect of terminal illness in the fairly near future. Sadie knows little about AIDS or HIV (except what she has seen on the television). Her family have not told her or her brother of the cause of the mother's illness. Sadie therefore sees her mother as cross, rejecting and highly demanding of her. At 10 years old, she has to hurry home from school to get the tea, helping with washing and ironing, shopping and the multiplicity of everyday chores which make up family life. On two occasions in the past month she has not been to school at all, because her mother felt too ill to be left and needed Sadie to be in the house to call the doctor, make cups of tea and generally to provide some basic nursing care.

Sadie's classroom teacher has seen the signs of tiredness, falling asleep at her desk, the reluctance to take part in after-school activities. She has also seen the little girl's sadness and dejection. She knows her mother is ill – and there is local speculation that she has AIDS. Few neighbours are unaware of the connection between HIV and haemophilia. But she hesitates to intervene. Sadie is well. Her brother is fortunate in not having HIV. But both children may be orphaned over the next few years and no one is allowed to plan with them for their futures. There are no easy solutions for children like Sadie – but schools need to be aware of the wider implications of HIV for *other* children in the family and (because of the association of HIV with family poverty) to be alert to young people becoming 'carers' and for the importance of having counselling and support services readily available. Where children are likely to be known to local Haemophilia Centres, their resources for marital, family and child counselling should be known to, and used by, schools.

Julie

In another school in another part of the United Kingdom, a grandmother was caring for Julie, her 6-year-old HIV-infected granddaughter because her daughter was terminally ill with AIDS. The mother had refused to tell her own family until she was seriously ill. The disclosure – first, of her illness, and second, of the cause through drug misuse – had proved double blows to the extended family, who found them virtually unacceptable. The grandmother adamantly refused to let the child visit her mother and, after her death, fantasised about the 'cancer' she had died from. She was quite unable to discuss her daughter's death with the granddaughter, to whom she was affectionate but totally controlling, in an effort to 'protect her from her mother's mistakes'. The family's fear of their local community knowing the cause of the mother's death meant that the child's school initially knew nothing about the family history. But the little girl's disturbed behaviour at school and her frequent references to her mother led to a home visit from the school. The grandmother broke down and related the story – expecting she would be asked to remove the child. The teacher's support was crucial, both in resolving the grandmother's unnecessary fears about the child's HIV status (which was negative, but the family had failed to understand the causes of HIV infection) and in persuading her to get support and counselling through a local community nurse. The child was referred to child guidance and a year later the family situation was said to be greatly improved.

Susan

Susan is the oldest of four children in her family. She is not HIV positive herself but her mother and father became infected with HIV through sharing infected needles in using drugs. One of her younger brothers is definitely HIV infected because the infection was passed on to him during his mother's pregnancy. Her 6-month-old baby sister is still showing signs of her mother's HIV antibodies in her blood but there is hope that these will disappear over time.

Susan's needs are often ignored and forgotten because of the overwhelming medical and social needs of other family members. In her early teens, she is desperate to discuss her family's problems and the forthcoming series of bereavements which she anticipates. Her grandparents refuse to discuss her parents' illness because of their own concerns at the previous drug-related lifestyles of the family. The child is fortunate in living in an area where bereavement counselling is available. Her need for counselling is exacerbated by her own age and the negative images of sexuality and death with which HIV is associated.

The most important ongoing source of help is her school, where one teacher knows of her HIV family status and is able – in confidence – to discuss a range of issues, including how she should handle teasing, how she can plan her schoolwork to take account of the increasing needs in the family home, and to discuss where she (and a healthy brother) may live if they survive the rest of their family members. The teacher, however, emphasised his need for support, for accurate information on HIV – and the sorrow and stress of being the only informed adult within a school with no permission to share knowledge or feelings with other staff members. An important issue for teachers in this situation will be the creation of networks (perhaps on a borough-wide basis) for mutual support by other teaching staff who are working directly with affected children or indeed with HIV-infected colleagues on the teaching staff.

Peter

In a third school, Peter, a 13-year-old boy with a drug-using older brother, found himself ridiculed and isolated by school-mates and their families because the brother's arrest by the local police for being in possession of drugs was regarded as a statement that 'he must have AIDS'. The younger brother refused to attend school and attempted suicide with an overdose of Paracetamol. He admitted his worries – and his anger and resentment at his brother – when in hospital and agreed to try school again. One of his teachers was sympathetic and able to visit him at home and in hospital. The school arranged a special 'whole school programme' about AIDS and HIV, with the local authority AIDS coordinator and a consultant from the local Haemophilia Unit (both well known in the community) to answer questions. The presentation focused on the importance of seeing people and families affected by HIV as *ordinary* people. It also stressed the need to avoid witch-hunts and the importance of schools supporting any pupil who was vulnerable or needed help with family life. Peter was able to return to school. The HIV status of his brother is not known, as he disappeared and is probably living as one of the many homeless young people who form a fringe community around the drugs world.

Margaret

Unfortunately, many of the images of health education are negative. Images of death, disease and ostracism may deter teenagers from trying risky activities like unprotected sex or intravenous drug use. But conversely they may be too shocking to be acceptable – and they may cause fear and anxiety in young people who regard themselves at risk because of incidents in their past. Margaret, 14 years old, was one such young woman. Attending a local secondary school, she viewed the sex education videos and literature provided at school with growing fear and horror. At the age of 10 she had been sexually abused by the teenage son of a neighbour. She had never told anyone of the incident, but the fear of AIDS as an additional consequence of that incident began to dominate her life. A bad attack of flu convinced her that she had an impaired immune system and she became deeply depressed, finally travelling to London secretly to have an AIDS test. The private clinic she had identified gave little counselling.

They accepted Margaret's stated age of 19. The results of the test were negative. Margaret finally told the school nurse, to whom she had been referred by her classroom teacher who was increasingly concerned about her anxieties over minor health problems and her evident depression. Margaret confessed that she had received little comfort from a negative test – the whole process had forced her to relive the original sexual abuse and her inability to tell her parents or any other trusted adult. She is now receiving counselling, refusing to consider criminal charges against the young man who has in any event left the neighbourhood. One year on she feels the whole process was perhaps positive – her fear of HIV made her acknowledge a much deeper problem. But the *school* has been forcibly reminded of the fears of teenagers who feel themselves to be at risk. Part of learning to live in the world of HIV is acknowledging the need to live with close friends' and family members' past histories. Teenagers are particularly vulnerable to anxiety about health and image amongst their peer group. They may also be unaware of the long-term consequences of having even a negative test for HIV. Importantly, the connection between sexual abuse and HIV is newly on the scene in the United Kingdom. Sensitivity and counselling will be essential when fears about both come together.

3 CONCLUSION

These case histories illustrate some of the diverse consequences for families affected by HIV, and for the schools working with their children. Partly because

HIV has been associated in people's minds with injecting drug use and being gay, parents may find it difficult to talk openly to schools. Schools themselves may experience the pain and isolation, with individual teachers also keeping secrets about particular children and desperately needing to talk through their often mixed feelings about HIV with an informed and sympathetic listener. Indeed, schools may not only feel concern about parents. An article in the *Guardian* (28 November 1990) highlighted the new dilemma of the HIV-positive teacher and the need to balance tolerance (not least of repeated absences on sick leave) with fears about the wider repercussions in the school if the cause of the illness was known. In effect HIV and AIDS are about *everyone's* family, and children and schools need to be part of the process of community awareness and support. If they are not part of the solution to living with HIV and AIDS, they will certainly be part of the problem.

NOTE

Further information for schoolworkers can be found in Honigsbaum (1991), Rogers (1989) and from the charity AVERT, PO Box 91, Horsham, West Sussex, RH13 7YR.

REFERENCES

Burger, H., Belman, A., Grimson, R., Koell, A., Flaherty, K., Gully, J., Gibbs, R., Phi-Ngu Nguyun and Weiser, B. (1990) 'Long HIV1 incubation periods and dynamics for transmission within a family', *The Lancet* 336 (8708), 134–6.

Chin, J. (1990) 'Current and future dimensions of the HIV/AIDS pandemic in women and children', *The Lancet* 336 (8709), 221–4.

Department of Health and Social Security (DHSS) (1991) *Communicable Diseases Report*, London: DHSS.

Honigsbaum, N. (1991) *HIV, AIDS and Children*, London: National Children's Bureau.

Norman, S., Studd, J. and Johnson, M. (1990) 'HIV infection in women', *British Medical Journal* 301 (6763), 1231–2.

Rogers, R. (1989) *HIV and AIDS: What Every Tutor Needs to Know*, London: Longman.

Chapter 25

Blood relations

Educational implications of sickle-cell anaemia and thalassaemia

Simon Dyson

Sickle-cell anaemia and thalassaemia are genetic conditions which affect people from Black and ethnic minority communities in much greater numbers than White people, and they remain ill-understood. In this chapter Simon Dyson explains how these two conditions affect the lives of the children and adults who have them and considers their educational consequences. The lack of resources allocated to tackling the conditions and widespread ignorance of their effects, Dyson argues, may indicate underlying racism.

1 INTRODUCTION

A child is made ill by being forced to take part in a cross-country run on a freezing winter's day. Another is dismissed as lazy and inattentive. A third regularly misses lessons, though the teachers do not know why. Yet all these children have serious inherited blood disorders. They are also from Black and other ethnic communities. How much progress have we really made since Bernard Coard (1971) argued that 'the West Indian child is made educationally sub-normal in the British Educational System'?

The serious inherited blood disorders are sickle-cell anaemia and thalassaemia. Although sickle-cell has its highest incidence amongst Black communities (Franklin 1990) and thalassaemia amongst certain Mediterranean peoples, both disorders also affect other groups.

Sickle-cell anaemia is the best known of the sickle-cell disorders. It occurs most frequently in people of African or Caribbean descent, though it may also occur in people from the Eastern Mediterranean, the Middle East, India and Pakistan. People who carry the trait for sickle-cell are usually perfectly healthy themselves but when both parents are carriers they can pass sickle-cell anaemia on to their children. The carrier rate varies between different social groups (see Table 25.1), but it is estimated that about 1 in 10 people of Afro-Caribbean descent carry the sickle-cell trait. When both parents are carriers there is a 1 in 4 chance in each pregnancy that a child will have sickle-cell anaemia and a 1 in 2 chance that the child will carry the trait. People with sickle-cell anaemia produce red blood cells which under certain conditions take on the shape of a crescent or

Table 25.1 Approximate incidence of sickle-cell and thalassaemia traits amongst different ethnic groups in N.W. Europe

	Thalassaemia trait (%)	*Sickle-cell trait (%)*
Italy	2–14	0–10
Greece	8	0–20
Turkey	0.2–6	0–12
Cyprus	16	1
Middle East	1–3	1–2
India	1–17	0–30
East African Asian	7	+
Pakistan	6.5	+
Bangladesh	1–3	—
South China	3	—
Vietnam	1–6	—
Cambodia	1–10	—
North Africa	2–3	1–3
Sub-Sahara	1–3	15–25
Afro-Caribbean	1–2	6–12

Source: Adapted from WHO (1988: 19).
Notes: + indicates trace too small to measure.
— indicates 'not known'.

farmer's sickle (hence the disorder's name), rather than remaining round and flexible. The rigid sickle-cells become stuck in narrow blood vessels, depriving that part of the body of oxygen and causing severe pain. These pains, together with the other main symptoms of episodes of anaemia and infection, are called sickle-cell crises. Some people get crises quite often, others may only have them once every several years. Crises require urgent medical help, and may require powerful painkillers. About 1 in 300–400 people of Afro-Caribbean descent have sickle-cell anaemia. World Health Organisation estimates suggest there are approximately seventy-five children with sickle-cell disorders born in the UK each year, with a total known number of people with sickle-cell anaemia of around 4,000 (WHO 1988).

Thalassaemia is a peculiarity of the blood which is found in many countries around the world, and particularly in people of Mediterranean, Middle Eastern or Asian origin. Thalassaemia is complex and covers a broad spectrum of disorders, but there are essentially two forms to consider here, thalassaemia trait and thalassaemia major. People with thalassaemia trait may be mildly anaemic, though otherwise healthy, and when both parents are carriers they can pass thalassaemia major on to their children. As with sickle-cell, different social groups have differing proportions of carriers of thalassaemia trait (see Table 25.1), but for example 1 in 7 of Cypriot origin and 1 in 10–15 of Gujarati origin are estimated to carry the trait, sometimes called 'thalassaemia minor'. The pattern of inheritance follows similar principles to sickle-cell. Children with thalassaemia major cannot make sufficient haemoglobin, and the red cells that are produced by their bone marrow are nearly empty. They therefore need complete blood transfusions once every three to four weeks. This transfused blood leads to an excess of iron which must be removed from the body using a drug called desferrioxamine. The drug is given by injection into the abdominal wall. The injection is given slowly over 10–12 hours and is controlled by a syringe-driver pump. The injection is given 5–7 times a week. As with diabetes some children with thalassaemia understandably reject this life-saving regime during their teenage years. The World Health Organisation estimates that in the UK there are fifty-eight children with thalassaemia major born each year, and that there are 350 known people with thalassaemia, projected to increase to 2,700 in the absence of genetic counselling and prevention of births (WHO 1988).

2 ALLOCATION OF RESOURCES

One study in 1985 surveyed screening and counselling facilities for sickle-cell anaemia and found that unlike newborn screening for phenylketonuria or treatment for haemophilia (4,000 to 5,000 sufferers in the UK) funding for sickle-cell was primarily through short-term inner-city partnership grants (Prashar *et al.* 1985). Since it might reasonably be argued that such special monies were the unconvincing panic response to inner-city rebellions of the early 1980s, themselves born of a sense of exclusion felt by such communities, the continued exclusion (as of 1991) of sickle-cell and thalassaemia from the type of mainstream NHS funding that is comprehensive and consistent across district health authorities almost beggars belief. The response to the racism of exclusion has been to continue to exclude Black and ethnic communities by encouraging them to bid for short-term piecemeal funding for issues whose equivalent in the White community are NHS-funded. Throughout the 1980s much of the responsibility for raising awareness about sickle-cell continued to fall on Black women and their unpaid community work (Bryan *et al.* 1985). The racism of NHS-funding has provided a convenient backcloth for schools and local education authorities to avoid their responsibilities to children with sickle-cell or thalassaemia. Earlier in the 1970s this was compounded as the activities of the National Front left Black community leaders feeling ambiguous about pushing sickle-cell on to the agenda (Dyson 1990).

3 EDUCATIONAL IMPLICATIONS

Neither sickle-cell anaemia nor thalassaemia usually involve a mental disability.

For example:

> If a stroke occurs . . . the function of the brain may be affected. Other than this sickle-cell does not mentally affect the sufferers who are just as capable and able as their peers.
>
> (Black and Laws 1986: 204)

Of the two disorders, sickle-cell is the more variable in the severity of the physical effects. The perceived effect of sickle-cell disorders on education is also variable. In one study in Newham, approximately one-third of people with the condition thought sickle-cell had no effect on their education, another third some effect and the final third considered their education had been greatly (and presumably adversely) affected by having sickle-cell anaemia (Black and Laws 1986). More specifically a number of issues may have an impact on a child's education.

Physical exercise

A Health Education Authority leaflet for teachers on sickle-cell anaemia advises:

> Make sure the child is always warm and dry. The condition may get worse in cold or wet. Never let a child with sickle-cell anaemia get chilled after PE or swimming. Cross country running and outdoor games should be avoided in cold or wet weather. However, you should encourage the child to join in with as much exercise as possible.
>
> (HEA 1987: 4)

The self-exertion of young children at play, who perhaps do not understand the implications of their condition is also a concern to parents (Black and Laws 1986). Children with thalassaemia may occasionally feel too tired and lethargic for strenuous physical exercise, particularly towards the end of the three- to four-week period between receiving blood transfusions.

Concentration

Children undergoing a mild sickle-cell crisis which does not require hospital admission are still going to find study difficult. If they become anaemic they are likely to become easily tired or lethargic, which may perhaps be mistaken for inattentiveness or laziness, particularly if overlaid with racist perceptions of Black children as underachievers.

Registers

In the Newham study there was concern at the keeping of a register of people with sickle-cell anaemia by a senior clinical medical officer (Black and Laws 1986). Clearly such registers, whether for sickle-cell or thalassaemia, must have a purpose, be accurate, be explained to parents and children and above all be accessible and open to amendment by parents/children if the abuses and inaccuracies consequential upon confidentiality are to be avoided. (Dyson 1986)

Support

By talking to children and parents, teachers may also be able, with the child, to learn to gauge the relative seriousness of crises and to avoid taking the child home or to hospital when this is not always necessary (Black and Laws 1986). They may also help the child manage its own medicines at school (painkillers, antibiotics or folic acid supplements may be required for example) as well as ensuring a greater intake of fluids (and more frequent trips to the toilet) than usual. Pastoral care support may also be necessary to help a child come to terms with a life-long condition. This is equally pertinent whether it is a child responding to the unpredictable nature of sickle-cell anaemia or a child with thalassaemia who rebels against the all too predictable daily routine of the syringe-driver pump.

Extra tuition

Children with sickle-cell anaemia or thalassaemia may miss lessons, days or even weeks of schooling. For both conditions there may be hospital out-patients appointments, and in-patient stays for blood transfusions. For sickle-cell anaemia there is also the constant possibility of painful crises, sometimes requiring periods of hospitalisation. Franklin (1990) argues that people with sickle-cell anaemia are not likely to be able to take up hard manual labour and that this makes a sound academic basis even more important than usual. Mohammed Farooq has also argued that:

> Being a Thalassaemic, one should have more incentive to do well in their education as in the long run this will make life easier.
>
> It would be unsuitable for me to do manual jobs which involve a lot of heavy lifting and long periods of standing etc. These kinds of jobs would be difficult to do when as a result of anaemia you are tired, lethargic and need longer periods of rest.
>
> (UK Thalassaemia Society 1990: 5)

In such circumstances, whether for sickle-cell or for thalassaemia, arrangements are clearly needed to enable children to catch up with work missed, to have home or hospital tuition and if required to have courses that are flexible enough to be taken over extended periods of time (a two-year course taken over three years, for example). Moreover, it is insufficient for individual teachers or schools to develop *ad hoc* responses on a local basis. LEAs need to have a policy which will guarantee the resources to teachers and schools to enable such needs to be met. It can therefore be seen that local management of schools could work to the disadvantage of children with either sickle-cell or thalassaemia.

Personal and social education

It remains to be seen to what extent personal and social education (PSE) or health education are abandoned by secondary schools under the pressures created by the National Curriculum. I wish to argue that schools have a duty to all pupils from ethnic communities, especially where carrier rates from sickle-cell or thalassaemia are high, to inform them of the possibility that they may indeed be carriers. Pupils also need an explanation of the disorders and their consequences, and advice about how and where they can have their blood tested for sickle-cell trait or thalassaemia trait. This empowering of pupils to make an informed choice about choosing partners and having children might be carried out most appropriately as part of a sex education programme located within a broader PSE/health education curriculum. For example, education about sickle-cell and thalassaemia raises difficult moral dilemmas, particularly around abortion. A woman's right to choose, never fully recognised in law and further diminished in 1990, is one extremely important dimension. The usual arguments are compounded further in the case of sickle-cell and thalassaemia. First, what messages are given to those children and adults with sickle-cell anaemia or thalassaemia major by the terminating of pregnancies where the foetus is known to have one of these severe disorders? And second, in a society where racism is arguably a long way from being eradicated, young people from Black and ethnic communities may mistake education about sickle-cell or thalassaemia as being part of a racist attack on the growth of the Black British population.

However, such education need not be lost even in the absence of a sex education programme, for there are many disciplines where the two disorders could be addressed. Biology lessons looking at the normal functions of the blood or at genetics could use sickle-cell and thalassaemia as illustrative cases. The patterns of genetic inheritance provide a relevant concrete example through which to teach the theory of probability in Mathematics. The origins of sickle-cell and thalassaemia trait in malarial areas of the world (the carrier status, though not the disorders themselves, offers a degree of protection against certain types of malaria) and the patterns of migration through slavery, labour shortages and post-colonialism that have increased the numbers of carriers in past colonial powers such as Britain, France, Portugal and the Netherlands (WHO 1988) could be addressed in History or Geography. Arts students have already been involved in producing videos, plays, poems and computer designs using sickle-cell and thalassaemia as the subject.

4 CONCLUSION

Much of the debate in the 1980s concerning learning for all was concerned with the issues of school placement and integration. The case of sickle-cell anaemia and thalassaemia, while sometimes involving unwanted placement of a young person in a segregated school (Dyson 1990), more often concerns the quality of integration in terms of sensitivities over physical exercise, concentration, compiling of registers, emotional support, extra tuition and pastoral care arrangements. The issue of educating whole communities of pupils, a proportion of whom may be carriers of a serious inherited disorder, extends the responsibilities on teachers, schools and LEAs to be proactive in instigating health education programmes, rather than merely reacting to issues which could unnecessarily be allowed to threaten learning for all.

REFERENCES

Black, J. and Laws, S. (1986) *Living with Sickle-Cell Disease*, London: East London Sickle-Cell Society, c/o Burning Hall, Earlham Grove, Forest Gate, London E7.

Bryan, B., Dadzie, S. and Scafe, S. (1985) *The Heart of the Race: Black Women's Lives in Britain*, London: Virago Press.

Coard, B. (1971) *How the West Indian Child is Made Educationally Sub-Normal in the British Educational System*, London: New Beacon Books.

Dyson, S. (1986) 'Professionals, mentally-handicapped children and confidential files', *Disability Handicap and Society* 1 (1), 73–87.

—— (ed.) (1990) *Report of the Community Conference on Sickle-Cell Anaemia and Thalassaemia*, 2nd edn, Leicester: Leicestershire Health Promotion Department, Leicestershire District Health Authority.

Franklin, I. (1990) *Sickle-Cell Disease: A Guide for Patients, Carers and Health Workers*, London: Faber and Faber.

Health Education Authority (HEA) (1987) *Sickle-Cell Disease: A Guide for Teachers and Others Caring for Children*, London: Health Education Authority.

Prashar, U., Anionwu, E. and Brozovic, M. (1985) *Sickle-Cell Anaemia: Who Cares?*, London: Runnymede Trust.

UK Thalassaemia Society (1990) *News Review*, no. 42, June.

World Health Organisation (WHO) (1988) *The Haemoglobinopathies in Europe: Combined Report on Two WHO Meetings (Brussels: 14 March 1986 and Paris 20–21 March 1987)*, Geneva: World Health Organisation.

Chapter 26

Hell guffawed

Joseph Meehan starts secondary school

Christopher Nolan

Source: Chapter 2 of Nolan, C. (1987) *Under the Eye of the Clock*, London: Weidenfeld & Nicolson.

Christopher Nolan is Irish, in his twenties and a writer, both of prose and poetry. His physical disabilities make it impossible for him to walk, talk or control his movements. This chapter is an extract from his autobiography Under the Eye of the Clock, *in which, as Joseph Meehan, he attends Mount Temple Comprehensive School for an interview and then for his first day as a pupil.*

Joseph Meehan leapt awake that morning. Crawling with nerves he cried out, 'Lord above, I've to go for that bloody interview today.' Then he cringed in fear. Slob that he was, he knew now before the day was out he'd have cooked his goose for good and all. He lay in his bed frightening himself and then relaxing himself. Wait till the headmaster sees you doing your war dance he teased himself, but right away he countered: maybe you won't be nervous at all, maybe you'll be grand and relaxed, you know it happens sometimes, remember the first time you ever received communion, that day you were as calm as the desert after a sandstorm. Vests of vanquished heaven bucked his boy's god-given loneliness but at the same time hell guffawed in loud mocking laughs.

Creaking with nerves he sat in his chair. His parents were preparing to take their zoo-caged son to meet John Medlycott, the headmaster of Mount Temple Comprehensive School. Don't worry, he whispered to himself, be brave, rest a-while. Desperate in the face of crying God's fear he waited to go on youthful trial. Plodding bravery abandoned him, Joseph Meehan now joined hushed criminals before the firing squad.

Matthew reversed the car out onto the road and switching on the radio he pretended that all was normal but his eye seemed to glance too often towards his son. Nora meanwhile supported her son's frame with her arm. He hugged her closer to his frail body as if he could draw strength from her courage. As the car eased into the gateway he glanced ahead at the spired school. A large clock face warned him that it had seen history recorded, but numb now he baulked before its long-handed beckoning. Matthew lifted him from his seat and placed him in his lonely chair. Then together parents and boy set off to find the principal's office.

Bidden to come in, the crippled wheelchair-bound boy braved it across the threshold of the headmaster's office. Seated at a desk he saw a bright-eyed, bearded man. What the headmaster saw could barely be believed, for, true to form, arms spread wide open, face suddenly locked tight in an expression of stupid-looking languor, Joseph Meehan made his grand entrance. The first attempt to smile at Mr Medlycott's welcoming words sent Joseph's body into spasm making facial muscles contort and making his arms and legs move violently just as a clockwork doll would move on being released to unwind. The poor headmaster must have been bewildered by what he faced, but Nora mastered his bafflement by candidly saying, 'As you can see Joseph is very nervous but he'll relax in a few minutes.' Fashioning a faith which was totally against his better instincts, Mr John Medlycott smiled convincingly and waved aside any need for further explanation. Just then a tall, bearded man stepped into the office. The principal introduced him as Jack Heaslip, the guidance counsellor. By this time Joseph had assumed a more relaxed state so he was able to pay attention to the teachers. Seconds passed into minutes and now Joseph was on the alert, storing away words and observations when suddenly the bombshell burst, bursting asunder all man's renegade constraints in dealing with disabled man. Gloriously grinning faith Mr Medlycott said, 'Well Joseph, when can you start?' Joseph acknowledged his question by assuming the stance of one about to levitate. He felt a surge of happiness rush through his heart, it melted all over his many rejections and schooled his resolve not ever to fail this warm-hearted schoolmaster. As if to establish a certainty in Joseph's mind Mr Medlycott picked up the house phone and said, 'Jim, would you come here for a moment?' The door opened again and brusquely a man breezed in. He was dressed in a thick-knit sweater and jeans and his deep copper coloured hair and beard seemed as if it was going to choke him. Joseph noticed not just the beard and smart haircut but creeping curls of red chest hair peeped up from inside his open-necked shirt. 'Mr Casey,' said the headmaster, 'I'd like you to meet Joseph Meehan', and turning to Joseph he said, 'Joseph, meet Mr Casey, he'll be your class tutor.' Mr Casey smiled and said, 'Welcome, Joseph, to this school', and turning he shook hands with Matthew and Nora. Then feeling for the youngster's excitement he said, 'Come on Joseph, I'll bring you on a tour of the school', and off they set, the friendly striding teacher and the wheelchair-bound, silent, though thinking boy.

Silence reigned in the corridors, murmurs could be heard in the classrooms as Jim Casey pushed him along. The teacher showed him the library, the art room, the dining hall and then taking his bunch of keys from his pocket, he opened the door of his own classroom. He eased the chair into the crowded room. Empty desks stood in packed rows, a big blackboard lined the wall, but it was the windows that caught Joseph's attention. They were placed up near the ceiling and Joseph wondered why so high, why get only a glimpse of the sky. Feeling for the young boy's curiosity, Jim Casey asked and answered questions that he felt might be racing through Joseph's mind. The boy was flummoxed by the teacher's imagination and as he listened he hurrahed silently, for Mount Temple was going to answer his dreams. Lighting flickered for a moment when Jim Casey switched it off, and then locking the door again the teacher and boy set about returning to the office. Between them the teachers decided then to introduce Joseph to two boys who would be classmates of his. Mr Medlycott had chosen them and asked them to help Joseph to fit in to life in Class 1L. The boys seemed nervous and ill-at-ease, but the contact had been made and each boy had now got time to think and adjust to their coming challenge. Joseph asked nothing but verily quaked at what was before him. As usual though, he heaved a prayer and manfully faced his future in Mount Temple Comprehensive School. Now it was time to go and Joseph dearly wished to thank the teachers, but even so spasms ruled out obvious vests of gratitude and instead grimaces, gutteral sounds and dancing foot movements were all that he could muster up. Hesitating on the threshold he made one last effort to express thanks. Steadying his head he looked Mr Medlycott straight in the eye and gave a series of staccato-rapid bows. John Medlycott was not found wanting and Joseph smiled naturally for the first time that day, but there would be other days, that he knew full well, for wasn't every opportunity about to be dragged forth to birth new light into his drab-dreamed world.

Accommodating Joseph's fears was Nora's job, and she sensed that sealed within him was a beautiful brittle sensitivity. She knew that he was disappointed with his personal showing in Mount Temple but on the drive home she chatted to Matthew about the size of the school, the great acreage of grounds, the obvious sports facilities and the awareness of the three teachers whom she had just met. Clearly declining any effort on Joseph's part to talk about restoring confidence after his highly cantankerous-looking display. Nora waited until they all arrived home. Then stretching reliable allowances she looked at Joseph and said, 'Well Joseph, how does it feel to have all that fuss behind you?' All his silent, pent-up despair burst wide open and poor Joseph cried out loud, forgetting the adage that big boys don't cry, very sure they must if life hellishly harasses them, and not giving a damn whether they did or not, he cried fulsome tears of thoughtful, shattered, bewildering bewilderment. How must I have looked to those sane men? How can I convince them of my sanity? Were they really shattered in the face of my mad body antics? Were they only extending the typical hand of Protestant Christian concern or were they as damnwell terrified of me as I was of facing them? And next time we meet I have to be geared to face eight hundred students as well. Yesteryear's tears certainly were the stuff of childhood but now today's tears were for bewildering now and castrated boy's future.

Feebly, Nora and Matthew tried to divine the depths of their sad son's despair but bravely they hotly confirmed his own summing-up. 'Yes,' said Matthew, 'you were tense, but what you don't realise is that those teachers were equally tense, but they could hide it. Better for them to see you at your worst, things can only get better for you and for them.' Nora, usually sympathetic, destroyed Joseph's scene by gleefully laughing at him. Never heeding his therapeutic tears she said, 'Come boy, you know you have made the first scrape on the canvas, wait and see what's in store.' Punching Joseph in the chest then she smilingly sauntered off to cook the dinner.

But nobody can choke back such salty tears, so Joseph continued snivelling for some time. He knew his parents slyly meant to shock him into manhood, but he was not going to give in just yet.

At dinner that evening Nora denounced her son for being a coward. 'Come on Joseph, don't be so damn dramatic,' she begged. 'Didn't you meet your teachers and two pupils, and didn't you get the feel of the school? Now be man enough to give yourself and them a chance.' Joseph was still feeling hard done by but he knew his mother was sealing the day by challenging him to think positively. Even so, he struggled between hope and despair. Feeling tired from the huge task of meeting and convincing the uninitiated, he eventually gave in. Counselling himself not to weary himself any more he grew calm. As usual consolation came and as usual it was bonded in beautiful boldness. What trestled his mind bore no resemblance to sadness, for as usual, and unasked, hollow, nebulous, clinging clouds of heliotrope happiness came to rescue the broken resolution in this young boy's battle.

Dead weary, Joseph went to bed that night thankful that his day for introduction to Mount Temple was over. Dearly he thanked his Master for numbing his voiceless despair. He pictured in his mind the great-hearted men that he had just met and he knew that they anointed him by first fastening faith in a future which would include a handicapped boy on their rollcall. Sizing up his future he counselled himself to describe what the past endured and what the future might hold. Look at your lessons boy, he chivvied. Consider how lucky you are. You have served your time to coldness in outlook. Now you have got your foot in the door, maybe you ought to panic. Think of the others gone before you – did they have fiery intellects? Were they stored away in a back room, dirty, neglected, frowned upon? Did sun ever tan their opaque skin? Did they ever see the night sky? Did kindness ever move them to tears? Did they ever delve their hand in cold water? Did someone ever feel for their clenched fists and gently prise them open, so that water could run between their withered fingers? Did they feel the cold nervous heartbeat of a damp frog? Did they hold a wriggling worm in the palm of their hand? Did they ever feel soft summer rain as it tickled down their face or the headbowed battle to breathe in the face of a blizzard? Did they ever gloat with pleasure in a warm bubbly bath and afterwards sneeze in an aroma of talcum powder? Did sunshine blind them from an early-morning golden-copper sun, or did they ever see winter-bared trees silhouetted against crimson shot with pastel blue evening skies? Did they ever hear a real sound of laughter free of innuendo coming pouring from a pal's heart? Did they ever feel absolute satisfaction when the golf ball they were let help to hit rolled straight as a die and plopped into the minuscule-sized hole? Did they ever have their father's company on lovely secluded walks as birds did their nut, each bird bursting forth its chest trying to outdo its neighbour's song-filled stand? Did they ever feel a dear sister's love when she spent backbreaking hours designing and painting an intricate Celtic drawing especially for them? Did they ever love a foolish dog and marvel at his happiness? Did they ever feel good omens? Did they ever heave a sigh of healthy feeling despite awful paralysis? Did they rush through breakfast to be in time for school? Did they wait for Santa unable to sleep, fretting that Santa wouldn't come if they were not asleep? Did they dare to carp if bad vibes came from their sister? Did they ever detect jealousy in their sister's clambering for bigger helpings, bigger toys, bigger slices of family attention? Did they ever get so much love that the able-bodied sister wished that she were crippled too? Did they ever? And if they didn't, was that the end of that? Nasty life cast a lonely shroud over their dreams, but years heard the silent cry of those bashful babes and cuteness cogitates years' findings. So, Joseph schooled his nerve, and so his resolve reverberated in the chambers of his soul.

Easing their car into the stream of morning traffic, Matthew and Nora filled in for voiceless Joseph. They wondered about the length of the day in school, about the subjects, wondered who would first befriend their son and wondered silently if he baulked inwardly. Joseph meanwhile sat and secretly fretted. He imagined what the pupils would be thinking when his voice would involuntarily ring out a screech associated with tension or what, he worried, will they think when my arms fly outstretched when they try pushing my wheelchair through the crowded corridors or, worst of all, will they think I'm bonkers if my hands suddenly fly forward and hit them in the face. As a gap developed in the traffic he felt the surge of speed as the car streamed forward bringing him ever-quicker towards Mount Temple. Slowing down now, Matthew swung in to the gateway of his son's school. Sampling the thronged, frantic-running students, the boy gasped with fright. Cringing, he cowered beside his mother, but still his eye fell anew on the great clock facing him from the spired, sober-brick building.

Arriving at the front hall, Joseph found Peter Nicholson and Eddie Collins waiting for him. He searched their faces but saw only boyish civility and confidence. 'Can we bring you to your first class?' enquired Peter, but Matthew detained them, for he was anxious to explain about his son's involuntary arm movements. Nora said nothing; seemingly she was depending on the three boys to make up their own minds about how to deal with their new problems. 'I'll be here in this little office if you need me,' said Nora as she glanced towards a yellow door, and with that the boys and their new classmate set off down the corridor. Joseph was schooling his body to stay calm, whilst the boys were negotiating how they'd manage to curtail his arms. 'We are bringing you to the music room for singing,' confided Peter and there at the end of a green corridor they came upon a group of pupils standing waiting for the teacher to unlock the door. He let the boys and girls pass inside and then conscious of his new pupil, he came towards him and taking his hand he shook it warmly saying as he did so, 'You're very welcome to Mount Temple. I hope, Joseph, that you'll be very happy here with us.' Eddie then eased the wheelchair into the room and class began. Seeming curious, cheeky-faced Joseph moved his gaze from one student to the next, whilst they, anxious not to seem afraid, quickly swerved away when his eye fell upon them. He smelt their utter fear of him but was anxious too not to add to their worry by getting tense and grimacing wildly as facial muscles twisted askew in spasm.

Prior to the end of class Peter and Eddie asked to be excused, explaining to the teacher that they needed a headstart in order to have the wheelchair delivered to the next class before the corridors became jammed with students careering in their hundreds at change of class. Casting around for something to talk about, Eddie and Peter faced their new charge and tried to include him in their conversation. All was going smoothly for the three boys, but nothing could have prepared them for what happened next. Suddenly the school siren blared bloody murder and, frightened out of his wits, his brain-damaged startle reflex gave an almighty leap frightening in turn poor Peter and Eddie half to death. Despite the fright the boys kept up a brave front. They recovered their confidence and asked Joseph if he was all right. Joseph grinned and silently cast his eyes towards the ceiling signalling yes.

Meeting Jim Casey the English teacher was next on the timetable. 'He's our class tutor, did you know that?' asked Peter as he wheeled Joseph into the English classroom. Glancing backwards into Peter's face, Joseph indicated yes. Smiling simple welcome, Mr Casey took the handles of the wheelchair and steered Joseph into a gap among the front row desks. Casting many a wary glance in Joseph's direction he commenced to teach his charges. School was taking on a new meaning for Joseph, and smartly he began to record his new insights. The silent boy watched and listened to Mr Casey's cradling of voiced moments in poetry, the likes of which he had never heard before. His method of recording was not very obvious, but with an acute and sensitive ear he listed and stored his findings. Mr Casey and his class were certain in their speech but their exchanges served his purpose for silently he too answered questions and waited then to see if anybody else shared his opinions.

Classes changed once again and History was the subject this time. 'We have the headmaster for History,' explained Peter as the three boys sauntered along. Silence in the corridors seemed to create a closeness between them and Joseph felt at ease in their company. The boys were first into the classroom and as the class members filed in Joseph sneaked sideways glances at them watching for fear to manifest itself, but more power to them, he found them reassuring in that they continued arguing, teasing and generally being their noisy selves. Mr Medlycott breezed in with a flourish as if to hint that yes he saw nothing unusual in his new class member. 'Now pay attention,' he said and determining where they were at in their history books he launched into his subject.

Breathing a sigh of relief, Joseph cast mental anguish aside as he and his charges headed up the corridor for the mid-morning break. Assessing pupils' attitudes towards him he feared the result. Poor-fashioned mannerisms plagued his appearance but he knew full well that great undertakings require great tender rescuers with great tender hearts, and young though he was he could feel the tenderness masked behind the seeming coldness of the teachers and now already some of the boys and girls in Class 1L.

As classes broke up for their fifteen-minute break, pupils eyed Joseph with great curiosity and bemusement. Peter and Eddie were by his side always, but childish-minded students classed both of them as gullible for wasn't it only too obvious that that boy was retarded.

Seeing the Irish teacher at the door of her classroom fencing a pathway in for the wheelchair made Joseph aware of something candid in the expression on the face of Miss Siney. She was dressed in grey but her eyes danced with friendliness. She spoke Irish as if her respect for it came not just from the fact that it was her native language, but that she relished the sound of pronunciation, in short she seemed to really love her mother tongue. Joseph caught Miss Siney's eye searching his face for a sign of interest in her subject, but all she saw was dull looks, dribbles and senseless sounds.

At five minutes to midday Peter and Eddie set off with their charge for Miss Craig's room for Environmental Studies. Breathing noisily from pure tension, Joseph steamed into the classroom. Voiceless, he could not convey his pleasure at meeting another new teacher, but Miss Craig beautifully bypassed the momentary embarrassment by carefully assisting the boys as they moved desks to make place for the wheelchair. Breathing quietly now, Joseph was able to size up his teacher. She emanated civil normal breadth of courage by creating an air of 'let there be no panic, I'm in control here', and on she went with her geography lesson.

Cheering wildly in the corridors, all 800 students broke free for lunch hour. A smell of cooking wafted from the dining hall but Joseph verily cheered too, for his first day in Mount Temple was over and he was free to go home and cast rollicking fun for himself and his family by drolly giving a blow-by-blow account of the teachers, pupils, attitudes and foul-ups of his first great day in an able-bodied man's wonderful world.

Each day of that first week narrowed down to a half-day was cast especially to cater for Joseph's needs. The teachers felt that his introduction to school and pupils needed to be done gradually. So it was that he charged home that first day, and so it was that he had the second half of the day for conversation, waffle, frankness and even some wound-licking.

Dark night was always waned by golden visions and the night of 20 February 1979 was no different. Just as always happened, Joseph Meehan saw his life pass before his sensitive mind's eye. Free-falling, he created grand gospels of boyish certainty. Washed by sedentary, snared sacrifice he descended within easy reach of hell, but severe despondency never could stop Joseph's mesmerised wold-waddling in ink-blue heaven's busy mobility of secrets. Cassettes played back the day's happenings sadly beckoning him towards despair, but fending off fright he beckoned instead towards students frolicking in dreamland and stole yesses from them before they ebbed notional no.

Part 5

Representing practice

Chapter 27

What counts as research?

Lawrence Stenhouse

Source: Edited version of the original paper in the British Journal of Educational Studies 29 (2), pp. 103–14, 1981.

In this chapter, originally given as a lecture in 1980, Lawrence Stenhouse, one of the most influential thinkers in British education in the second half of the century, offers a non-technical definition of research as 'systematic self-critical inquiry'. He compares the relevance of science and history as models for research in education which can influence practice, and he examines the possibilities and limitations of experimental social science as a basis for educational action. Stenhouse looks at the conditions for objectivity in research, and argues for a central place for teachers in the conduct of research in education. He sees publication as an essential part of research, but his definition of publication is wide. It includes discussion in teacher groups and application in action. Publication for Stenhouse involves the subjection of research to critical tests of its claims.

1 INTRODUCTION

I shall begin by hazarding a minimal definition: research is systematic self-critical inquiry.

As an inquiry, it is founded in curiosity and a desire to understand; but it is a stable, not a fleeting, curiosity, systematic in the sense of being sustained by a strategy. When Jane Goodall confronted a chimpanzee with a looking-glass, the animal, after gesticulating at its own image, felt behind the glass in order – may I say loosely – to understand the situation; but after a few moments it had passed on to other activities. Not so the researcher, who has bred a persistence of sequential inquiry by curiosity out of patience. And fundamental to such persistence of inquiry is a sceptical temper of mind sustained by critical principles, a doubt not only about the received and comfortable answers, but also about one's own hypotheses. [. . .]

The utility of research generally brings to people's minds the hard science that lies behind their kitchen equipment or television, but my homeland is history. I see history as the archetypal utilitarian research. It lies behind our recipe books rather than our cooking pots. While the hard sciences produce our hardware, history produces our software: it is the expression of a systematic critical inquiry into the fruits of our experience. In the broadest sense the physical and life sciences pursue research into the *context* of experience: history is concerned – again in the broadest sense – with research into the *content* of experience.

You will be clear that I am not using the term *history* in the narrow senses sometimes adopted in schools and universities. I am distinguishing between the researches of science, which characteristically seek laws or theories not narrowly conditional upon time, and those researches cast in a historical perspective, which recognise time as an essential variable in the accounts they give. Once we are in time there is no account of the present. Both science and history are given to generalisation – in spite of the disclaimers of some historians – but science aspires to generalisations which are predictive and universal, whereas historical generalisation is retrospective and summarises experience within boundaries of time and place.[1]

The position I have sketched is clearly problematic at many points, but I must be highly selective in the problems I take up. Since all are united – I assume – by an interest in the relevance of research to the practical activity of education, I must ask some questions about the relevance of science and history to practice, and, by implication, to future practice. And I can only sketch some answers to these questions. Then, I must look at the 'human sciences' of psychology and sociology to locate them in the wider picture of research. Finally, I shall turn to the problems of values and interests in research.

I have, I must confess, withheld to this point a problem concerning my simple definition of research, which I now bring out into the open. In a paper[2] I have described research as 'systematic inquiry *made public*'. What is the role of report in research? What is the status of research-based action? What is the relation of report to discourse and to practice? These questions, as well as those set out in the previous paragraph, deserve at least a glance before I turn to the practical problem which I have assumed to be the hidden agenda lying between the lines of the letter inviting me to contribute this chapter: what credible force can we give to the slogan, *Teacher as Researcher?*

Scientists attempt to account for consistencies of occurrence or of the conjunction of occurrences over time or for events which are regarded as inevitable outcomes of preceding causes. Or, to put it another way, scientists are interested in the power of laws and theories which are general and predictive to organise and summarise data derived from observations. Whether or not the laws of science are invented by mind or discovered in nature, together with many other controversies, need not concern us for the moment.

The first and most obvious application of science to practice rests on the capacity of predictions to provide us with information about the context of action. To put it crudely, I can plan my farming on the prediction that there will be seasons, or my navigation on the prediction that there will be tides. Such predictions do not guide me by telling me exactly what to do, though they may tell me clearly what I should not do. A simple way to express them is to say that they set the conditions of the game: they are the field of play and perhaps the rules in their barest form.

The second application of science to practice works through the possibility of applying general laws to the problem of predicting the outcomes of specific acts. This enables me to design acts on the basis of a more or less reliable estimate of their outcome: to calculate that my bridge will stand or that my glue will stick.

These two applications of science strengthen, but do not supersede, common sense. Nor do they tell us whether to build our bridge, for all that they predict the traffic flows and assure us that we can construct a bridge that will stand.

History has an application close to the first application of science suggested above. It helps to define the conditions of action by summarising experience in such a way as to suggest the considerations we shall have to take into account as we make judgements as to how to act. We must attempt to understand the complex web of social variables which contextualise our actions and influence the outcomes. Historical analyses which support such understanding are more useful across time than is sometimes recognised: the speeches arguing for and against war in Thucydides' history of the Peloponnesian War are no bad introduction to an understanding of the ground rules of present conflicts. Judgements of relevance to our acting in any given case can be founded on such stock-taking, 'state-of-the-nation' reports, which are 'contemporary histories' in the sense that they are accounts of a past as close to our present – or perhaps, better said, to our future – as we can make them.

History is also able to summarise the experience of action in such a way as to strengthen judgement and revision of judgement in planning acts. It enables us to make judgemental predictions of how events will go and to revise those predictions in the face of surprise by rapid reassessments. Paradoxically, history both predicts that events will be substantially unpredictable and supports our attempts to narrow the bounds of unpredictability both by judgemental predictions and by contingency plans. Further, it offers to make us adept at reading the significance of the unexpected and reacting shrewdly to it. It helps us to play what, by analogy with chess, we may call 'the middle game'.

Science and history have a great deal more in common than is sometimes believed: both help to define the context in which people act, and both help to anticipate the outcomes of actions. But when we apply science, we premise high predictability, and when we apply history we premise low predictability. I believe that the acts and thoughts of individual human beings contain essentially unpredictable elements owing to the human capacity for creative problem-solving and the creation of meanings. Others, of course, will see unpredictability in human action as the wilderness beyond the advancing frontier of a social science, a wilderness to be colonised in the future.

2 SOCIAL SCIENCE AND PRACTICE

Although social science begins with an attempt to apply the methods of natural science to social phenomena in the confidence that human action is lawfully predictable, it would be quite unjust to burden contemporary social science with this heritage. In practice, experimental and analytic social science seeks to ride the assumption of high predictability as far as it may, while observational and naturalistic social science attempts to work in areas where the assumption of low predictability seems stronger. There is nothing ultimately contradictory in nibbling that bit of string from both ends.

The application of the work of the analytic experimentalists to practice is at two levels, corresponding broadly to two research traditions. A laboratory tradition seeks general laws and theories which are analogous to those in certain areas of the natural sciences. The area of learning theory is a good example of this kind of work. Concepts such as recency, frequency, reinforcement, proactive and retroactive inhibition and so forth are pretty well anchored and contribute to synthetic theory. In my view the interest of this kind of work is currently underestimated by educators, but its relevance to practice is rather in defining ground rules than in discriminating action. It draws attention to some of the variables at work in a complex multivariate situation, but it does not enable us to predict outcomes in such situations.

It is in part this shortcoming which presses the social scientist to come out of the laboratory and undertake field research of a kind which faces real situations with their full multivariate complexity. Quasi-experimental designs[3] are applied directly to practice, usually to attempt to predict the effects of actions, the crucial tools being the statistical procedures which allow estimates of reliability, of internal and external validity, and the use of analysis of variance and correlational techniques. This tradition of field experiment fails to discriminate the effects of specific actions on specific cases. What it yields are indications of trends, that is, actuarial predictions for populations; and often in educational research these predictions suffer from weak external validity. For example, Bennett's work on *Teaching Styles and Pupil Progress*[4] fails to control the LEA as a variable, while the Humanities Project experiment in teaching style revealed the LEA as a crucial factor.[5] Moreover, when it comes to the problem of how to act as an individual teacher in the light of the Bennett research, it is not clear whether one should adopt the formal style which gave the best mean results or the informal style which gave an excellent, perhaps the best, single result.

In short, it seems that, while social science applied to education can produce results which help us to understand the ground rules of action, it cannot provide the basis for a technology of teaching which offers reliable guidance to the teacher. Predictions based upon statistical levels of confidence are applicable to action only when the same treatment must be given throughout the entire population. This condition does not apply in education. It is the teacher's task to differentiate treatments.

It is in part the recognition of this problem that accounts for the spread of interest in naturalistic or ethnographic styles of educational research. The portrayal of cases offers to inform the judgement of actors – the administrators, teachers, pupils or parents – rather after the manner of history, by opening the research accounts to recognition and to comparison and hence to criticism in the light of experience. Such a refinement of experienced practical judgement eludes the psycho-statistical model which strips the data of recognisable characteristics and context, and presents 'findings' or 'results', which are accessible to criticism only by replication or by technical attack on the design or conduct of the research.

However, naturalistic styles of social research, in contrast to laboratory or field experiments, do appear to accept real time as a dimension and the question arises: is naturalistic research simply and necessarily history?

To my mind the extent to which naturalistic studies should draw on the traditions of history or of social science is one of the most important issues in contemporary social research. I have written elsewhere on the topic and this is not the place to explore it at length. But one issue has central relevance here: the status of theory.

History, though not wholly atheoretical, is none the less parsimonious of theory. In particular, historians point up issues as often by ambiguity as by stating hypotheses. Since their accounts are not conspicuously theoretical, the historians take most of their terms of art from their subjects. Thus, the historian of parliament will use the terms of parliamentarians, the historian of music, the terms of musicians, and so forth. One great strength of history is that its vocabulary is accessible to those who are interested in the topic under discussion.

Social scientists, even naturalistic social scientists, appear to be much more interested in theory than are historians. Even when they are not hotly in pursuit of laws they still have a taste for theory, for they seek generalisations which go across the boundaries of human interests and hence of interest-linked vocabularies. They are, to simplify the matter a little, interested in human and social and political behaviour rather than the behaviour of parliamentarians or musicians or beekeepers or teachers. Social scientists themselves are a group with their own language (which others often criticise as jargon) which not only arranges their world so that they can communicate with one another, but also relates discourse to action. But the act to which the discourse relates is primarily the social science research act. The discipline of social science, expressed in the language of social science, organises social science knowledge in such a way as to point up promising lines of research and organises understanding of methodology and method to support the planning of the research act. To apply social science to teaching most often requires a translation and one difficult enough for researchers to yearn for a richer literacy of the consumer.[6]

The question arises: could we have an educational science? It is a question that can be construed in many ways, but here I mean: could we have a study of educational phenomena which opted neither for the common language of education nor for the language of social science theory, but instead for a theory which related directly to educational practice? Not a sociology, nor a psychology, but a pedagogy.

For the moment, I shall leave that question hanging.

3 VALUES AND INTERESTS IN RESEARCH

I need to take up the issue of objectivity in social research, and it is not an issue I am well equipped to handle, partly because I personally have been untroubled by the problem. I am content that human and social research (and probably also all research that is interested in interpretation or theory rather than mere brute facts) should aim to ground discourse in dependable intersubjectivities. For me disciplines of knowledge or complexes of research are founded on 'arrests of experience',[7] limitations of aspiration which allow us to order experience within conditional boundaries. To name something is, in any event, to make it accessible to discussion at the expense of both oversimplifying it and rendering it ambiguous.

It is commonplace that research is attacked on the grounds that researchers allow an intrusion of their values. It will help my analysis, as well as suit my inclinations, if I consider the perspectives given to research not by researchers' values but by their interest. I use the word *interest* in two dictionary senses which are clearly related: 'being concerned or affected in respect of advantage or detriment' and 'feeling of concern for or curiosity about a person or thing'. Now it is clear that the second of these definitions accords pretty closely with what I have suggested is the impulse behind all research – curiosity – and I believe that such curiosity is almost inevitably associated with considerations of advantage or detriment.

In particular, it should be noted, interest figures prominently in applied sciences: we build a bridge because it is advantageous to us to do so and that advantage breeds a curiosity about bridges. Moreover, the building of a good bridge is to our advantage not only in the primary sense that it lets us cross the river, but also in the secondary sense that successful achievement rewards us in terms of reputation, material payment and future opportunities. In most cases these interests do not impel us to falsify our formulae and build bridges that fall down. The collapse of a bridge is difficult to hide: we do not fudge our process when it is impossible to falsify our result.

The prime problem of interests (and values) in research is this: when the tests of our hypotheses or interpretations are not rigorous, there is a temptation to make dubious claims which appear likely to promote our reputation, increase our material rewards, better our future prospects or endorse some policy to which we are devoted independently of the research.

All researchers are beset by temptations of interest which may blow them off course. The crucial problem is the strength of the critical process which controls such temptations, and such a critical process is essentially social as well as methodological. The person who is too powerful to be questioned – like the person who is too clever to be understood – cannot be controlled by the adoption of methods which purport to support objectivity.

Inquiry counts as research to the extent that it is systematic, but even more to the extent that it can claim to be conscientiously self-critical.

4 THE TEACHER-RESEARCHER

The basic argument for placing teachers at the heart of the educational research process may be simply stated. Teachers are in charge of classrooms. From the point of view of the experimentalist, classrooms are the ideal laboratories for the testing of educational theory. From the point of view of the researcher whose interest lies in naturalistic observation, the teacher is a potential participant observer in classrooms and schools. From whatever standpoint we view research, we must find it difficult to deny that the teacher is surrounded by rich research opportunities.

Moreover, there is in the research field of education little theory which could be relied upon by the teacher without testing it. Many of the findings of research are based on small-scale or laboratory experiments which often do not replicate or cannot be successfully applied in classrooms. Many are actuarial and probabilistic, and, if they are to be used by the individual teacher, they demand situational verification. The application of insights drawn from naturalistic case studies to a teacher's situation rests upon the quality of the teacher's study of his home case. Using research means doing research. The teacher has grounds for motivation to research. We researchers have reason to excite that motivation: without a research response from teachers our research cannot be utilised.

And, after all, much medical research even in universities is conducted by practitioner-researchers. We pay them more and call them clinical.

There are, however, a number of objections to the teacher as a researcher.

First, it is said that tests of the accuracy of teachers' self-reports suggest that teachers do not know what they do. Although this shortcoming can be exaggerated, it has substance. Teachers lay the foundation of their capacity for research by developing self-monitoring strategies. The effect is not unlike that of making the transition from amateur to professional actor. Through self-monitoring teachers become conscious artists. Through conscious art they are able to use themselves as instruments of their research.

Second, it is claimed that involvement in the action of school and classroom gives teachers an interest in the tendency of research findings and condemns them to bias. This is not in my view a sustainable objection. In my experience the dedication of professional researchers to their theories is a more serious source of bias than the dedication of teachers to their practice. Teachers whose work I have examined at master's and doctoral level seem to me to achieve remarkably cool and dispassionate appraisals. I see more distortion produced by academic battles than by practical concerns. But I must concede that there are forbidden areas for most teacher-researchers, and that these are mainly where the exposure of persons and personal relationships is at stake. In general, however, professional researchers seem to me more vulnerable because of their distance from practice and their lack of responsibility for practice than teachers are by virtue of their involvement in practice.

Researchers sometimes regard teachers as theoretically innocent. But much professional research drawing on, if not feeding, the disciplines is also theoretically innocent. This is true of most surveys, field experiments and evaluations. You can partly detect them by the sign that all the theoretical work of their authors is methodological. On the other hand, some teachers are theorists, hot from Ph.Ds or having informally developed theoretical interests. What teachers most often lack is confidence and experience in relating theory to design and in the conduct of research work.

The most serious impediment to the development of teachers as researchers – and indeed as artists in teaching – is quite simply shortage of time. In this country teachers teach too much. So research by teachers is a minority activity, commonly stimulated and supported by formal degree structures at master's and doctoral level, or by participation in a research project with the teacher-research concept built in. In rare persons the interest and activity is sustained. In a number of cases teacher research develops as someone turns to immersion in work as a response to bereavement or other crises. Much clearly needs to be done to ameliorate the burdens of the teacher prepared to embark on a programme of research and development.

5 PUBLICATION

Earlier in this chapter I mentioned that a full definition of research might include the qualification that it be made public. Private research for our purpose does not count as research. Partly, this is because unpublished research does not profit by criticism. Partly, it is because we see research as a community effort and unpublished research is of little use to others. What seems to me most important is that research becomes part of a community of critical discourse. But perhaps too much research is published to the world, too little to the village. We need local cooperatives and papers as well as international conferences and journals. And in any case we need more face-to-face discourse. It's a pity, perhaps, that in this country the doctorate is not publicly defended.

Here is a description of a particular model of a critical community:

> One type of deliberative college which seeks to incorporate the necessary technical competence to work realistically has been described elsewhere, where I spoke of what happens on the editorial boards of certain reviews, which function as cultural circles at the same time as editorial boards. The circle criticises in a collegiate way and so contributes towards developing the work of individual members of the editorial staff whose own task is organised according to

> a rationally worked out plan and division of labour.
>
> Through discussions and joint criticisms (consisting of suggestions, advice, indications of method, constructive criticism directed towards mutual learning), by which each man functions as a specialist in his own subject to improve the collective competence, the average level of each individual is raised. It reaches the height or the capacity of the best trained and assures the review not only of ever better selected and organic contributions but creates the conditions for the rise of a homogeneous group of intellectuals trained to produce regular and methodical literary activity (not only in *livres d'occasion* and partial studies, but in organic general works as well).
>
> Undoubtedly in this kind of collective activity each job produces the capacity and possibility for new work, since it creates even more organic conditions of work: card indexes, bibliographical notes, collections of basic specialised works, etc. A rigorous struggle is required against habits of dilettantism, improvisation, oratorical and declamatory solutions. It is important for reports, and this applies to criticisms, to be made in written form, in short succinct notes. This can be ensured by distributing material in good time etc. Writing notes and criticisms is a didactic principle rendered necessary by the need to combat habits of prolixity, declamation and sophistry created by oratory . . .[8]

Publication has two functions. It opens work to criticism and consequently to refinement; and it also disseminates the fruits of research and hence makes possible the cumulation of knowledge. When systematic inquiry is shared in groups whose character approximates Gramsci's deliberative college, it enjoys the advantage of criticism, but it does not necessarily disseminate outside the collegiate group. Work undertaken in such a context must, in my view, count as research. Indeed, the critical process in the group might with advantage act as a filter. If publication were more selective, we might be in less danger of cumulating the redundant or ephemeral.

There is, however, a less obvious implication of Gramsci's idea. His deliberative college is dedicated to action (in this case running a newspaper). In this it might be compared to a school or teachers' centre group or to an opera company or to a cooperative workshop. The question arises: can research be expressed in performances or actions? I think it can if its force is to make action hypothetical or problematic. To the extent that a substantive action is an expression of a research inquiry, it tests the hypothetical outcome of the inquiry; and this is one understanding of action research.

Alongside our received academic notion of what constitutes publication, we must, I think, allow that research can find other utterances – in critical groups or in action – which can be subject to disciplines which test its claims. Indeed, it could be a weakness of much research in education that it is insufficiently tested in action, too readily accepted by its mere survival in the academic debate.

6 WHAT COUNTS AS EDUCATIONAL RESEARCH?

Research, I have suggested, is systematic and sustained inquiry, planned and self-critical, which is subjected to public criticism and to empirical tests where these are appropriate. Where empirical tests are not appropriate, critical discourse will appeal to judgement of evidence – the text, the document, the observation, the record. In applied or action research the test or evidence may be provided by substantive action, that is, action which must be justified in other than research terms.

I conclude by asking: what counts as research in education? I mean by research *in* education, research conducted within the educational intention and contributory to the educational enterprise. There is, of course, in history, philosophy, psychology and sociology, research *on* education conducted from the standpoint of the disciplines which contributes to the educational enterprise incidentally if at all. It is, one might say, educational research only in the sense that Durkheim gave us suicidal research.

Research is educational to the extent that it can be related to the practice of education. Whether this relationship is to be made by a theory of pedagogy at some level of generalisation or by an extension of experience which informs practice or by providing the framework for action research as a tool to explore the characteristics of particular situations or by critical evaluation of practice, or by all of these appears an open question. But two points seem to me clear: first, teachers must inevitably be intimately involved in the research process; and second, researchers must justify themselves to practitioners, not practitioners to researchers.

NOTES

1 There is a sense in which historical generalisations are predictive but such predictions are predictions of what further research is likely to reveal.
2 Stenhouse, L. (1979) 'Research as a basis for teaching', Inaugural Lecture, University of East Anglia.
3 Campbell, D. T. and Stanley, J. C. (1963) 'Experimental and quasi-experimental designs in research on teaching', in N. L. Gage (ed.), *A Handbook of Research on Teaching*, Chicago: Rand McNally.
4 Bennett, N. (1976) *Teaching Styles and Pupil Progress*, London: Open Books. Editor's note: In this study, Bennett examined the link between different teaching styles in junior schools and the attainments of pupils. He concluded that a style which was characterised as traditional was associated with higher attainment in general, although the teacher whose pupils had the highest attainment had a style described as progressive. All the schools were drawn from one LEA, so the study was unable to assess the significance of the policies and practices of the LEA for teaching style or for pupil attainment.
5 Editor's note: The Humanities Curriculum Project was an influential project developed in the late 1960s under the direction of Lawrence Stenhouse. It sought to teach about controversial issues, such as war, poverty and law and order, to lower-attaining 14 to 16 year olds. The methods involved active, collaborative learning, class and

group discussion and the use of first-hand evidence. The project ran in a number of LEAs. The evaluation found that the outcomes of the project depended greatly on the particular school and LEA in which it was implemented. See MacDonald, B. (1971) 'The evaluation of the Humanities Curriculum Project: a holistic approach', *Theory into Practice* 10, 163–7; and Stenhouse, L. (1971) 'The Humanities Curriculum Project: the rationale', *Theory into Practice* 10, 154–62.

6 Halpin, A. W. (1966) *Theory and Research in Administration*, London: Collier/Macmillan.

7 Oakeshott, M. (1933) *Experience and its Modes*, Cambridge: Cambridge University Press.

8 Gramsci, A. (1967) 'The organisation of education and culture', in *The Modern Prince and Other Writings*, New York: International Publishers.

Chapter 28

Finding a voice

Extracts by Micheline Mason, Ved Mehta, Doug Mellor and Rosemary Sutcliff, with an introduction and discussion by Patricia Potts

To maximise the participation of all children and adults within the education system, listening to all their varied views has to be encouraged and valued. One way to explore and communicate our own views is to describe and discuss our own experiences of education, to tell our own story.

In this chapter, Patricia Potts has collected together four examples of first-hand accounts of experiences of school. Micheline Mason is a writer, illustrator and disability rights worker and she describes how the comradeship of other disabled teenagers enabled her to begin to develop a positive self-image. Doug Mellor is a tiler and he describes the terror of his adolescent illiteracy. Rosemary Sutcliff, the author of historical novels for children, refused to learn to read when her parents thought it was high time. Ved Mehta, a writer, was blinded by meningitis at the age of 4. He describes his life in a residential school for poor blind boys in what was then part of India and how he wanted to be able to run like the sighted boys.

Reading these four stories gives their authors a voice. Listening to what they say about their experiences of school makes it possible for us to enter into and share their different perspectives. And it may help us to find our own voices.

1 INTRODUCTION

Patricia Potts

If all children, young people and adults who are learners in our education system are to enjoy an appropriate curriculum in settings which do not reduce their status as full members of the mainstream community, then everyone has to be seen to be of equal worth, not only in principle but also in practice. The structure of power-relationships within education denies this full participation to various groups of pupils, as well as to groups of teachers and other adult workers.

One way to increase the participation of devalued or excluded groups is to make it possible for them to speak for themselves, taking a more active part in shaping what they see as appropriate provision. This means encouraging people both to tell their own stories and to listen to those of other people. Making it easy for people to express their views, to retain control over the use of personal information and to reach the audience they want must all be included among the aims of an inclusive system of education.

Listening to what people have to say about their experiences of school makes it possible for us to enter into and share their different perspectives. If teachers listen to more accounts told by adults about their time as pupils, then perhaps it will be easier to enter into the worlds of their own students, whatever their age. Being a learner is, after all, an experience that we share with everyone. Remembering what learning was like for us may make it easier for us to let other learners speak for themselves. And in giving others a voice and sharing more of their perspectives we may find a stronger voice for ourselves.

2 MICHELINE MASON

Micheline is a freelance writer, illustrator and disability rights worker. This extract comes from a contribution she made to a collection of autobiographical pieces entitled *Images of Outselves: Women with Disabilities Talking*.

> Animals have it easy. I mean, for example, that it is very unlikely that a horse wastes much time wondering if she is really a horse, whilst human beings seem disposed to spending vast amounts of totally unproductive time wondering if they are really human beings at all. Well, some do.
>
> The first time the doubt that I belonged to this particular planet struck me, was a glorious, calm, blue-skied day when I was twelve years old. Lying flat on my back in the garden, staring at the sky, I was thinking about growing up. Until that moment I think I had somehow believed that when I grew up I would become 'normal', i.e. without a disability. 'Normal' then meant to me, 'like my big sister', pretty, rebellious, going out with boys, doing wonderful, naughty things with them, leaving school and getting a job, leaving home, getting married and having children. That momentous day I suddenly realised that my life was not going to be like that at all. I was going to be just the same as I had always been – very small, funnily shaped, unable to walk. It seemed at that moment that the sky cracked. My vision expanded wildly. My simply black and white world exploded into vivid colours which dazzled and frightened me in a way in which I had never been frightened before. Everything familiar took on an ominous hue. At that point I saw life, especially with regard to other women, as a huge competition, and I believed that I was just not equipped to compete. My girl-friend from next door came out and suggested a game as she had done many times before. I remember her look of confusion and hurt when I said I didn't want to play any more. [. . .]
>
> I guess when you go about feeling like a mouldy artichoke, people tend to react to you as though you were one. I was so shy, especially with boys, that very few managed to overcome their reactions to my disability and my self-consciousness enough for any conversation to last more than five minutes, thus affirming my belief that I was unlovable. However, one or two confident

souls broke through to me despite all this. I experienced my first real kiss when I was fourteen. I didn't like it much, but I think from that moment on the grey clouds began to part. At some point during those two years, I worked out that the cosy future my family had planned for me would be so boring that I would rather die than make their gloomy prophesies come true. When the chance came for me to go to a boarding school for girls with disabilities, I jumped at it. I saw it as the beginning of my road to freedom.

Our boarding school had rows of adjacent loos. One day, very soon after my arrival at the school, I was sitting in one loo whilst a new friend was sitting in the loo next door. 'Micheline,' she said, 'Do you think you will ever get married?' A flood of relief came over me then. I knew the question was coming from someone who had asked herself the same question many times already. There were other people who had gone through all that doubting too! Nice people! Other young women who had had their self-image as women so severely damaged that they too had wondered if they were entitled to anything life had to offer. My three years with nearly one hundred young women with disabilities began a slow healing process. We laughed and cried together. We experienced illness and even deaths amongst us. But we felt so strong! There I realised how strong women are, especially when we have to fight to overcome something – in our case our disabilities. There I discovered what sharing meant, and accepting people's differences whether they be of colour, class, religion or experience of disability. I began to accept my differences, my uniqueness, as something to be proud of.

(Campling 1981: 24–7)

Drawing on her own resources and the solidarity that the shared experiences with other young women at her boarding school gave her, Micheline managed to peel off the layers of 'mouldy artichoke' and develop a positive self-image. Micheline challenges our narrow view of what it means to be 'human' and describes the damage this does to disabled people. I find her language and imagery strikingly candid, both humorous and sharp, a concise, straightforward but moving account of coping with everyday oppression.

Micheline now has a daughter, who also has a disability and who attends a mainstream school. Micheline is a founder member of the Integration Alliance, which includes parents of children and young people with disabilities or who experience difficulties in learning, parents with disabilities, teachers with disabilities and education workers committed to developing an inclusive system of education. Micheline is co-editor, with Richard Rieser, of *Disability Equality in the Classroom: A Human Rights Issue* (ILEA 1990), and wants to extend her work as a coordinator of disability awareness training for workers in educational and other services.

3 DOUG MELLOR

Doug describes himself as a tiler and member of his local Conservative club. This extract comes from a contribution Doug made to a book of short, autobiographical pieces spoken or written by men and women who had become literate as adults.

The fear of not being able to read and write stems from the age of, I would say seven or eight. That's when it first starts to build up.

I remember a day in school, probably the worst I had when I was in school, when our form teacher called me out to read out the English lesson. What I used to always do was learn a page. Oh, I was just cheating myself really, but I always used to learn a page. I knew this page without even looking at it really. I went to his desk and he says, 'Right, start reading.' But he opened the book and he said, 'Not that page.' Obviously he must have known. So I was stuck at a new page. I was struggling through it and I got stuck at this word and he got really ratty about it. He said 'I told you that word not two minutes ago,' so I said, 'Well I'm sorry sir, I've forgotten it.' He says, 'Well right, you go down to Miss Blackburn's class.' It used to be A, B, C then and I was always in the C class. But this was the B class. I had a lot of friends in that class. So what he asked me to do was to go and ask Miss Blackburn what this word was. So I thought, 'God ... what am I going to do?' I walked in and like a fool, I read this page out that I knew, and she said, 'Very good. Off you go.'

I got back to the classroom and Mr Parry says, 'Right Mellor, what's that word?' I says, 'I don't know sir, I didn't ask her.' He says, 'Right, stand over there,' gets out of his desk the big strap and he bloody leathered me. That was the first and only time that I actually cried. It was so, I thought, humiliating in front of the class, what he did to me for not asking this word, that's what stuck in my mind. But it was great, for all the class gathered round me and, I don't know, I suppose comforted me, come to me and said 'Oh, he's a rotten pig.' He was a real swine, that teacher. I was 14 then ...

The compensations

The compensations for being in the C class, or for not being able to read and write, was you had to be tough and hard, so you could be the 'I don't care' cock of the school. So you got respect that way, rather than being clever. [...]

Nightmare

When I had English exams at school I would have nightmares and sleep-walk the night before. I always had the same nightmare and it stopped when I left school. It was cushions, big cushions and everything in the room would look far away, as if it was about 20 yards away, but it was weird. I tried to study

> this dream, this nightmare. I could feel myself going into it and it was always before an exam, and sometimes before the English lesson, for that's one lesson that used to terrify me, was English. I could feel myself going asleep and I'd open my eyes and I could see the room going away and I could say to myself, 'I'm wide awake. I'm going to figure it out', but obviously I used to go deeper into it. I used to always go for a window to get out. My aunty saved me once from literally jumping out of the bedroom window. She just managed to grab me before I jumped out.
>
> (Mellor 1983)

This is what I'd call a blow-by-blow account. The details of direct speech, his own thoughts and the present tense for the teacher's actions make his description uncomfortably vivid. From the passage as a whole, I felt the force of Doug's fear and panic, the humiliation of his teenage illiteracy and the injury that his low educational attainments were allowed to inflict on his self-esteem and social value.

Why does streaming by ability persist as a way of grouping students in schools when we know how harmful is the experience of being in the C stream? Is it because arguments about the 'efficiency' of supposedly homogeneous teaching groups outweigh the feelings of the 'lower ability', lower status students? Or is it because people accept arguments about reducing the pressure on these students by removing them from 'more able' competitors and filter out these other things that we know about their experience?

4 ROSEMARY SUTCLIFF

Rosemary Sutcliff is a writer of historical novels for children. This is an extract from her autobiography *Blue Remembered Hills: A Recollection* (1983), 'the only record', she tells us, of the years before she began to keep a diary, before her first novel was published.

As a child, Rosemary had Still's Disease, a form of arthritis, which prevented her from walking. Because of her disability and because her father's job in the navy meant that her family moved house frequently, Rosemary did not go to any kind of school until after she was 7. Her mother was bringing her up with 'rigid naval discipline', which included corporal punishment and total, unquestioning obedience. Rosemary was an only child and writes that her mother treated her like the sons she did not have. Under her mother's strict regime, Rosemary benefited from a great deal of attention and recalls the pleasure, particularly, of her mother's talent and enthusiasm for reading aloud. However, her attempts to teach Rosemary to read were fruitless. Eventually, someone in the town in which they were then living, recommended a 'small, private school'.

> It seems to me now surprising that with so much else going on, I was also having lessons. Or more truthfully, sitting through lessons with practically nothing to show for them afterwards. That was not my mother's fault. She tried so hard; she had begun trying when we first went to Sheerness, and had

been at it ever since. Actually, I had absorbed quite a lot. Under the heading of General Knowledge, I think I would have done quite well in a TV quiz. I knew the meaning of the three white bands round a sailor's collar, I knew the proportions of an iceberg above and below water, and the name of Apollo's mother. From a lovely book about a little boy going on a voyage round the world with his toys, which I had on long loan from grown-up cousins (very long loan; I have it still) I had accumulated quite a lot of geography. From *Flower Fairies of the Seasons* I had gathered nearly as much botany as I have now; and I seldom find myself at a loss where flowers and trees are concerned. I had a smattering of child's-version history from *Our Island Story*, in which Queen Boadicea rebelled against the Romans because they had beaten her and been rude to her daughters. But I could add two and two together three times and get a different answer each time. And I could not do the one thing on which everything else depended.

I could not read.

Neither could Rudyard Kipling until he was nine years old; but neither my mother nor I knew that at the time; and my mother was at times near to despair. My failure really *was* her fault, for the odd reason that she herself read too well and too willingly. I have noticed that a child who has a willing adult to read to him is often late in learning to read to himself, simply because, when being read to, he can cope with stories well in advance of those he could read for himself; and so learning to read means, in an odd sort of way, a step backwards. My mother started to read to me when I was very young indeed. She read aloud beautifully and never got tired, and she would never, from the first, read anything that she could not enjoy herself, which cut out all the poor quality writing which every right-minded child loves when he can get it. Her only concession was one weekly comic, 'Rainbow'. But apart from that, I was reared on a fine mixed diet of Beatrix Potter, A. A. Milne, Dickens, Stevenson, Hans Andersen, Kenneth Grahame and Kipling – especially *Puck of Pook's Hill* whose three magnificent stories of Roman Britain were the beginning of my own passion for the subject, and resulted in the fullness of time in *The Eagle of the Ninth*. Hero myths of Greece and Rome I had, in an unexpurgated edition which my mother edited herself as she went along, and Norse and Saxon and Celtic legends. There were Whyte Melville's *The Gladiators* and Bulwer-Lytton's *Last Days of Pompeii* and Weigal's *Egyptian Princess*; for my mother loved historical novels – history of any kind, though her view of it was always the minstrel's rather than the historian's.

When I was about six, she decided that the time had come for me to learn to read. And that was when she made her mistake. Instead of merely sitting me down in front of *Peter Rabbit*, *The Secret Garden* or the Jungle Books and telling me to get on with it, she provided a dreadful book about a Rosy-Faced Family who Lived Next Door and Had Cats that Sat on Mats, and expected me to get on with *that*. I was outraged – I, who had walked the boards with the Crummles, and fought beside Beowulf in the darkened Hall of Heriot [sic].

I took one look, and decided that the best way of making sure that I should never meet the Rosy-Faced Family or any of their unspeakable kind in the future was not to learn to read at all. So I didn't, and my mother never quite had the hardness of heart to stop reading to me. We had lessons and lessons and lessons; and we got practically nowhere.

I still had my spinal carriage, which now lived in the front porch for afternoon rest sessions only, for I could walk quite well, even, given time, the whole length of the terrace. And I still had my inability to read. My father now joined the battle, and had small serious talks with me.

'When you can read to yourself, old girl, you will find a whole new world opening up to you.'

'Yes, Daddy,' said I. Polite but unconvinced.

He resorted to bribery. I longed to model things. He bought me a box of 'Barbola' modelling clay with all its accompanying paraphernalia, and promised me I should have it when I could read.

'You can't go on like this for *ever*!' he said.

'No, Daddy,' I agreed. I had every intention of going on like it for ever.

'Don't say "No, Daddy".'

'No, Daddy.'

But, at last, help was at hand; somebody told my mother of a little private school in the town. Maybe, if Miss Beck would take me, I might learn better among other children. It was worth trying. Anything was worth trying.

And, oddly enough, I was all for it. I had no real desire to learn to read, but the dignity of schoolgirlhood appealed to me strongly. So there, on a day, was I, my chest swollen with the importance of myself and the occasion, passing for the first time through the doorway of Miss Beck's Academy.

In a small back room with peeling wallpaper, under the eye of a gaunt elderly maid, I was stripped of my coat, leggings and tam-o'-shanter, in company with twelve or fourteen others of my kind. And with them, all on my own, so grown up, I filed through into the schoolroom, to be received, as Royalty receives, by Miss Beck herself, who sat, upright as Royalty sits, in a heavily carved Victorian armchair.

My schooldays proper had begun.

Looking back with warm affection at that first school of mine, I can hardly believe that it was real, and not something dreamed up out of the pages of *Cranford* or *Quality Street*. I suppose nowadays it would not be allowed to exist at all. Miss Amelia Beck had no teaching qualifications whatsoever, save the qualifications of long experience and love. She was the daughter of a colonel of Marines, in her eighty-sixth year when I became one of her pupils; and for more than sixty years, in her narrow house overlooking the Lines at Chatham, she had taught the children of the dockyard and the barracks. She accepted only the children of service families. Oh, the gentle snobbery of a bygone age; bygone even then, and having less to do with class than totem. It was her frequent boast that she had smacked, in their early days, most of the senior officers of both services. Both, not all three, for the RAF was too young as yet to count for much in Miss Beck's scheme of things. But I do not think that it can have been true, unless she had gentled greatly with the passing of the years. For I never knew her to smack anybody during the year that I sat at her feet. [...]

Any elementary schoolteacher of today would have fallen into strong hysterics or sat down with a banner in some public place after one look at our schoolroom, though I don't think we ever had much fault to find with it. It had mud-coloured walls with damp stains in the outer corners, three shelves of limp and weary school-books, a bit of unravelled carpet on the floor. We had no desks; we sat round a vast kitchen table with the initials of long-past admirals and generals carved with illicit pocket-knives among the inkstains on top and down the legs, and we worked our sums and wrote our exercises on slates, with squeaky slate pencils. Some of us ate a good deal of the slate pencils; but myself, I never cared much for the taste. And Miss Beck sat at the head of the table in her carved Victorian chair, with a patchwork cushion made out of crocheted squares, and watched us with a quiet but commanding eye.

We coloured in chalks the elaborate kaleidoscope patterns which she drew for us on our graph paper or with a pair of compasses. We learned deportment, the boys to bow and the girls to curtsey, when we shook hands morning and evening. I, who had stiffened knees and could not curtsey, bowed with the boys; and to this day, I never hand a pair of scissors to anyone without consciously remembering Miss Beck's instructions to do so with the points towards myself and the handle towards the other person.

From a tattered old volume of Grimm's *Fairy Tales* passed round among us, we learned to read, even I, at long last, discovering suddenly what the mystery was all about. I have no recollection of the actual process; I do not know how or why or when or wherefore the light dawned. I only know that when I went to Miss Beck's Academy I could not read, and that by the end of my first term, without any apparent transition period, I was reading, without too much trouble, anything that came my way.

(Sutcliff 1983)

Rosemary's experience of the world was restricted by her limited mobility, but expanded both by moving from place to place and by the stories that her mother read aloud. There was a lot going on in her young life, without school.

Rosemary's mother loved history and legends and this passion obviously communicated itself to Rosemary. But when her parents thought that it was time for Rosemary to learn to read for herself, she resisted, realising that the distant worlds recreated for her by her mother were described in language that would be beyond her beginner's grasp. For Rosemary, reading for herself would involve taking a step backwards, sacrificing a rich world of imagination while she learned the basic skills.

However, Rosemary's apparent inability to read, though irritating and puzzling to her parents, does not seem to have dented anyone's view of Rosemary's worth as a person. Rosemary deliberately resisted learning to read, but risked nothing central to her self-esteem. Unlike 14-year-old Doug, who would probably have loved to have been able to read easily and who perceived that his illiteracy was a major reason for his low social status and the brutal rejection by his teacher.

Rosemary learned to read when placed in a new context, one where reading for yourself was what was expected and where the adult sat calmly at the head of the table. Presumably, Rosemary's motivation changed with the setting and she ceased to resist learning to read. Even so, she still learned with a minimum of help, without a lot of attention, positive or negative, being paid to her progress. She herself hasn't a clue about how or why she learned to read at Miss Beck's. She felt secure, at ease, entertained, not damagingly different.

Doug's teacher had no idea why he couldn't read and Doug certainly made no progress while he faced ritual public humiliation. He felt insecure, ill-at-ease, stigmatised and despairing. Illiteracy was the all-defining characteristic that had swallowed up the rest of his personality in the context which then dominated his life. Perhaps Doug too would have benefited from a change of scene, one where, unlike his secondary school (or Rosemary's home?), reading was less of a conscious obsession, an end in itself and more of an incidental means to a pleasurable or purposeful end.

5 VED MEHTA

Ved Mehta is a novelist and essayist. He was born in what was then India, but became Pakistan after partition in 1947 and he is now an American citizen.

Ved had meningitis when he was 4 and was left blind as a result. At that time in India the prospects for a blind person, even from a Civil Servant's middle-class home, included working as a musician or begging. Ved's father was anxious for Vedi to receive an education and so, when he was 'scarcely five', Vedi was sent 1,300 miles away from home to an orphanage for blind children in Bombay, an institution that his father had not visited but had only had a 'perfunctory correspondence' with its Principal. The Principal, however, had been trained at the Perkins Institution for the Blind in Boston, USA. This extract comes from the first volume of his autobiography, *Vedi*:

> One afternoon, Mr Ras Mohun took those of us boys who were totally blind behind the school building, past Abdul's boa-constrictor tree, to a little vacant area by the wall of the Tata Mill. Here he let us feel four waist-high metal wires and what he called the starting and finishing posts, between which the wires had been strung. The wires formed three long lanes, each a few feet wide. Each wire had a hoop around the size of a thick bangle hanging from it.
>
> 'This is a racing track,' he said. 'I have modelled it on a racing track for the

blind which I saw at Perkins, in America. We will have races for you here every week.'

We were excited. At school, the most we could do was to run up and down the boys' stairs, and even that we were not supposed to do, because the Sighted Master didn't like the noise we made. When we went for our outings, we had to hold on to the partially sighted or half-sighted boys and walk slowly. But here, Mr Ras Mohun said, we could run, and by ourselves.

Mr Ras Mohun positioned Abdul, Reuben, and me in separate lanes, at the starting posts, and showed us how to catch hold of the metal hoop by a string that hung from it, and then run with the wire as our guide.

'No, no, Reuben, don't hold on to the string with both hands,' Mr Ras Mohun said. 'Just catch hold of the string loosely with your right hand, like this.'

'I don't need the string, Uncle,' I said. 'I can run just holding on to the hoop.'

'You need the string for a certain amount of leeway,' he said. 'Let's have a trial race, and you'll see what I mean.'

I prayed to Jesus, Mary, and Joseph that I would win.

Mr Ras Mohun called out, 'Ready, steady, go!'

I had never run so fast. I imagined myself an arrow flying from one post to the other.

'Oh, my God, they're going to kill themselves!' I heard Mr Ras Mohun exclaim as I fell sidewise, almost wrapping myself around the finish post, and hitting my mouth on it.

'Any of you badly hurt?' Mr Ras Mohun asked, running up to us.

All three of us had bleeding mouths and bleeding foreheads. There had been no way for us to know when we were coming to the end, so we had all fallen down and hurt ourselves on the finishing posts.

Mr Ras Mohun sent for tincture of iodine and bandages, and after he had attended to our injuries he said, almost to himself, 'Bless me, I can't remember how they prevented such mishaps at Perkins.' He paused, and then went on, to us, 'I know. I'll station the Sighted Master at the finishing posts with my bell. He can ring it during the races. From the sound of the ringing, you'll know how close you are to the end. As an added precaution, I'll have a nice, strong rope stretched across the lanes, at the height of the wires, just before the end, so that if you fall you won't hit the finishing posts.'

After that, every Saturday we had races at the racing track. Mr Ras Mohun would stand at the starting posts and get us off, and the Sighted Master would stand at the finishing posts, behind the newly stretched rope, and ring the bell. Abdul, Reuben, and I were the three fastest runners, and whenever the school had visitors – missionaries and benefactors, Bombay notables and government officials – we three would be asked to put on a special racing exhibition, running different kinds of races we had learned. We would put on the Biscuit Race: Mr Ras Mohun would give us each a hard biscuit, and when he said

> 'Ready, steady, go!' we would eat the biscuit quickly, show our mouths to him, and then run. We would put on the Leapfrog Race: we would leap frog-fashion along the racing track, hanging on to the string. We would put on the Dog Race, with two dogs, Bobby and Robby, which Mr Ras Mohun had just acquired for us to play with: Mr Ras Mohun would line up Bobby and Robby as best he could outside the lanes, and we would all race against one another. The Dog Race was not as satisfactory as the Biscuit Race or the Leapfrog Race, because Mr Ras Mohun never quite succeeded in starting Bobby and Robby at the right time and getting them to run exactly as he wanted them to.
>
> As time went on, the boys from a sighted school nearby occasionally came and joined us at our Saturday races. They would run outside the lanes. I was so eager to compete with them on even terms that now and again I would slyly let go of the string and hurl the hoop forward, so that I could run along the track like them for a time.
>
> (Mehta 1982)

When I first read this passage I was struck by the energy of the boys and by the ingenuity of the wires and hoops which enabled them to race. The scene contrasted with the severe deprivations of classroom and dormitory life remembered by Ved and with the physical sufferings of many of the other children he describes, especially two boys, both of them blind and deaf.

Ved describes how wonderful it felt to run freely on his own. He also describes how much he wanted to be able to compete on equal terms with sighted boys, to be able to overcome the handicap to running presented by his disability. His joy was to become more like the sighted boys, not to take pride in his differences.

This short passage brings alive the chaotic hilarity of Ved's experiences of running. It could be part of a novel. Ved is not, here, concerned to reflect on how he felt about his blindness or the sighted boys he wanted to emulate in the way that Micheline, for example, reflects on what it means to be 'normal'. Her main purpose in writing autobiographically could be described as political, additional to the task of writing well or of creating a literary work of art.

6 FINDING A VOICE

From these four narratives we have learned that school can be exhilarating or frightening, that corporal punishment can be devastating or unremarkably routine, that, for these writers, the experience of illiteracy can be a greater barrier to self-esteem than having a physical disability. How do their experiences resonate with your own?

Before writing *Vedi*, Ved Mehta had written two books about his parents, which did include some of his childhood experiences. In his preface to *Vedi*, he describes how he had changed since those earlier writings and how the very act of writing stirred his memory, so that he literally learned about his life as he wrote:

> That, however, was before I had quite found my voice as a writer and before I had acquired even the rougher implements of the craft. It was also before I had realized that memory expands by some kind of associative process, so that a remembered scene that at first seems hardly worth a line grows in the act of thinking and writing into a chapter, and this full-blown memory uncovers other memories, other scenes, which in their turn expand and multiply.

Ved's project was to create a series of literary works based on the lives of himself and members of his family. The interweaving of the processes of writing and remembering enabled him to define himself as a writer.

Rosemary's autobiography is a recollection of her early life. She set out to preserve a vivid personal account of the years that would otherwise not have any record written from her own perspective. Like *Vedi*, *Blue Remembered Hills* was written by a mature literary artist.

Doug wrote about his experiences of school to communicate for the first time to a wider audience how he managed to overcome the huge obstacles to learning that he encountered.

Micheline traces the evolution of her self-image through her childhood and school experiences, thereby taking control of the process of defining who and what she is, not allowing other people to do this on her behalf any more, however benevolently.

Micheline and Doug are finding their voices as we listen to them. Rosemary and Ved are using their voices to reflect back on their experiences and preserve a personal account. I feel that it is easier to enter into the worlds of Micheline and Doug, perhaps because, despite the great differences between their experiences of school and my own, there are fewer imaginative hurdles to leap than with the lives of Rosemary and Ved. I suppose that the measure of how far we share the perspective of other people will be the nature of our future response to those to whose stories we listen.

But autobiographies can have many purposes. What kind of story would you like to tell about yourself? One of the most salient facts about my own experiences of school is that I attended the same one for thirteen years – such a thorough process of institutionalisation that I may never really get away from it. Another all-embracing feature of my schooling is illustrated by the headline of an article in the local paper at the time of the centenary of the old-girls' association (I thought that it was the school itself that was a hundred years old and so did most of the people who turned up for the party). The article was headed 'The Could-Do-Better-Girls'. It is a characteristic of selective education that the competitive sorting out does not end at the school gates, but carries on into the deepest recesses within. This is true, not only in schools which select students on the grounds of high ability but also in schools which select students on the grounds of low ability. Most special schools for students who experience 'severe' difficulties in learning have 'special care' classes separated off from the other classes. Recently, I was talking to a friend I met through singing in a choir. We were chatting about school and it happens that my sister also sings in this choir, as does a woman who taught both of us and who we have therefore known for nearly thirty years. I mentioned to my friend that we were the 'could-do-better-girls'. She understood perfectly.

REFERENCES

Campling, J. (ed.) (1981) *Images of Ourselves: Women With Disabilities Talking*, London: Routledge & Kegan Paul.

Mehta, V. (1982) *Vedi*, Oxford: Oxford University Press.

Mellor, D. (1983) 'If you don't read from school, you're teaching yourself to do something else, that's to deceive', in *Where Do We Go From Here: Adult Lives Without Literacy*, Manchester: Gatehouse Project.

ILEA (1990) *Disability Equality in the Classroom: A Human Rights Issue*, London: Inner London Education Authority.

Sutcliff, R. (1983) *Blue Remembered Hills: A Recollection*, Oxford: Oxford University Press.

ACKNOWLEDGEMENTS

The extract from *Where Do We Go From Here: Adult Lives Without Literacy* is reproduced by permission of Gatehouse Books, Gatehouse Project, St Luke's, Sawley Road, Miles Platting, Manchester M10 8DB (books available by mail order). The extract from *Blue Remembered Hills* is reproduced by permission of the Bodley Head Ltd, and the *Vedi* extract by permission of A. P. Watt Ltd.

Chapter 29

Close observation

Extracts by Patrick Easen, John Joseph Gleason, Robert Hull and James Pye, with an introduction and discussion by Patricia Potts

This chapter contains four examples of detailed observations of children and curricula. Patrick Easen describes two secondary pupils having problems with subtraction. John Joseph Gleason observes the play of two boys with profound disabilities. Robert Hull gives an account of a science lesson whose temporal organisation created learning problems, and James Pye watches who gets attention in a French lesson. Together the extracts show the benefits of a close observation and recording of teaching and learning, with an emphasis on the learner's viewpoint.

1 INTRODUCTION

Patricia Potts

If we are interested in finding out how children learn and when and why they experience difficulties in learning, then watching them at work and at play, trying to see things from their point of view, would seem to be a fundamental strategy. However, given that a complete record of what people say and do is impossible and that observers do not always agree about what it is they have jointly seen, observation is not nearly as straightforward a procedure as it might seem. Learning from observation inevitably involves reporting that is selective and interpretations that reflect the view of the observer. Further, when we say that we want to observe children's learning, what exactly do we mean?

I have collected together four examples of detailed reporting and discussion of observations of children. First of all, Patrick Easen takes us carefully through the individual experiences of two pupils struggling with mathematics. Next, we sit back with John Joseph Gleason and watch part of an afternoon's play session between two young boys identified as having 'profound and severe' difficulties in learning. Then we join a first-year secondary group for a lesson in what happens to naphthalene when it is heated. Finally, we join a class of middle-school pupils for a French lesson, reported for us by James Pye.

Patrick Easen and Robert Hull both entered into discussions with the children they were observing, encouraging them to talk about what they were doing and why. John Joseph Gleason did not participate in the game Thomas and Danial played. The boys were unable to talk to him and he wanted to concentrate on what he saw to build up his picture of what the boys' game meant to them. James Pye, moving from lesson to lesson with one class, tried to avoid participation as he sought to make sense of the children's behaviour, both as individuals and as a whole group.

What each of the four observers was watching was a relationship – either between an individual pupil and his or her task; between pupils, their teachers and a task; or between two children and their self-initiated task. What each of them discovered was that the capabilities of many of the children they observed were significantly underestimated by their teachers or care staff. A more accurate appreciation of the children's abilities would therefore seem to depend upon the opportunity for teachers and other workers to become as familiar with the children's own perspectives as these observers. How are such opportunities to be created?

None of the observers I have included approached their own task armed with clip-boards loaded with checklists. They did not plan their studies according to precisely worded hypotheses and predictions. They did try to absorb what they saw and heard in such a way that understandings and insights could emerge from the action they observed. All this was in the context, though, of their own previous experience of similar situations and their reading of other people's published work. James Pye kept a count of certain behaviours in his charting of the visibility and invisibility of pupils in the class he observed, but otherwise the extracts represent qualitative approaches to the interpretation of detailed observations. They are taken from individual narratives, stories told about children in styles which reflect the interests and literary talents of each author.

All four of the observers are men. They are all teachers or ex-teachers, some now education department academics. I wanted to include the work of teachers, rather than psychologists. James Pye uses a lot of theatrical imagery in his account of his career as a teacher and his observations of the children in what he calls 'Nomansland' and he talks about the 'limelight' that classroom life generates. It would seem that the limelight generated by fluency in the writing-up of observational studies of children is enjoyed disproportionately by men. Of course, men have traditionally done the watching.

2 THE DIFFICULTIES OF DOING SUBTRACTION

Patrick Easen

Let's begin with Mandy. She's thirteen and having difficulties at her comprehensive school. She is trying to take 70 away from 109, so she sets it down like this:

$$\begin{array}{r} 109 \\ -\ 70 \\ \hline \\ \hline \end{array}$$

She begins:

Mandy: 0 from 9 you can't do ... go over to the 1 and cross it off ...

writes $\begin{array}{r} {}^{0}\not{1}09 \\ -\quad 70 \end{array}$

that's a 0 ... that's a 1 ...

writes $\begin{array}{r} {}^{0}\not{1}{}^{1}09 \\ -\quad 70 \end{array}$

cross that off ... 10 off ... that's a 9 and a 1 ...

writes $\begin{array}{r} {}^{0}\not{1}{}^{1}0{}^{1}9 \\ -\quad 7\ 0 \end{array}$

At this point she pauses, frowns, screws up her nose and sucks her lip. Then she slumps back with a puzzled look, bites her lip and screws up her face.

Mandy: Gone wrong.
Teacher: Would you like to start again?

Mandy writes out the sum again and then sits there looking puzzled. She bites her lip.

Teacher: What are you looking at now?
Mandy: The 0
Teacher: What are you trying to decide?

Mandy pauses and then, with a sheepish grin, whispers, 'How to start'.

Her classmate Nicola is in even worse trouble. She sits looking at the sum, sucks her lip, blinks, looks up and then, hesitantly, begins and, as she does so, explains what she is doing:

Nicola: You can't do 9 from 0 ... so you cross out the 0 and put a 9, put a 1 at the top ...

writes $\begin{array}{l} 10{}^{1}9\ - \\ \ \ 7{}^{9}\not{0} \end{array}$

... 19 from 9 is ...

She closes her eyes and her lips move silently as she counts in her head, '10?' She looks up in the hope of some confirmation and then continues:

Nicola: Then put the 0 in there and the 1 under here. 0 from 7 you can't do, so cross out the 7 and put a 9. Put a 1 at the top ...

writes $1^{1}0^{1}9$

$9\not{1}\not{0}$

———

0

———

$_{1}$

10 from 9 leaves 1, 2

writes $1^{1}0^{1}9$

$9\not{1}\not{0}$

———

20

———

$_{1}$

[. . .]

Both Mandy and Nicola were using 'incorrect procedures', but their mistakes were not random. Each of them was trying to work with a rule concerning zero and subtraction; the trouble was that they only remembered certain aspects of how to achieve the desired surface features for their calculation. Thus for example:

Mandy: 0 from 9 you can't do . . . go over to the 1 and cross it off . . .

As a recitation of a sequence of moves in this type of sum it is almost perfect; what a pity she got the 0 and the 9 the wrong way round! Nicola, on the other hand, got the recitation 'right' – 'You can't do 9 from 0 . . .' – but she had a penchant for subtracting digits in the top line from those in the bottom line.

[. . .]

Now, there are many things that could be said about the mathematics asked for or, indeed, actually being used in these two cases, but the thing that really struck me when watching these two girls was the despair. When confronted by mathematics, some people (not just pupils) experience stress, and inevitably they try to develop ways of coping with it. I am inclined to agree with those who believe that unhappiness is a cause for concern, and yet, in all these cases I am going to describe, there was a sadness, a feeling of depression, pain. How can you learn mathematics if it makes you feel like that? And how can we know what someone else thinks or feels without focusing upon the individual involved? Even then it is dificult enough, but it is the most promising starting-point.

Children do not walk into the mathematics classroom as a textbook example of this or that particular learning difficulty; they walk in as children. We, as teachers, do not therefore begin by solving a technical problem; we begin by observing the child and we are dependent on innumerable tacit recognitions, judgements and skilful performances on our part if we are to map our categories of existing theory onto features of the living classroom. We need to look for what is there, what gaps exist and how the individual bridges them.

(Easen 1987: 25–8)

3 THOMAS AND DANIAL AT PLAY

John Joseph Gleason

Thomas and Danial experience the full breadth of human expression within the constraints of their handicap and the environment in which they live. The context for the interaction or event determines its social meaning. The messages contained within their behaviour are the signs of what they are doing and can be understood through the consideration of context. In the following example, the context is the rest period. The event is in one sense what these two 'get away with'.

The descriptions which follow illustrate a range of interactional behaviour and events in which the boys participated during the conduct of the study. The examples focus on qualities of the interaction between the residents, the richness in the ability to participate in play when left to themselves, the complexity of their involvement and execution of movements and behaviours, the simple enjoyment inherent in activities and events when they engage each other. The descriptions also demonstrate purposeful and intentional qualities in their behaviour. These are of course not the only examples of the boys' behaviour, nor are they illustrative of the entire range and the depth of each boy's ability. Not all of the residents play and socialise in the manner described below. Each resident demonstrates his own interactional ability and participatory ability within the constraints of disability on functioning. What each resident demonstrates is the ability to understand and act in social interactions with others. [...]

> In a series of three rolls, Danial finds himself head-to-toe with Thomas. Thomas manoeuvres parallel to Danial. Thomas's legs angle behind him. Danial's legs rest just to one side of Thomas's head. Each holds a toy lawn mower. Each brings it around in front of him to hold parallel to the other. Looking into each other's knees, they can look down the length of the other's torso to see the second lawn mower. The toys and their hands appear to obstruct direct eye contact.
>
> Danial has the white-handled lawn mower and Thomas the blue-handled lawn mower. The toys are identical. Danial lifts the white-handled lawn mower up to and over his face. It shields his face. With this, Thomas grips the blue-handled lawn mower resting loosely in the palm of his hand. He inches closer to and down towards the chest and head of Danial and within an arm's length of Danial's white-handled lawn mower. As Thomas is moving down towards him, Danial takes the lawn mower down from his face and pushes it toward Thomas, who grits his teeth. Danial quickly withdraws it. Thomas himself moves in closer to Danial, positioning his lawn mower next to Danial's. Letting his own drop to the floor, Thomas quickly reaches for the white handle of Danial's lawn mower. Danial pulls it back towards him as soon as Thomas lunges toward it. A moment elapses in which neither one does anything except stare. Then Danial pushes the lawn mower towards

> Thomas while moving himself away from Thomas. Thomas grabs at the white handle but cannot get it out of Danial's grip. Maintaining his grip Danial reaches over and tries to grab the blue handle of Thomas's. Danial misses. Neither one has succeeded in grabbing the other's toy. Thomas slowly reaches for the white handle of the lawn mower. Suddenly, he dramatically throws himself towards Danial and grabs the white-handled lawn mower. In the process, he jerks back quickly, pushing his own blue-handled lawn mower away from him. Recovering from the movement, he drags the white-handled lawn mower from Danial. Danial seizes the opportunity to grab the blue handle of Thomas's lawn mower, and pulls it swiftly back towards himself, keeping an eye on Thomas. Then with a smile, he lifts the blue-handled lawn mower over his head, holds it in a flag position, and then lets it drop to the floor. Thomas turns his head away from Danial and rolls the white-handled lawn mower on the floor beside him. The musical ditty plays and Thomas watches the balls jump in the cylinder, ignoring Danial. [...]

In the next series of interchanges in the event, each boy tries to sneak up on the other while guarding his own toy. Thomas grabs hold of the approaching lawn mower and pushes it into Danial's chest. Each boy relinquishes his lawn mower in the space between them. Each observes momentary calm.

> The two lawn mowers lie side by side in the space on the floor between the two boys. The two are startled by the turn of events. Thomas moves closer to the toys, picks up the white-handled lawn mower and pushes it into Danial's stomach. After the jab, he picks it up and swings it over Danial's head. It wavers and falls close to Danial, but never touches his head. Danial does not reach for the toy over his head, but for the blue-handled toy in front of him. He pushes it toward Thomas. With this, Thomas withdraws the white-handled toy from over Danial's head.
>
> Precisely at the time the toys are being withdrawn, an attendant enters the activity area from the office, looks down at the boys and says, 'What are you fighting for?' She at once separates Thomas from Danial. She picks up Thomas by sliding her arms underneath his armpits, bending him up to her waist and dragging him across the floor a distance of twelve feet, with his legs trailing behind him. Danial immediately pulls the blue-handled lawn mower into his chest to protect it and shield it from sight. As he is being lifted, Thomas grabs for his own white-handled lawn mower, just in time to maintain it. The attendant returns and picks up Danial in the same fashion, to move him away from Thomas. Unwittingly, although she tries to distance them from one another, she places them on mats almost directly across from each other and separated only by the aisle.
>
> Each boy drops his toy in the aisle between the mats, unable to sustain a grip. Thomas drops his while hunched over and bent from the attendant's position. It lands in the aisle. The attendant pushes Danial's lawn mower out

of his hand when it wedges between them on the move. Danial lets go just on the edge of the mat.

On the mat, Danial immediately rolls over in the direction opposite to the toys and toward the wall into the sunshine. Thomas, on the other hand, moves into the aisle between the mats, and picks up the blue-handled lawn mower, not the white-handled one he had taken from Danial. He holds it high in the air, straight up as far as his arm can reach. With the lawn mower stretched up into the air, he starts to grunt, squirm, grit his teeth, and flap his other hand. He sways the lawn mower in the air in a very slow circle and stares up at it.

Danial rolls over towards this scene. Looking at Thomas, Danial reaches out and takes back the white-handled lawn mower near him. He pulls the white-handled lawn mower underneath him and rolls over in the opposite direction again. Thomas stares at the circles he makes in the air. Thomas gradually lowers the lawn mower, laughing and gritting his teeth. He rests with the lawn mower to his side.

After a pause, the play resumes. Thomas again challenges Danial by raising the lawn mower over his head. It seems Danial does not want to play right now. He pushes his lawn mower over toward Thomas, who immediately withdraws the lawn mower from over Danial's head.

At this point the attendant enters and separates the two. The attendant looks and asks them, 'What are you fighting for?' Moving the boys and dropping the toys sets the stage for continuing interaction, although this intervention is not directed, planned, or programmed. What is interpreted by the attendant as a fight is cooperative play.

(Gleason 1989: 93–101)

4 GETTING ON IN FIRST YEAR SCIENCE

Robert Hull

The lesson I shall comment on was about the effects of heating on various substances. One of its purposes was to introduce the notion of 'subliming', the vaporising of substances when heated without their passing through a 'melting' stage. I shall discuss parts of the lesson first, and later look at the overall structure, with particular regard to its temporal aspects.

The teacher performed the demonstration experiments at his bench, while pupils watched. [. . .] [We join the lesson after the heating of sulphur has been discussed. We are well into a double period.]

Naphthalene was the next substance to be heated.

T: Right, now for the second ... a substance called naphthalene.... What does it smell like?

P1: Apples.

P2: Mothballs ...
T: *YES!*

They went on to describe its structure and appearance, and the teacher wrote: 'Naphthalene is a soft white crystalline solid', adding orally, 'If something is a crystal, we call it crystalline.' (A pupil had produced the word 'crystal'.) Note that 'smelling like mothballs' is already edited out from what naphthalene 'is'. Then it was heated.

T: What was the first thing that happened?
P1: It turned red.
T: Did it? If it did, it must have been the bunsen.
P2: It melted.
T: If it turns to a liquid, how would you describe it?
P3: Transparent.
T: What colour? Has it got a colour?
P4: No.
T: What would you *say* it is? [his emphasis].
P5: Colourless.
T: Right, colourless.

And he wrote: 'When naphthalene is heated, it turns to a colourless liquid.'

It was heated further, and it was noted on the board that 'it began to boil' and that 'white fumes of naphthalene vapour were formed', and finally that 'when the glass was allowed to cool naphthalene crystals are seen to form on the cooler parts of the glass'. (The regularity of those summaries makes them function as temporal boundaries.)

Here again we see the form of the pupils' observations shaped by the retroactive effect of the résumé-to-be. The redness that one pupil observed 'must have been the bunsen', 'transparent' becomes 'colourless'. Of three contributions, one goes into the description, one is dropped and another modified.

The third substance to be heated was iodine. First, the description:

P1: Small lumps.
T: Let's describe it more scientifically than that.
P2: Small crystals.
T: What colour?
P3: Shiny.
T: Iodine is a shiny black ... [pause to wait for the next word] crystalline solid.

[Normally during the résumé the teacher didn't wait for pupils to offer terms.]

Heating produced dense purple fumes, and one pupil asked, 'What colour is it, sir?' The strange hesitancy here (strange since it was a flagrant and obvious purple, even if a few pupils might not have a word for purple) represents the kind of undermining of pupils' confidence in their own constitutive speech that could be produced by recognising the precarious status of their contributions. The question might well mean, 'What colour is it appropriate to call it?' The teacher's somewhat sibylline reply was: 'Something different happened to that.' [. . .]

T: What *didn't* happen to the iodine?
P1: It didn't form fumes.
T: Oh, yes, I think it formed fumes. What happened to the naphthalene?
[Two indistinct but evidently wrong answers.]
T: Then what happened to the iodine?
P2: It melted.
T: No, it didn't melt.
P: Sir, smoke's coming up the neck!
T: We'll come to that. Yes, so it's turned straight from the solid to a vapour. And it does this at quite low temperatures.

The résumé on the board was: 'Iodine when heated forms iodine vapour without melting. It is said to *sublime.*' He accompanied this orally with, 'That's what we say when we mean . . .' and so on, and added a written comment: 'When a substance turns from being a solid into a vapour without melting it is said to *sublime*', adding, 'Put that in brackets because that explains the first word.'

A pupil then asked, 'Why was that yellow and the others purple?', and was told, 'It's just the state of the glass.'

Finally a diagram was drawn, which the class was to copy, and the title 'Some Effects of Heating' written up. The bell went as the children were drawing the flask.

The double lesson discussed above would amount to about one-seventeenth of the teacher's actual teaching time. It is a complex lesson in many ways, but in particular it is highly structured temporally, in an informal way. A plot of the lesson shows this.

Stage 1 Résumé of last week's lesson.
Stage 2 Introduce subject of this lesson.
Stage 3 Sulphur – oral description, with pupils.
Stage 4 Write up 'definition', have it copied.
Stage 5 Heat sulphur.
Stage 6 Oral description of heating at melting stage, with pupils.
Stage 7 Résumé of melting.
Stage 8 Oral description of vaporising.
Stage 9 Résumé.
Stage 10 Oral description of cooling.
Stage 11 Résumé.
Stage 12 Exit to fume cupboard.

These twelve stages were distinct; the divisions were marked by the teacher's decisions to move on, or divert, what was happening. There were these twelve stages with sulphur, then a further eight with naphthalene and six with iodine.

Most of the lesson time (about half) was taken up by the sulphur part. After these further fourteen stages, there followed:

Stage 27 Written notes on '*sublime*'.
Stage 28 Drawing and notes on 'some effects of heating'.

What seems striking is the way in which the lesson's structure, rationally derivable from the course of which it is a part, produces – despite its overall 'simplicity' in some respects – such a series of discrete events temporally bounded. I say temporally bounded because while an explicit timetable of stages is not necessary, since no synchronisation with others is involved (not within the lesson, though a good deal of synchronisation with lab assistants and three other science teachers would have been needed to decide on it originally), the teacher's own decisions about what different things will be done have imposed an informal distribution of lesson time available through the stages. He wants, clearly, all three materials to be heated since 'they're all different'; he wants some discussion to take place; he wants all this gathered together; and he wants a final drawing. Admirably careful and thorough though it is, some of the directional closures commented on are perhaps entailed by such planning. The various learning problems arising (misunderstandings about the conservation of one substance behind appearances, the undermining of pupils' natural ways of speaking about what they see) could only have been confronted at the expense of the structure as a whole.

(Hull 1985: 129–39)

5 OBSERVING A CROWD IN A MIDDLE SCHOOL

James Pye

The school was small by secondary standards: some 400 strong. Its atmosphere was warm and friendly: walls were covered with paintings; children tended to smile at me; teachers were hospitable, and the head and his deputy were very welcoming and helpful. I am very grateful to them, and to all their colleagues who let me sit in their classes and watch.

I wanted to do just that: to watch; to see what sort of children seemed prominent, what sort less so; to see how teachers approached their pupils, and how pupils avoided and approached their teachers. [...]

What I set out to do was to record, by manic writing down of everything I saw, every contact made between a teacher and a pupil. I could not hope to catch every single contact. But I did aim to do a gross arithmetic of the relations between teachers and pupils that I saw being enacted before me. I devised a code, and a way of writing briefly and quickly a description of what I saw. And I included all sorts of contact, from a question asked, to a reprimand given; from a meaningful shake of the head, to a shared laugh without words.

There were moments when so much contact was being made so fast – for instance, during a French lesson, when questions were being asked about a text the class had read, and hands were shooting up to answer them – that I must have missed some contacts made. But there were more frequent phases of lessons when contact was less often, and much more easily recordable. Moreover, the phases of most rapid contact tended to be with the same pupils, again and again. In French, to take the best example, the teacher waited for hands to go up before asking her quick-fire questions; and the same hands tended to go up on each occasion. And interestingly, when she chose people to read, or to stumble out loud through what they had written, she chose the same people, the question-answerers. So I am pretty sure that I missed contacts only with those pupils whom teachers tended to contact most frequently, rather than with the elusive and least-often contacted.

Nomansland was visibly there to be watched – where skulked some crafty boys, and douce and biddable girls. Passivity was there, as a style, a demeanour, a ritualised way of being. Anonymity was there; or not there. Without thinking it out very clearly, I decided not to ask teachers for the names of the pupils I was watching, so that I could become acquainted with names naturally, according to the frequency of their use. I disobeyed my own rule stupidly with one girl, Mona, who intrigued me so much from the start that I asked a teacher for her name, before I could stop myself. But otherwise I knew no names until I heard them used.

One girl's name I still did not know after two weeks and over seventy lessons. Several girls' names I did not know until well on in the second week. Only one boy's name escaped me till then; and I knew his by the first day of the second week.

The disparity between the most and the least contacted was startling – amazing. A boy, Darren, scored 123 contacts. A girl, Jenny, scored only 7. Boys on the whole made more contact with their teachers than girls. There were twelve boys in the class and they achieved in total 626 contacts. There were more girls in the class – sixteen – but they made only 489 contacts.

It was also interesting that those towards the top of the list of contacts – the active, the attractive – tended to volunteer, to initiate contact; but those from the middle of the list downwards were, on the whole, more contacted than contacting.

Those at the bottom of the list were barely contacted at all, nor did they make contact. They spoke not, neither did they attract. The last eight on the list – ranging from 16 contacts to 7 – were all girls. [. . .]

I certainly saw boys getting a great deal of attention. The two who made most contacts were in every way attractive. They were good-looking, articulate, naughty in an agreeable way, willing to make fools of themselves, willing to help, willing to speak even if they had nothing of great relevance to say.

There is a sequence in a French lesson which is relevant. The French teacher had a persuasive, pleasant, warm manner. She smiled. She encouraged. She praised a good quick answer. She seemed to have the knack of making her pupils relax enough to risk saying something in French. She herself seemed relaxed, and to be enjoying what she was doing.

But admirable though she was in all these ways, she was unusually partial in her choice of participants. Teaching a language depends on participation: on pupils speaking, asking, risking. If she chose a pupil to speak, she chose either the always willing – like Darren or Nevin, the two 'top' contacters, neither of whom seemed especially gifted at French, but both of whom were happiest in the limelight; or she chose those who did seem gifted at French. But even these pupils – and one girl, Marilyn, in particular – she 'used' less than the two boys.

More often than not, if she were seeking answers to her questions, or the meaning of words in a text, the teacher would ask: 'Et Monsieur Dupont, qu'est-ce qui'il faisait hier, qu'est-ce qu'il faisait?' and wait for hands to go up. She would then, with unerring regularity, choose the owner of the most vociferous hand, or the hands of those she knew would give an accurate answer. Often, in the competition to be chosen, the two boys would win, and give inaccurate answers.

My notes do not tell me exactly how one particular lesson began. But soon afterwards a vocabulary test had to be done. By that time, Darren had already spoken twice, in a loud voice. The lesson began at 1.07 p.m., and the test began at 1.09 p.m. Twice then, in two minutes, Darren had frolicked in the limelight.

He had been the first of the pupils to speak to me uninvited. My profile – sitting at the back of the room with my clipboard and my carefully neutral expression – was as low as I could make it. But to Darren I was another, probably sympathetic, person to engage in conversation. 'How are you, all right?' he asked. Thereafter he would always acknowledge me in some way.

He was slightly overweight; he liked to get out of his seat and walk about, if possible – usually finding a legitimate reason to do so. He smiled, joked, laughed. He would always put his hand up and volunteer an answer to a question, even if he had not heard the question properly. His demeanour was in every way the opposite of the disengagement and passivity of Nomansland.

It became obvious that he irritated his teachers. His French teacher, the second time he spoke, had to shut him up: he was not speaking to her but to someone at the other side of the room. But she and his other teachers liked him too; and they depended on him. It was obvious that his French teacher – as I did – put a very high value on liveliness. She needed lively pupils to generate the sort of atmosphere she liked. With Darren, in whom was no malice, her irritation was less important than her appreciation.

The test finished. Then more vocabulary was tested – out loud. The class, all twenty-eight of them, had read a page of 'the book' for homework and had been asked to learn the new words.

I shall quote from my notes:

Question and Answer – teacher asking for volunteers.
Darren answers

Terry
Malcolm
Darren shouts out
Darren again – tremendous enthusiasm at having got a right answer.
This sequence of male participation is followed by:
1.17 p.m. Two girls in front of me still haven't said a word.

What a contrast these two girls were to Darren in all the French lessons, and in all lessons. The code for one of them was 'TH' until well into the second week: TH standing for 'tailhead', to illustrate the minuscule pigtail she wore as a relish to her short haircut. Not once in the French lessons did she contact or was she contacted.

My next entry says that Darren is waving his arm madly to answer the next question. He answers it, again with pleasure at getting it right.

Then the teacher asks to see the exercise books of those who have queries about the written part of the homework – questions to answer about the dread Duponts. Who are at the head of the line waving their books? Darren and Nevin. They and three other pupils stand at the teacher's desk. 'Très bien', I hear her say, in her warm friendly voice.

The two girls in front of me, heads well down, murmur discreetly to each other. Then the next stage of the lesson begins. The text is to be read aloud: another thrilling day in the lives of the Duponts. The text requires two readers. Darren and Nevin are both chosen.

The prominent and the ignored

It seemed to me that what had happened was that Darren, from the beginning of the lesson, had made sure that his teacher knew he was there. At first she has to admonish him – lightly – for being too noisy. But twice he answers her questions correctly, and rewards her with his delight at his success. So that when she roams the room looking for readers, his face, name, presence are pleasurably clear in her mind, and it is inevitable that she chooses him.

In all, the teacher contacted ten pupils in this lesson, out of twenty-eight. She sought out those who attracted and rewarded her, and avoided the rest. She also sought out those who, to be controlled, need a large share of the limelight. Darren is attractive; but she and his other teachers also know that if they do not give him plenty of attention, he will create his own limelight on another part of the stage.

The corollary of this suggests why the passive girls are so pleasant to teach. I have made the point already: they please because they present no problem, but *the pleasure they provide is limited.* They are not attractive enough to be rewarding; and it is as if they are trapped by the mild pleasure they provide, which confirms their timidity and the ideas they have already learnt about how to behave.

(Pye 1989: 91–7)

6 DISCUSSION

Patrick Easen wanted to understand why children found the learning of mathematics so painful and why their calculations were often wrong, even when they did have some idea of the appropriate method. John Joseph Gleason became caught up in the play activities of two boys living in a long-stay hospital in the USA for people identified as 'profoundly mentally retarded' as he gradually realised that what he saw in front of him was not meaningless or mindless but a complex social action. Robert Hull observed pupils and teachers to try to understand why communication was so rarely accomplished. James Pye was looking out for those pupils who were invisible to their teachers, to try to make sense of how and why this happens with such regularity. In the course of their observations, they made use of videotapes, audiotapes, children's work, notes taken down at the time, diaries written up later.

The four extracts consist of four very different kinds of narrative. The proportion of material gathered at the time of observation as compared to comment and interpretation varies and the style in which the two are put together as a report reflects each observer's aims and individuality. For example, John Joseph Gleason describes his approach as 'ethnographic' and his detailed fieldnotes form the core of his method of recording his observations. These notes are written up in the present tense and occupy more space in the passage quoted here than his commentary. Gleason based his developing perceptions on the non-verbal behaviour of Thomas and Danial. Does this approach seem rather passive to you, particularly when you compare it with the obviously autobiographical style of James Pye or the richly annotated reporting of Robert Hull? Or do you feel that only by including extended extracts from notes taken at the time of observation can authors provide their readers with enough material for them to be able to make up their own minds about what was seen and so be able to form their own critique of the report? Or is this going to remain difficult for readers who weren't there alongside the authors, leaving us dependent upon the authors' own interpretations?

John Joseph Gleason's narrative builds up to the surprise of discovering that Thomas and Danial were enjoying an elaborate game of horizontal tag. His observations challenge the basic assumptions of the hospital staff and ask for a redefinition of the boys' capabilities. Robert Hull and James Pye looked at the verbatim detail of classroom life to see if they could build up any generalisations about patterns and recurrences. Their general understandings are rooted in vivid particulars. Despite four very different approaches, each of these observers made significant discoveries that would otherwise have remained unknown.

REFERENCES

Easen, P. (1987) 'All at sixes and sevens: the difficulties of learning mathematics', in T. Booth, P. Potts and W. Swann (eds), *Curricula for All: Preventing Difficulties in Learning*, Oxford: Basil Blackwell.

Gleason, J. J. (1989) *Special Education in Context*, Cambridge: Cambridge University Press.
Hull, R. (1985) *The Language Gap*, London: Methuen.
Pye, J. (1989) *Invisible Children*, Oxford: Oxford University Press.

ACKNOWLEDGEMENTS

The extract from *Special Education in Context* is reproduced by permission of Cambridge University Press, and the *Invisible Children* extract by permission of Oxford University Press.

Chapter 30

Approaches to interviewing

Patricia Potts

Interviewers can adopt a wide variety of approaches, from the tightly structured to the very informal, depending upon what they see as their main task and the relevant characteristics of their interviewees. In this chapter, Patricia Potts argues that what can be learned from interviewing does not just depend upon the kinds of questions asked and the kinds of people interviewed, but also upon the nature of the social relationship, however apparently superficial, that develops between interviewer and interviewee. Further, because social relationships are never static, the information that an interviewer receives from a single interviewee will vary from occasion to occasion; the responses given on any one occasion cannot be seen as the whole, nor the only true, story.

First, Patricia Potts examines some of the reasons for conducting interviews. Then she examines the argument that interviews should be seen as a relationship rather than simply a process of extracting information. Finally, she looks at some examples of interviews carried out within an educational context.

1 INTRODUCTION: WHY INTERVIEW PEOPLE?

If you have the opportunity to make your own enquiries into some aspect of the education system that interests, puzzles, annoys or delights you, then talking to people from whom you expect to learn something relevant is very likely to be one of the activities you will undertake. We call this talking 'interviewing' when we want to shape our talks with other people around the topic that is the focus of our enquiry, asking questions and recording answers in a structured and controlling way. Listening to the answers we receive may be delayed to a later stage, when we try to analyse and make sense of what we have been told.

But, by talking to them, what can we learn about, or from, other people that we could not learn by any other means? Why should we interview people face to face when we could send out questionnaires to a far greater number of people in the same time?

We might want to talk to someone because what we hope they will have to say doesn't exist elsewhere, in written or audio-visual form. It could also be that our interviewee prefers talking to any other medium of communication. It might be that what we want to find out about is, precisely, what only our interviewees themselves know, that it is their own perspectives that interest us, making them unique sources of this information, which, perhaps, has never been asked for before. It may be that we want responses, therefore, that will help us to fill what we see as gaps in existing accounts.

You may want to observe how your interviewees cope with your questions, realising that all kinds of nonverbal information may be useful to you. You may want to secure an immediate response to your questions, deliberately not giving your interviewees time to write a considered answer. You may want to learn from your interviewee directly, rather than have someone else respond to your questions on their behalf. You may think that if you ask for a written response you'll never get it, whereas turning up in person to conduct an interview may guarantee at least some sort of response. Besides, an interview is a 'live' way of making enquiries and even in a tightly controlled situation can be seen as paying attention to the interviewee and therefore positive. You may believe that talking to someone is the best way to ask about intimate or controversial subjects.

2 INTERVIEWS AS A SOCIAL RELATIONSHIP

There is a wide variety of reasons for wanting to interview people in the course of making enquiries. But why should anyone agree to be interviewed? What could be in it for them? What if the subject-matter under discussion is painful or threatening or the interview is seen as intrusive, exploitative, taking without any giving?

In a long article on women interviewing women, Ann Oakley (1981) discusses what she sees as the contradiction inherent in conducting interviews for the purpose of research. In so far as a successful 'research' interview is seen as both a collection of 'data' or information and as a conversation based on the rapport between interviewer and interviewee, then it is a contradictory activity because you need to be objective, distant, on the outside for the former, but warm, reciprocal, on the inside for the latter.

Ann Oakley compares interviewing to marriage: 'everybody knows what it is, an awful lot of people do it, and yet behind each closed front door there is a world of secrets' (Oakley 1981: 31). She takes a critical look at what the textbooks say about 'proper' interviewing and decides that, for her, the contradiction had to be resolved in the direction of establishing 'sisterhood' with her interviewees if, as a 'researcher', she is to learn anything from them.

When Ann Oakley's interviewees asked *her* questions, she felt she had to answer them and, as a result, develop a closer, more personal relationship with them. This would not be condoned by many researchers who aim to operate a method of making enquiries that fits into a paradigm of social 'science', in which the validity and reliability of what interviewees say – that is, the possibility of what they say being 'true' – can only be achieved by maximum control and prediction on the part of the researcher.

Ann Oakley describes the conventional interviewer–interviewee relationship as a 'rationalization of inequality; what is good for interviewers is not necessarily good for interviewees' and her own experience leads her to conclude that this is 'morally indefensible':

> It becomes clear that, in most cases, the goal of finding out about people through interviewing is best achieved when the relationship of interviewer and interviewee is non-hierarchical and when the interviewer is prepared to invest his or her own personal identity in the relationship.
>
> (Oakley 1981: 41)

The women interviewees who asked questions of Ann Oakley when she was interviewing them began to ask questions when they had already had more than one round of interviews. This made possible a two-way give and take of learning from each other.

Jocelyn Cornwell (1984) describes how she set out to put Ann Oakley's approach into action as she recorded the accounts of health and illness given to her by men and women from East London. A central feature of her study was repeated rounds of interviews with a fairly small group of people:

> My priority in composing the schedules for the interviews and interviewing people was, as much as possible, to take my cue from them, to let them direct the course of the interview and to follow their interest in the topics I proposed to them.
>
> (Cornwell 1984: 12)

Jocelyn Cornwell goes further than Ann Oakley to stress that the effects of social and professional differences between interviewer and interviewee should not be underestimated and that several rounds of interviewing help people to move away from polite, safe, 'public' accounts of their views and experiences towards more significant 'private' accounts.

Jocelyn Cornwell acknowledges that 'the interviewer cannot simply be a "recording instrument" because who she is, what she is like and the relationship she has with the interviewee affects the content of the interviews' (Cornwell 1984: 17).

Wendy Hollway (1989) reflects on the experience of carrying out and interpreting the 'research' she undertook for her Ph.D. thesis. At first she was anxious that her way of talking to people would not be regarded as 'good research practice'. She aimed to 'talk with people in such a manner that they felt able to explore material about themselves and their relationships, past and present, in a searching and insightful way. I did not feel skilful because it came so easily . . . Now I can believe that this made for good research practice. At the time I was anxious that it was a bit of a con' (Hollway 1989: 11).

Wendy Hollway was interviewing people about their social relationships. It may be that any interviewing you become involved with will not have personal relationships as an explicit topic for investigation and that you will not have the time to spend developing a relationship with your interviewees. It may also be the case that your interviewees do not want to develop this kind of two-way communication, not seeing it as relevant to your enquiries or to the nature of the relationship which does exist between you. Wendy Hollway's description of her experiences of interviewing make them sound therapeutic:

> It was also because of who I was, that is, someone in a similar situation to them, someone who did not withhold my own experience and feelings and someone who not only was happy to listen endlessly but who asked helpful questions and used an analysis which made sense of their confused experience.
>
> (Hollway 1989: 12)

However, feeling at ease with her style of informal, mutually supportive conversations, did not mean that Wendy Hollway had no worries at all about her approach. She argues that the desire to respect the personal accounts of individual people's experiences should not be confused with a belief in their truth – that is, that what her interviewees said to her, although valid in itself, should not be seen as the whole truth, the only account that they could have given:

> What is not considered is the status of the account in relation to the infinite number of things that were not said.
>
> (Hollway 1989: 40)

Understanding the relationship between events and experience and people's personal accounts of them is an extremely complex process. Nevertheless, Wendy Hollway is particularly concerned that the interpretation of women's accounts of their experience should be liberated from orthodox social psychological methods which see the meaning of these accounts as 'unproblematic' (Hollway 1989: 42). So where does this leave us and our own, perhaps very small-scale, enquiries?

We may wish that we had the chance to take several years to pursue our enquiries in sufficient breadth to set our interview material into an adequate context for interpretation. We are probably faced with the chance of a few lunch-hours or snatched sessions after work. We can feel lucky enough to find the time to talk, just once, to someone whose story we believe to be relevant to our enquiries. But if we are not likely to learn enough to set what they say about their professional responsibilities into an appropriate context, for example, what hope can we have of making sense of our interview?

However, as I read on I came across what seems to me to be a useful strategy, whatever the scope of our enquiries: 'We need to understand the ways in which the terms we use to recount our experience are not neutral' (Hollway 1989: 46). So, part of interviewing an individual or a group of people will be this exploration of the meanings assigned by the interviewees themselves to the events and feelings that they describe.

3 INTERVIEWING IN PRACTICE: FINDING OUT ABOUT PEOPLE'S EXPERIENCES OF EDUCATION

I have suggested that interviewing is not just a matter of asking questions of people you believe can tell you something relevant to a topic that interests you. Trying to see what meaning the whole conversation has for your interviewees and what there is in it for them to talk to you should also be seen as central.

One advantage of undertaking to interview people systematically, for example as part of a research project, is that we get to talk to people with whom we might not otherwise be able to spend much time. These may include people whose higher status has made them inaccessible, as well as those for whom we ourselves are relatively inaccessible.

Jane, a student on an Open University Advanced Diploma course, works as an art teacher in a school for students who experience 'moderate learning difficulties'. She had ten weeks to complete a project in her school and she had decided to develop ideas for a whole-school policy for her curriculum area. She discovered that there were other issues which had to be discussed in detail first – for example, the school's commitment to planning by individual behavioural objectives, which made group work or following the students' own interests difficult. Jane had to modify her initial topic, therefore, and investigate the rationales for the school's views about curricular issues in general.

Jane was a newcomer to the staff and saw herself as an outsider, feeling particularly constrained by her low status when she talked to senior members of staff. In her Open University project report (unpublished), Jane had this to say about her experience of conducting interviews:

> Firstly I put out feelers to gauge staff response to being interviewed. Whilst all were pleased to co-operate they *all* expressed a wish to have the questions given in advance in a written form. One member of staff expressed a strong wish not to be recorded by tape, therefore I took notes which were difficult to do because (a) they took too long and I was unable to record every word and therefore some of the meaning was lost, and (b) created a difficult atmosphere because if I looked at the person I couldn't take notes and if I took notes I lost important eye contact.
>
> With the Head I was totally passive and very aware of his and my status ... I felt more relaxed with the rest of the staff. It is worth noting that the interview with the Head took place in his office and that he sat behind his desk, whilst the other interviews took place either in my room or their room.
>
> Time was a major handicap to all the interviews apart from the Head's. I spoke to him after school and for well over an hour. However, there were quite a few interruptions which affected the flow as well as creating intervals where we both relaxed momentarily. (It was just after one such interruption that the Head inquired about the anonymity of my interviews.)
>
> The Deputy Head had also stayed behind on the same evening and wanted to be interviewed despite the lateness. He had made notes while I was with the

Head and read from these. Unfortunately it stifled the conversation and I became disheartened as the interview progressed. It was particularly upsetting because the previous evening the Deputy Head and I had had a lively and unrecorded conversation which would have been far more interesting.

The rest of the staff arranged lunchtime meetings (I didn't feel I could ask staff to see me after school time) which were only brief and I'm sure affected the depth of some of the answers. Also it is difficult to shut out the noise and disruption of a school lunch hour and as a result concentration and line of thought was often interrupted.

However, despite the difficulties, I do feel that the interviews provided a very valuable insight into many aspects of the school as well as providing substance to my project. I also feel that it has helped me with my personal relationships with staff – I have been accepted and taken more seriously more quickly. It also provided an opportunity for me to ask questions that I would not have asked normally.

Jane has four main points to make about interviewing in a school: first, that interviewing is difficult due to lack of time and the constant interruptions; second, that participation was negotiated on the basis of advanced notice of the questions she intended to ask, which proved disastrous for the interview with the Deputy Head; third, that people do not always feel free to talk and so may keep their responses on a superficial level; fourth, that her own inexperience as an interviewer was an initial obstacle.

We can probably imagine what it would be like to interview a selection of colleagues – particularly those senior to us – and what kinds of problems might arise before we both felt at ease. What about interviewing students then? Should we assume that this will be more straightforward than interviewing colleagues? Especially if we remember to be open with them and try to make the conversations as enjoyable as possible for everyone? Tom Logan (1984) discusses the problems of talking to teenagers about their experiences of school, particularly when these experiences have not been very rewarding and the young people are critical of the education they have received. He had wanted to listen, to be responsive rather than directive, not to have preconceived ideas about the students and to share biographies. However, there were difficulties with such an unstructured approach, despite the aim of trying to equalise power relationships, because personal revelations were encouraged to which the interviewer in reality could not respond:

> My mistake was to assume too much – that his [the teenage interviewee's] image could stand the probing he had demanded of mine. The rest of the interview reverted back to honest response, but no self-analysis.
>
> Shared biography as a strategy to democratise an otherwise threatening interview is one thing – and an essential thing. But it is another to live with shared biography if reciprocity means the relatively powerless losing even more power. No matter how much they might desire to share biography as

> people, unless the authority relationship is equally negotiable, equally reciprocal, then it will be rejected, pitied, or even resented (many interviewees have complained of teachers going on about their own lives or opinions, wasting pupils' time).
>
> (Logan 1984: 24)

Reflecting on his experiences of interviewing, Tom Logan says:

> Each interview is new and one cannot rely on either previous assumptions or one's complacency due to experience. Sometimes failure and sheer accident are the best teachers. For example, at the end of a particularly slow starting interview, two fifteen year old girls and I discover that the last twenty minutes of the tape has been lost (in fact switched off accidentally by someone making coffee). They were very disappointed and seeing the spare tape-recorder, asked if they could 'do it again' while I went off to my next scheduled interview. On returning I find they have accomplished little. They claim not to know what to say, despite having just done it because 'it was you that was asking the questions. We don't know what to say *now*. We don't talk about things like that unless someone is there.' In listening to their efforts later, it became obvious that these girls have a model of an interview in their heads. Each took turns in asking questions, adopting a completely uncharacteristic 'posh' voice and reflecting my choice of words and phrases; one was 'the area': 'tell me Marie, and what do you think of de aireeaa?' This statement ended with a screech of laughter. In their fifteen years they had heard Kirkby called 'Newtown', 'the Ponderosa' and less printable names, but never had they heard it referred to as 'the area' and it amused them. The other phrase, which they couldn't even say was 'the work situation': 'And now Shirley, tell us what you ... you think of ... de ... de work sit ... [laughs uncontrollably].' The lesson was to re-think the question, to translate it into understandable language, and thus allow them to respond.
>
> (Logan 1984: 24)

Tom Logan accepts that the students he interviewed need to retain some control over the language of the interview and that he must listen carefully. This is the way to discover what their stories mean to the story-tellers.

4 CONCLUSION

From the work of Ann Oakley, Jocelyn Cornwell and Wendy Hollway the following main points emerge: first, that what you learn from other people when you talk to them depends upon the social relationship between you (Jocelyn Cornwell found that people gave her different kinds of information and in different kinds of words on different occasions, according to how well they knew, liked and trusted her); second, that talking to people several times allows the relationship to develop so that deeper layers of experience and opinion can be revealed as interviewees abandon formal and superficial statements for more intimate, critical and honest accounts; third, that each individual account needs to be set into context if it is to be fully understood. Tom Logan adds a further point: that interviewees need to trust the curiosity of the interviewer, believing that talking about their experience will be rewarding for them, that what they say will not be taken away by the interviewer and used in an alienating way.

I have referred to two kinds of interviewing: the once-off question and answer session and an extended series of conversations between two people or between a group. In the first, the interviewer controls, or tries to, the structure and content of the interview, assimilating the interviewee's responses to his or her own line of enquiry. In the second, the interviewer uses preparatory researches to encourage the interviewee to define what is important, adapting to the interviewee's perspective during the interview. How far the material gathered from either approach is 'true' has to be assessed in the context of what else you can discover about the relevant contexts of your interviewees. The garrulity or economy of the speech of your interviewees will be no guide. However, we have to ask questions if we are to find out anything. Despite the complications that I have described, interviewing is obviously an indispensable way of learning from other people.

REFERENCES

Cornwell, J. (1984) *Hard Earned Lives*, London: Tavistock.

Hollway, W. (1989) *Subjectivity and Method in Psychology: Gender Meaning and Science*, London: Sage Publications.

Logan, T. (1984) 'Learning through interviewing', in I. Schostak and T. Logan (eds), *Pupil Experience*, London: Croom Helm.

Oakley, A. (1981) 'Interviewing women: a contradiction in terms', in H. Roberts (ed.), *Doing Feminist Research*, London: Routledge.

Chapter 31

Le mot juste: Learning the language of equality

Caroline Roaf

In this chapter Caroline Roaf considers the language used to describe and define the groupings, successes and opportunities of students at Peers School, a 13–18 comprehensive, where she works as special needs coordinator. Class groups there are balanced according to gender, race and attainment in the first year (Year 9), with choice of course having a greater influence thereafter. She suggests that particular attention should be given to the way young people are talked about when they reach the end of the period of compulsory education.

1 INTRODUCTION

In a school committed to equality of opportunity staff need to examine and question how language is used to imply differences in capabilities and worth. Some of these linguistic developments are obvious, well tried and are becoming natural ways of talking in certain sections of society and in some schools. The extremes of racist and sexist language have been under attack for some years, not least because they have been the subject of legislation, although alternatives for phrases such as 'Christian name', 'manning' and 'flesh coloured' are less often heard and alternatives for a word such as 'master'/'mastery' defeat most of us (try 'control') and never seem to trip off the tongue easily. What is important, at a personal level, is the speed and naturalness with which one can adapt one's language to fit one's developing thought. Until a form of words has been fully internalised, practised, corrected and recorrected, there will be hesitation and clumsy circumlocution.

My own first rude awakening to this came when I moved to my present school, Peers, in Oxford. I was well aware when I went there that I would, so to speak, have to be careful not to let my linguistic slip show. And sure enough after about a week it did. 'Would there be a problem about manning the stall (or whatever) during the lunch hour?' I asked. Instant correction: 'We say "staffing" here.' Well of course, naturally ... Until that moment I don't think I had realised, in a practical way, quite how important it was to change a sloppy habit nor quite how painless it was to be corrected quickly and gently. So the first important step for a school is to encourage an intelligent interest in the use of words as a worthwhile, even entertaining, habit in its own right. When this is tied to a policy which recognises the connection between language and thought, attitudes and behaviour, and insists on appropriate language, then equal opportunities is really in business.

2 STUDENT GROUPING

Deciding how to group students and to discuss these groups also challenge thoughts which are antipathetic to equal opportunities. This has been recognised for several years at Peers and plenty of attention is given to it. The greatest concern centres around the criteria on which decisions are made about grouping. If on the grounds of 'ability', ability in relation to what? Phrases such as 'low ability', 'the more able', 'mixed ability' are meaningless unless used in relation to specific skills or talents (although it takes time to become adept at avoiding their use in both speech and writing).

Setting

The setting used in many schools employs criteria which are based on a retrospective view of what a child has achieved rather than what might be achieved in the future. At Peers it is recognised that grouping by 'ability' is too problematic to be worth doing. Most seriously, grouping by 'ability' encourages the language, attitudes and behaviour of 'top' and 'bottom' sets. Young people are encouraged to accept a powerful external analysis of their worth rather than being helped to develop their own analysis of strengths and weaknesses at the stage where self-esteem is still very fragile.

Often, setting is the norm, while random (not even balanced) groups such as tutorial sessions, Art or PE are formed in some areas. In such circumstances, setting becomes even more closely associated with high status and random groups with low status. The net effect is to privilege, irrationally, some subjects and students at the expense of others.

Balanced groups at Peers School

In devising groups for the first year at Peers (Year 9) we considered but rejected random grouping except in certain limited circumstances for we do not wish to deny differences between students and treat them as if they are all exactly the same. Instead we try to devise balanced groups in which relevant differences are noted. Each teaching group contains a mix of students differing in race, gender, attainment and social and personal characteristics, such as family stress, which can affect the whole group's learning. We respect existing friendships. We accept that secondary schools are strongly based in year groups and do not consider mixed-age groups.

Our groups are a mixture of balanced tutor groups, in which Year 9 students may spend up to half their lessons, and balanced rearrangements of these to allow, for example, five tutor groups (half a year group) to be blocked across six Science classes to achieve smaller groups. In Years 10 and 11, some choice of course is introduced preceded by a clear course description and guidance. It is made clear to students that, in principle, they choose their courses though inevitably teachers and parents do guide the choices of some students.

The existence of balanced groups in a school does not preclude the formation, from time to time, of other groups for specific purposes of positive discrimination such as a single sex group, groups to follow a particular specialist course, interest or whatever. The point is that such groupings are formed for specific purposes and for specific lengths of time, using criteria which are rational and based on accurate and up-to-date information. Such groupings are formed against a background which insists that equality is the norm.

Needless to say, Peers staff are not wholly united on this issue of balanced groups and there is enough healthy dissent to keep the discussion alive and ensure that the reasons for our school policy on groupings are well rehearsed. At present, it does not seem likely that setting will be established.

Reviewing group membership

In all three years the formation of groups is subjected to careful scrutiny by both curriculum and tutorial staff. This has the additional benefit of providing opportunity for information exchange on student progress, attitude and behaviour which allows for the discussion of factors affecting learning which might not otherwise get an airing. In how many schools is it accepted that students may need help and counselling to overcome difficulties over different teachers' style or manner? Yet this is the sharp reality for some students and appropriate support and advice can make all the difference between success and failure.

3 SUCCESS AND ACHIEVEMENT

What then about the language of success and achievement which perhaps underpins all else? And what is to count as success? If schooling is viewed as a competition between students there can be little equality of opportunity to experience success. Success will be reserved for some and failure for many. The teacher may argue that the students are treated the same, but this ignores relevant differences between the students, such as their ability to write to dictation or read a text, and simply compounds the inequality.

The teacher whose class is organised so that individual differences are recognised and catered for, and where cooperative effort is valued, opens new fields in which to record success and achievement. Such a class more readily allows entry to students who would otherwise have been excluded because of physical disability or difficulty in learning.

At Peers we have widened the range of activities through which the success of students can be recorded by restructuring the curriculum. Curriculum initiatives in which we have been involved include Oxfordshire's Skills Project, New Learning Initiative (Oxfordshire's version of the Lower Attaining Pupils' Programme), Records of Achievement, the Technical and Vocational Education Initiative, integration programmes with local special schools, active community liaison, the use of support staff in lessons and an emphasis on outdoor and residential education. By broadening our ideas of achievement we have tried to counteract the pressure, inevitable in our exam- and test-laden secondary school curriculum, to use academic attainment as a yardstick of value.

4 LEAVING SCHOOL

Post-16 education is a further area in which a review of terms is necessary. The language we habitually use to discuss the future with teenagers is hopelessly fatalistic and seems to accept low expectations of young people by the government, by society and by the young people and their families. It thus fails to challenge assumed ideas about their worth and their future. How does one express an alternative to the all too familiar 'when you leave school', 'your final year at school' (used almost invariably to those assumed to be leaving at 16), or the question 'Are you staying on?' The notion of the 15-year-old 'school leaver' shows how difficult it is for teachers in this country to develop words to express a desire for students to continue their education, at the very least until the end of their entitlement to free education, still less until their full potential has been reached.

Clearly, other structures, such as an examination system which is, in effect, a school leaving certificate, do not help, but how we handle conversations with students about their post-16 education and training can be very significant. This really does challenge the thought behind the words. Cutting out phrases which suggest that education ends at 16 and using instead phrases such as 'next year', 'after GCSE', 'continuing education', takes time. The fact that we find it so hard reveals a frightening degree of collusion with the traditional class structure of society.

It would be interesting to compare language use in this respect with that used in other European countries or in Japan, where very much higher percentages of school students do remain in full-time education until 18. We have tried hard to change the attitudes of students and of ourselves to post-16 education at Peers. We have been able to double the staying-on rate within the last two years. This is no mean achievement for a school serving the least advantaged areas of one of the most socially divided cities in the country.

5 WHOM DO WE TEACH?

Finally, how about the language we use to describe those taught? Our last head teacher promoted the language of equal opportunity, but our present one has introduced a further element, the language of mutual respect and recognition of worth. We now speak of 'students', no longer of 'kids', 'children', 'pupils' or any of the other more or less patronising words habitually used to subvert the essentially professional relationship between teacher and student. This seems to challenge something very deep in an adult's attitude to children. If you are a teacher, try selecting a suitable word appropriate to the age group you teach and see how long it is before you slip!

Chapter 32

Writing clearly

Contributing to the ideal comprehensibility situation

Margaret Peter

In this chapter, Margaret Peter, editor of the British Journal of Special Education, *puts in a plea for plain writing.*

It is a truth not universally acknowledged that writers on education in the late twentieth century tend to advocate integration in segregating prose. However, gobbledegook, more widespread in North America than in Britain, is not confined to the issue of integration. It pervades other aspects of education but its use seems at its most paradoxical in writings which promote the principle that children with special educational needs should be educated in the mainstream together with their peers.

Jargon-laden language separates the uninitiated from those who understand and the writers who perpetrate it are likely to be teachers turned educational psychologists/researchers/lecturers in higher education. Exposed too often to what, at its worst, is academic gibberish, its victims may end up as 'reading failures' alienated from the printed page and from any desire to try to relate published research to classroom practice. The authors, poor innocents, fail to see that they are shooting themselves in the foot.

The worst examples come from American research journals, reporting comparisons of mainstream and segregated settings and other investigations in schools. Titles like 'The effect of textual proximity on fourth- and fifth-grade LD students' metacognitive awareness and strategic comprehension behaviour' (Simmons *et al.* 1988), far from encouraging proximity, will fail to lure many readers over the threshold of the text; those who persist, often in mounting bewilderment, may be poleaxed by conclusions which are equally obscure. A recent issue of the *Journal of Learning Disabilities* (Made *et al.* 1990) reports on the social effects of two levels of integration of pupils with learning difficulties in Washington States. Its third conclusion states breathlessly, 'Graphs indicate that reciprocal choices as a preferred peer occurred considerably more frequently in the ICM, and non-reciprocal choices, wherein a special education student preferentially selected a regular education peer, but was indicated as least preferred by that same peer, happened more often in the resource room model.' (Something is rotten in the State of Washington!)

Nor is the British literature free from gobbledegook. Even when books and journals make determined efforts to resist what the OED defines as 'pompous official or professional jargon' occasional outbreaks occur. In *Preventing Difficulties in Learning* (Booth *et al.* 1987) Annabel Mercer (1987), reporting on an integration programme in Lothian, describes a hemiplegic pupil as 'being completely non-participating in the gym' (Mercer 1987: 137). A research paper on social integration among junior age pupils in the *British Journal of Special Education* (Rose 1981) concludes that it is important to know what 'interpersonal sensitivities a teacher needs to possess in order to facilitate the social adaptation of the handicapped child'. Neither string of words is beyond comprehension, both are needlessly obscure.

Why do teachers, psychologists and members of many other professions resort to jargon? Ernest Gowers in *The Complete Plain Words* (1973) suggests, among other explanations, the instinct for self-preservation ('it is sometimes dangerous to be precise'), the desire to show off (to dazzle by the choice of language if not by the quality of thought and laziness ('clear thinking is hard work'). All three are plausible and all three may be closely linked. Lazy thinkers shield themselves from exposure by using technical and impressively long words – gems of ignorance are protected by impenetrable prose.

Other explanations occur, to do with professional identity. In the absence of other insignia, jargon can become the verbal badge of the profession. At its most defensible it is a time-saving shorthand to trade with fellow professionals, at its worst it is pathetic. An armoury of technical terms, often incomprehensible to the outsider, is seen as enhancing professional status and lends a spurious distinction to what may be trivial or unsound. It is also yawningly boring. While yuppie city dealers can invent macho terms like 'dead cat bounce' (shares rise slightly, then fall back) and 'shark repellents' (to fend off unwanted take-over bids) in order to enliven the dullness of life at a city desk (Johnson 1990), teachers are unlikely to warn their school leavers about becoming 'basket cases' (collapsed executives poured into baskets to prevent their lives from falling totally apart) or to bracket pupils of certain vintages with the 'pig in a python' (post-war baby boom).

Unlike law or mathematics, or other disciplines with long-established bodies of knowledge, the jargon of education draws heavily on loan words coming from medicine (diagnosis, cases), psychology (cognitive and IQ) and, increasingly, from information technology (interface, input) and business management (marketing policy, quality control). Other terms are merely pompous like 'giving a presentation' (why not a 'talk'?), the 'teaching situation' (try dropping the second word), 'prestigious organisations' (smacks of the smug and second rate) and 'non-reciprocal speaking and listening situations' in the National Curriculum Working Group's report on *English for Ages 5 to 16* (DES 1989). The group should have known better than to descend into drivel when what it meant was 'radio, television' etc. Beneath these attempts to build up an armoury of academic jargon lie feelings of professional inferiority. Education is low in the hierarchy of academic disciplines (some would question if it is a discipline at all) and teaching is rated less highly in the professions' league table than it should be. Is it significant that, both in conversation and in print, teachers frequently refer to the 'real world' beyond school? What is 'unreal' about teaching children in the formative school years from 5 to 16 is unclear. Most children are at day schools and even children in residential schools usually go home in the holidays. Are their experiences in the family, in the street, in weekend jobs and in leisure activities not part of the 'real world' either? It would be interesting to know if teachers in countries where education is more highly valued use the same self-denigrating jargon.

The danger is that the disease will spread. The National Curriculum and local management of schools are the latest developments to add new weapons to the armoury. 'Cross-curricular dimensions' and 'profile components' will divide teachers who know from parents who don't, while 'performance indicators' and 'quality control' may raise barriers of hostility between budget-handling governors and their teachers. Nor is there any reassurance in the new LEA designations like 'line manager' and 'head of the quality assurance division' (a number of senior officers have recently been rebaptised).

Much of the new jargon treats education as a commodity like junk food; it can be bought and sold by the hungriest bidders. It does not suggest a public service to which all children (*not* clients) have a right and in which integration is a serious goal. A typical example, from the School Examinations and Assessment Council (SEAC 1990) sounds more like the fast food industry than a government bent on raising the standards of teaching and learning. 'Orders . . . will be placed' for standard assessment tasks by LEAs and these 'will be delivered directly to schools' – a sort of 'you ring, we bring' service, but less appetising.

Who is to blame for the contagion? If Gowers is correct in saying that gobbledegook is a disease contracted in early adulthood, university and college lecturers should be purging their own vocabularies and inoculating their students with jabs of Plain English vaccine. Books and journals are equally at fault, failing to filter manuscripts finely enough, rejecting some jargon while allowing other dregs to seep through. (All editors have their '*bêtes noires*'; my own resolve to root out 'facilitate' and its derivatives has hardened with the discovery that a 'facilitator', according to Green (1987), is 'a member of the Rogerian group who quickly suppresses anyone who attempts to offer a less than enthusiastic statement by smothering them with calming embraces and general expounding of the group philosophy'. If this is what facilitators do, what expectations might a 'coordinator' arouse?)

In the end it is up to teachers to develop the self-confidence to use plain words and to recognise that polysyllables and a prolix style will obscure the message, whether it concerns integration or anything else. To return to the beginning and to Jane Austen, they should take pride in clear and simple prose and rid themselves of the prejudice that an abundance of jargon means high professionalism. It does not.

REFERENCES

Booth, T., Potts, P. and Swann, W. (1987) *Preventing Difficulties in Learning*, Oxford: Basil Blackwell.

Department of Education and Science (DES) (1989) *English for Ages 5 to 16*, London: DES.

Gowers, E. (1973) *The Complete Plain Words*, London: HMSO.

Green, J. (1987) *Dictionary of Jargon*, London: Routledge & Kegan Paul.

Johnson, M. (1990) *Business Buzz Words*, Oxford: Basil Blackwell.

Madge, S., Affleck, J. and Lowenbraum, S. (1990) 'Social effects of integrated classrooms and resource room/regular class placements on elementary students with learning disabilities', *Journal of Learning Disabilities* 23 (7), 439–45.

Mercer, A. (1987) 'Help where it is needed: support across the primary curriculum', in T. Booth, P. Potts and W. Swann (eds), *Preventing Difficulties in Learning*, Oxford: Basil Blackwell.

Rose, C. (1981) 'Social integration of school age ESN(S) children in a regular school', *British Journal of Special Education* 8 (4), 17–22.

School Examinations and Assessment Council (SEAC) (1990) *National Curriculum Assessment: Assessment Arrangements for Core Subjects at Key Stage 1. Responsibility of LEAs in 1990/91*, London: SEAC.

Simmons, D. C., Kameenui, E. J. and Darch, C. B. (1988) 'The effect of textual proximity on fourth- and fifth-grade LD students' metacognitive awareness and strategic comprehension behavior', *Learning Disabilities Quarterly* 11 (4), 380–95.

Index

Note: Most entries imply teaching/teachers and learning/pupils, and these are generally omitted as main entries, except where references are particularly significant.

ability, grouping by 341
abortion 282
access to National Curriculum *see* microtechnology
ACE *see* Aids to Communication and Education
achievement, language of 342–3
adolescents and HIV risk 253–69; and drugs 257–60; and heterosexual sex 263–5; knowledge of and attitudes to 260–3; policy 265–7
adults: in hospital school 200–10; literacy 137
age: and bullying 229; and National Curriculum 92–4
Ahmed, A. 69, 70
AIDS *see* HIV
Aids to Communication and Education centres 163
Ainscow, M. x; on reflective teaching 171–82
anaemia *see* sickle-cell anaemia
answering back and girls in 'bother' 214
appearance and girls in 'bother' 218–19
APU *see* Assessment of Performance Unit
area support centre 175–6
art *see* drawing and painting
Asian children, deaf 151–5
Assessment of Performance Unit 67
ATs *see* attainment targets
attainment levels and National Curriculum 98–9; origin and nature of 86–90
attainment targets 95–6; defined 99
attendance problems 137
audio-visual aids: and history teaching 23, 26–7, 28, 33; and physically disabled 160, 167; and science 57; and writing 46–7; *see also* computers
autobiographies of school experiences 304–16

balanced tutor groups 341–2
Barnard, M. x; on HIV risks 253–69
Barnes, D. 10
Beardshaw, V. x; on conductive education 183, 190–1
behaviour problems 24; in hospital school 202–8; modification 195, 202–8; *see also* bullying; trouble
Bennett, A. x; on mathematics teaching 63–75
Bennett, N. 296, 302
Better Mathematics 69–70, 71–2
bias in research 299
bilingual pupils, deaf children as 150–5
bilingual pupils, developing English of 124–35; drawbacks and advantages of support teaching 132–3; feeding into mainstream 129–30; improving support teaching 130–2; mainstream teachers' attitudes 133–4; support teaching and withdrawal balanced 128–9; support teaching and withdrawal compared 126–8

Biott, C. 10
blindness 312–14
Bolton 124
Booth, T. x, 1–5, 348; on HIV and AIDS 270–1
'bother' *see* trouble
boys *see* gender
Bradford 124
British Sign Language (BSL) 150–1, 152, 153, 155
Bullock Report (1975) 124
bullying in two comprehensives 224–35; results of research 226–32; comparison with previous research 233–4

Campbell, D.T. 302
Campling, J. 306
care, children in 249–52
Careers Service 244, 245
CEUKS (Conductive Education UK Style) 184
cheekiness and girls in 'bother' 214
Children Act (1989) 249
choice: negotiated 16; of youth training scheme 244–7
Clare, A. x; on child with Down's syndrome 143–9
class *see* working class
classroom *see* collaborative; in-class
climate of classroom and science in primary school 60–1
closed curriculum in special education 173
Clough, D. 10
collaborative classrooms 9–22; background 9–11; National Curriculum implications 20–1; not 'group work' 11–14, 21; range and quality developed 17–20; self-supporting framework created 15–17
commitment 16
commodity, education as 347
Community Education 137
Community Homes 251
comprehensible language, need for 345–8
comprehensive schools: children with disabilities in 284–90; *see also* bullying; equality; secondary schools
computers *see* microtechnology
concentration problems and sickle-cell anaemia 280
conductive education 183–92
construction work in primary school 9, 10–11, 18
containment in early special schools 194–5
Corbett, J. x; on 'special care' 193–9
Cornwall, J. 334, 338
counselling: and HIV 272, 274; and sickle-cell anaemia 279, 281
Coventry 176–8
Cox Report (1988) 125
critical community 300–1
crowd, close observation of 326–30
Curriculum for All, A 3, 84; *see also* National Curriculum

databases: in science 57; *see also* microtechnology
deaf people 189; Deaf Instructors for 151, 153–5; *see also* signing
death and poetry 39, 41
DES (Department of Education and Science); classification of children 98; and English as Second Language 124–5; and special schools 172; and traveller children 137, 141; *see also* National Curriculum
disability and handicap: categories 98; and multi-media scheme 76–82; play 321–3, 330–1; *see also* blind; deaf; physical disabilities; special education
disease *see* haemophilia; HIV and AIDS; sickle-cell anaemia
'Distance Learning Packs' 137
diversity, teaching for 4; *see also* collaborative; history, learning; mathematics; multi-media; National Curriculum as system; poetry; science
doodles 47
Down's syndrome and support teaching 143–9
drawing and painting: and collaborative classrooms 10, 18; by child with Down's syndrome 144, 146–7; and history teaching 30, 31; and poetry writing 47; in science 55–6
dress and girls in 'bother' 218–19
Driver, R. 55
drugs and HIV risk 252–3, 256–6, 266, 270, 274
Dudley, project in *see* history, learning
Dulay, H. 127
dysfunction concept 184–5
dyslexia 38
Dyson, S. x; on sickle-cell anaemia 277–83

Earth and space 56, 60
Eason, P. x; mathematics observed 318–321, 330
Edinburgh 208, 253, 264; Leith girls in 'bother' *see* trouble
Education Act (1981) 84, 98, 99, 105, 150, 176
Education Reform Act (1988) 2, 83–6, 94
Education Supervision Orders 249
Educational Interpreters 151, 152–5
Elton Report (1989) 224
emotions: and bullying 229; and poetry 36, 39, 41
employment training *see* training, youth
encouraging classroom success 179–82
English: listening by deaf Asian child 151–5; and microtechnology 159–61; and National Curriculum 90, 156, 159–61, 346; as Second Language 124–35; *see also* bilingual pupils
environment for collaboration, creating 13–14, 19–21
equality, learning language of 340–4; leaving school 343; pupils 344; student grouping 341–2; success and achievement 342–3
equity issues and microtechnology and access to National Curriculum 164–6
ERA *see* Education Reform Act
ESN (educationally subnormal) ca‘ :gory 98, 171
ethnographic style of research 297
Europe, sickle-cell anaemia in 277–8, 282
evaluating support teaching 105–13
evaporation 59–60; observing 54–5
everyday language, power of 57–9, 345–8
expectations of leaving school 241–4
experience: of school and youth training 236–41; and science in primary school 59–60
experimentalists 296
explanation and science in primary school 59–60
extra tuition for people with sickle-cell anaemia 281

fellings *see* emotions
Fibonacci sequence 70–1
fighting and girls in 'bother' 216–17
films *see* audio-visual aids
Fletcher-Campbell, F. x; on children in care 249–52
food and science 58
Foundation for Conductive Education 184, 188
fragmentation problem of children in care 251
French lesson, teacher–pupil contacts in 327–30
Freyburg, P. 55
further education 242; *see also* training
future: hospital school 207–8; support teaching of traveller children 141–2

GCSE 2
gender: and attainment 88; and attitudes to HIV 263; and bullying 227–8, 229, 230, 231–2; and pupil–teacher contacts 327–30; of school leavers 237, 241, 248; of teachers 220–1; and trouble 220–1
geography and National Curriculum 89
girls *see* gender: trouble
Glasgow *see* adolescents
Gleason, J.J. x; play observed 321–3, 330–1
Goacher, B. 251
gobbledegook 345–8
Gowers, E. 346, 347
Gramsci, A. 301, 303
Green, J. 347
groups: discussions in science 56–7; discussions on HIV risk 254–65; and equality 341–2; and multi-media scheme 76–82; 'special care' 192–9; 'work', collaborative classrooms not 11–14, 21; *see also* conductive education; history, learning; poetry

haemophilia and HIV 270, 271–4
Halpin, A.W. 303
handicapped people *see* disabled and handicapped
Harland, L. x; on support service 114–23
Harperbury Hospital School *see* hospital school
Hart, S. x; on collaborative classrooms 9–22; on evaluating support teaching 105–13
heterosexuality *see* sex
Hewett, D. x; on hospital school 200–10
hierarchies, subject, National Curriculum and creation of 90–2
history: learning through talk 23–35; and research 294–5, 297
HIV and AIDS: impact of 270–6; risk *see* adolescents

Hollands, R. x; on youth training 236–48
Hollway, W. 334, 335, 338
homosexuality and HIV 252, 270
hospital school 200–10; developing curriculum critique 200–2; emergence of new curriculum 202–3; future 207–8; 'intensive interaction' teaching described 203–5; theoretical rationale 205–7
Hull, R. x; science observed 323–6, 330–1
Humanities Curriculum Project 302–3
Hungary *see* Institute for Conductive Education

illiteracy, personal experiences of 307–8, 315; *see also* literacy
improvement of support teaching 130–2
in-class support teaching: English as Second Language 124–35; evaluated 105–13; reading 118–22; *see also* mainstream
independence in collaborative classrooms 16
India 312–14
individual: approach to in-class support teaching 106–11; work and collaborative classrooms 11, 13, 16–17
inherited disorders *see* haemophilia; sickle-cell anaemia
initiatives, curriculum 343
in-service education of teachers (INSET) 20, 84; *see also* training for teachers
Inspector for Special Educational Needs 115
Institute for Conductive Education of Motor Disabled (Hungary) 183–5, 190, 191
integration: in special schools *see* 'special care'; *see also* mainstream
'intensive interaction' teaching 203–8; *see also* social interaction
interests: mathematical, building on pupils' own 68–9; and research 298–9
International Conference for deaf 189
interpreters for deaf children 151, 152–5
interviewing 322–9; about HIV risk 254–65; in history teaching 27–30; in practice 336–8; reasons for 332–3; school leavers 236–48; as social relationship 333–5

jargon 345–8
Johnson, D.W. 10
Johnson, M. 346

labelling: and school leavers 237–8; in special schools 195–6
LAMP *see* Low Attainers in Mathematics Project
language: development of child with Down's syndrome 144–6, 147–9; English as Second Language 124–35; everyday, power of 57–9, 345–8; writing poetry in foreign mother tongue 19; *see also* equality, learning language of; listening; reading; talking; writing
learning difficulties *see* disability; special education; support teaching; *and also* preliminary note to index
LEAs (local education authorities): and conductive education 188–9; and microtechnology 163–4, 165; and sickle-cell anaemia 281; and support teaching 114–23, 136, 137, 139, 171, 175–6
leaving school 343; *see also* training
Leeds primary school, talking and signing in 150–5
legislation: children 249; *see also* Education Act; Education Reform Act
Leonardo of Pisa (Fibonacci) 70, 72
levels and National Curriculum 92–4
light and science 58
listening: and microtechnology 159–60; and National Curriculum 90–1; to poetry 36–40
literacy: adult 137; *see also* illiteracy; reading; writing
Lloyd, G. x; on English 159–60; on girls and 'bother' 213–23
LMS *see* local management of schools
local authorities *see* care; LEAs
local authority staff development programme (SNAP) 176–8
local management of schools 86, 115, 121
Logan, T. 337, 338, 339
London 105, 252–3
Low Attainers in Mathematics Project 63–4, 69–70, 75

MacDonald, B. 303
McKeganey, N. xi; on HIV risks 253–69
Madge, S. 345
mainstream: deaf children in 150–5; feeding bilingual pupils into 129–30; help for special pupils in *see* support

teaching; teachers and bilingual pupils 133–4; temporary integration from special school *see* history, learning; *see also* in-class
Makaton sign language 145–6, 147, 148
make-up and girls in 'bother' 214
Mason, M. x; experience of school 305–6, 315
mathematics 63–75; by child with Down's syndrome 147; joint exploration 67–8; and microtechnology 161–3; and National Curriculum 87–8, 91, 93, 156, 161–2; pupils' interests, building on 68–9; pupils' own strategies developed 72–4; 'rich mathematical activities' 69–72; subtraction difficulties closely observed 318–21, 330; as teacher and learner 63–7
Meehan, Joseph: starting secondary school 284–90
Mehta, V. x; experience of school 312–15
Mellor, D. xi; experience of school 307–8, 315
menstruation and girls in 'bother' 215–16
Mercer, A. 346
microtechnology: and access to National Curriculum 156–68; and collaborative classrooms 10; and English 159–61; equity issues 164–6; and mathematics 161–3; participation and control issues 166–7; and physically disabled 156–68; possibilities and problems 156–9; and science 57, 162–3; support network 163–4; and technology 162; and writing 47; *see also* audio-visual aids
middle schools, reading support teaching in 118–20
Mills, C. xi; on traveller children 136–42
MLD (moderate learning difficulties) category 98, 171
mobility *see* peripatetic; traveller
moderate learning difficulties *see* MLD
modern languages: and National Curriculum 88, 89, 165; observed 327–30
Morris, C. xi; on history learning 23–35
multi-media learning scheme, student participation in 76–82

National Curriculum 2–3; access to *see* microtechnology; and collaborative classrooms 9; and English 90, 156, 159–61, 346; and geography 89; implications of collaborative classrooms 20–1; and jargon 346–7; and listening 90–1; and mathematics 87–8, 91, 93, 156, 161–2; and modern languages 88, 89; and reading 115–16; and sickle-cell anaemia 282; and 'special care' 198–9; and talking 90–1, 167; and traveller children 141; and writing 95–7, 100, 164; *see also* National Curriculum Council; National Curriculum as system
National Curriculum Council 3; and children with special needs 84–5, 87, 98, 97; *see also Curriculum for All*: National Curriculum
National Curriculum as system of classification 83–101; attainment levels and targets 86–90, 95–6, 98–9; extending system 94–7; levels and ages 92–4; subject hierarchies created 90–2; *see also* National Curriculum
National Health Service 163; *see also* hospital school
National Writing Project 24, 35, 97, 100
naturalistic style of research 297
NCC *see* National Curriculum Council
negative attitudes *see* prejudice
nervous system, residual capacity in 185, 187–8
network, support, microtechnology and access to National Curriculum 163–4
new role for support service 114–23; before policy change 114–15; after policy change 115–16; general consequences 122–3; successes and problems 116–22
New York 252–3
Nind, M. xi; on hospital school 200–10
Nolan, C. xi; on starting secondary school 284–90
normality concept and disability 183, 187, 188, 189, 190, 207
Norway, bullying in 224, 226, 233–4

Oakeshott, M. 303
Oakley, A. 333–4, 338
objectivity in research 298
observation 317–31; crowd 326–30; play 321–3; and science 53–4, 323–6; subtraction difficulties 318–21
Oldham 163
Olesker, S. xi. 78; on multi-media learning 76–82

Oliver, M. xi; on conductive education 183, 187–90; criticised 190–2
Onions, C. and R. xi; on microtechnology and National Curriculum 156–68
open curriculum in special education 173
oppressiveness of normality concept 188
organisation of collaborative classrooms 16
orthofunction concept 184–5, 187–8
Osborne, R. 55
Oxford 163

Pakistani Sign Language 151
parents: and conductive education 189, 190–2; and deaf children 151; and girls in 'bother' 222–3; and HIV 271–3, 276; involvement lacking 24; and 'special care' 194; and traveller children 138, 140
participation and microtechnology 166–7
Peers School *see* equality, learning
peripatetic support teaching 115, 136–42
personal experiences: interviewing about 333–9; of school, examples of 304–16
personal questions and girls in 'bother' 222
Personal and Social Education module 139
Peter, M. xi; on writing clearly 345–8
physical activity: for blind 312–14; and sickle-cell anaemia 280
physical disabilities: and microtechnology 156–68; personal experiences of 305–6, 312–15; starting school 284–90; *see also* conductive education; deaf; disabled; hospital school; 'special care'; special education
'picking on' girls 220
planning: lessons and in-class support teaching 110–11; in special education 173–5
plants and science 59
play: close observation of disabled children 321–3, 330–1; and learning in hospital 202–8
Plowden Report (1967) 141
poetry 36–52; and collaborative classrooms 10, 19; and history teaching 30–3; listening to 36–40; reading 40–2; writing 42–7
policy, educational *see* National Curriculum; new role; support teaching
Portsmouth College of Art, Design and Further Education multi-media scheme 76–82
Potts, P. xi; on close observation 317–18, 330–1; on experience of school 304–5, 314–16; on interviewing 332–9
practice: interviewing in 336–8; and research 294
prejudice: and HIV 273–5; racism 276; and traveller children 138–40
pressure, children and young people under 4; *see also* bullying; care; HIV; Meehan; sickle-cell; training; trouble
primary schools 157; Leeds, talking and signing in 150–5; reading support teaching 116–18, 120–2; science in 53–62; special school pupils temporarily integrated *see* history, learning; teaching styles 302; and traveller children 138–9; *see also* collaborative classrooms; poetry; science
problems: of microtechnology 156–9; solving in primary school 10
professionals and jargon 346
profile components 96–7, 99, 100
public, research made 294
Punjabi-speaking children 151–5
pupils/students: behaviour *see* behaviour problems; grouping *see* groups; interests and strategies in mathematics 68–9, 72–4; and language *see* bilingual; language to describe 344; participation *see* multi-media; *see also* preliminary note to index
Pye, J. xi; crowd observed 326–31

quality of collaborative classrooms developed 17–20
questionnaires on bullying 225–32

racism 276
Raising Achievement in Mathematics Project (RAMP) 63–4, 69–70, 75
random grouping 341
Ranford, V. 25
range of collaborative classrooms developed 17–20
Ravenstonedale School 143–9
reading: by child with Down's syndrome 147; and collaborative classrooms 10; in English 160–1; and microtechnology 160–1; and National Curriculum 115–16; poetry 40–2, 43; refusal 308–12; and support teaching 114–23
realities of leaving school 241–4
recording *see* audio-visual aids

Rees, S. 166
Reeves, J. 49
reflective teacher, becoming 171–82; curriculum development in special school 171–6; encouraging classroom success 179–82; local authority staff development programme 176–8
registers of people with sickle-cell anaemia 280–1
reinforcement in collaborative classrooms 15–16
remedial work 114–15; *see also* special education; support teaching
representing practice 4–5; *see also* equality; interviewing; observation; personal experiences; research; writing clearly
reputations and girls in 'bother' 218
research defined and described 293–303; publication 300–1; social science and practice 296–8; teacher-researcher 299–300; values and interests 298–9
resources, lack of 141, 194
'rich mathematical activities' 69–72
Rieser, R. 306
Roaf, C. xi; on language of equality 340–4
roles *see* new role
Rose, C. 346
Russell, P. xi; on HIV and AIDS 271–6
Russells Hall School *see* history, learning
rusting, observing 53–4, 56
Rutter, M. 252

SATs *see* Standard Assessment Tasks
SAWA *see* Special Attachment Welfare Assistant
Schmidt-Rohlfing, B. xi; on signing and talking 150–5
School Examinations and Assessment Council 99, 347
school leavers 236–48
science and research 293–5
science teaching: appropriate classroom climate created 60–1; close observation of 323–6; everyday language, power of 57–9; experience and explanation 59–60; and microtechnology 162–3; and National Curriculum 49, 88, 89, 91–3, 156, 162–3; observation in 53–5; in primary school 53–62; Science Processes and Concept Exploration 53, 55, 62; strategies to enable expression of ideas 55–7
Scotland 208; girls in *see* trouble; and HIV risk *see* adolescents; support teaching 110–11, 115
SEAC *see* School Examinations and Assessment Council
secondary schools 157; and English as Second Language 124–35; in-class support teaching evaluated 105–13; mathematical problems 318–21; and traveller children 139; *see also* bullying; comprehensive; equality
'secret' book 155
Sedgwick, F. xi; on poetry teaching 36–52
Seebohm Report (1968) 251
self-critical enquiry, research as 293–4
self-knowledge and poetry 48–9
self-supporting framework of collaborative classrooms created 15–17
SEMERCs *see* Special Education Microelectronic Resource Centres
setting 341
sex/sexuality: denied in intensive interaction 207; and HIV risk 252, 261, 263–5, 266–7, 270–1
sickle-cell anaemia and thalassaemia 277–83; care and attention 279–82
signing: and child with Down's syndrome 145–6, 147, 148; and multi-media scheme 77, 81; Sign Supported English 151–2; and talking in Leeds primary school 150–5
silence, importance of 43
Simmons, D.C. 345
slagging and girls in 'bother' 218
Slavin, R. 10
Smith, P. xi; on bullying 224–35
smoking and girls in 'bother' 214–15
social interaction/relationships: in French lesson 326–30; 'intensive interaction' teaching 203–8; interviewing as 333–5; social education for people with sickle-cell anaemia 282; *see also* groups
social science and practice 296–8
SPACE *see* Science Processes and Concept Exploration
space control and girls in 'bother' 216
Spastics Society 184, 187, 188
spatial skills 65
speaking *see* talking
Special Attachment Welfare Assistant and child with Down's syndrome 143–4
'special care' integrated within special school 193–9; success proved 197

special education 4; active approach to mathematics teaching 63–75; and reflective teachers 171–5; Statement of Special Educational Needs 87, 94, 98; temporary integration for history lessons *see* history, learning; *see also* conductive education; disabled; hospital school; National Curriculum as system; reflective teacher; 'special care'; support teaching
Special Education Microelectronic Resource Centres 164
Special Needs Priority Action Programme (SNAP) 176–8
spelling: and National Curriculum 96; unimportant 43, 46
Spender, S. 48–9
spontaneous collaboration 11–13
SSE (Sign Supported English) 151–2
staff *see* teachers
Standard Assessment Tasks 90–2, 141
Stanley, J.C. 302
Statement of Special Educational Needs 87, 94, 98
Statements of Attainment 91–2, 94–7; defined 99
Stenhouse, L. xi; on research 293–303
strategies, mathematical, developing pupils' own 72–4
students *see* pupils/students
subject hierarchies creation and National Curriculum 90–2
success: encouraging classroom 179–82; language of 342–3; and problems of support service 116–22
support: in collaborative classrooms 15–17; for people with sickle-cell anaemia 281
support teaching 4; evaluating 105–13; *see also* bilingual; deaf; Down's syndrome; microtechnology; new role; special education; traveller
Sutcliff, R. xi; experience of school 308–12, 315
Sutton School *see* history, learning
Swann, W. xi; on conductive education 183–7; on National Curriculum 83–101
Swann Report (1985) 124–5, 141
swearing and girls in 'bother' 214
systematic self-critical enquiry, research as 293–4
talking: by child with Down's syndrome 145–6, 148–9; and collaborative classrooms 10; in English 159–60; and history *see* history, learning; and microtechnology 159–60; and National Curriculum 90–1, 167; and poetry 36, 41; and science 56–60, 61; and support teaching 174; *see also* signing
Tann, S. 10
tapes *see* audio-visual aids
Task Group on Assessment and Testing 86–9, 92–3, 97
task-series in conductive education 185–7
Teacher of Deaf 151
teachers: and bullying 228–9; and collaborative classrooms 13–14, 19–21; as fellow learners in mathematics 63–75; girls' relationships with 219–23; HIV-positive 276; and hospital school 200–8; prejudice against traveller children 138–40; presence as contaminant 41–2; as researchers 299–300; and 'special care' 194–6; staff development programme 176–8; staff development programme (SNAP) 176–8; *see also* reflective teacher; *and* preliminary note to index
team teaching 198
technology *see* microtechnology
television *see* audio-visual aids
textbooks 119
TGAT *see* Task Group on Assessment and Testing
thalassaemia *see* sickle-cell anaemia
theory: and rationale of hospital school 205–7; and research 297, 300
Thucydides 295
time: brief duration of collaborative work 13; control and girls in 'bother' 216; poetry's power over 40
Todd, F. 10
toilets and girls in 'bother' 215–16
training for teachers: support 116, 136, 171, 175, 176–8; *see also* in-service
training, youth 77, 236–46; 'choosing' scheme 244–7; expectations and realities of leaving school 241–4; schooling experiences 236–41
transition from school 343; *see also* training, youth
traveller children and support teaching 136–42; countering negative attitudes 138–40; future 141–2; parental

expectations 140
trouble at school, girls in 213–23; reasons for 214–19; relationships with teachers 219–23
truancy and girls in 'bother' 216

unemployment 243, 256
unfairness of teachers 220
United States 252–3, 345

values and research 298–9
victimisation *see* bullying
videos *see* audio-visual aids
vision and science 58
vocationalisation 239

Wadsworth, P. xi; on primary science 53–62
War, Second World, project about 23–35
Warnock Report (1978) 84, 105, 172, 176
Whittall, L. 25
whole curriculum approach to in-class support teaching 106–13
Williams, H. xi; on mathematics teaching 63–75
Williamson, J. xi; on English with bilingual pupils 124–35
'winding up' teachers 221–2
withdrawal and support teaching: balanced 128–9; compared 126–8; and English as Second Language 124–35; reading 114–15, 117–18; return afterwards *see* mainstream, feeding
working class school leavers 236–48
World Health Authority 278–9, 282
writing: clearly, plea for 345–8; and collaborative classrooms 10, 16–18; by deaf children 155; and child with Down's syndrome 146; drafting 44, 45, 46–7; and English 161; and history teaching 30–3; and microtechnology 161; and National Curriculum 95–7, 100, 164; National Writing Project 24, 35, 97, 100; about personal experiences of school 304–16; poetry 36, 42–7, 48–9; and science 53, 54, 56; *see also* language

Yates, C. xi; on bullying 224–35
Youth Opportunities Programme 245
Youth Training Scheme (YTS) *see* training, youth